T0401342

An unorthodox history

Manchester University Press

An unorthodox history

British Jews since 1945

Gavin Schaffer

MANCHESTER UNIVERSITY PRESS

Published by Manchester University Press
Oxford Road, Manchester, M13 9PL

www.manchesteruniversitypress.co.uk

British Library Cataloguing-in-Publication Data
A catalogue record for this book is available from the British Library

ISBN   978 1 5261 6547 3   hardback

First published 2025

The publisher has no responsibility for the persistence or accuracy of URLs for any external or third-party internet websites referred to in this book, and does not guarantee that any content on such websites is, or will remain, accurate or appropriate.

EU authorised representative for GPSR:
Easy Access System Europe, Mustamäe tee 50, 10621 Tallinn, Estonia
gpsr.requests@easproject.com

Typeset
by New Best-set Typesetters Ltd
Printed and bound by
CPI (UK) Ltd, Croydon CR0 4YY

For Mum and Dad

Contents

Introduction   I

1 The last Jew of Merthyr and other *bubbe meises*: Jewish history and heritage in flux   20

2 *Meshuga frum*? Devotion and division in religious practice   39

3 'We speak for them': political activism in the Six-Day War and the campaign for Soviet Jewry   72

4 'These wicked sons': Israel-critical Jews and the Zionist majority   90

5 *Oi vay* – I'm Jewish and gay: queer Jewish lives and the struggle for recognition   109

6 The (un)forgivable sin: intimacy, love and interfaith marriage   130

7 The nice Jewish boy (who believes in Jesus): Jews, Christianity and the challenge of Messianic Judaism   150

8 The last outpost of the British Empire: youth movements and kibbutz *aliyah*   174

Conclusion: ending, schmending   193

Acknowledgements   197

List of figures   199

List of abbreviations   200

Notes   201

Select bibliography   245

Index   253

Introduction

In my hometown, Birmingham, stands Britain's 'oldest functioning example' of a cathedral synagogue.[1] Dating from 1856, Singers Hill is a Grade II listed gem, recently recognised by Historic England as one of the nation's ten most beautiful synagogues.[2] Designed by Yeoville Thomason (famous as the architect of Birmingham's prominent Council House), it is without question one of the city's primary architectural assets, as well as a vibrant hub of community and worship. You cannot, however, simply wander into Singers Hill, whether you are Jewish or not. While school trips are catered for and interfaith events encouraged, the synagogue is generally inaccessible to the public.

In another world there would be gift shops, cafés and exhibitions, tourists with selfie sticks and guides pointing out the Italian Renaissance design. Singers Hill would be touted on the Birmingham tourist trail, its members bogged down in discussions about how to manage as a working synagogue amid the tourist hullabaloo. That is not, however, the way things are for British Jewry. Instead, amid concerns about community safety and terrorism, the synagogue functions, like the great majority of British Jewish institutions, behind a high fence and locked doors, with no external signage bar a discreet Hebrew inscription on the building itself. Singers Hill does not advertise itself to passers-by. If you don't know that it is there, you are unlikely to notice it at all.

In this way, this striking building reflects something of the feelings of those who have prayed within its walls. While much has changed of course over the lifespan of Singers Hill, many British Jews remain wary about drawing attention to their Jewishness in public and are selective about where and when they do so. In a twentieth century where the forced public badging of Jews in Europe was a prelude to genocide this is perhaps unsurprising, but the disinclination to shout about being Jewish in Britain long preceded the Holocaust.

An unorthodox history

European Jewish immigrants to Britain, many of whom had arrived in flight from racial violence in Russia, suspected that their Jewishness would be tolerated in the new society only up to a point, and were encouraged by the established Jewish community to believe that success and safety stemmed from playing down Jewish difference.[3] Almost all of the big beasts of British Jewry were well connected in non-Jewish circles, anglicised, and practised their Judaism as a matter of private confession and personal association. This approach reflected an environment where the accentuation of Jewishness was seen as undesirable and dangerous, and often as un-British. Reflecting the contemporary legacy of this outlook, public declarations of Jewishness remain challenging for many British Jews, who still think carefully about where and when it is appropriate to tell. Jewishness, Devorah Baum has argued in this context, 'is no sooner uttered aloud than it seems to leave a faint trace of embarrassment on the faces of everyone within range'.[4] Asking someone if they are Jewish, actor Adrian Schiller told the *Jewish Chronicle*, is 'a very intrusive question'.[5]

All of which, perhaps, begins to explain why it has taken me so long to put the British Jewish community at the front and centre of my work. Yet my reticence about 'doing' Jewish history has also been shaped by a feeling that the subject is not considered particularly interesting or significant among historians of modern Britain. As Tony Kushner put it in *Anglo-Jewry since 1066*, among communities of historical scholarship, 'British Jewish history has been regarded as being of minor importance'.[6] Earlier generations of historians defended the subject's worth in terms of the stellar contribution that Jews had made to the nations in which they resided, arguments that were obviously rooted in the desire to justify Jewish presence in non-Jewish societies, and protect the community's reputation in climates where the desirability of a Jewish population was very much a matter for dispute.[7] In this way, Jewish history was recruited to the cause of Jewish survival, as tales of loyalty, ability and service were harnessed in a battle against poisonous antisemitic tropes of Jewish parasitism, internationalism and inferiority.[8] Writing in the interwar period, historians such as Cecil Roth tightly knitted Jewish history into narratives of the British past, arguing in so doing that British and Jewish heritage were 'interwoven inextricably', so that any attempt to pull Jews and Britons apart would see 'the tree of western culture ... mutilated'.[9] In an era when some thought Britain would be better off without its Jews, the reasons for Roth's inclination to use scholarship to defend his community were obvious.

Generations later, such defensive thinking lurks within my work too. In a world where antisemitism continues to linger, I am unable to escape the feeling that writing Jewish history remains a political act laden with risks and responsibilities, similar to the pressures I feel when writing about other racialised communities in Britain. Nonetheless, working in a different age to Roth, I have the luxury of conceiving and constructing Jewish history somewhat differently. This book builds intellectually from the confident and challenging Jewish histories written by the 'new' historians of the 1980s and 1990s, who did so much to help us break away from apologia and paint a richer picture of Jewish experience in Britain.[10] Working from these foundations, there are now different reasons to see British Jewish history as important and to champion its practice; specifically, to explore the significance of British Jews in the global Jewish world, and the centrality of Jewish history in the story of multicultural Britain.[11] Here, in terms that Roth would have appreciated, Jewish history remains a constituent part of the nation's story, developing and evolving within a framework of broader British change.[12] Recognising that this was the case, pioneering historian of local Jewish lives Bill Williams argued that pointing Jewish history outwards was the biggest challenge facing Jewish studies. Jewish historians had too often, Williams regretted, been stricken with the 'disease' of 'introversion', not realising the broader implications of their work.[13] Jewish history, he cautioned, should never be studied in 'an ethnic vacuum'. It was British history at its core and spoke to a raft of broader pasts and historiographies.

Beyond the work of historians, British writers and commentators have been confident in asserting this broader relevance of the Jewish past and present. As migrants *par excellence*, the story of Jews, it has often been argued, opens a window on to a broader range of migrant and refugee experiences and emotions. The Jewish experience, studied through this lens, seems to offer up the human condition of dislocation and marginality, a situation that led one British Reform rabbi to claim that 'the Jew represents anybody who breathes on this earth'.[14] Jews, as seekers, sufferers and survivors, have been held up as a symbol of humanity writ large. As the character Rabbi Leo explains, in Gerda Charles's novel *The Crossing Point* from 1961, 'the Jew is man's nerve, extending and touching everywhere ... the connector without whom the whole flies apart'.[15]

This reading of the British Jewish experience, however, is not easy to swallow. Of course, much in Jewish history chimes with the experiences of non-Jewish minorities. Yet the assertion, made recently in one Jewish community history, that Jews, as migrants, 'trod the same path as others' doesn't necessarily ring true, despite its comforting political resonances.[16] For sure, Jewish migration can and should be studied in the context of other communities.[17] But to assume that Jewish history offers a narrative that speaks for all, that migrants all tread 'the same path', risks silencing both the specificities of Jewish pasts and the complexities of other migrant journeys.[18] Reflecting a lack of certainty in Jews as brokers of universal experience, this book calls for a British Jewish history that asserts a relevance and resonance beyond its Jewish core, but also allows for a turn inwards; introspection that begins by questioning who are the Jews of post-war Britain, and how one might best write their specific history.

Jews in post-war Britain

In the post-war period the British Jewish community assumed a heightened significance in terms of world Jewry that it did not have prior to the Holocaust.[19] After the murder of six million Jews across the Channel, Britain's modest community of 400,000 people found itself (for twenty years) the largest in Europe, bolstered further by Jewish migration from Eastern Europe and the Middle East. This reality thrust British Jewish society into the international limelight as a global hub of Jewish life.[20] As Moshe Davis, from Hebrew University, explained to a 1962 conference on Jewish life in Britain, 'the British Jewish community stands out, by the will of God – as a brand maintained whole after its plucking from the fire'.[21] In the immediate aftermath of the war, British Jewry also assumed an importance on the global Jewish stage as interlocutors between the British government and the 'surviving remnant' of Jewish refugees headed for the mandate territory of Palestine.[22] British Jews challenged and fought British restrictions on immigration to Palestine at home and abroad, but they also represented Britain in its government, its military, its polity.

British Jews lived in a post-war atmosphere of increasing uncertainty about the relevance of religion. Just as Callum Brown has pointed to the 'unprecedented rapidity' of declining Christian religiosity from the late 1950s onwards, so too British Judaism experienced a similar turn away from some forms of traditional religious practice.[23] This turn threw up big questions for the growing number of non- or minimally practising Jews who instinctively saw (or thought they should see) ongoing value in their Jewishness, but didn't really know what to do with it. In a controversial article in the *New Statesman* in 1965, journalist Bernard Levin questioned the relevance of Judaism in a secular age, asking whether modernity had 'entirely dissolved … the word Jew', and concluding that his own practice had indeed 'ceased to have any meaning' at all.[24]

The numerous responses to Levin, and the anger that his piece undoubtedly caused, suggested that he had touched a nerve, that the secular turn was causing existential anxiety for some Jews, felt in terms of loss and guilt.[25] One reply highlighted the horrors of antisemitism as a reason why Levin was not right to even pose a question about the ongoing relevance of Judaism. 'There is a simple and irrefutable answer to Mr Bernard Levin's tragic (and ridiculous) dilemma: Am I a Jew? He can ask himself what Hitler would have thought.'[26] Yet Levin's dilemma was far from his alone, instead reflecting a broader current of uncertainty about secularism and its impact on the old faith. A generation later, Howard Katz, the eponymous character in Patrick Marber's 2001 play, cried in conversation with his dead father, telling him, 'I'm scared... I don't know how to be ... tell me what to do.'[27]

The question of why mostly secular Jews continued to care about their Jewishness, and about Jewish history, remains pertinent. Today's Jewish communities, it seems, are worried about disappearing, whether into gas chambers or the contemporary equivalent, or into the sea of humanity, diluted beyond recognition into other populations and peoples. The first of these concerns has had an enduring impact. The legacy of the Holocaust looms large in contemporary British Jewish subjectivities. In her British Jewish family, novelist Linda Grant recalled, the Holocaust lingered as 'a darkness in us we couldn't be rid of'.[28] After the war, Jewish communities latched quickly on to threats against fellow Jews at home and abroad. As we shall see, British Jews speedily mobilised in support of the State of Israel when they perceived it to be threatened in 1967 and 1973, and have been similarly committed to helping other international Jewish communities under attack (thus the sustained support for Soviet Jewish 'refuseniks' in the 1970s and 1980s). These actions were rooted in solidarity, but also in Holocaust-informed guilt and fear, feelings that created something of a dissonance between perception and reality within and beyond Jewish communal life. Communities that looked to all intents and purposes strong and safe could instead feel weak and vulnerable, a situation described as 'ironic' by recent scholars of international Jewish life, but true nonetheless.[29] In this atmosphere, threats against Jewry seemed to Jewish communities to be the norm, 'a familiar routine' that justified (as shown in the responses to Levin) the point of being Jewish.[30]

Fear and anxiety have shaped modern Jewish life in ways not always realised by communities themselves. What does it mean 'to need Pharoah?', American activist and scholar Leonard Fein asked his readers, arguing that it was the 'winds of others' hatred' that held Jewish communities together.[31] This is an idea that is also underpinned by the seemingly opposite problem of secularism and acceptance. If non-Jews stopped hating us, if we could just blend in among them, what then? Jews, for generations, have feared these challenges, which are hyperbolised, in Simon Rawidowicz's famous formulation, into obsessive narratives of an 'ever-dying people'. This fear, Rawidowicz has argued, has suppressed Jewish culture, exercising 'a most paralyzing effect on our conscious and subconscious life, on our emotions and thought'.[32] In the thinking of many community leaders around the Jewish world, fears of threat/violence and acceptance/assimilation blended together, along with the idea that the latter betrays those whose fate was the former. Judaism thus becomes, as expressed in Levin's provocative analysis, 'nothing but a conditioned reflex to a conditioned stimulus'.[33] Jews need to be, because not being is a betrayal of the past.

In the post-war period many Jews were scared of losing their Judaism or having it ripped from them, despite ostensibly being a settled and secure part of Britain. Jews have frequently been labelled as neurotics, and we have often constructed ourselves (with varying degrees of seriousness) in this way. When, in Bernice Rubens' novel *The Elected Member*, the tragic Norman Zweck remonstrates with God for using Jews as the 'scapegoat for all Your neurosis', he argued a case with which many will identify.[34] But the reduction of narratives of fear to neurosis seems to me to be a slip into antisemitism, taking on the clothes that Jews have so often been given to wear, as well as a somewhat smug refusal to recognise the impacts of recent and present dangers on Jewish communities. For Jews did not (and do not) need to seek out threats or terrors; they were (and are) real enough. Jews in the post-war period have been frightened for good reasons, and taking these fears seriously must be the starting point, in many cases, when opening up Jewish stories and lives. And just as threats against Jewry were real, the idea that many Jews were drifting away from traditional Jewish communities, and that Jewish culture and practice were rapidly changing, was real too.[35]

This book will attempt to capture this state of flux while trying to resist what Salo Baron would have described as a lachrymose reading of what Jews have been, and what we may become. Resisting the lachrymose feels immensely important when trying to understand Jewish history. As the Chief Rabbi, Jonathan Sacks, put it in 2009, the post-war Jewish tendency to feel 'alone' and 'surrounded by enemies' was 'understandable' but 'dangerous'.[36] Aside from leading us away from much of the richness of Jewish lives, it would be profoundly depressing if identifying Jewish fears and their impacts were all that this book achieved. British Jewish communities cannot be explained or understood simply in terms of their anxieties; Jewish lives are much more interesting than that. While it will rear its ugly head in many places, I have declined in this book to offer a history of British antisemitism. This focusing away from antisemitism is not designed to undermine or delegitimise the fears that Jews might justifiably feel, but to show that prejudice and discrimination are not, after all, the glue that holds us together.

An unorthodox history

In an atmosphere of relative prosperity, safety and acceptance, Jewish lives sprawled in different directions across post-war Britain. As religious, family, sexual and social norms changed, Jews changed too, leading some to claim that British Jewry was unravelling into disparate threads. In 2001 an Institute for Jewish Policy Research (JPR) report described British Jewry as 'a community of communities', following the thinking of the ex-president of the Board of Deputies Israel Finestein that to speak of one community was 'misleading'.[37] Sociologist Barry Kosmin had made just such a suggestion over twenty years earlier, noting that 'the plural term communities is increasingly a much more accurate description of the sociological reality than the singular noun'.[38] This issue vexed Jonathan Sacks during his time in office.[39] For him and his predecessor, Immanuel Jakobovits, division was the 'worst disaster that could strike Jewry', when Jews did not 'recognize the others as brothers belonging to a common tribe'.[40] Whether or not division spells disaster, this book argues that there remains value in seeing and understanding the Jewish community as a unitary whole, and that the different paths taken through post-war Britain do not diminish this case. The case studies that follow in this book point to a strong nexus of shared thinking, concerns and values, despite the breadth of Jewish practice. Division and discord, moreover, have historically been so constant in Jewish life that there is no compelling reason to worry about a coming apart now. Jews have always sought out different paths, argued and splintered into separate spheres and congregations. Yet a core of unity remains.

In this 'unorthodox history', I consciously seek out the stories of Jewish Britons who have not been afforded much attention in existing scholarship, those who have lived beyond the parameters of Jewish community and communal organisations and/or who have not met stereotypical expectations of post-war Jews. Certain narratives, voices and places have come to dominate British Jewish history, a reality that has allowed some stories to emerge but silenced others, skewing history towards the rich and famous, towards London, towards heterosexuals, Ashkenazim and men.[41] This book sets out to complicate these dominant narratives, focusing on stories that bring into Jewish history at least some of those who have frequently been left out. The devotions and lives of Ashkenazi (straight) men is not, after all, the story of British Jewry. Too often, however, it has been served up as just that. Jewish post-war history has been oversimplified into a tale of a gentrifying community on the up, neglecting working-class voices, and leaving people feeling cast adrift from a suffocating narrative of Jewish success. Painting a more diverse picture means leaving London. Bill Williams did more than most to check the assumption in Jewish history that other parts of Britain were represented only as 'pale reflections' of the capital.[42] Mindful that this has indeed frequently been the case, I have tried to decentre my analysis, to focus on the plurality of Jewish experiences in Scotland, Wales and Northern England, as well, of course, as London.

I have also sought to ask questions about what being Jewish really means, striving for an inclusive definition of community. To Baum, analysis of 'the Jewish Question' in modern societies has more than anything been a matter 'of categorization'.[43] What/who were/are these people living within the tapestry of modern Britain? A religious community? An ethnicity/race? A cultural or associational group? And how can scholars get to grips with any such questions when the people involved keep moving, both geographically and conceptually. When, in 1966, statistician Marlena Schmool sent notes to her collaborator Maurice Freedman (following the Board of Deputies' establishment of a Demographic and Statistical Research Unit), she offered a range of ways that Jews might be defined for analysis. Jewish community, Schmool wrote, 'could be taken to mean':

a. All persons who have a Jewish mother, or
b. all persons who have some, recorded contact with the organised community, or
c. all persons who have one Jewish parent, mother or father, or
d. all persons who call themselves Jewish, or
e. all persons whom other Jews consider to be Jewish[44]

This list highlighted the challenge facing scholars of Jewry in the post-war period, which is not dissimilar to the one now facing me. How does a researcher decide, in a study of British Jews, who should be included? For Orthodox Jewish communities, and those influenced by Orthodox thinking, the simple answer to Schmool's question is 'a'. Judaism operates a matrilineal descent system, so that you are a Jew if your mother was one (or if you formally convert), a state of affairs that can and must be policed by the rabbinic authorities. There is little scope, in this worldview, for negotiation. As Immanuel Jakobovits explained in 1958, 'it would be preposterous and utterly chaotic to transfer the prerogative of effecting admissions to Judaism (or Jewishness) from the jurisdiction of competent legal authorities to the arbitrary choice of private individuals'.[45] Orthodox Jews, Jakobovits argued, 'can and will never depart from the age-old legal definition of what constitutes a Jewish person'.[46]

But for post-war statistical, and for that matter historical, enquiry, this definition feels very unsatisfactory. For one thing, Reform and Liberal congregations in Britain, at different moments, have formally embraced patrilineal descent, meaning that definition 'a' excludes a raft of people who recognise themselves as Jews and have been formally recognised as such by a set of British synagogues, as well, of course, as a greater number of unaffiliated people who considered themselves to be Jewish in terms of their ancestry, culture or practice.[47] Here, synagogues and rabbinic courts are not the only arbiters. Families, individuals, social groups designate Jewishness in a myriad of ways, so that the lived religious experience of British Jews differs significantly from the way it might look from the pulpit of an Orthodox synagogue. Noting that the majority of those in the USA who identify as Jewish will soon be intermarried Jews, Baker has thus argued that we are witnessing an era in which the parameters of 'Jew' are being 'expanded and transformed'.[48] Of course, this idea is hard, if not impossible, for many Orthodox Jews (and non-Orthodox Jews) to swallow, but it seems important to explore the stakes in the discussion.

Can you really be a Jew if many other Jews don't think you are one? This question comes up most frequently as regards patrilineal Jews, but is nowhere more incendiary than as regards Messianic Judaism (as we shall see below), wherein Jews believe in Jesus but passionately assert their Jewishness, a definition of self seen by most other Jews as a contradiction in terms, even as an offence. In an age where the primacy of self-definition, when it comes to personal identities, could hardly be more apposite, how all-embracing can 'Jew' as a moniker be? Are there any people to whom it is appropriate to deny, against their wishes, the label 'Jew'; and, in a period when any such definition is unstable, permeable, evolving, who gets to decide? The difficulty of these challenges has pushed Jewish studies back time and again towards a stable, easy-to-interrogate centre. For Norman Cohen, reporting on trends in Jewish religious life at a conference in 1962, the impossibility of charting 'with any reliability' numbers of non-affiliated Jews meant that community bodies had little choice but to exclude them from their thinking. These Jews, he explained, 'have probably passed the point of no return and they can be ignored in any consideration of communal conditions'.[49] As a result, therefore, of what it was possible to study and categorise, Jewish studies has focused mostly on specific and stable communities.

This story of the Jewish centre, of middle-of-the-road, United Synagogue Jews, has pushed British Jewish history in a certain direction, specifically towards an analysis of decline, which has been difficult for some to resist. Changes in affiliation and patterns of devotion among such Jews have led some scholars to paint a morbid picture. To David Vital, 'the majoritarian secularist trend' has meant a 'cultural vulnerability that is more than likely, ultimately, to prove fatal' to the British Jewish community.[50] Such readings, however, are missing something, seeing endings where there are instead changes, decline where there is in fact regeneration. My alternative narrative is rooted in two interlinked contentions: first, that different Jewish cultures have been emerging from the old, that it is necessary to look away from the historical centre to understand the full richness of modern Jewish lives.[51] Second, that British Jewry is so deeply woven into the nation that it could never be removed (exactly as Cecil Roth had argued). Whether, of course, such Jewish cultures are seen as vibrant, even as Jewish, is in the eye of the beholder. But to me, British Jewry sprawls and thrives.

To interrogate the sprawl of British Jewry is the aim of this book. The next chapter opens this question by focusing on the Welsh town of Merthyr Tydfil and its Jewish history, arguing that we have been too quick to pronounce the end of Jewish life in the town (because people of Jewish descent still live there), and, ultimately, that an inclusive definition of Jewishness makes it highly unlikely that Merthyr will ever be bereft of Jews and Jewishness. Jewish roots now lie so deep in every part of Britain that they cannot conceivably be absent in any near future. In the second, third and fourth chapters, I draw out the ways in which Jewish belief and activism have sprawled in line with evolving religious and political cultures, reflecting on how being (and doing) Jewish has meant very different things to different people across the post-war period. From there, the book dives deep into Jewish histories which could be dismissed as marginal. Queer Jews, Jews who have married non-Jews and Messianic Jews are one by one pulled into our understanding of the British Jewish whole. Finally, in 'The last outpost of the British Empire', I move away from British shores, looking at Jews who are no longer in Britain but remain very much British, having made new lives for themselves in Israel.

Taken as a whole, these chapters explore paths less travelled in British Jewish history. Nonetheless, they each, in their way, take us closer to the heart of British Jewish post-war experience. There are many ways to be Jewish and many Jewish histories to be written. My aim is to expose some new edges in what is a vibrant and resonant history, following in the footsteps of those previous historians who believed that Jewish stories are worth telling for their own sake, and speak to much more than the sum of their parts. I write in hope of a proliferation in British Jewish studies that will create a rich tapestry, so that we can begin to capture the complexity and diversity of the global Jewish past and contribute more broadly to the history of modern Britain.

The personal and the communal

My history of British Jews will be as close to everyday Jewish lives, a history of the ordinary and 'banal', as possible.[52] I want to question what happens to people and their families when they are remembered primarily as a constituent of something bigger, within a community narrative. What happens to me, to the Schaffers, in such a history? When Brits of the future visit Jewish museums, read Jewish histories and take walking tours of Jewish neighbourhoods and buildings, assuming they can be bothered to do any such thing, what or who will they hear and see, and what will it tell them about the Jewish world that I know?

Such worries, at one level, make unreasonable, even laughable, claims on the future. I am reminded of a story told to me by the historian Pam Fox about criticism of her social history of Golders Green, condemned by one irritated reader for failing to mention his grandfather! Histories, after all, can only give voice to a tiny minority of lives. They cannot give space to all our grandfathers, much as I understand the personal desire for commemoration. But recognising that this is the case, that some kind of imperfect collective must hold space for the multiplicity of our experiences, doesn't reduce the challenge. The tension between the personal and the communal comes to the fore in the stories we choose to tell, the events which are held up as emblematic of our history in books, museums and other repositories of our pasts. Jewish communities and their leaderships have their own evolving agenda, which individual stories enter (and do not enter) in relation to overarching community narratives. As Keith Kahn-Harris and Ben Gidley have noted, 'the urgent desire to ensure Jewish continuity leads to ambivalence regarding research on the lives of individual Jews'.[53]

Community history, at all times, has its own rhythms and needs. In his analysis of Jewish family histories, Stephan Feuchtwang has drawn attention to the construction and importance of 'caesurae', defining events which are used to 'mark the moment of creation of a relative past, the before of a given event and the after of a new present'.[54] Looking at British Jewish history, a few caesurae loom large, doing the heavy lifting that makes sense of all that follows. The pogroms and poverty that brought so many Jews to these shores, the Holocaust, and key moments in Israeli history (the foundation of the state and the Six-Day War in particular) provide the before and after moments of our Jewish communal story, and help to explain the how, when and why in terms of what the Jewish community in Britain has become.

In the chapters that follow, these communal caesurae are ever present, especially the Holocaust (a reality that inadvertently stifles the commemoration of many Mizrahi migrant journeys). Post-war Jewish writers have often presented British Jewish lives in this way as trauma histories, deploying characters who cannot shake off the horror of what happened to Europe's Jews. In Alexander Baron's *The Lowlife*, the protagonist, Harryboy Boas, is haunted by his knowledge of the Holocaust, which intrudes at every stage on the world he sees around him.[55] In Howard Jacobson's *Kalooki Nights*, the narrator, Max Glickman, grows up in Manchester with '"extermination" in my vocabulary and the Nazis in my living room'.[56] In these fictional worlds, Jews could not escape the overpowering horror of the Holocaust, and sometimes personal histories tell a similar story. In Adam Andrusier's recent account of his own Jewish family, he recalls how his father collected postcards of European synagogues because they 'made him feel like a rescuer, a witness'.[57] This kind of feeling, powerful and persistent, resonates in community histories, is one of the organising themes of British Jewish heritage, and dominates much of our communal rendering of our past.

But in my own family, and in the Jewish communities in which I have grown up, the Holocaust and Israel assume a smaller space. This is not because the Jewish people I know would ever be indifferent to these overwhelming histories, but because the key events that punctuate personal histories are inevitably different. Here, a more mundane set of markers hold sway – births, deaths, marriages, personal moments of triumph and disaster. And looked at through these lenses, Jewish life is rendered in a very different fashion, as much more like the lives of non-Jewish Britons, whose personal worlds are built around the same kinds of life events. That this is the case can be seen in the hard work of Jewish communal bodies to draw us back to our collective responsibilities. The annual cycle of campaigns to ensure support for Israel and to remember the Holocaust suggest that Jewish people need reminding, that we are otherwise distracted by a different set of priorities. Put simply, Emil Fackenheim's famous 614th commandment, that Jews must not give Hitler a 'posthumous victory' by neglecting Judaism or forgetting 'the martyrs of the Holocaust', only makes sense if there is a real risk of such a possibility in our everyday lives.[58]

This divergence of paths between the personal and the communal matters because the stories we choose to tell, and what we make of them, shape what our Jewish history becomes. Children emerge into their family history as characters in 'an ongoing story', and this, of course, influences our understanding of our Jewishness long before any synagogue, history book or museum has the chance to have its say.[59] On these terms, our stories shape expectations of the future as well as curating our past. Championing hitherto under-recorded histories serves thus as a corrective measure to ensure that future generations see the breadth and diversity of what British Jewry is, and has been. In this way, I want to use personal stories to distance us from communal narratives, not just to bring the old stories to life but to draw us to new ones. In this book, by mapping out the borders of the Jewish community and how they have been policed, broader patterns of feeling and faith come into view. Even the kinds of insults that we throw at each other (self-haters, traitors, apostates, not being real Jews) seem important, telling as they do of our beliefs, fears, prejudices and insecurities. In this way, I have tried to capture outsider experiences and set them alongside more conventional accounts of Jews coming together. In all these histories, I strive not to lose sight of the individual, mindful that as we lose personal stories in our history, we lose the community too.

Historians tend to shy away from idiosyncratic family stories, ever fearful of the 'so what?' question. We all know the feeling of being bored to death by tedious tales of little-known relatives. But every family has such stories, and it would be a mistake to think that their telling and retelling has no purpose.[60] These histories are less likely to speak immediately to the community caesurae, but instead might pull us in new directions. That said, the personal and communal do not stand entirely separate. As a story below from my own family illustrates, the bigger picture encroaches at every stage, shaping a history at the point of its first telling and every point after. It's a history that has stuck in my mind, evolving with me as a listener, its retelling now saying as much about my beliefs and interests as about those who came before me.[61]

The story begins with my great grandfather, Marks (or Mark) Bernstein. Marks was born in Suwalki in eastern Poland, or at least that is what is recorded in the 1901 census. In 1911 his birthplace is recorded as Hamburg, some twelve hours' drive westward. Marks sought out his future in Britain, marrying his wife Fanny, and setting up home in the Welsh valley town of Merthyr Tydfil, making his living as a door-to-door salesman of clothes, and raising nine children, the youngest of whom was my grandmother, Sophie. This personal history is at one level tragically typical of Jewish British experience. Immigrant Polish door-to-door salesman, cryptic and contradictory census data, not even being entirely sure about a first name are all about as stereotypical as British Jewish history gets. In such a narrative, poor Marks's name and birthplace get mixed up by census officials not understanding (or respecting) what they were told and making their own assumptions about the stranger in front of them (Marks spoke very limited English by all accounts). British and American Jewish family histories are full of such stories, of unfeeling bureaucrats playing fast and loose with the Jewish past, changing names, anglicising, making things up.[62]

A man with a long history of heart problems, Marks passed away in 1928 at the age of 62, sixteen years before my father, his grandson, was born. The manner of Marks's death was unusual to say the least. My dad tells the story in terms of a death 'in unfortunate circumstances', and certainly, for Sophie, who witnessed it and who told me the story herself many times, it must have been extremely upsetting. Below is the story in my father's words.

> well my Mum was 13 and the family were making quite a bit of money, they worked the markets at that time, and my uncles were all very good salesmen most of them and on the weekend on a Sunday particularly, if it was a nice day they would drive to Porthcawl, which is a very nice seaside, park there, put out a couple of rugs in the carpark and have a picnic ... and they had a nice day and loaded up the car, which was a new Vauxhall they'd bought, and got back in the car, and started to drive home when mum, who was sitting next to her dad, said, 'Mum, Dad's awful quiet'. And they looked round, and he'd had a heart attack and died in the car.

The story continues in terms of the difficulty of managing Marks's death, in a Jewish way, from the outskirts of Porthcawl. Men had to come from Merthyr and Cardiff to ensure that the handling of the body and its transfer back home complied with Jewish laws around death and burial. They managed in the end, because Marks is buried in the Jewish cemetery of the Merthyr congregation in Cefn Coed, next to his wife, Fanny, who survived for a further thirty-two years. The family grew in Merthyr through the Second World War, and Sophie, in 1937, married a Londoner, my grandpa Sid.

Sophie and Sid set up home in the London suburb of Edgware in 1950, arriving via Stamford Hill, another highly typical Jewish immigrant trajectory from my grandpa's origins in the East End of London. The couple met after the Merthyr family had sent Sophie to visit relatives in London (in the hope that she might meet an appropriate Jewish partner), and the rest, as they say, is history. After spending the war in the relative safety of Merthyr, where my dad was born, the family moved back. A builder originally, Sid was persuaded by his new family that there were easier ways to make a living. He set up a business selling fabrics and making them into underwear, the materials coming from the family back in Merthyr. The new enterprise was in Balham, South London, and he named it Balham Bargain Stores. He bought a four-storey terrace house on Hildreth Street which enabled him to operate a shop and a small factory. The top floor was rented out to Edward Bryan, a nightwatchman, and his wife, Annie, who were living there with their 34-year-old son, Leslie. On 5 May 1961 disaster struck.

My dad remembers being woken in the middle of the night by a phone call from the emergency services. The shop was on fire and Sid was asked to attend. All the family drove to Balham to be greeted by a scene of devastation. Dad remembers how they 'got dressed quickly, got in the car, drove to Balham, and there was this shell of a shop … the only thing that was left was the basement really and the front wall'. A local newspaper report confirmed the assessment. 'The whole place', it told readers, 'was gutted.' A neighbouring family had first raised the alarm when their infant daughter woke up coughing at 2.30 a.m.[63] Soon the fire brigade from Tooting, Clapham and Streatham were on the scene, attempting to rescue the Bryans, but they were 'beaten back by flames shooting … through the roof'.[64] A neighbour explained to the local press that the firemen had no chance of saving the family. 'It was impossible to get inside the premises which together with the adjoining storeroom was a blazing furnace.'[65] Other nearby residents were more fortunate. A newspaper report told of how 'a turn-table ladder was used to evacuate some of the families in adjoining premises while firemen were fighting flames that were twelve feet high at times'.[66]

So dreadful was the fire that its wreckage became something of a distasteful local attraction. A week after the tragedy, according to the *Balham and Tooting News and Mercury*,

> Hordes of sightseers made a macabre pilgrimage ... to the burnt-out shell of a building in Hildreth Street, Balham, where three people were trapped and burned to death in a top-floor flat on Friday. They came in dozens at a time to point to the top floor and air their own theories as to how the victims ... met their death.[67]

This question, of course, was brought before a coroner. Annie and Leslie Bryan, he recorded, along with Leslie's friend Bernard Clarke, a labourer who was staying the night with the family, died in their sleep, seemingly without knowing anything of what was happening around them. The firemen finally managed to retrieve their bodies at 4.30 a.m. Cause of death was given as 'Asphyxia due to inhalation of fire fumes'.[68] Edward Bryan survived the tragedy because he worked at night. Returning from his shift at 8 a.m. the following morning, he found his family and home totally destroyed.

What happened to cause the fire was never really known. Sid thought the shop had been 'struck by lightning', but that turned out not to be the case.[69] The fire, the coroner heard, had started at 'the floor of the staircase on the ground floor', and could have been caused by a gas ring or cigarette or match from the shop, or when 'one of the occupants on the third floor had dropped a lighted cigarette or a match near the foot of the stairs'. Given that one guest of the Bryans, who left their flat at 12.15 a.m., gave evidence that there was no smell of smoke on his departure, the coroner felt that 'a fire inside the enclosure could be ruled out'.[70] Over a dropped cigarette, it seems, three people lost their lives, a family was destroyed, with their neighbours having a lucky escape because a little girl woke up and smelled the fumes.

The story of the Hildreth Street fire, however, evolved differently in my family. Here, the deaths of the Bryans and Bernard Clarke receded, and instead the story became primarily one about the shop, the damage, and how my grandfather navigated what was undoubtedly a financial disaster. At the outset, Sid was, of course, mindful of the terrible loss of lives. He told the local newspaper: 'I was terribly shocked when I heard about those poor people – my tenants – being trapped in the top floor. You just don't think of tragedy striking people you know in this way.'[71] And yet, perhaps inevitably, his and the family's thoughts soon turned to the business and what was to be done.

Introduction

Because he didn't want to pay high premiums, the shop had been significantly under-insured and Sid 'lost thousands and thousands'. All the stock was pretty much destroyed and bills needed to be paid. To solve these problems, Sid speedily put a plan into operation. He had a banner made and hung it over the shop's façade: 'Balham Bargain Stores: Down but not out'. He recovered the damaged fabrics that had survived in the basement, sodden with water from the fire hoses, and sold them, at cut price, from an improvised stall in front of the shop. He tasked my dad with trying to mend the damaged sewing machines and with setting up a new workshop in Vauxhall to continue making the underwear. Meanwhile, he and his brother started to rebuild the shop themselves.

Following the rebuild, the story of the fire was seldom told, and when it was it became a tale about responding to crisis and about my grandfather's personality. A man who had little time for institutions (insurers in this instance), Sid would solve problems in his own way, with his own resources. He called upon family as and when he felt he needed them, and he managed everything himself. In my dad's words: 'That was exactly how he lived his life. He made the decisions, and my mum went along with him.' With this focus, the story of the fire became a tale of resilience and rebuilding, of a certain spirit and attitude. The real story, the terrible loss of life, vanishes in this rendering to the point that the present teller, my dad, is foggy on the details. 'I knew nothing about it at the time', he told me. 'I think I was told the old guy up there died in the fire, and he was smoking and fell asleep.'

The Hildreth Street fire, in my family story, has thus evolved to focus almost entirely on the impact of the event on my family. This myopic rendering offers a cautionary tale about family history writ large. By focusing our histories on those we hold dear, and telling stories about them, we risk losing much of the world in which they lived. And might we not extrapolate to see this risk in the writing of Jewish history more broadly? When we historicise ourselves as Jews, what becomes of our neighbours? Are they drawn in only as persecutors, or in bit parts? Do they get left out entirely, even when the real story is about them?

My family story, moreover, has evolved within those pervasive communal parameters regarding what Jewish immigrant stories are and should be. Marks's death, in this context, is a story of strangers in a strange land, a tale that casts its Jewish protagonists as vulnerable outsiders, out of their comfort zone. Had Marks stayed where he belonged, in the bosom of kosher Merthyr (or even better kosher Suwalki), he would not have been exposed to such an uncouth ending. Instead, speaking no English, in poor health, he died like a fish out of water, leaving his family with the not inconsiderable challenge of trying to return his body to a Jewish environment. But while Marks couldn't survive his outing to Porthcawl, there is another story here too, about children who were adapting and thriving in their new home. With their new Vauxhall for weekend outings, their picnics and trips to the seaside speak to the hegemonic Jewish immigrant experience: working hard, fitting in, getting on. Marks may have been lost on the journey, but the journey itself continued.

This entrepreneurial rendering of the Jewish past rears its head in Hildreth Street too. Undaunted by losses that would have wiped out another businessman, the Jewish shop owner carried on, got back on his feet, striving for prosperity and security against all odds. It wasn't only my family who evolved the story in this manner. To some extent at least, even in the immediate aftermath, the fire was presented as a tale of Jewish resilience in the local press too. A week after it happened, the *Tooting and Balham Gazette* described the scene thus: 'Business was as usual in the Hildreth Street market area on Friday – with one exception. An extra stall was there. It was being used by Mr Shaffer [*sic*] proprietor of the destroyed shop who was busy helping in salvage operations.' Here, then, was the story; the Jewish immigrant, down but not out, carrying on, refusing to give up.

This matters for a number of reasons. First, and most obviously, it offers a warning about what is so easily lost in family history (that is, people not in the family) and about the place of non-Jews in Jewish history. By failing to foreground the deaths of Leslie and Annie Bryan and Bernard Clarke, our story loses its very essence. Without the contextual picture, beyond the struggle of Jews making their lives in Britain, history loses its meaning. Jewish stories, meanwhile, continue to be moulded by the community caesurae. These creep in, uninvited and unobserved. So really Marks's death is a story of immigrant Jewish vulnerability, the Hildreth Street fire one of immigrant durability. Both begin really in the pogroms of Eastern Europe and tell of Jews trying to rise from oppression, striving against the odds to get on. Taking our places as characters in such stories obscures our real selves and pulls into sharp focus the risk that our personal histories are all too easily bound up, and ultimately lost, in such an overarching narrative.

Instead, we need history that recognises that Jewish lives in modern Britain started and ended on innumerable disparate paths and are not easily captured within any monolithic community experience. Jews in post-war Britain, Rabbi Lionel Blue understood, 'live[d] in the untidy workshop out of which a new

Judaism [was] being born'.[72] Here, new lives and new cultures were made, histories that speak to the diversity of the makers and the world they lived in. Many generations after most Jews came to these shores, this past and present cannot be pulled apart from broader British history and society, of which Jews have long been a constituent part. After hundreds of years, Jews and Jewishness live in the bones of the nation. This unorthodox history sets out to tell some of their stories.

1

The last Jew of Merthyr and other *bubbe meises*: Jewish history and heritage in flux[1]

Nudrat Afza is not Jewish. Originally from Pakistan, she migrated to the UK with her mother at the age of 10, setting up home in the Yorkshire city of Bradford. Here, she raised her own family, and developed a professional reputation as a social documentary photographer. In 2019 Afza exhibited a collection of photographs documenting Jewish lives in the city. Entitled *Kehillah* (the Hebrew word for community or congregation), this exhibition offered a down-to-earth, everyday portrait of Jewish worship, focused on Bradford's small Reform congregation.

Afza's involvement with, and focus on, Jewish people grew organically, stemming from personal relationships, and, only later, professional curiosity. Long-term friendships shaped her awareness of Jewish history in the city, eventually leading her to pick up her camera and photograph Bradford's Jews. Through a hospital visit she developed a bond with a Jewish woman, Faye Kramrisch, who, it turned out, had lived in Afza's house as a child. Twenty years of friendship ensued, incorporating another Jewish friend, who one day asked Afza to drive her to the Orthodox synagogue so that she could attend the community's final service. Committed as she was to recording decline and change in Bradford, Afza wanted to photograph the synagogue. She remembered: 'I kind of knew that the building would go, or it would change, so a few months afterwards I went to take pictures of it from the outside.' In the following months she gained permission from the synagogue's chairman to take pictures inside the building as well, which was soon afterwards demolished. In its absence Afza's pictures survive, recording the change, showing a building empty of worshippers, in her mind offering a 'poignancy' and a 'haunting quality' that left her with a desire to juxtapose these images with those of the living Bradford Jewish community. The city's Reform congregation, one of the oldest in the country, was still operational in its striking nineteenth-century building. Creating her *Kehillah*, Afza took pictures of the community there, having secured an Arts Council grant for the project.

The beauty of Afza's *Kehillah*, grainy natural shots taken on fast film to compensate for the low light in the building, attracted national attention. We see an old man, the then 93-year-old Rudi Leavor, poised over his prayer book, a woman in the dark blowing out candles on a menorah as if it is the last action of a generation. But, as Afza envisaged, we also see day-to-day community, friends posing outside shul, a young boy with his tallis bag, a smiling lady with a cup of coffee. And yet it is the idea of decline, of a community on the way out, that really gives *Kehillah* its punch. Presented in black and white, the pictures ooze 'nostalgia' and 'romance'. They could, Afza explained, have been 'taken sixty years ago'. The project, to her mind, 'documented a culture that's disappearing and a community that's disappearing'.[2]

The Reform synagogue in Bradford opened in 1881 (some fifty years after Jews came to the city) and is indeed in serious decline.[3] When Rudi Leavor passed away in 2021, he was the last of twelve singers in the synagogue's choir, in a community that now only gathers around fifteen people for monthly services.[4] Money from friends of the synagogue, and notably from local Muslim supporters and the Heritage Lottery Fund, enabled Bradford Reform to avoid closure in 2013. As Rudi told the gathered crowd at the opening of *Kehillah* in 2020, it now 'just about ticks over, in slow motion'.[5] For Afza, this sentiment sums up Bradford more generally. 'I've been in Bradford for a long time and I saw it kind of being vandalised and destroyed in the 60s when I arrived, although I was young, I didn't understand and then again, it happened again in the 80s…'[6] For many of the visitors to *Kehillah*, however, and much of the press, the story of decline was specifically a Jewish one, as the Bradford setting receded.[7] In the exhibition's comments book, visitors recorded their feelings that *Kehillah* was 'a fine tribute to a lost world', 'a priceless record of a disappearing way of life', 'a bygone age', which they were glad to see 'before it disappears'. This lens for seeing Jewish life is far from Afza's and Bradford's alone. Just across the Pennines in Manchester, Rachel Lichtenstein's recent curation of the photographs of Jewish photographer Shloimy Alman tells a similar story. Alman's photos of Jewish life in the city in the 1970s, she explained, offer 'a unique record of a disappeared world'.[8]

The instinct to see, capture and preserve Jewish life in an atmosphere of decline and disappearance is the subject of this chapter. Looking across and beyond Jewish communities in Britain, I want to interrogate Longfellow's *Legend of the Dead*, the persistent, determined vulnerability and morbidity that seems so often to shape the ways that we view Jews and Jewish communities.[9] Why, as Josh Glancy asked in a *Jewish Chronicle* column, is the idea of 'the last Jew' so compelling? Glancy quipped, 'Try googling it: the last Jews of Libya, the last Jews of Cochin, the last Jews of Alexandria, of Burma, of Cuba, of Baghdad. The joke about the *New York Times* is they will eventually publish a piece about the last Jews on the moon.'[10] People love dead Jews, Dara Horn recently told us.[11] But why? This chapter will reflect on how British Jews and non-Jews engage with the idea of 'dead' and 'dying' Jewish spaces – cemeteries and disused synagogues – arguing that the ways in which such spaces are understood tells us a considerable amount about Jewish life in Britain.

The whine of decline

To Stephen Brook, Jewish decline was 'the problem that worrie[d] almost all sections of the Anglo-Jewish community' in the post-war period.[12] At one level, this was a very British worry. As numerous scholars of post-war history have attested, concerns about decline were politically and socially prominent across a nation highly anxious about its waning relevance and power.[13] At another level, Jewish communal anxiety reflected the realities of demographic change. The number of Jews in Britain fell from a peak in the 1950s of over 400,000 to somewhere beneath 300,000 people. In certain towns and cities, and Bradford offers a key example, this decline was dramatic. Where once communities existed and even thrived, they now, as Leavor put it, 'tick[ed] over', where they existed at all. Change was particularly pronounced in provincial Jewish spaces, where Jewish communal life often seemingly vanished. In South Wales, once a bustling Jewish hub because of the industrial revolution, communities dwindled after the war. In 1954 the marriage secretary of the Aberdare and Aberaman community asked the Board of Deputies if he could return the marriage register, noting that his towns had 'not had a marriage officiated since August 1942' and that there was 'no prospect of any wedding taking place in my time'.[14] Close by, the honorary secretary of the Brynmawr Hebrew Congregation told the Board, 'we have ceased to exist. This is happening, as you are no doubt aware with quite a number of smaller communities.'[15]

At the heart of these changes was generally not the international migration that had characterised the nineteenth- and twentieth-century Jewish past, and it was not, as was the case in so much of the rest of Jewish Europe, a story of genocide. Instead, Jewry 'ceasing to exist' in places such as Brynmawr was an everyday consequence of second- and third-generation migrants moving across and beyond Britain in search of better social and professional opportunities, and more frequently living outside formal Jewish communities. As Ursula Henriques asserted in her study of South Wales Jewish life, 'The history of the Jews of South Wales is one of rise and fall. But it is largely a rise of destitute immigrants and largely a fall of well-educated, middle-class families looking for business and professional openings.'[16] On these terms, Jewish communities dwindled in some places, while large communities such as Manchester and especially London continued to thrive. Overall, the community has recently been growing again in number.[17]

Yet amid this everyday reality there has been something alluring about capturing Jewish communities in their final throes, in weakness and vulnerability, illuminated by a persistent morbid fascination with South Wales's Jewish past and present. In 1989 Chaim Bermant's article in the *Jewish Chronicle*, 'Last Jews of the Valleys?', captured neatly the affection and attention given to Jewish communities which, in Bermant's words, were 'fading away'.[18] The narrative explained that while Jews used to be found 'everywhere' in South Wales, and where there was once 'almost a minyan of Rabbis and shochetim and chazanim', now 'the rabbi is all on his own'. A week later, Bermant was criticised in the newspaper for an analysis that sounded 'ominously like an epitaph'.[19] Epitaphs were, though, the order of the day, nowhere more so than in coverage of the Welsh Jewish community in Merthyr Tydfil. This community was portrayed in a 1997 *Sunday Telegraph* article by Tony Scotland, entitled 'The Last Jew in Merthyr'.[20] Scotland's narrative focused on a barber, George Black, who was in the process of retiring to Manchester. Here, Jewish history was again captured in its last act, as Black told Scotland that he would return to Merthyr only to be buried in the Jewish cemetery. 'Oh yes. I've paid for the plot up at the cemetery. But I don't know when. That's the only phone call I haven't made.'[21]

In Scotland's story, Jewish Merthyr was presented in a tone both mournful and romantic. The disused synagogue, built in 1872, was described as 'a fairy-tale castle' bringing happiness to a town of Jews who had found an unlikely 'new Jerusalem' in the valleys. Merthyr's community ceased to operate in the 1980s, but regret at its demise, and a desire to reverse it, have persisted to the extent that the Foundation for Jewish Heritage has now purchased the disused synagogue building and is working to create within it a 'Welsh Jewish Heritage Centre'. To the Foundation, this restoration is 'saving Jewish history', fighting against 'oblivion'.[22] But while this narrative obviously scratches a communal itch, and while it can hardly be understood as an attempt to undermine Jewish history, it is in some ways both stifling and silencing. For Jewish life did not end in Merthyr with George Black the barber. Nor has it ended anywhere in Britain, and nor is it likely to do so. Jewish people, Jewish stories are saturated into the fabric of the nation. Hundreds of years of history have made quite sure of that. The most recent UK census in 2021 recorded five people in Merthyr who declared their religion as Jewish, as against four in 2011 and fifteen in 2001. Given that these data might well miss people who consider themselves Jewish on other terms than religion (such as ethnicity, culture or heritage), it seems clear that 'Last Jew' stories in Britain are just that. Aside from their questionable accuracy, such narratives remove at a stroke from our collective history those inconvenient people whose lives don't fit the mould, who refuse to disappear. In Merthyr, siblings Steve Shipman and Jackie Edwards lived in the town through the period of Scotland's story, and still do.

Steve and Jackie are the children of a Jewish man from Merthyr, Alfred Shipman, and a non-Jewish Welsh woman from Abercanaid, Elizabeth (Betty) Evans, who met Alfred when she came to work in his mother's shop in the town. Initially, Alfred and Elizabeth's interfaith romance was resisted by both sets of families (Alfred was sent away to work in London in the hope that he might change his mind). In 1940, however, when Alfred was working to support the war effort in Bristol, his relationship with Elizabeth reignited and the couple married, returning to live in Merthyr after the end of the conflict. Brought up in Merthyr's Jewish community, Steve and Jackie were taken to the cheder and the synagogue, Jackie recalling that she loved attending with her cousins and going to her grandma's for dinner 'every Friday night'.[23] Both sustain relationships to this day with other members of the Jewish community, including the daughter of the 'last Jew', George Black, who often comes back to visit. Unlike many of the town's Jewish people, Alfred Shipman hadn't wanted to leave Merthyr, and lived out his days there, finally being buried in the Jewish cemetery in Cefn Coed in 1977. Similarly, Steve cannot see himself leaving a town which has firmly become the family's home. He told me: 'I won't be leaving Merthyr.'[24] Indeed, both Steve and Jackie still live in the town, and Jackie's daughter until recently resided in the house formerly owned by Alfred's mother, Rose.

The story of Jackie and Steve problematises the idea that Jewish life ended in Merthyr and also helps us to understand changes in British Jewish demographics. As these two life stories indicate, any decline in the number of Jewish people in Britain needs to be understood as a decline in Jewish affiliation.[25] Of course, people with Jewish antecedents have not reduced in number in this period. Instead, as has been the case outside Jewish communities too, decline has occurred in the context of an increasing number of people eschewing religious affiliation, and slipping into the secular stream of non-affiliated multicultural Britain.[26] Steve told me, 'we feel multicultural in the family'.[27] This trend, Geoffrey Alderman has argued, rendered the post-war years a time of 'seemingly irreversible ... demographic decline' for British Jewry.[28] As a result of growing secularism, he argued, 'much of what we now regard as modern British Jewry will disappear, concealing itself behind a cloak of secular ethnicity', reducing recognisable Jews to 'a strange and largely suburban dwelling remnant'. This construction, however, does not capture fully the diversity of complex Jewish identities in twentieth-century Britain. Drifting out of communities did not necessarily mean that people ceased to see themselves as Jewish, or to practise Judaism on their own terms. Jewishness has never left Jackie and Steve or their Merthyr home, for example. After her marriage ended, Jackie told me of her urge to 'go to synagogue again', while Steve still prays for his family daily to 'the same God as Moses, which is the Hebrew God'.[29] For many analysts, however, as our introduction showed, non-affiliation and intermarriage really did signal the end of Judaism (on the presumption that the children of non-affiliated Jews were unlikely to step back into communal Judaism). In the post-war period, the fear of losing such Jews caused considerable concern. Academics, activists and leaders pored over the declining numbers of Jews marrying in synagogue, increasing rates of intermarriage, the number of Jewish circumcisions, and the tendency of young people not to affiliate with religious communities.[30]

Anxieties about Jewish decline have reflected realities on the ground, but they have also served a purpose, and continue to do so. To some scholars, decline anxiety has been little less than the binding force of Jewish communities over generations. In this atmosphere, Leonard Fein contended, survival became 'the principal consensual aim' of post-war Jewish life, fear of decline the key motivator of Jewish leadership.[31] For this to be the case, of course, such fears needed to be productive, and indeed they were. The 'constant vision of the end', Rawidowicz argued, helped Jewry to 'overcome every crisis'.[32] In what they have described as a 'reflexive turn', Kahn-Harris and Gidley have argued that British Jewish leaders from the 1990s 'publicly stressed the weaknesses ... of Anglo Jewry ... to nurture the insecurity that was deemed necessary to motivate action to ensure Jewish survival'.[33] Put simply, decline anxiety could serve as a spur to action, persuading otherwise apathetic people that today was the day to act as Jews, that any delay risked tarring present custodians of the faith with the unparalleled guilt of breaking the age-old chain that had after all been maintained by forebears in much tougher times. Through this lens, anxieties about the loss of the past can be seen as a leadership strategy to maintain a community that was reluctant to engage with its history and chose to keep a good distance from memories that were anything but happy in many cases. As Linda Grant put it, forgetting/ignoring the past had been a choice for many British Jews. 'Of course when they said, "I can't remember"', she quipped, 'they remembered all too bloody well.'[34] Indeed, it seems unarguable that for many British Jews (in all but the last quarter of the twentieth century), engaging with the past was not at all on their agenda.

The fall and rise of Jewish heritage

The day-to-day challenges facing many Jewish immigrants and their descendants were substantial, as people worked hard to get on and escape poverty, and had little time for anything else.[35] As Grace Paley neatly put it, describing aspiring Jewish Americans, 'their past [wa]s a pincushion, future the eye of a needle'.[36] When, in the 1960s, some individuals attempted to persuade the Board of Deputies to prioritise the matter of unmarked Jewish graves in Britain, they were informed in no uncertain terms that dealing with the community's present and future was the priority. The secretary of the Board told one such enquirer in 1963: 'I do not think anybody who realises the tremendous claims on the resources of the Community for the urgent needs of the living, would regard a national fund for unmarked graves as ranking high in the order of priority.'[37] So far as the Board was concerned, the British Jewish public were unlikely to be persuaded that commemorating the Jewish dead was all that important. Similarly, the preservation of archives and records was not afforded a prominent place in the community's thinking.

In his pioneering study of British Jewry, the American scholar Lloyd Gartner expressed a concern that archives were not being properly preserved.[38] In Manchester, local historian Bill Williams was appalled by the seemingly casual 'indifference' shown by the Jewish community to its own history, inaction that left him struggling to comprehend 'the disjunction between the honour bestowed on distant traditions and the desecration of heritage'.[39] In the East End of London Tony Kushner concurred, asserting that Jewish history and heritage were 'being destroyed without thought'.[40] When Anthony Joseph, later co-founder of the Jewish Genealogical Society of Great Britain (JGSGB), went up to Cambridge and joined the Genealogical Society he remembered being the only Jewish member. Very few Jews at the time, he recalled, were 'interested in the slightest in their ancestry or their background'.[41] Similarly, one of Scotland's leading Jewish heritage experts, Harvey Kaplan, remembers that at Glasgow University there was 'no sort of Jewish history group in any shape or form and I didn't really know anybody else who was interested in Jewish history'.[42] For some, looking back into the Jewish past seemed futile. Having moved around so much, it felt perhaps as if the search for roots would prove impossible, that the level of dislocation in Jewish history was 'not conducive to the preservation of records'.[43] In his account of his own childhood in Hackney, East London, Morris Beckman, in this context, recalled, 'Few Jews have been fortunate enough to have survived several generations in one tolerant climate which is why family trees are rare and curiosity in ancestry remains pragmatically non-existent.'[44] In similar terms, Anthony Joseph remembered his father's incredulity when asked about his own family tree. 'Don't be silly. We're immigrant Jews … You'll find nothing.'[45]

It wasn't only the migration, but its drivers and outcomes, that curtailed Jewish interest in the past. For many Jews, the key lesson of their history was to try to blend in as far as possible with the new society. Kaplan explained: 'Wherever you went, whether it was Britain, America, whatever, first thing that the immigrants wanted to do was blend in and not stick out as immigrants.'[46] Amid such efforts, too great a knowledge of Jewish antecedents was seen by some as an impediment, a danger, or at least an embarrassing irrelevance. For Williams, it seemed as if local Jews saw their past as a 'time of foreign and inferior ways: habits which the community had given up and of which it did not want to be reminded'.[47] The issue here was not simply embarrassment but also fear and trauma. Joseph recalled that some Jewish people would avoid their family history 'because of a fear that a discovery of their roots would lead to persecution'.[48] For others, memories were painful and best forgotten. Beckman, remembering his father's disinclination to talk about the past, explained, 'the lands whence they escaped were abominations. They never wanted to talk about them, think about them.'[49] Like Richard Rabinowitz's own immigrant Jewish mother, many British Jews 'had had enough of history for one lifetime'.[50]

Times, however, gradually changed as ethnicity became, for a new post-war generation, a badge 'of pride, not shame'.[51] Key here was evolving Holocaust consciousness, which drove a heightened desire to embrace the memory of pre-Holocaust European Jewry. Groundbreaking television programmes such as the 'Genocide' episode of *The World at War*, first aired on Thames

Television in 1974, and the subsequent British broadcast of the NBC miniseries *Holocaust* in 1979, brought respectively the tangled history and the emotional punch of the Holocaust into British living rooms, adding up to a 'formative moment in the history of Britain's Holocaust consciousness'.[52] In British Jewish communities, wherein migration and its attendant insecurities had mostly become a grandparent's memory, a new generation became more determined to preserve the past, more curious about family histories about which they often knew little. This rising interest had a Jewish specificity, but also resonated with a broader enthusiasm for personal and family history in British society. A key moment often cited in this context was the publication and televisual adaptation of Alex Haley's *Roots* in the USA in 1976–77.[53] *Roots* used a blend of fiction and Haley's own family history to tell the story of Atlantic slavery, from Kunta Kinte, an eighteenth-century African adolescent captured in The Gambia, enslaved and transported to the USA, all the way to Haley in the present day. The broadcast of *Roots* as a miniseries on BBC 1 in 1977 was watched by one-third of the British population, not quite the size of the record-breaking US audience but highly significant nonetheless.[54] *Roots*'s story offered a powerful and timely introduction to the savagery of Atlantic slavery, yet it also showed both possibility and purpose in the personal family histories of subaltern people (even though the accuracy of Haley's research was subsequently heavily disputed). After *Roots* aired on British television, Anthony Joseph recalled, 'local societies sprang up everywhere … People read the book and thought, gosh, if he can do it, we can.'[55] In this context, Michael Sharpe recalls how 'record offices were besieged by visitors wanting to search out their own roots, and family history societies were inundated with letters and enquiries'.[56]

Roots seems to have struck a specific chord with Jewish communities.[57] Although the tale of an entirely different historical trajectory, some Jews, it seemed, saw something of themselves in Haley's narrative. As Rachel Gross put it, 'the Jewish diaspora would be to Jews what Africa was to Haley'.[58] Taking a trip to see far-flung family in the USA in the 1990s, Harvey Kaplan remembers the *Roots* inspiration. 'I felt like Kunta Kinte because they would sit me down and bring their extended family in and I was to tell them their family history.'[59] Haley's story, the *Jewish Chronicle* reviewer commented, was bound to make Jewish readers' 'think' as they worked through their own histories of dislocation. After all, there was a 'whole generation of Anglo-Jewish young people growing up with no knowledge of their antecedents beyond discarded fragments overheard from parents'.[60] Commenting on the impact of the drama on the Jewish affection for 'mishpochology' (studying one's family), another *Chronicle* columnist explained how British genealogists could now 'have substantial expectations of a whole new clientele of people digging for roots to establish an identity'.[61] In 1977 Haley was awarded an honorary fellowship by the Hebrew University in Jerusalem. Israel, he told the assembled guests at the ceremony, was where the 'real roots' were.[62]

The *Roots* phenomenon both reflected and inspired a broader trend in the rise of genealogy and family history in Britain. The subject's popularity was already gathering pace in the post-war period, spurred on by the opening up of public records and microfiche (and later computer) technologies. Technological innovation was driven in particular by the work of the Church of Jesus Christ of Latter-Day Saints in the USA. Having tasked itself 'to create an accurate and comprehensive genealogical tree of the entire human race, primarily in order that they could move a dead person from one status in the celestial world to a higher realm', the Church prioritised the collection of family records and invested in technology to support research.[63] Its innovative Computer File Index (later renamed the International Genealogy Index) offered a game-changing resource for global genealogical communities, and was purchased by Britain's Society of Genealogists in 1977.[64]

Across Britain, a growing number of local family history societies were united in a National Federation in 1974. Catalysed by *Roots*, the BBC broadcast its own family history series (*Family History*) in five parts on BBC 2 in 1979, a programme which saw newsreader Gordon Honeycombe foreground his own search for his great grandfather's life story. This programme, as *Roots* had done, served to inspire greater numbers of British people to begin to dig into personal pasts.[65] By the 1980s family history had become big business. In 1984 130 groups were members of the Federation, which boasted a total membership of 50,000.[66] In the Jewish community, gathering interest led to the establishment, in 1992, of the JGSGB.[67] In its first year the Society gathered over 130 members, gaining nearly 300 by the end of 1993 and stabilising at around 1,000.[68] An increasing interest in Jewish personal and social histories across Britain in the 1980s also triggered a substantial proliferation of heritage activities and collecting: 1985 saw the beginnings of the Scottish Jewish Archives Project in Glasgow, soon permanently housed in Garnethill synagogue; 1983, the opening of the Museum of the Jewish East End in the Manor House (later the Sternberg) Centre in Finchley. One year later Manchester opened its own Jewish Museum in the old Spanish and Portuguese synagogue in Cheetham Hill, following years of research 'in the Manchester Studies department of

Manchester Polytechnic in the 1970s'.[69] Significantly, these new endeavours were mostly focused not on the history of community elites or 'ritual objects' but instead much more on the social history of ordinary Jewish people.[70] In advance of the launch of the Museum of the Jewish East End, David Jacobs, the Association of Jewish Youth employee who started the Jewish East End Project in 1979, called for people to 'look into their cupboards and send anything that shows what ghetto life in the East End was like'.[71] In Manchester, the new museum collected 400 'life story' oral history interviews with Jewish Mancunians and thousands of personal photographs.[72]

It is significant that key players in the growth of Jewish heritage in the UK were scholars such as Bill Williams and Jerry White, who had been heavily involved with the History Workshop movement.[73] Scholarship of this nature set out to challenge working-class exclusion from heritage and (in a Jewish context) to convince 'ordinary' Jewish people that their history had a value. As Williams recalled, 'Like all working people, they had been led to believe that real history was about influential people and significant events.'[74] The rising tide of social history was key also to setting Scotland's Jewish community on a new, more inclusive heritage path. Harvey Kaplan's involvement in the establishment of the Archive Project in Scotland began when the Gorbals Fair Society wrote to the *Jewish Echo* asking for Jewish participation in its new social historical study of the area.[75] Tony Kushner, then working for the new Manchester Jewish Museum, presented the collection in terms of its working-class and immigrant histories, proudly advertising the museum's 'good collection of union cards, reports, rulebooks and photographs showing the transformation of specifically Jewish unions such as the Manchester Jewish Tailors at the turn of the century, into general unions in the post-1918 world'.[76] This kind of collecting in Glasgow, London and Manchester stood in sharp contrast to the earlier elitist stance of London's Jewish Museum, for which 'social history, certainly of the Jewish poor, [was] not a major concern'.[77] From the 1980s onwards, more and more Jewish people began to feel as if their history mattered, and was worth preserving and researching.

This growing interest in family history occurred in a period of rising secularism. In this context, it seems that history and heritage came to serve an important purpose, offering a new way for people to be Jewish, and do Jewish, which pulled people back to or held them in Jewish communities from which they might otherwise have been lost. In this atmosphere, more and more Jews seem to have seen their Jewishness in terms of ethnicity not practice. Outside devoted Orthodox communities, as Geoffrey Alderman put it, 'ethnic identity is much stronger within Anglo-Jewry than religious commitment, and it is the former, not the latter, that appears to motivate religious observance'.[78] In early editions of *Shemot*, the magazine of the JGSGB, this agenda was plain to see. Explaining his own involvement, chairman Richard Jaffe argued that genealogy was 'an essential part of my Jewishness – a way of ensuring that future generations are aware of their heritage'.[79] Searching for your ancestors, another enthusiast explained, was a way to 'show a commitment to our past and your own heritage'.[80] In these terms, family history and genealogy was, as Kaplan put it, a way to 'plug in' to the community, crucially important amid a decline of religious devotion.

Of course, this plugging in did not only have to involve an interest in one's own family story, but could and did extend to taking an interest in British Jewish history more broadly. Here, the history of Jewish cemeteries and disappeared/disappearing small communities assumed a new prominence.

Raising the dead

Jewish cemeteries, as we have seen, had once been regarded as a low priority, palmed off as they fell into disuse on to the Board of Deputies, which would try to visit 'at least once a year … in an effort to ensure proper care of the last resting places of the members of previous generations of Anglo-Jewry' (a responsibility later shared by synagogue organisations).[81] Growing anxieties about such cemeteries in the last quarter of the century reflected a rising instinct among British Jews to mark out their history, amid a growing belief that the footprint of Jewish presence in Britain should not be lost. In 1991 one article in the *Jewish Chronicle* complained that in places such as Derry and Ebbw Vale, 'nothing exists … as a reminder that Jewish communities once existed'.[82] To an increasing number of Jewish people this vanishing was undesirable; after all, with unparalleled permanence, graves marked out Jewish existence and contribution, creating the longest-term marker of Jewish presence in Britain. In Bernice Rubens' *I Dreyfus*, the protagonist understands his parents' graves as a 'small plot of land [that] gave the Dreyfus family a territorial right on the country of their exile'.[83] To a migrant community, graves could be, and increasingly were, seen as roots, a link to a spiritual home in times of uncertainty.[84]

In a community increasingly seeking such anchors of identity and belonging, changing attitudes to cemeteries were epitomised by activists such as Alfred Dunitz and Nicholas de Lange, who led efforts to preserve and protect Jewish graves, emphasising their importance to contemporary Jewish life. Dunitz, honorary officer of the United Synagogue and member of the Burial Society, toured British Jewish graves for fifteen years, fighting campaigns to save burial grounds that were threatened by development or neglect. It was work, he explained, that was 'keeping alive another page in the history of Anglo-Jewry'.[85] Similarly, de Lange, Cambridge scholar and rabbi, set himself the task of visiting 'all the older cemeteries in Britain on behalf of the Anglo-Jewish Archives, with a view to recording the inscriptions'.[86] De Lange's work caught the imagination of Canadian short story writer Norman Levine, who captured his efforts and energy in a piece published in a *Jewish Chronicle* Supplement in 1983. The protagonist in the story, Jonathan Singer, outlined the importance of his keeping a record of Jewish cemeteries as he sought help to find the correct location of Jewish graves in Penzance in Cornwall. 'Other people will come after me', Singer (de Lange) explains, 'and make something from this information ... I'm doing this for the Jewish community.'[87] Yet interestingly, it was not only the community-minded motivations of de Lange that came through in the story; it also captured a more personal motivation. The research, Singer confides, 'is also something I enjoy. When I am in one of the cemeteries, I feel a sense of continuity. These are my people.' In response Levine tells his wife that Singer 'looks so secure' in his quest, 'so happy in what he is doing, in knowing where he belongs'. Here indeed was a way to 'plug in', and to respond to fears about decline in Jewish life. Alf Dunitz explained his work in the context of the 'grim reality of Britain's dying Jewish communities. Congregations everywhere are getting smaller and older.'[88]

Of course these were extraordinary individuals, but work of this nature was catching on more broadly. In 1973 young Jewish people on summer camp holidays were enlisted to clear disused cemeteries in Great Yarmouth, the East End of London and Bath.[89] In Manchester, the Reform community 'turned out in force to weed our section of Southern cemetery' which had become overgrown.[90] In recent years, the community's focus on its cemeteries has continued to grow, albeit inconsistently. For genealogists in JGSGB, a 'cemetery project' was started, promising an 'ongoing series' of visits to make a 'complete record' of Jewish headstones.[91] In Leicester and in Willesden, Heritage Lottery funding has supported cemetery projects which tell the stories of Jewish communities for a broader public.[92] Death, it seemed, could be productive for Judaism, pulling people back with its gravity and permanence.

This pull was all the more potent amid anxieties about antisemitism, and Jewish responsibilities in the wake of the Holocaust. Writing to the Chief Rabbi, Malcolm Slowe expressed his exasperation:

> Jewish history records many massacres of the living, and often they were followed by attacks on the dead in their graves and by wanton destruction of the tombstones, so that no trace of the Jews should be found among the living or the dead. Jewish cemeteries are not now the subject of wanton destruction by our enemies but they are the subject of wanton neglect by Jews themselves.[93]

This kind of guilt lay heavily. Writing in *Shemot*, Harold Lewin questioned whether those Jews who lost family in the Holocaust were 'contented with the thought that the names and personal histories might follow the victims to the incinerator'.[94] On these terms, Jews needed to preserve their own histories as a matter of self-respect, and not internalise the hatred of others. The neglect of heritage, to the founder of Ireland's Jewish Museum, in the end added up to 'a unique form of antisemitism among Jews'.[95]

Communities struggling to maintain buildings and burial grounds often articulated their need for funds in the context of the history of antisemitism, which lingered in the background as decisions were made about what to preserve and where. In particular, the longevity afforded to Jewry by a tolerant Britain was mobilised as something worth commemorating in and of itself. Thus, leaders of the Exeter Jewish community, struggling amid dwindling numbers to meet the costs of maintaining their synagogue, called on British Jewry for help to preserve the experience of British tolerance. In a circular to mark the 200th anniversary of the community, Rose Sabel, synagogue secretary, argued, 'We do not leave many memorials, except perhaps tragic ones, but the Exeter synagogue is a living reminder of the deep roots of Jewry in this tolerant English soil.'[96] In Britain, it was argued, the heritage of Jewish life could (and should) be preserved in sharp contrast to the destruction that had occurred across much of the rest of Europe. Describing the need to preserve Birmingham's Singers Hill synagogue in 1998, Jewish heritage expert Sharman Kadish explained, 'Equivalent buildings ... were erected in France and Germany from the 1830s onwards and precious few have survived.'[97]

Amid a desire to offset the damage done in the Holocaust and preserve Jewish life, in an atmosphere of growing interest in roots and identity, and as a way to be Jewish in a secular landscape, heritage and family history grew in British Jewish communities. Indeed, the idea of the dying Jewish community, and the need to preserve it, has pulled people together far beyond burial grounds. Genealogy, Catherine Nash reminds us, is ever a process of 'self-definition and self-making', which does not merely describe those who went before but also generates 'social and familial relations'.[98] Plotting out our history, Eviatar Zerubavel explains, means more than 'passively documenting who our ancestors were, they are the narratives we construct to actually make them our ancestors'.[99] But interest in Jews as dead, dying, declining went far beyond the actions and thinking of communities themselves, seeming to capture something of the way that Jews have recently been seen and valued in Britain by non-Jews too.

In 2017 Historic England published a new list championing English history through 100 'irreplaceable' sites around the country.[100] Across different categories, Jewish history entered the list at various points, through discussion of the Cable Street mural and as past custodians of the mosque in Fournier Street in Whitechapel. But the only 'irreplaceable' Jewish site was listed in the 'Faith and Belief' category, where the Jewish cemetery at Penryn near Falmouth was singled out and listed (alongside the adjoining nonconformist cemetery) as a place which offers 'an important reminder of how different faiths commemorate their dead'. Of course, in a list that celebrates the history of faith and belief in Britain one would hope and expect that British Jews would receive a mention, but it is interesting that it was not one of the nation's grand synagogues, such as Bevis Marks or Singers Hill, that caught the eye, but instead a cemetery.

Delving deeper, it is possible to see in the Falmouth listing a story about Jewish decline and death which transcends the beauty of long-standing headstones. The cemetery, Historic England's Joe Flatman explained in a podcast accompanying the designation, revealed 'a quiet community, perhaps trying to find its way a little tentatively in the world, perhaps a little bit concerned about drawing attention to itself'.[101] What comes through here is a perception of Jewish vulnerability. The site, we are told, is 'very fragile'. Cornish Jews, in this rendering and elsewhere, have been repeatedly constructed as rare, vulnerable and on the brink of extinction, when in fact there remains a proud and secure Cornish Jewish community. Tony Kushner, reviewing a number of academic works on the county's 'Lost Jews', warned in this context of an 'unreconstructed and romanticised anthropological gaze' which rendered lost people who had 'never really been missing'.[102] Responding to a journalist who recently claimed to be 'the only Jew in the village' in Cornwall, letter writers in the *Jewish Chronicle* criticised the failure to acknowledge a Jewish community that is 'spread right across the county', with members from 'right across the spectrum of Jewish life ... But why let facts get in the way of a supposedly good story?'[103]

*　*　*

There is, it seems, a persistent tendency to write about Jewish pasts in terms of decline and vulnerability, of doing Jewish heritage as a service to preserve a doomed, yet beautiful, old thing; treating Jews, in Kushner's parlance, like 'a trustworthy old dog'.[104] As with Historic England in Falmouth, those who stepped forward to preserve the Jewish community in Bradford seem to have ascribed an almost holy meaning to marking and slowing Jewish decline. In Falmouth, the Jewish bones empower storytelling about the *longue durée* of British multifaith and multiculture, reminding us that while it might seem 'strange' and out of place, 'there are people of different faiths all over the place'.[105] In Bradford, keeping the breath in the Jewish community seems to have served a purpose for contemporary Muslim culture in the town in a similar way. Helping to preserve the shul, Rudi Leavor explained, provided a valuable way for the local Muslim community to challenge racist perceptions of extremism and intolerance. 'On the whole Muslims are frightened of being thought to segregate themselves and here's a Jewish person who is actually reaching out to them and being friendly with them and they appreciate that ... These people can say ... I'm friends with the Jewish people in Bradford.'[106] Of course, there are plenty of Jewish friends to be made down the road in Leeds, where numbers are much more buoyant (and where there are numerous examples of positive interfaith relationships), and Britain is hardly short of buildings that illuminate the Jewish presence in the nation. Supporting the preservation of Jewish life in its final throes, however, seems to retain a special appeal. Here, we return to Dara Horn's observation about the lure of dead Jews; this fascination across and beyond the community bears careful consideration.

Ultimately, stories of Jewish communal decline, of endings and death, offer a weepy nostalgic lens that renders Jews not as vibrant and contemporary but as belonging to some past place that has now forever been lost. For Gross, nostalgia has assumed a primary place in the practice of Jews, akin to the religious practice of previous generations.[107] For sure, the legend of the dead, of dying and dying-out Jews, seems still to matter greatly across and beyond the community. This chapter has questioned at length why this is the case, highlighting the traumatic nature of the recent Jewish past, and the rise of family history and genealogy, as key factors. But could it be that narratives of dying and decline are just more comforting and less unsettling for Jewish communities in the face of the inherent uncertainties and rapid change of the present and future? One recent case in Glasgow (along with the story of Steve and Jackie in Merthyr) seems to point to just this conclusion.

In 2014 the Orthodox synagogue of Langside in Glasgow closed its doors for the final time. Established in 1915, in the end it struggled to maintain a viable congregation, and the striking synagogue building, not listed for preservation but far from uninteresting, was put up for sale.[108] Yet this was not to be the end of the story, for Langside synagogue became embroiled in an unpredictable afterlife. In the wake of its closure, a local Jewish anarchist group, Irn-Ju, set up a petition and protested outside, demanding the building's return to use as a synagogue, highlighting its potentially ongoing value to the community. Explaining their actions, one of the campaigners told the BBC, 'The fact that there is a synagogue which we could use so close to us – but which we are denied from using – is painful.'[109]

Irn-Ju's actions met with incredulity from some Scottish Jewish activists. Harvey Kaplan, for example, struggled to understand the challenge, coming as it did in the wake of generations of slow decline at Langside. 'Where were you', he asked of the new protesters, 'four years ago when it was struggling so much that it had to close.'[110] But of course, as an 'anarchist diasporist Jewish collective' of predominantly queer people, Irn-Ju members would probably not have felt at home in the community that was Langside. As one of the collective made clear, 'a lot of Jewish life excludes people like me'.[111] Instead, in a manner that perplexed more traditional community members, Irn-Ju could only really make their case after the old community had gone, in the vacuum created. Their argument was simple. If your Jewish community has ended here, could ours begin in its space? With few resources and a brand of Judaism that alienated many traditional observers, it was never likely that Irn-Ju would succeed in gaining access to the Langside synagogue building, but their challenge certainly raised questions.

Irn-Ju's actions point to a community in a state of flux more than terminal decline. Perhaps, moreover, their challenge tells us a little more about why the idea of decline remains so potent. For if the future of Judaism looks so different, perhaps for some there is greater comfort in the idea that Judaism died in the traditional homes of a safer Jewish past.[112] Rather than embrace a future that threatens to break down divisions between Jews and non-Jews, that is secular or at least radically different in terms of religiosity, where gender and heteronormativity might be challenged, some British Jews will opt for the graveyard and the museum, for narratives that saw us perish or move but not change. Similarly, thriving (ultra-) Orthodox communities might offer a vibrant future for British Judaism, but it will be a future that many Jews don't appreciate, and one in which they are unable to recognise themselves. In this atmosphere there is comparative safety and stability in harking back to a past that was anything but safe and stable, but that can, at least, be rendered familiar and recognisable as our Jewish history. In this way, discussions are presently taking place about rehousing the Langside synagogue Ark in the restored synagogue in Merthyr, as a museum piece. Here, it would have pride of place, marking the lives of Jews of the past (albeit not actually Welsh ones), and enabling visitors to see how Jews used to be.

Steve and Jackie's lives in Merthyr tell a similar story. As Jewish history in the town came to attract greater public attention, a local historian led a walking tour of the 'vanished' community, keen to visit the memorial to victims of the Holocaust outside Merthyr's central library. Out in the street, Steve emerged from the gathered crowd to have his say. The historian didn't know, Steve complained, about 'our family [and] not just our family'. Keen to offer a more nuanced immigrant history, he ended up leading the crowd in an impromptu tour of Merthyr's multicultural past and present.[113] After all, as Tony Scotland's article had earlier explained, the Jewish experience in Merthyr was very much the norm; migrant Jews took their place among a 'ragbag population of gold-digging Highland Scots, West Country English, Geordies, Irish, Italians and Spanish'.[114] Instead, however, of mixing Jewish history into a melting pot of British multiculturalism, for many Jews and non-Jews it has felt important to ringfence the specificities of a distinct Jewish story, to see Jews as separate and different. Jackie told me that she could still feel the presence of her Jewish grandmother, Rose, in her daughter's house (which had once belonged to her Jewish great grandmother). When her daughter put candlesticks on display in the lounge, she explained, they fell down when her non-Jewish husband entered the room. Here, to Jackie, Rose's spirit lived on, a ghost who 'didn't like anybody else being there, only Shipmans'.[115]

Rose, however, cannot have her way. Jewish people and Jewish history are core constituents of Britain's diverse multicultural past and present, and hold this space in a messy unity with other people and traditions. To this end, Jewish heritage and history must locate itself within the tapestry of British migration history and recognise the ongoing vivacity of Jewish Britain in all its shades and complexities. Far from dead, the sprawl of Judaism and Jewishness continues apace in all kinds of religious and secular spaces across the country, posing challenging questions to old communities, and offering exciting and divergent futures to all those who are not yet ready to take their place in the past, or be consigned to the museum and the graveyard. As letter writers to the *Jewish Chronicle* explained, Cornwall hadn't lost its Jews. Instead, 'the vibrant and thriving … Kehillat Kernow' was a 'warm and welcoming community, full of "ruach" (spirit) and "chesed" (loving kindness)'. Here, in a nutshell, is the British Jewish community writ large. Transcending the worldview of those who went before, evolving beyond what many post-war thinkers expected and accepted, British Jewry thrives.[116]

2

Meshuga frum? Devotion and division in religious practice[1]

On 26 December 1982 a fiery exchange took place between the Glaswegian rabbi of St John's Wood United (Orthodox) synagogue, Cyril Harris, and Hugo Gryn, Holocaust survivor and rabbi of Britain's oldest Reform congregation, the West London. The row was broadcast on Michael Freedland's weekly Sunday morning show on Radio London, *You Don't Have to Be Jewish*.[2] Freedland had invited the two prominent rabbis, both regular contributors to his show, to discuss critical comments, initially made by the Manchester Beth Din (Rabbinic Court), about the legitimacy of Jewish rites of passage as carried out under the auspices of Reform Judaism, specifically relating to marriage, divorce and conversion. The Beth Din, Freedland paraphrased, had made the case that Reform marriage wasn't 'worth the paper it's written upon'.

In a tense conversation, Harris told Freedland that the Beth Din had been right to take a firm position. It was a stance, he argued, that reflected the views of the 'vast majority of traditional rabbis in this country who utterly repudiate the violence which Reform and Liberal so-called rabbis are doing in the name of Jewish law and Jewish tradition'. Indeed, issues relating to rites of passage were key points of tension between denominations amid Orthodox fears about the creation of invalid Jewish statuses; people who claimed to be Jews, or to be fit for Jewish marriage, when this was not the case according to Orthodox interpretation of Jewish law.[3]

The tone of the radio discussion was brutal, but what really hurt Gryn was the Orthodox refusal to recognise the theological integrity of non-Orthodox Judaism in any sense. To Harris, Progressive Judaism was 'an abnormality which we would rather do without'. Upset by the attack on his community and rabbinical status, Gryn said that he could only understand it as *Sinat Chinam*, the sin of bearing a causeless hate. As the conversation turned ugly, Gryn characterised the Orthodox position as 'an outbreak of Ayatollaism', while Harris countered that some Reform converts did not know the difference between the first letter of the Hebrew alphabet and a swastika, comments that Gryn dismissed as 'nasty' and that a subsequent letter in the *Jewish Chronicle* labelled 'distasteful'.[4] The Orthodox position on Reform (notably towards accepting converts) was not, Gryn argued, 'a million miles from being quite racist'.

In the aftermath of the broadcast, Gryn expressed 'his profound sense of hurt at the abuse to which he had been subjected'.[5] On the Orthodox side, however, attempts were made to play down the row as a normal part of Jewish life. In private comments which served (possibly not inadvertently) to legitimise the Progressive point of view by stressing the familial nature of the argument, the Chief Rabbi, Immanuel Jakobovits, quipped that the broadcast had been 'very mild as compared for example with the confrontations between Belz Satmar and Lubavitch, which had from time to time turned New York into a battlefield'.[6] Perhaps more important, however, was the Orthodox opinion that this argument needed to be had. There was no point, Rabbi Jeffrey Cohen asserted, 'covering over cracks that existed'.[7] In this spirit, the broadcast was one of a myriad of attacks made on Progressive Judaism by Orthodox activists and rabbis in post-war Britain. To some within Orthodox communities, the Reform Judaism preached by Gryn posed an existential threat, described by one rabbi as 'reminiscent of the disputations that Jews had to have with Christians in the Middle Ages'. Here, Progressive Judaism was presented not as an alternative path but as an entirely different faith, 'a new religion which bears no relationship to Judaism'.[8]

To Harris and many others, British Jewish conservatism in the face of the Progressive challenge had been the community's 'trump card' over generations. Now, they feared, the traditional loyalty of British Jewry to Orthodox Judaism was in jeopardy. Arguably, this Orthodox anxiety was overstated. Since the first British Reform congregation opened its doors in 1842, the great majority of synagogue-attending Jews in Britain have continued to associate with Orthodox communities of various shades, although Progressive Judaism grew significantly over the course of the twentieth century (especially in the post-war period). Research in 1970 revealed that over three-quarters of synagogue-attending Jews in London were still members of Orthodox congregations, statistics that have changed only slowly since then.[9] Commenting in 1977, Chief Rabbi Jakobovits asserted that British Jewry was 'the most stable community in the world' and remained 'staunchly traditional and predominantly Orthodox'.[10]

Whether or not British Orthodoxy remained ascendant, the Progressive challenge caused worry and consternation. Matters again came to a head when Gryn died in August 1996. One of the most high-profile Jewish figures in Britain, Gryn was held in the highest esteem across Progressive Judaism and far beyond it. To Jonathan Wittenberg, leading rabbi of Britain's Masorti community, Gryn was 'irreplaceable. In a great many areas, he was the moral leader of Jewry and of wider society, in this country and beyond.'[11] Gryn was not only an eminent rabbi and public Jewish figure, but also a Holocaust survivor, seen as a role model and representative of Jewry in the wake of the genocide. The emeritus Chief Rabbi Jakobovits paid tribute to Gryn as 'a leading spokesman in our community for the Holocaust and an exceptional communicator'.[12]

Gryn was, though, first and foremost Britain's pre-eminent advocate for Progressive Judaism, a reality which for some severely restricted any willingness to eulogise his passing. To letter writers in the Orthodox *Jewish Tribune*, Gryn's death was no reason to pay respects. One such writer criticised those Orthodox rabbis who had seen fit to issue condolences, warning readers, 'To so eulogize one who personified the Reform movement and all it stands for, can only help further distance the wider Jewish communities from true Torah values and allow them greater licence to patronise Reform ideologies.'[13] Gryn, in this context, was held responsible for legitimising a range of sinful practices and separating naive congregants from true Judaism. Similarly reluctant to pay homage was the *Tribune*'s columnist, Ben Yitzchok (Joe Lobenstein), who refused to celebrate a man 'who for 30 years led a community which denies the authenticity of the Torah, condones intermarriage and solemnises marriages which are not *k'das Moshe v'Yisroel*'.[14]

In this atmosphere, Jakobovits's successor as Chief Rabbi, Jonathan Sacks, made the decision that he could not attend Gryn's funeral (although his wife, as well as a representative of his office, did go). Senior figures of the United Synagogue also declined to attend. These absences, especially that of the Chief Rabbi, were applauded by some but caused fury among others, who felt that Sacks's decision was disrespectful and revealed a deep crisis in the way British Jews dealt with each other. For *Jewish Chronicle* columnist Chaim Bermant, it 'highlighted the mean minds, the mean souls and the mean principles which govern' the United Synagogue.[15] Of course, Bermant explained, he had expected little more from what he termed 'the extreme right', those devotional communities too religious for affiliation with the United Synagogue, but what bothered him was the 'mean minds muddying the mainstream'. Unsurprisingly, the reaction from Progressive Jews was even more angry, and threatened a deepening divide in British Jewry. David J. Goldberg, rabbi of the Liberal Jewish synagogue in St Johns Wood, told the *Jewish Chronicle* that Orthodox failure to accept the 'pluralism and diversity of Jewish belief' could collapse 'the fragile consensus – whereby we non-Orthodox Jews have tolerated inequality in order to project an illusion of communal unity to the outside world'.[16]

The discord caused by Orthodox responses to Gryn's funeral, like his earlier exchange with Cyril Harris, provokes important questions. This was not a row desired by senior figures in the United Synagogue nor the Chief Rabbi, a reality reflected by the attendance of Elaine Sacks at the funeral and by other conciliatory gestures in the aftermath. Instead, the Chief Rabbi's decision to absent himself needs to be seen as part of a long-term pulling of British Jewry in different directions (in which the Chief Rabbi was stuck in what he perceived to be the centre).[17] Indeed, the post-war period has most frequently been characterised by historians of British Jewry as a period of schism and polarisation, during which a growing diversity of practice and belief undermined Jewish unity.[18] Geoffrey Alderman has argued that by the beginning of the twenty-first century, 'Anglo-Jewry had come apart', with Todd Endelman concurring that the end of the century saw a religious community 'more diverse, fractured, and contentious than in any previous period'.[19] According to this kind of thinking, traditional British Jewry, moderate, middle-of-the-road, Orthodox, was being pulled by Progressive Judaism on the one hand, and more conservative and strict Orthodoxy on the other.

This pulling away from the centre had been understood by Chief Rabbi Jakobovits in terms of a generational shift. The children of United Synagogue members, he argued, were either 'recruits for enrolment in Jewish day schools and even yeshivot or seminaries' or hanging out 'at coffee bars' where they would 'wear off their Jewish identity to the point of complete disengagement'.[20] Jakobovits illuminated the challenge facing the post-war generation, confronted with the question of how to be Jewish in an increasingly secular society. Disparate Jewish responses to these changing times were accentuated by the arrival of European Jewish refugees fleeing Nazism and the Cold War. These refugees often brought with them traditions and practices that accelerated the pulling in different directions. Of course, the influence of European immigration had informed British Judaism over a much longer period. But the arrival of refugees from Nazism and subsequently from the Eastern Bloc accelerated shifts to both Progressive Judaism and stricter Orthodoxy, strengthening 'the outer poles of Anglo-Jewry'.[21]

Orthodox Jews in Manchester (interviewed by Bill Williams and Ros Livshin) highlighted the impact of refugees from Nazism on their religious culture. Chaim Heilpern, whose father was one of the founders of the Manchester *Machzikei Hadass* (which strove for stricter standards of Orthodoxy), recalled the refugees as 'a great fillip to the orthodoxy in Manchester'.[22] Jack Morgenstern remembered their impact in similar terms:

> a lot of German Jews came over from Frankfurt. And they were very very frum [religious] in Frankfurt. There's been a foreign influence, an incursion, and they brought it across. Polish Jews brought it across in the beginning and then, the Hitler period.[23]

It was not, however, only Orthodox communities that benefited from the absorption of the refugees from Nazism, who included thirty-five Reform rabbis.[24] Their arrival in Britain fuelled Progressive expansion by providing a new quality and quantity of leaders. As Anne Kershen and Jonathan Romain explained, 'When synagogues needed ministers, or even when small embryonic groups began to arise, it was the refugee rabbis who began to serve them from 1940 onwards.'[25] Armed with this new strength, Progressive Judaism grew apace in post-war Britain.

This chapter will explore the post-war growth of British Orthodoxy and the Progressive Judaism of the Reform movement, focusing on the (largely fraught) relations between these two growing communities. I want to question whether polarisation is the most appropriate way to describe the changes that have taken place, for it is possible to argue that a set of common concerns, and similar patterns of thinking, have underwritten devotional changes across the spectrum of Jewish life, a reality which has led me to wonder whether British Jews are as different from one another as they seem to think. I also want to explore what this ostensible pulling in different directions might tell us about the changing nature of British Jewishness and religiosity more generally, in a climate where Christianity and other faiths have experienced similar tensions and challenges. As we shall see, conflicts of Jewish faith in this period spoke to broader social angst about our understanding of God in post-war Britain.

Orthodox disaffection and the emergence of a new right block

Jewish immigrants from Europe in the late nineteenth and early twentieth century were frequently unsure about the merits of the British Jewish synagogue.

In an anglicised atmosphere, the soul of Judaism could be seen to be missing. Fellow of the Institute for Higher Rabbinical Study in Gateshead, David Miller, spoke on behalf of many in immigrant communities when he explained that he was left cold by the 'Minister in his clerical collar and the Cantor in a pom-pom hat'. 'What is left after all the pomp and ceremony? – spiritual insecurity, koved, self-aggrandisement, artificial decorum, snobbery and religious sterility.'[26] To such Jews, the anglicised British rabbinate didn't look or sound authentically Jewish, Louis Jacobs recalling that one of his teachers at Manchester Yeshiva had 'nothing but scorn for English ministers and their head, the Chief Rabbi'.[27] Here, the anglicised nomenclature was as much a problem as anything else. The teacher, Jacobs remembered, 'loved to scoff at the Chief Rabbi's grandiose title. "If a Reverend is a goy", he would say, "it must follow that a Very Reverend is a great goy" (a grosser goy).'

But the difference between themselves and established British Jewry, for many religious immigrants, went beyond appearance, titles and atmosphere. There was a deep anxiety that Jewish practice in Britain was diminished and inadequate, lacking the appropriate rigour and devotion. Looking at the day-to-day lives of British Jews, immigrants from Orthodox communities frequently saw degrees of change and compromise that caused considerable angst. As Chaim Heilpern remembers, 'There was laxity in the community, people were keeping their businesses and shops open on shabbas [the sabbath], people were not being particular about foods etc.'[28] British synagogues were administered by lay leaders in many cases, men who were not so much religious as well established and dedicated to their communities. For some devotional Jews, such leadership did not sit well. Another Manchester migrant, Dayan Golditch, remembers his dissatisfaction that business could be conducted 'bare-headed' in Orthodox synagogues. Looking at this practice in contrast to the Reform, he asserted, 'There wasn't a great deal of difference between them.'[29]

As a result of these anxieties, not feeling at home in British communities, a whole host of new synagogues and institutions were created by immigrants. Many established small, separate congregations, sometimes in private houses, where they could pray without compromise in an atmosphere more akin to their pre-immigration homes.[30] In the post-war period, Mizrahi Jews from former British colonies followed a similar pattern, setting up their own communities such as the David Ishag synagogue in Wembley, the Aden Jews Congregation in Stamford Hill and Od Yosef Hai synagogue and yeshiva in Hendon.[31] Unaffiliated and usually small, congregations such as these survived through membership subscriptions, which frequently did not stretch far enough to pay for a full-time rabbi or substantial premises. With the support of banker Samuel Montagu, many of the early Ashkenazi communities affiliated with a new Federation of Synagogues from 1887, a grouping which enabled them to access funds for development and a burial society, and assert more of a voice in British Jewish affairs.[32] By the interwar period, the Federation had become the largest 'synagogal body' in the country, although the United Synagogue would recover its supremacy after the Second World War.[33]

These new voices in British Jewry often called for higher standards of Jewish practice. In 1891 members of two new small communities in London came together to establish the *Chevra Machzike Hadath* to express their concerns about standards of *shechita* (kosher animal slaughter) as supervised by the Chief Rabbi.[34] Failure to agree led to the establishment of a separate congregation with its own *shechita*, a marker of the willingness of new communities to go their own way when they felt that their religious practice was threatened. In 1901 the *Machzike Hadath* affiliated with the Federation. A generation later, in 1925, Jews in Manchester established their own *Machzikei Hadass* organisation (and later a synagogue) over similar concerns.[35]

Other significant new groupings similarly supported more Orthodox Jewish practice. In 1909 a group of independent-minded Orthodox Jews in North London made an approach to Hungarian Dr Avigdor (Victor) Schonfeld (working at that time in Vienna) to become rabbi of a new synagogue, *Adath Yisroel*.[36] Schonfeld was keen 'to strengthen the practice of traditional Judaism' in Britain, and in 1926 set up a new organisation, the Union of Orthodox Hebrew Congregations (UOHC), to allow like-minded independent synagogues to affiliate.[37] The UOHC's aim, as stated in its 1931 Constitution, was 'to protect and to further in every way the interests of traditional Judaism in Great Britain'.[38] The UOHC's outlook linked closely to the vision of *Agudath Israel*, a global movement of Jewish (anti-Zionist) Orthodoxy established in Poland in 1912. By the early 1970s the UOHC incorporated 40 affiliate communities, comprising some 3,000 families.[39]

The UOHC offered a point of affiliation for strictly Orthodox communities, which grew in number in Britain following the arrival of refugees from communist Eastern Europe, many of whom were pious Chasidim.[40] The UOHC also came to represent the main seat of Orthodox Jewish learning in Britain, the Gateshead Yeshiva, which had been established by Rabbi Dovid Dryan, who had arrived from Radun (seat of the eminent rabbi Yisrael Meir Kagan, known as the *Chofetz Chayim*) via Port Talbot in South Wales in 1929, as well as ultra-Orthodox Jewish communities in Stamford Hill and Broughton Park.[41]

Cooperation and collaboration within and between these organisations and groups was limited, and this was a conscious decision. Wary of the British Jewish establishment, these were Jews who feared that overarching associations, especially when led by lay people, would diminish religious integrity and threaten communal purity. Here, the most obvious example of what not to do was the United Synagogue. Discussing the impacts of the United on British Jews, David Miller asserted that while 'the amalgamators' of the nineteenth century might have had 'the best of intentions', the large organisation had created a Judaism for 'passive spectators rather than active participants'.[42] This atmosphere, Miller claimed, diminished true faith. Amid a 'machinery to handle any problem, a constitution that is coterminous with all of life', there was 'hardly any need for the Messiah'.[43]

The UOHC was set up on an entirely different basis. Its constituents were not asked to come together any more than was necessary and were largely left to set their own religious practice. Solomon Schonfeld (who succeeded his father as the organisation's presiding rabbi) laid out this difference clearly in 1972:

> Our first principle is: 'divide and rule' – ourselves, not others. We have but little centralization. You can't force real Jews to toe the line. Warm Orthodox Jews do not lend themselves to regimentalization.[44]

UOHC members, he quipped, would 'meet in the end in the same Beis Olom [cemetery]', but until then they were to be left apart as far as possible. The thinking here was well understood by members of Manchester's *Machzikei Hadass*, who set out to avoid the kind of compromises that they saw as inevitable in big organisations. 'A large community', Dayan Golditch argued, could not 'apply strict standards to everybody'.[45] Instead, Chaim Heilpern explained, religious Jews became 'convinced that the only way to have an existence was to be entirely independent, your own rabbinate, your own shechita, your own synagogue'.[46] The leaders of *Machzikei Hadass* in Manchester were thus content that their members came together only to discuss key issues and could remain (even after the establishment of their own synagogue) in separate congregations. Similarly, the constitutional principles of the UOHC highlighted the extent to which Jewish unity was not a primary concern. 'Whether it is essential that all these fifty groupings should actually meet together, is an open question which time alone will answer.'[47]

This principle of separation was inspired by the example of Rabbi Samson Raphael Hirsch, who had outlined the desirability of an *Austrittsgemeinde* (seceded community) in Germany in 1864, as an attempt to separate Orthodox Jews from the lax majority and preserve an unadulterated Orthodox tradition.[48] Describing themselves as a 'kind of successor community' to Hirsch, the *Jewish Tribune* explained in 1965 the value that British Orthodox Jewry saw in the principle of separation. 'To us "Austritt" is a spiritual wall which is seen only by those who voluntarily seek its shelter but remains completely invisible to those outside.'[49] Amid this kind of thinking, some Orthodox communities in Britain and indeed globally (often described as Ultra-Orthodox or *Haredi*) have in some ways evolved as separate from non- (or less) Orthodox Jewish communities, and from the non-Jewish world.

The instinct of the Lubavitch/Chabad Orthodox sect to reach out to all Jews, in a holy mission to bring them back to God, offered the exception that proves the rule amid these kinds of religious cultures.[50] Thus, the Orthodox communities that have grown in Stamford Hill, Gateshead and Broughton Park are only outward-facing in a limited way, and generally tend to view the non-Jewish world, and the less religious Jewish world, with suspicion.[51] With their own schools, synagogues and a raft of internally sustained social services, such communities can and do limit contact with the outside world to a significant degree. Yiddish is frequently the language of choice, which serves 'to linguistically isolate the pious from the outside world'.[52] Such Jews seek community among co-religionists with similar traditions and outlooks across the world more than with other local people. As a policeman in Stamford Hill explained in a 1991 Channel 4 documentary, 'they're most probably closer to their relatives and contacts in places like New York and Jerusalem and other centres of Orthodoxy throughout Europe than they are with the rest of the community around them'.[53]

In her study of newly Orthodox Jewish women in America, Louise Tallen highlighted the prevalence of a 'fear of contamination from the secular world' which shaped behaviours and attitudes, a view echoed by Rabinowicz in his study of British Chasidim.[54] This concern came through clearly in Livshin's and Williams's interviews with Orthodox Jews in Manchester. Many, they found, had had grave doubts about the sagacity of moving away from the Eastern European Jewish heartlands in the first place. Dayan Golditch recalled his father asking the Belzer rebbe for an introduction which would enable him to migrate to Antwerp and the rebbe's negative response, laced with fear that his Jewish congregant 'might be led astray there because going to the West was abandoning the Chassidic strongholds and being exposed to the temptations of western civilisation'.[55] Migrants such as these, Rabinowicz argues, 'feared to expose their children to the spiritual dangers of the godless countries even more than they feared the violent and murderous mobs at home'.[56] Having made the leap, new Orthodox migrants in Britain were often determined to stay strong to their traditions and resist change. This could and often did mean refusing to dress in an English fashion and even reverting to the religious Jewish dress of previous generations in an attempt to preserve that which had been lost in Europe. Recalling the determination of post-war Orthodox migrants to maintain their Jewish appearance, Chaim Heilpern explained, 'when a person's uprooted from his land, from his family, from his home, either consciously or subconsciously he feels he's got to preserve what's left'.[57]

Some Jews were wary even of allowing their children to attend school. Dayan Golditch remembered that his father kept him at home for a year for fear that he would have to 'sit without a yamulka [skullcap]' in the classroom, not wanting his son to 'get contaminated that way'.[58] Concerns often focused on the risks of educating daughters outside the community. For them to embark on further education, Rabinowicz explains, was seen as a risk that might 'delay their early marriages, and expose them to alien influences'.[59] Compromises in the end were made based on the need to train and make a living, but here a line was drawn. Religious Jews, Miri Freud-Kandel argues, were prepared to 'compartmentalise' their lives and engage with the outside world 'for the sake of one's livelihood'. Any further intrusion on the 'dominant Jewish aspect of one's mind' was not, generally, welcomed.[60]

Thus, for such Orthodox Jews, priorities in education looked slightly different. In religious circles, 'secular educational achievements' were sometimes dismissed as 'goyim nachas, pleasures only for the Gentiles, of a wholly inferior order'.[61] In Chasidic communities, Rabinowicz argues, 'secular subjects are Goyishe (non-Jewish) subjects, and both parents and children regard them as a burden and as a concession to the secular authorities' requirements'.[62] Even for rabbis, one UOHC paper concluded, non-religious education needed 'to be balanced by exceptional maturity' to ensure that it worked 'for avodas Hashem, rather than to unbalance the judgment of its graduate owner'.[63] Fearing the influence of the secular world, the use of English as a medium of instruction could signpost a threat. Mitchell cited an article from a London Yiddish newspaper published from the Beis Rokhel Girls School, which argued that it was '"dangerous" for [women] to learn gentile languages lest they come under foreign influences which are hostile to Judaism'.[64] In a similar spirit, Dayan Golditch recalled how his father, 'if he caught me reading an English book … would throw it on the fire'. Here, the English language was very much the problem. 'It made no difference to him what kind of book it was.'[65]

Such parents were often committed to their children's education, but with a focus on Jewish learning to the extent that priorities could seem very different from the mass of British Jewry.[66] A different set of educational programmes were developed, amid priorities which limited interactions with the outside world and ensured a focus on traditional Jewish study. Such devotion to Torah learning could not easily be satisfied within mainstream British Orthodoxy, even within its centre of rabbinical training, Jews' College. With its emphasis on producing leaders for the community, Jacobs noted, the College was looked at as 'an institution which taught heresy', so that any attending student would be seen as 'a traitor to the ideal of Torah study for its own sake'.[67] Instead, at the heart of Orthodox commitment to learning was the *yeshiva* (religious seminary) and the *kollel* (seminary for married men). In the twentieth century, numerous such institutions opened in Britain, most famously in Gateshead but also in Sunderland, Liverpool, Glasgow, Leeds, Manchester and London. 'The yeshiva, bastion of the book and palace of the rabbis', was, Samuel Heilman noted, 'the embodiment of haredi life'.[68] Study at British yeshivot was nearly exclusively in Yiddish. 'It was inconceivable', Dayan Golditch recalls, 'that a Rosh Yeshiva should have taught us in any other language.'[69]

It would be wrong, however, to dismiss these divergent educational paths as an out and out abandonment of broader British Jewry. They are perhaps better understood as an attempt to pull British Jewry towards more traditional and conservative Jewish practice, which, as we shall see, had a considerable impact on mainstream British Orthodoxy. After all, such communities of learning (often in conjunction with bigger international players) went on to train many of the leaders of the post-war United Synagogue. By the 1990s half the pulpits of United's communities were held by rabbis schooled in Lubavitch seminaries, mostly in the United States and Israel.[70] For Bernard Homa, the arrival in Britain of more religious immigrants had converted 'a semi-assimilated and religiously declining group of some sixty-five thousand … into a thriving and virile community of nearly half a million'.[71]

While this impact is oversimplified, it is no doubt true that migrant Jews pulled the British Jewish centre back towards stricter religious practice in post-war Britain (epitomised by their influence on the office of the Chief Rabbi and the United Synagogue), as piety increasingly became a benchmark of 'authenticity in Orthodoxy'.[72] Chief Rabbi Brodie, Chaim Heilpern claimed, told him that this had been the case, specifically that communities such as

Manchester's *Machzikei Hadass* had kept 'the United Synagogue on the right path'.[73] Certainly these kinds of influences strengthened the rigour around Jewish law (and especially *shechita*). To Abraham Heilpern, the Manchester Beth Din now operated 'much more in accord with the strict line than it would have been 50 years ago' with 'far far far stricter' rules on Kashrut.[74] Indeed, Chaim Heilpern quipped, the founders of Manchester's Great Synagogue would 'have a fit' if they knew how religious it had become.[75]

This pull to the right, however, was not the only force operating on British Jewry, or indeed on the Chief Rabbi, in this period. For there were two significant centres of growth in religious Jewish communities in the post-war period, both of which squeezed and threatened the unstable foundations of 'middle of the road' traditional Jewry. Just as Orthodoxy grew apace in post-war Britain, so too, on an impressive scale, did Progressive Judaism, most notably in the form the Reform Synagogues of Great Britain (RSGB).

The rise of Reform

Reform Judaism grew amid a climate of insecure yet substantial changes in Jewish/non-Jewish relations in late eighteenth-century Europe. Across several states, barriers which had long prevented Jewish political and social participation were gradually removed or reduced, a development that led some Jews to seek a model of religiosity that better reflected their aspirational status as loyal European subjects, and emphasised the compatibility of Judaism with the Christianity of their peers. In a short history of Reform Judaism, Rabbi Michael Leigh highlighted the foundational work of Israel Jacobson in Seeson in Lower Saxony. Jacobson opened in 1801 a non-sectarian boarding school and later a synagogue, creating services with a greater emphasis on congregational decorum and sermons in German.[76] The opening of the Seeson synagogue, in 1810, has thus been described by Michael Meyer as 'a social statement: Jews worship as do Christians; they are their equals in religion as in civil life. No longer an Oriental, foreign faith transplanted to Europe, Judaism – like Christianity – is homeborn.'[77]

The growth of Reform, however, was not only shaped by a hunger to respond to the changing political environment but also by Jewish scholarly engagement with the Enlightenment. Jewish thinkers were inspired by new approaches to philosophy and history, which questioned the roots of religions and probed their texts as historical documents. The establishment in 1819 of the Society for the Advancement of the Science of Judaism in Berlin, which sought to introduce scientific method and criticism to Jewish learning, has been pinpointed as the beginning of a wider movement of *Wissenschaft des Judentums*, 'the scholarly study of the Jewish religion and people'.[78] This new approach to Judaism was key to Reform, prompting calls for changes in practice and influencing the development of a series of religious seminaries. The practice of this growing Reform movement in new congregations was never consistent but did lead to widespread patterns of devotional change: greater use of the vernacular in prayer and sermons, abbreviation of the service and the use of organs and choirs.[79]

In Britain, the first congregation that would go on to be described as 'Reform' had opened as the West London Synagogue of British Jews in January 1842, following the establishment of a 'kind of "Reform Club"' in 1840, which produced a declaration of disaffection with the status quo.[80] The concerns of these Reformers were in some ways like those of their continental peers, especially as regards their desire for a more dignified service with better congregational decorum. Yet far from being a significant theological schism, the issue that drove the establishment of the West London was irritation on the part of both Sephardi and Ashkenazi Jews that their synagogue authorities would not support the creation of new communities closer to their homes.[81]

The actual reforms instigated were modest, focused on the principle of 'discourses in the English language, length of service and the use of Portuguese pronunciation'.[82] As Leigh's history noted, the new synagogue did not allow men and women to sit together (until after 1919), did not initially incorporate an organ (until 1859), and made only 'very meagre' changes to services.[83] Nonetheless, the removal of the Second Day celebrations of certain festivals was sufficient to lead to a joint 'denunciation' of the West London by Sephardi and Ashkenazi authorities in 1841, which added up, Leigh argued, to a 'Herem or ban on the seceders'.[84] The West London soon employed David Woolf Marks (assistant reader and secretary of Liverpool's Orthodox Congregation) to lead them.[85] Marks held the view that the Oral Law should not be considered divinely given, an idea that fuelled his personal readiness to engage with the new, more open-minded congregation.

Beyond the West London, the initial growth of Reform Judaism in Britain was modest. The nineteenth century saw the establishment of only two further British congregations, in Manchester in 1858 and Bradford in 1873. These further communities, Jacobs has argued, owed more to the European Reform movement than had been the case with the very British West London.[86] The majority of East European migrants, however, were not Reform-minded, so that the growth of Reform communities remained small. Prior to 1933 only the East London Settlement synagogue added to the number of congregations.

More radical innovation in British Progressive Judaism came in the form of the Liberal Jewish synagogue which formally began in London in 1909. The synagogue was preceded for nearly a decade by informal meetings of a Jewish Religious Union, which grew after an article by Lily Montagu in the *Jewish Quarterly Review* called on the Jewish public to renew their relationship with Judaism and reassess the old faith in the context of modern society.[87] Driven by the intellectual vision of Claude Montefiore and Israel Abrahams, and the leadership of Lily Montagu, Liberal Judaism offered a more radical departure from Orthodoxy, promoting a level of change that went far beyond the West London (in which Montefiore had grown up), not least in terms of its clear commitment that the Bible had been written by human beings, and thus did not merit unequivocal obedience.[88] The new community's manifesto laid bare this radical stance as a core feature of Liberal identity: 'even before we open the Book, before we open the Code, we know it cannot be for us an infallible and eternal authority'.[89] To Jews such as these, it was the responsibility of every generation to engage with, add to and amend Jewish practice, which they felt was not encapsulated in any reading of a perfect past. Montefiore argued that 'perfect righteousness, perfect truth, are not capable of being embodied in any book, or of being contained in any single generation or in any human mind'.[90]

Under Rabbi Israel Mattuck (who was recruited from the USA by Montefiore and historian of science Charles Singer in 1912), liturgy was substantially altered, as was the order of service.[91] For Mattuck, it was the values emanating from Jewish scripture and tradition that were important to maintain. He explained, 'Those who do not accept the literal authority of the law do accept its fundamental principles.'[92] While membership numbers at this new congregation soon outpaced the West London, it would take some time for Liberal Judaism to witness a substantial take-up among British Jews, who generally remained wedded to their traditional Orthodox communities. The interwar period, however, did begin to bring change, as the children of migrant communities started to seek out Jewish practice that aligned better with their less religious, more assimilated lives. By the 1930s the Settlement synagogue in the East End of London was attracting 400 people on Friday evenings and a thousand on High Holy Days.[93] As migrant Jewish lives sprawled out of the areas of initial settlement, new Reform congregations opened in the suburbs of Edgware and Golders Green, as well as in Glasgow.

British Reform Judaism crystallised as a movement during the Second World War. Before the war, relations between mainstream Orthodox communities and the Reform synagogues had been comparatively amicable. In 1878 United Synagogue authorities had 'sounded out' the Reform congregations about a possible joining together, and while this and later similar initiatives were not pursued, it gives some indication of the limited distance between United and Reform leadership, which was bolstered by 'close family ties'.[94] More important was 'the tolerant liberal tradition of Orthodoxy' in late nineteenth- and early twentieth-century Britain.[95] In the 1940s, however, relations began to strain, coming to a head over what Reform leaders perceived as Orthodox intransigence over the education of displaced children during the Second World War. In the 1930s steps had been taken towards sharing practice on educational provision (between different Jewish denominations), which paved the way for a wartime Joint Emergency Committee for the Religious Education of Refugee Children led by the Board of Deputies.[96] The marginalisation, however, of Reform education within this committee led to a breakaway gathering held at the Midland Hotel in Manchester in 1942. Alliance between Reform congregations was needed, the minutes of the Manchester meeting recorded, because of the 'failure of the synagogue to persuade the Deputies that their scheme should not be confined to sponsoring orthodox teaching'.[97]

Hugo Gryn, looking back on the movement from its Jubilee Celebration in 1992, recalled this beginning as an 'act of faith', taken out of 'concern for the next generation', while Leigh claimed that 'it was felt that the six congregations united by a common Prayer Book and outlook should form some loose association'.[98] In reality, the meeting seems to have been driven more than anything by exasperation that the Reform synagogues were not being granted equal status alongside the Orthodox, a snub which it was felt required a collective response. Reform synagogues were keen to assert their own traditions, and to be included in communal leadership and decision making, especially because so many of the refugees who needed educational support came from Reform backgrounds. The Manchester meeting resolved to establish both an Educational Committee and a Standing Conference of the members, known as the Associated British Synagogues. Soon, however, the group evolved their name to the Associated Synagogues of Great Britain (ASGB).[99]

The absence of the descriptor 'Reform' in the title of the new association highlighted the limits of agreement between the synagogues, and a broader disinclination to categorise themselves away from the centre of Jewish practice. As Rabbi Reinhart (of West London) argued in 1946: 'the progressive quality of Judaism was traditional and had always been inherent in its very nature ... to adopt any label such as "Progressive" was to invite the suggestion that their Judaism was not traditional'.[100] After all, most of the changes made by the West London synagogue in the 1840s, Reinhart claimed at a later conference, had now 'been adopted by the majority of Anglo-Jewish congregations'.[101] This disinclination to recognise a divergence between reforming tendencies and Jewish tradition had been present throughout Reform history, on the grounds that Jews had always adapted their faith.[102] In 1958, however, the word 'Reform' was finally included in the grouping's nomenclature, as it renamed itself the Reform Synagogues of Great Britain (RSGB).[103] Still, delegates such as Rabbi Van der Zyl (of the North Western Reform synagogue) spoke in opposition to the change, fearing that the prefix might suggest 'a sectarian movement' and 'did not convey any positive meaning'.[104]

The values of the Reform movement were laid out, under the auspices of the ASGB, at an executive meeting in 1948. As the group set out to expand, advertisements were taken out in the Jewish press, describing British Reform Judaism according to the following 'four principles'.

The "ASGB."–

1. Promotes and fosters a robust and living Judaism for the worship of God and for the fulfilment of His holy Law as a way of life.
2. Safeguards our ancestral faith by the earnestness and sincerity of Divine Services (in Hebrew and English) in the Synagogue, and of religious observance in the home.
3. Interprets the Torah for Jews and Jewesses who seek an expression of Judaism relevant to life in our day.
4. Represents a positive, constructive, and progressive view of Jewish tradition, stressing integrity and courage in religious expression.[105]

These principles tell us much about the movement as it was evolving. The commitment to building a 'living Judaism' and celebrating faith that was 'relevant to life in our day' reflected the key difference that had been emerging between Progressive and Orthodox theology. For Reform Jews it was both acceptable and necessary for people to look at their Judaism and reassess its practice in the contemporary environment. As Ignaz Maybaum explained, 'In each age we must translate the eternal and unchangeable word of God ... into the language of the civilisation surrounding us'.[106] The founder rabbi of the *Beit Klal Yisrael* congregation in North Kensington, Sheila Shulman, explained the process of her own engagement with Jewish theology. 'We need to be both loving and critical, and make the text ours.'[107] For Rabbi Jonathan

Romain, Reform Judaism provided for Jewish people in this period a newly relevant way to engage with their ancient faith. Reform Jews, he argued, weren't 'rejecting Judaism, it's just that they wanted a format that was more akin to their new lifestyle and social involvement'. This flexibility, for Romain, aligned Reform theology with the thinking of most British Jews in an increasingly secular post-war environment. Most Jewish people, he argued, did not believe in the 'literal word of the Torah anyway'.[108]

To support its development, the Reform movement strove, early on, to train its ministers through what was soon named Leo Baeck College in London. The idea of a Reform training seminary was supported by the Associated British Synagogues conference in 1946, and it opened in 1956.[109] Through the college, a generation of new rabbis emerged from British Progressive Judaism, although its early educators were often refugees from Nazism who brought with them much from the German Reform tradition. Graduates from Leo Baeck would soon have a transformative impact on Progressive Judaism in Britain and beyond. From 1964, at which point the college was formally shared between Reform and Liberal communities, Leo Baeck 'became the training ground of religious leadership for Reform communities throughout the continent'.[110]

Newly ambitious and clearly in tune with a significant subset of British Jews, Reform Judaism grew rapidly in post-war Britain. By 1992 the membership of RSGB had grown by 'over 500%' since its 1942 beginnings, so that RSGB was, behind the United, the second biggest synagogue block in the country.[111] For a movement that did not initially set out to be radical, the contribution of Reform to British Jewish practice has been substantial. For example, it has enabled the training and placement of female rabbis and openly gay rabbis. In both cases, concerns within the leadership of RSGB, and worries about who their congregations would and would not accept as religious leaders, slowed the pace of change, which occurred with less opposition in the smaller, but more radical, Liberal movement. Thus, for rabbis such as Elizabeth Sarah, conservative Reform resistance to her participation as an openly gay female rabbi ultimately drove her from RSGB to the Liberals.

The first woman to graduate as a rabbi from Leo Baeck College was Jackie Tabick. Tabick applied to, and was accepted by, Leo Baeck for rabbinical training in 1971. She graduated in 1975, going on to serve in the West London synagogue as its assistant rabbi, having been employed as 'education director' because Hugo Gryn 'initially did not dare put her to the vote'.[112] While Tabick hoped that her presence 'made little difference' at Leo Baeck, it was clearly not entirely uncontroversial. After some early test cases, the college had formally approved in principle the acceptance of female candidates for rabbinical training in 1967.[113] Tabick, though, recalls delays in her application process, and that RSGB's ultimate decision on her candidature was perhaps made more palatable by her initial reticence about whether she intended to practise as a rabbi (Tabick's plans at the time were to take a teaching post at the end of her studies).[114] In the end Julia Neuberger from the Liberal movement, also trained at Leo Baeck, became the first female rabbi to have her own congregation in Britain, the South London Liberal synagogue, from 1977. Nonetheless, despite its hesitations, RSGB was opening the way for women rabbis in this period, so that many followed in Tabick's wake.[115]

Similarly, Rabbi Lionel Blue, who held several high-profile positions in the Reform movement having been one of the first graduates of Leo Baeck, became Britain's first openly gay rabbi when he came out in 1980, creating a path for others to follow.[116] Sheila Shulman, who declared on her successful application to Leo Baeck College that she was a lesbian and radical feminist, went on to create the 'predominantly gay and lesbian' community *Beit Klal Yisrael* soon after her ordination, a community initially affiliated with RSGB before switching to Liberal Judaism.[117] All in all, while conservative communities did sometimes express a preference for male, straight rabbis, the ability of RSGB and Liberal Judaism to adapt Jewish tradition and principles paved the way for a new set of religious leaders, and struck out a new direction for Jewish religiosity.[118]

Reform Judaism, moreover, brought new people into Jewish communities as it developed a different set of practices and principles with regard to conversion. At many points RSGB and its predecessors took a conservative stance when it came to allowing non-Jewish people to join its communities. In an atmosphere where Progressive Judaism was frequently derided as less than rigorous by Orthodox critics, Reform leaders (and members) were sometimes reluctant to allow their congregations to be presented as a soft touch on conversion, or as being made up of people who weren't 'real' Jews. 'The greatest obstacle to proper integration of converts', Dow Marmur complained, was 'the non-cooperation of many congregations and congregants.'[119] Anxious about the Reform process of conversion, the Manchester Reform community insisted on retaining full independence when it came to deciding who to admit into its congregation.[120] Speaking at a conference in 1956, Manchester's rabbi Selwyn Goldberg defended 'the discouragement of proselytization' as a principle of Judaism.[121] Making clear the nature of their concerns on the issue, another

Manchester delegate argued that his community felt membership 'should be for people who wished to worship as progressive Jews and that they should not be used as a "dumping ground" for conversion'. This concern reflected a broader conservative tendency regarding conversions. In notes of discussions at a session on 'Reform Judaism in the provinces' at the annual RSGB conference in 1973, it was recorded that all the communities 'seemed to have the same problem – conversion – we must not let it become the majority in a congregation'.[122]

Yet despite these concerns, RSGB's position on conversion emerged as radically different to that of Orthodox Judaism. Even as they sought to maintain a high bar, Reform thinking and process ensured a different start and end point for procedures around joining the community, most obviously rooted in a more positive position on accepting those who wanted to join because their partner was Jewish. So far as the Orthodox Beth Din was concerned, wanting to marry a Jew (or having already done so) was not a case for conversion. Indeed, it was feared that taking a soft position on this particular issue might lead to more intermarriage if couples thought that the Beth Din could 'make good' a decision to 'marry out'. For the Reform, however, marriage to a Jew (so long as it was backed up with a sincere desire to join) was increasingly seen as a good reason to become Jewish, one which was perhaps more likely to lead someone to maintain a Jewish life than if they merely had a personal theological desire to adopt the faith. Jonathan Romain explained:

> I have a much greater preference for somebody who has got a Jewish partner than somebody who is *lishmah* and comes to it just for the spirituality, because the person with the Jewish partner, a. is going to unify the family, b. they've got that support group, they've got that home base, they've got that family.[123]

Taking a positive attitude towards potential converts with Jewish partners, Reform leaders realised, could help to stem the flow of Jewish people from Judaism at a time when interfaith marriage was becoming more common. Here was a practical reason to take a different line to the Orthodox, rooted not so much in theology as in the realities of post-war British life. As one delegate from North Western Reform synagogue questioned in 1956, was it not 'better to accept a proselyte for the purpose of marriage and ensure that the children came into the fold, or to discourage the applicants – who would doubtless all the same marry out of the faith – and lose them completely'.[124] As was often the case, Reform theology blended practical and theological rationales for change. Rabbi Van der Zyl made the case that the love expressed through marriage was a strong starting point for entry to Judaism. 'Out of that bond of love could arise the sincere conviction of one partner to share the faith of the other.'[125]

Attitudes towards non-Jews joining the community reflected a broader inclination among Reform Jewry to engage with the non-Jewish world. Progressive Jews in post-war Britain frequently led the Jewish community in interfaith dialogue and represented Judaism to non-Jewish society. Indeed, Orthodox leaders sometimes became irritated that Reform theologians became the go-to contacts for media companies when a Jewish position was sought. Rabbis such as Hugo Gryn and Lionel Blue became household names, particularly for their contributions on radio. The popularity of these high-profile figures reflected a commitment to sharing with the non-Jewish world which went right to the grassroots of Progressive Jewish communities. Gryn himself highlighted the importance to Reform Judaism of interfaith work as he surveyed the challenges facing RSGB in its Jubilee Year of 1992. 'In the pluralistic society in which we now live', he argued, it was necessary to be 'effective in forging harmonious relationships with as many communities of other faiths as possible'.[126] This work was 'essential to the well-being and safety of our society'. Here, the motive of fighting antisemitism was plain to see. Manchester's Reform congregation at Jackson's Row synagogue made a point of inviting non-Jews into the community, especially to witness festivals. This work, the president of the community argued, was valuable 'not only in providing education and understanding to our neighbours but nipping in the bud incipient anti-semitism'.[127]

This desire to reach outwards from the community also had a theological dimension, whereby it was recognised that there were lessons to be learned from other faiths, and that Judaism was not the sole repository of God's wisdom. As Finchley Reform's minister, Jeffrey Newman, explained: 'God breathes outside the Jewish world as well as within it, and we need this energy wherever it is available.'[128] On these grounds, Jackson's Row occasionally invited Christian theologians to address the congregation, including the Catholic Archbishop of Westminster, John Heenan, in 1967.[129] No one represented this open-minded approach more than Lionel Blue, who was unapologetic in his belief that God could, and should, be sought by Jews in the wisdom of other faiths. 'Retreat houses', he argued in 1975, 'whether Christian, Hindu or Sufi could help people to pray.'[130] Blue recalled with satisfaction that Leo Baeck had reassured him that 'Judaism is your religious home, it's not your religious prison.'[131] Feeling as though he had 'touched heaven' sitting in a church, he allowed himself not to worry too much about it. 'If the magic worked, I was with it.'[132]

In the end, the differences between Progressive and Orthodox Judaism were sufficient to ensure significant tension and a perception of deep division. As Jonathan Sacks put it, the Reform platform added up to a 'fateful break … not only with the letter but with the whole spirit of Jewish law' and risked a future in which Orthodox Jews would see Progressive Judaism as 'a different religion'.[133] There had been opposition from the moment that the West London opened its doors, but as the Reform movement expanded in the post-war period, amid a lurch to the right within Orthodoxy, relations began to sour on a new scale.

A growing divide?

The 1940s witnessed increasing Orthodox opposition to the establishment of Reform congregations, especially outside London. As Glasgow sought to embed a Reform community, hostility from the local Orthodox leadership made things difficult. A note from the Conference of Associated British Synagogues in 1944 recorded that Glasgow's new communal rabbi had 'informed a large audience that Liberal and Reform Synagogues were churches for Jewish Christians'.[134] These kinds of slurs delegitimised Progressive communities, as did the Orthodox denial of basic Jewish services to Reform congregants. Glasgow, for example, refused to allow Reform ministers to officiate at the Jewish cemetery, meaning that Reform Jews could only access Jewish burial 'conducted by orthodox ministers in accordance with the strictest orthodox ritual'.[135] In Cardiff, 'overt hostility' from the Orthodox congregation meant that Reform members on 'several' occasions had to secure a 'London mohel' to perform their children's circumcisions.[136] Local rivalries could be petty. In Hull, the Orthodox minister called an Extraordinary General Meeting at three days' notice to prevent his members from attending a scheduled lecture by the Reform rabbi to which the whole community had been invited.[137]

For some Orthodox Jews, the abandonment of traditional rules in Progressive Judaism put it completely beyond the pale. It was a religion, an editorial in the *Jewish Tribune* complained, where one 'can eat trefa [non-kosher food] on Yom Kippur, refuse circumcision, marry out of the fold and still be regarded as a good "progressive" Jew'.[138] Amid this perceived dereliction of duty, Reform Jews were sometimes cast as not Jewish at all. At the ASGB Executive in 1957, discussion took place about how to respond to teachers at the Orthodox

London Hasmonean School, who had described 'people who practiced Reform Judaism' to their pupils 'as not being Jews'.[139]

Underpinning this Orthodox position was perhaps a fear that Progressive Judaism might be contagious if they allowed themselves (or vulnerable people in their communities) to come into contact with it. The challenge posed by Progressive theology could not be ignored or tolerated, but instead 'needed to be faced with determination and a planned counter-offensive'.[140] Readers of the *Jewish Tribune* wrote in to urge the newspaper to take on these dangerous forces. One advised:

> You would be doing a great service if you devoted more space to enlightening the Community to the dangers and pitfalls of Reform and Liberal Judaism... Many people attend their services because they do not see the dangers involved. Children from orthodox homes are invited to attend Bar Mitzvah or Bath Mitzvah celebrations and in sheer ignorance join their friends at the 'Simcha'.[141]

Students, it was feared, were particularly at risk. It was likely, another letter writer warned, that Reformers would 'go over onto the offensive ... for the minds and allegiance of the student-world'.[142]

The solution often proposed, alongside propaganda against Progressive Judaism, was a ban on any contact, especially at the level of rabbis and other leaders. This push for separation posed significant challenges for those who sought to engage across the Jewish community, notably the Chief Rabbi. Israel Brodie, who held the role from 1948 to 1965, was generally regarded, in Orthodox circles, as being suitably hostile towards Progressives (not least, as we shall see, because of his handling of the Jacobs Affair), but concerns arose about his successor, Immanuel Jakobovits. While Jakobovits was respected as an Orthodox figure, he began to attract criticism because of his view that it was appropriate to engage with Progressive Jews on community matters beyond religion (such as Israel, antisemitism, interfaith relations). One such attempt at communal unity in 1979 saw the Chief Rabbi attend an event for Israel alongside Progressive leaders, a decision that sparked a furious response in some Orthodox circles. A small group of religious Jewish leaders, including rabbinical heads of Britain's yeshivot, the leader of the UOHC's Beth Din, the rabbis of Manchester's *Machzikei Hadass* and London's *Adath Yisroel* synagogues, collectively going under the name of EMETH (Emunah Mitzvah Torah), published an advertisement in the *Jewish Chronicle* which congratulated the UOHC on having made a declaration criticising Jakobovits's attendance at the event. The EMETH advert made it clear that, for them, Progressive

Jewry was completely untouchable, and that any engagement with such Jews was an act against Judaism.

> Their followers have rejected Divine Authority, their beliefs are heretical and the very existence of such groups is a denial of the Written and Oral Law given to us at Sinai… Any participation with these movements and their leaders gives them moral support and undermines our own firm adherence to Torah. Anyone who imagines that these dissenters can be brought back into the fold by consorting with them is deluding himself and misleading others.[143]

To Jakobovits, what the EMETH signatories failed to understand was that British Jews expected him (and the community more broadly) to strive for unity, and not the kind of separation called for by EMETH and the UOHC. 'Come with me on any of my communal visits to meet the grass-roots', he told one letter writer, 'and you will find out that the chief recruitment agents for Reform are the signatories to the recent pronouncement.'[144] Supporting the Chief Rabbi's stance, a report in the *Jewish Gazette* (Manchester), which asked Jews in Sedgley Park about the controversy, found 52 out of 60 urging cooperation between Orthodox and Progressive communities.[145] In an atmosphere where concerns about antisemitism persisted, and where Jewish communities strove to maximise support for Israel and Soviet Jewry, most Jews did not see the need for such in-fighting. Engagement between Orthodox and Progressive Judaism often cut across family and friendship groups and was largely seen as a matter of personal preference, not meriting ostracism or public argument. As Ben Azai (Chaim Bermant) put it in the *Jewish Chronicle*, 'you pay your membership fee and you sit through the service of your choice'.[146]

Recognising that this was the case, Jakobovits's tolerance of Progressives in certain spaces was a pragmatic response to the thinking of his flock, a tactical accommodation more than a theological recognition, a point not lost on leading Reform rabbis who expected him to go further. Dow Marmur, who worked with Jakobovits on the Consultative Committee on Jewish-Christian Relations, wrote to the Chief Rabbi to express concern that Jakobovits only seemed to be distancing himself from the EMETH signatories and their like out of expediency. Jakobovits conceded that it would be 'sheer hypocrisy for Jews [such as himself] who held traditional beliefs and practices as sacred to regard doctrines denying these commitments as equally authentic'.[147] Similarly, his successor, Jonathan Sacks, was clear that his position could not be seen as 'halfway between Orthodoxy and Reform, halakhah and the rejection of halakhah'.[148] Nonetheless, Jakobovits assured Marmur that his stance on

Progressive Judaism was born of conviction (about recognising the authenticity of all Jews) as well as a strategic desire to maximise Jewish unity. This position was enough to reassure the Reform leader, while others in Progressive Jewry seem to have appreciated the line being held by Jakobovits at least in comparison to what was being asked for by EMETH. As for EMETH's challenge, Liberal rabbi John Rayner returned the religious incomprehension and fury when he railed in his St John's Wood pulpit against the 'strange kind of zeal which defends the Torah by violating the Torah!'[149]

The fault line between Orthodox and Progressive Jews, with the Chief Rabbi stuck in the middle as an Orthodox leader seeking communal unity, came to a head in the internal politics of the Board of Deputies. As the Progressive movements grew in size in post-war Britain, so too increased their desire to be afforded proportional and appropriate recognition on this body of British Jewish representation. The RSGB newsletter of 1967 highlighted a push to encourage communities to take up their places on the Board, which led to 15 new Reform synagogues sending delegates, increasing their overall representation to 36.[150] Reform enthusiasm to engage was bolstered by the ascendance, in 1967, of Michael Fidler as the Board's new president, and the change of Chief Rabbi from Brodie to Jakobovits.[151] Fidler, in his previous role as chair of the Council of Manchester and Salford Jews, 'spoke out strongly' against Orthodox attempts in Newcastle to marginalise the Reform community, an action which led Reform leaders to believe that he would serve their interests well on the Board.[152] Yet despite the perceived potential for change, the end of the decade brought 'a series of perceived snubs' to Reform leaders, highlighting the extent to which they continued to suffer 'second class treatment' on the Board.[153] In particular, it was felt, Reform rabbinic authorities had not been afforded appropriate recognition, in contrast to the Chief Rabbi and the Haham (the spiritual leader of British Sephardi Jewry). For example, when ecclesiastical advisors were sought for an education conference with the Israeli Prime Minister Levi Eshkol, no invitation was afforded to any Reform rabbi. In a letter to the Chief Rabbi, Alan King-Hamilton (who had led an internal strategy committee bridging Reform and Liberal Jews) argued that it was time to reconsider who spoke for the religious conscience of the British community in recognition of its changing make-up.

> There is, and has been for many years, a strong and growing progressive community and to ignore it is to shut one's eyes to the obvious. Accordingly, it is not accurate for you and the Haham to describe yourselves in such a way as to convey the impression that you are the sole 'spiritual leaders of Anglo-Jewry'.[154]

This issue was brought to the Board in the summer of 1970 in an attempt to amend Clause 43 of its constitution. This clause invested Jewish ecclesiastical authority solely in the Chief Rabbi and Haham, restricting the Board to consultation with these officers when it sought a rabbinical ruling. The proposed amendment held that Reform authorities too should be consulted where a particular matter would affect their congregations. This amendment secured a simple majority of the deputies but failed narrowly to secure the two-thirds needed to change the constitution. Opposition to the change was fierce among representatives of Orthodox synagogues affiliated with the UOHC and the Federation. Counsellor Joe Lobenstein, of the UOHC, told the *Jewish Tribune* that no Orthodox Jew could 'give any recognition to a religion of convenience which has deserted the sanctity of our heritage'.[155]

Here, the Chief Rabbi and Haham were caught in the middle, seeking compromise. The matter was, Jakobovits felt, 'largely artificial' and risked diverting 'the community's attention from the more urgent challenges facing us'.[156] Board leaders sought a solution, but by the following summer RSGB and ULPS (Union of Liberal and Progressive Synagogues) delegates had reached a state of exasperation whereby they threatened to leave the Board unless a compromise could be agreed, an outcome, Fidler felt, that would be 'one of the gravest blows to communal unity and to the vital work of Anglo-Jewry'.[157] The solution worked out by the Board left the Chief Rabbi and the Haham named as the 'ecclesiastical authorities' but committed the Board to consult with other religious leaders where matters affected them. This, to both the Chief Rabbi and the Haham, avoided what they perceived as red lines, that the Board should not afford 'religious recognition to Progressive Judaism and its spiritual leaders' or make statements 'on behalf of the community which flout the halacha'.[158] But to the Orthodox block of deputies, this compromise was far from acceptable. As Bernard Homa put it in a letter to Jakobovits, 'the additional requirement to consult with other "religious leaders", can only mean that these are now being put on a par with the Ecclesiastical Authorities of the Board'.[159] For Lazar Dovid Brunner, president of the (London) *Machzike Hadath*, it was 'the thin end of the wedge'. 'Today', he told the Haham, 'they are asking for consultation, in five or ten years' time the demand will be for the inclusion of their "rabbis" amongst the "ecclesiastical authorities" of the Board.'[160] When the compromise motion passed in October 1971, 80 Orthodox deputies resigned on behalf of their communities (most returned in 1973 following further discussion).[161]

This crisis highlighted the difficulty of the Chief Rabbi's position. To some on the Orthodox right his willingness to compromise revealed weakness, made worse by it being rooted in what some saw as a broader pattern of sympathetic behaviour towards Progressives. One 1971 letter writer accused the Chief Rabbi of having embarked on a 'pre-conceived journey' of 'rapprochement with the Progressives'. Amid a litany of charges, Jakobovits, it was noted, had participated in Solomon Teff's committee 'to reconcile different elements in Anglo-Jewry', lectured at Leo Baeck College, and given the Lily Montagu memorial lecture, all signs of the Board of Deputies compromise that was to come.[162] The Chief Rabbi responded by asserting that he 'never had, or ever will have, any desire to recognise [the Progressives]'. Instead, he argued, he was merely responding to the pressures of the period. His predecessors were 'never confronted' by the 'permissive society', which had ushered in an atmosphere where Jews were 'no longer content simply to accept affirmations of Judaism' because he felt them 'to be the only legitimate expression of our faith'.[163]

Jakobovits presented his position to critics on the right in terms of his obligation to accept reality, in contrast to their idealistic unworldliness. Those deputies who had walked out of the Board, Jakobovits advised in a joint statement with the Haham, 'could do so with an easy conscience since they knew full well that Orthodox interests would continue to be protected by the vast majority of Orthodox Deputies who remained on the Board'.[164] Writing to Bernard Homa, who had just resigned as a deputy and as head of the Board's Shechita Committee, Jakobovits accused him of showing 'complete disregard for the spiritual responsibilities imposed on me for the tens of thousands of "middle-of-the-road" Jews within mainstream Orthodoxy'.[165] The expulsion of the Progressives, Jakobovits explained, would 'alienate' this mainstream body of Jews and make the Progressives look like 'martyrs' and 'underdogs' in a way which would 'only boost their popularity'. Moreover, Jakobovits felt, men such as Homa owed him religious loyalty as the Chief Rabbi. 'By denying this loyalty to me, you undermine the very halachic authority which you claim to defend.'

Indeed, this conflict highlighted the weak bonds that tied Orthodox Jews to the Chief Rabbi. The Orthodox representatives who resigned from the Board did so following the guidance of their own rabbinic authorities. As Homa, in his reply to the Chief Rabbi, made clear, his own decision had been guided by 'three independent expert Rabbinic authorities in this country'. Homa reminded the Chief Rabbi that the community he represented on the Board, the *Machzike Hadath*, 'agreed in 1905 to "recognise … the jurisdiction and authority … of the Chief Rabbi … for the time being … provided he acts in accordance with the Shulchan Aruch" … The advice I have now received relieves me of this obligation.'[166] Stuck between a rock and a hard place, there was little Jakobovits could do except express his dismay at the situation and try to talk the Orthodox deputies back to the table.

What was at stake here was little less than the correct way to be Jewish in the face of modernity. As British Jewish communities adopted radically different approaches to modern life, the Chief Rabbi tried to bridge the gap, but it wasn't easy. Perhaps more than any other, the core theological issue related to the God-given nature, and thus the unchangeability, of Jewish scripture. For Progressive theologians the challenge was to adapt Jewish practice and learning for modern times, and engage with biblical criticism and historical analyses of the Jewish past. As Montefiore put it in 1923, what was needed was a Judaism that could 'look science in the face without flinching'.[167] Even Progressives, however, accepted that it was not easy to keep God in Jewish lives through such a journey. 'Righteousness', Lionel Blue conceded, could survive the distance from 'medieval piety to enlightened materialism', but 'holiness' was 'a more delicate plant' whose life was 'precarious'.[168] Despite Jonathan Romain's claim that most of British Jewry no longer believed in the literal word of the Torah, for many Orthodox Jews the Written and Oral Law came from God and it was heresy to see things otherwise. Differences of opinion on this issue challenged relations between Orthodox and Progressive Jews but also caused significant conflict within Orthodox communities, reflected most obviously in the 'Jacobs Affair' of 1961.

This controversy saw Chief Rabbi Brodie decline to support the appointment, as principal of Jews' College, of Rabbi Louis Jacobs in 1961. Jacobs had strong Orthodox credentials after studying in Gateshead and Manchester and had ascended to the post of minister and preacher in the New West End (United) synagogue in 1954. He had then taken up the post of Moral Tutor and Lecturer in Pastoral Theology at Jews' College in the expectation of becoming principal after Isodore Epstein's retirement.[169] In the event, however, Chief Rabbi Brodie refused to consent to the appointment, a decision that ultimately led Jacobs to resign from his teaching post, sparking wide-scale fallout, which continued as the Chief Rabbi declined to allow Jacobs to return to his old pulpit at the New West End when he was invited to do so by its management board in 1964.[170] With support from over 300 members of his London community, Jacobs broke away and established in 1964 a new congregation, the New London, in the character, Alderman has noted, of the 'United Synagogue of pre-war days'.[171] Followed subsequently by a small number of further congregations, the New London marked the beginnings of what would emerge as Masorti Judaism in Britain in 1980, a congregation similar to the US Conservative Jewish movement.[172] For his part, Chief Rabbi Brodie responded by denying the New London the right to certify marriages, a decision speedily reversed by Immanuel Jakobovits after his ascent to office.[173]

Brodie's refusal to endorse Jacobs was rooted in objections to his published work, most obviously *We Have Reason to Believe* in 1957 and *Jewish Values* in 1960. While *We Have Reason to Believe* had not initially been particularly controversial (Brodie himself, Jacobs recorded, had accepted a copy 'without the slightest objection'), concerns were soon expressed at its openness to biblical criticism, and specifically its analysis of whether the Written and Oral Law was handed over complete, directly from God.[174] Looking back on the controversy, Jacobs explained that he felt it right to acknowledge modern scholarship which had 'demonstrated to the satisfaction of many believers that the Torah did not simply drop down, ready packaged, so to speak, from heaven but has evolved over the ages, partly, at least, in response to, and influenced by external conditions'.[175] Such analysis made sense to Jacobs but was seen by Brodie as a fundamental threat to Jewish values: 'An attitude to the Torah such as this which denies its Divine source and unity (Torah min Hashamayim) is directly opposed to Orthodox Jewish teaching and no person holding such views can expect to obtain the approval of the Orthodox ecclesiastical authority.'[176] The pulling away from traditional religious certainties in Jacobs's analysis reflected discussions also taking place in British Christianity, most obviously the 1963 publication of *Honest to God* by John Robinson, a text which sent shock waves through Christian circles because of its willingness to re-evaluate the relationship between God and the Church. While James Parkes was quick to point out that Jacobs's theological challenge was modest in comparison, it nonetheless spoke to a similar belief that religious leaders needed to be open to radical modern questioning if they were to futureproof their faiths.[177] Thus, the *Daily Telegraph* opined, 'We have been warned against regarding Rabbi Louis Jacobs as a sort of Jewish Bishop of Woolwich. Yet that, mutatis mutandis, is rather what he is.'[178]

Parkes, though, was right that Jacobs's intention was not to undermine Orthodoxy. Instead, Jacobs aimed to strengthen the Torah's legitimacy by not shying away from engagement with modern scholarship. In Jacobs's words:

> The modern Jewish theologian, true to the tradition, has to try to understand how, now that Judaism is seen to have had a history (which means there is a human element in revelation), the traditional view of Torah Min Ha-Shamayyim can be reinterpreted while still retaining its ancient vigour and power.[179]

Jacobs had initially considered this view 'fully compatible with the somewhat tepid Orthodoxy' of British Jewry.[180] Yet, as we have seen, British Orthodoxy in this period was lurching to the right, so that the argument of *We Have Reason to Believe*, not helped by its author's cordial relationships with Progressives, was painted as heretical by some of the Chief Rabbi's advisors.[181]

For the *Jewish Chronicle*, the fallout was a 'symptom of a fundamental cleavage in Anglo-Jewish religious attitudes'.[182] Editor William Frankel was a 'close personal friend' of Jacobs who had been 'instrumental' in supporting the rabbi both at the New West End (where he was an active member) and at Jews' College.[183] To thinkers such as Frankel, rightist forces within the Beth Din had pressurised the Chief Rabbi, 'at variance with the benevolent Anglo-Jewish traditions of tolerance and reasonableness'. Accusations were laid at the door of foreign-born and trained refugee rabbis, who, it was argued, were determined to drag British Jewry to un-British levels of religious extremism. It was, Alfred Sherman argued in the *Telegraph*, a 'counterattack by the elderly East European trained dayanim – second rank religious administrators – who see their world crumbling around them under the onset of anglicisation'.[184] While it was no doubt true that Brodie had come under pressure to block Jacobs at Jews' College, blaming others for the stance he took (and especially blaming foreign-born rabbis) fails to paint the full picture of a crisis that was a long time in the making. By the time of the Jacobs Affair, the Chief Rabbi did not so much acquiesce to change but exemplify it. 'His mind', the Dayanim of the London Beth Din explained, 'was at one with ours.'[185] Indeed, as Jacobs himself understood, when it came to blocking his return to the New West End, it was Brodie calling the shots while the Beth Din urged reconciliation.[186]

Following Brodie, Immanuel Jakobovits attempted to pour water on the flames, but he could not easily do so (as the Clause 43 crisis would go on to show). On Jacobs and Clause 43, Jakobovits's instinct was to conciliate so far as possible in a spirit of religious ecumenism, which, he felt, was most likely to leave Orthodoxy in the ascendancy. When he started in post, he recalled, the Jacobs Affair had been 'a major threat to the Orthodox community'. By refusing to exacerbate the crisis (by allowing marriage certification to Jacobs's new community), he believed he had reduced the risk of contagion. 'I have never regretted it', he told one right-wing critic. 'The moment they could no longer claim that they were ostracised or dealt with unjustly, the whole movement collapsed and it has never bothered us since.'[187] This was an exaggeration, but Jakobovits was certainly right that the Masorti community did not (then or now) dominate the Orthodox centre ground. Instead, the growth of British Masorti Judaism might be seen as reflecting a response to the movement of what had previously been the Orthodox centre ground to the right. Within this new right, many Jews felt disinclined to compromise with reformers of any hue. For some, as expressed in an editorial in the *Jewish Tribune* in 1965, the battle with the middle-of-the-road 'older-type Anglo-Jew' was a 'vital and holy war', which needed fighting 'for the sake of the very future of our own children and children's children'.[188] These were Jews who thought their predecessors were 'always greater', and had created an unchallengeable model for 'today, tomorrow, and forever'.[189] Criticising the moderation of Jakobovits, Salmond Levin explained that attempting to hold the middle ground was doomed to failure:

> People are in the middle of the road because they want to cross over to the other side. It is happening on a large scale. Statistics are now available indicating that within a generation there will be left only a Sheerit in Anglo Jewry. They will be the orthodox, who stood firm and did not compromise.[190]

Amid such thinking, the Orthodox centre felt consistent pressure not to yield in the face of rising secularism and the growth of Progressive Judaism. Instead, the sharp divide highlighted by the Clause 43 row, and earlier by the Jacobs Affair, reflected the polarisation thesis that was outlined at the outset of this chapter.

* * *

In the context of the substantial growth of both Progressive and Orthodox Judaism in post-war Britain, and amid mounting hostility between the two, it is tempting to see British Jews, as Alderman has done, as a 'house divided', with the Chief Rabbi and diplomatic Board of Deputies officials attempting to bridge a widening gap. To some extent this thesis is difficult to dispute. Yet for me it does not tell the whole story of changing religious culture in Jewish Britain, and in some ways it serves to obscure the stakes of religious disagreement. Of course, there was (and has remained) a seemingly unbridgeable distance between those who see the Written and Oral Law as the word of God and those who do not. And yet, as the challenge of Louis Jacobs demonstrated, this was no simple dispute between Orthodox and Progressive theologians. Instead, the Jacobs Affair served to illustrate a deeper issue, which transcended Judaism and is perhaps best understood as symptomatic of the post-war tensions between religion and modernity writ large. Religious thinkers of different hues in this period were scrambling to answer the same question: how should one preserve the old faith in a new age? For the Orthodox (or at least for some Orthodox thinkers), the correct response was the 'rabbinic slogan: *af al pi chen*. We must carry on regardless.' For Progressives, significant change was needed to keep Jews 'within the fold, in a dislocated world'.[191] And yet the fact that Jewish thinkers were all confronting the same challenge itself tells a story. As Lionel Blue put it, Jewish unity didn't stem from an Orthodoxy wherein Jews believed 'the same things' but from 'an orthopraxis, where we all work together for the same things'.[192] Indeed, there has been much in common in the motivations and thinking of seemingly disparate Jewish religious communities in post-war Britain.

Religious divisions, moreover, changed shape and focus depending on the vantage point of the enquiry. Devotional differences that ran within families and social groups perhaps too easily obscured greater commonalities, which, when considered, allow a less fraught image of British Jewry to come to the fore, different both in tone and substance from what one might imagine from high-volume national disputes. At a local level, religious community could look very different. In Bournemouth, long-serving Reform rabbi David Soetendorp explained, years of 'breaking down barriers' had brought together Reform and Orthodox communities on the Representative Council, seen them share childcare and old-age support services, and provide advice and encouragement to one another.[193] This kind of cooperation promoted a different reading of religious Jewish life, highlighting that, in many ways, devotional Jews across the religious spectrum still had much in common.

For one thing, the contrasting beliefs and behaviours of Orthodox and Reform communities have often been rooted in the same anxieties, driven by a belief that they were the last defenders of Judaism holding back a tidal wave of secularism and assimilation. In both cases, this sense of responsibility was firmly rooted in a post-Holocaust determination not to allow, in Fackenheim's famous parlance, a posthumous Nazi victory in the form of the disappearance of Jews and Judaism.[194] This was, as the *Jewish Tribune* explained, 'an orphaned generation' of Jews, very much conscious of its 'spiritual and material weakness'.[195] For Hugo Gryn, the Holocaust had left 'unfinished business', and British Jewry was engaged in a 'process of healing' which would 'take generations'.[196]

At an institutional level, the creation of new religious seminaries (both Orthodox and Progressive) was rooted in a desire to repair these devastated communities. Leo Baeck College, Ruth Cohen attested, 'was founded to replace the seminaries destroyed by the Nazis'.[197] Similarly, the expansion of colleges in Gateshead was explained in these terms, as 'Torah centres to replace those in Europe, whose loss threatened disaster for the whole of Jewry'.[198] To the post-Holocaust generation, Chief Rabbi Israel Brodie argued at an anniversary dinner for the Sunderland Kollel in 1972, fell 'the privilege as well as the challenge to ensure that there should be a future for Judaism'.[199]

Although Brodie was speaking to (and no doubt thinking of) Orthodox Jews, this was a challenge felt across the British Jewish community, driving ambition and anxiety. The response, in Progressive communities, was (in Gryn's words) to 're-affirm our commitment to the opening of our doors to all those who wish to enter the Jewish community', an attitude that saw the modification of a range of policies and practices to make Judaism more appealing and inclusive and reverse 'unhappy trends' of communal decline.[200] To Ignaz Maybaum, Progressives were working to 'try to save as much as possible' of a 'rich past that has been destroyed'.[201] For Orthodox Jews, a different approach was taken to solve the problem. Here, it was most often thought, the remedy was to hold fast and not bend to the prevailing winds. By maintaining the highest level of religious observance, some Orthodox Jews saw their role as 'to defend a small corner of spiritual territory of Judaism, to maintain a faithful remnant'.[202] In so doing, they not only honoured the lost generation of the Holocaust, but had the best chance, they thought, of inspiring the next.

In this anxious atmosphere, as Orthodox and Progressive Jews engaged in what they similarly perceived as a battle for a Jewish future, they served a useful purpose for each other. To Progressive Jews, adaptability and inclusivity were presented as essential responses to intransigent and closed-minded Orthodox attitudes, which risked driving Jews out of the faith. For the Orthodox, the case for maintaining strict religious standards and preserving traditions was made in terms of resisting the dangerous pressure being exerted by Progressive Jews. Yet beyond using each other as bogeymen, and beyond very real divisions of thought and practice, this was, for the most part, a community that still recognised each other as family, however much they disapproved of each other's choices. On these grounds, Orthodox insults about Progressive Jews not being real Jews should be seen as just that; 'nasty' words, as Gryn might have put it, designed to antagonise and rebuke, not ultimately intended as statements of fact. Indeed, one could argue, determined in-fighting itself pointed to the ultimate unity of the community. For, as Barbara Myerhoff has explained, 'fighting is a partnership, requiring cooperation. A boundary-maintaining mechanism – for strangers cannot participate fully – it is also above all a profoundly sociable activity.'[203]

British Jewry grew from multiple national, class and religious backgrounds, so that it had never been neatly comprehensible as one group. This did not change in the post-war period, but neither did the community radically come apart. Instead, the growth of Progressive and Orthodox Judaism should be seen both in terms of the long-term impact of immigration, and as evolving responses to the changing place of religion that was causing concern across all faith communities, and in which the identified problem – the decline of traditional Jewish community – was in many ways agreed upon. Across and within families and flocks, Jewish practice varied, as had always been the case. But using these disparities and arguments as evidence of polarisation foregrounds religious belief in a period in which Jews increasingly explained and understood their Jewishness in different, and less divisive, terms, as a fight against anti-semitism, as Zionism, as the preservation of culture and tradition. For sure, some Jews bickered bitterly about religion, and believed other Jews to be on the wrong path. Yet for all but the most religious Jews in post-war Britain, relations with God and with formal religious institutions were increasingly personal, informal and idiosyncratic.

3

'We speak for them': political activism in the Six-Day War and the campaign for Soviet Jewry

Three days before the Six-Day War between Israel and its Arab neighbours began in 1967, in an atmosphere of high tension, Jewish *Daily Mail* journalist Bernard Levin used his column to launch a scathing attack on the British Chief Rabbi, Immanuel Jakobovits. Levin was furious about the role that the Chief Rabbi ascribed to British Jewry in the imminent Middle East conflict.[1] Speaking to the Board of Deputies, Jakobovits had argued that British Jews should be at the service of the Israeli state. 'If they want us', he asserted, 'we will be there at their command.'[2] For Levin, this offer was nothing short of an outrage. Dismissing Jakobovits's comments as 'dangerous nonsense' which threatened to raise a 'dreadful ghost' of dual loyalty allegations against British Jews, Levin told readers that any fighting he did in the future would be 'in defence of my own country'. He explained, 'My allegiance, legal and emotional, is to the country of which I am a citizen by birth: Britain.'[3]

Levin's stance represented the traditional position of many British Jews. From the earliest days of Zionism others had expressed similar opinions, a reality that led some Jewish leaders to lobby against the Balfour Declaration in 1917 (and to succeed in softening its tone), and significantly restricted British Jewish support for Zionism until the late 1930s.[4] For many Jews, especially those who were long established in the country, unequivocal and unambiguous loyalty to Britain was owed and demanded, evidenced through demonstrations of patriotism and, in particular, military service in British wars.[5] Despite a high level of support for the State of Israel after its birth in 1948, many British Jews remained convinced that their primary and overriding loyalty should be to Britain. Eleven years before the Six-Day War, during the Suez Crisis of 1956, all seventeen Jewish MPs from Labour's opposition (including Barnett Janner, who was chair of the Board of Deputies) voted with their party against the action, despite Israeli involvement, a decision that saw Janner face a vote of no confidence at the Board of Deputies (which he won overwhelmingly).[6] For these MPs, loyalty and priority was owed to their constituents and their nation. Maurice Edelman, Labour MP for Coventry North, explained his stance: 'As British citizens, we have an unquestionable and undivided loyalty: that is to Britain.'[7] This kind of tension around the obligations of British Jews reflected long-standing debates and conflicts within and beyond Jewish communities. Underpinning Jewish thinking, in many cases at least, were anxieties about the way Jews were seen by other Britons. Like Levin, some feared accusations of dual loyalty, insufficient patriotism and clannishness. Amid a long history of European antisemitism, such fears were often well founded, and shaped the behaviour of a migrant community that very much wanted to be accepted and protected.

By the time of the Six-Day War, however, Levin's position was out of step with the majority. Jack Omer-Jackaman, in this context, has asserted that Levin was one of 'only two isolated Jewish outliers' in Britain who worried that 'dual loyalty' charges might be levelled against British Jews who supported Israel in this conflict.[8] Instead, the Six-Day War revealed a heightened British Jewish commitment to the Jewish state, best understood as a transformative moment of diasporic consciousness, an 'immensely powerful collective experience'.[9] In the midst of a conflict that many British Jews saw as a matter of life and death for Israel, Levin's comments about Jakobovits were most frequently dismissed as 'utterly contemptible'.[10] And in the wake of the dramatic Israeli victory, the matter could and did become something of a joke. *Daily Mail* cartoonist John Musgrave-Wood drew the Israeli triumph with the caption, 'What Really Hurts, Abdul, is that They Managed It without Bernard Levin.'[11]

This chapter will explore post-war British Jewish engagement with global politics, looking specifically at how British Jews evolved their relationship with, and obligations to, the wider Jewish world. To this end, it will consider two different, yet linked, international Jewish crises: the Six-Day War and the thirty-year campaign for Soviet Jewry. British Jewish activism in these crises, I argue, reveals communities with growing confidence, ready to use their position as established Britons on behalf of other Jews in a way that (as Levin's intervention suggested) jarred sharply with some of the previous rhythms of British Jewish life. Amid a post-Holocaust determination to prevent any further destruction of Jewish people and society, this activism amounted to a new way to be Jewish in a climate of growing secularism and reflected broader

British approaches to political campaigning in an era when direct action and single-issue politics became more common across the nation.

New campaigning? New confidence?

The Six-Day War has been described as a '"watershed" moment' as regards the way that Jewish people understood their place in the post-war world and their relationship with Jews in other countries.[12] Following a period of mounting tension, the war began with a decisive Israeli air strike on Egypt after the Egyptian president, Gamal Abdel Nasser, had mobilised his troops on the Israeli border and ordered UN peacekeepers to leave the area. As Israel took on and swiftly defeated five Arab states, the speed and drama of the victory drew euphoric reactions from relieved and proud Jewish communities who had feared the worst for the young state. The level of peril faced by Israel in the war is a matter of historical debate, but 'the fear [of the state's destruction] had been real' both in the country itself and abroad, among communities still deeply traumatised by the Holocaust.[13] In the aftermath, British Jewry basked in Israel's victory, which served to bolster Jewish confidence and correspondingly reduce anxieties about public displays of solidarity with international Jewry. To MP Emanuel Shinwell, the Israeli victory gave new value to Jewishness and restored Jewish pride worldwide. He told a 2,000-strong victory rally in Manchester's Opera House: 'At last we Jews can look the whole world in the face ... I glory in what the State of Israel and its people have done ... If I have spoken in what may appear an arrogant fashion, it's because I feel somehow it's worthwhile being a Jew.'[14]

This was far from an isolated feeling. Looking back on his early Zionism, Jewish community scholar and activist Antony Lerman recalls 'almost a sense that every Jew's personal status was enhanced' by the Israeli victory.[15] To a people humiliated by feelings of impotence in the face of the Holocaust, and frequently historicised as weak and timid over a far longer period, Israel's pugnacity proved irresistible and even captured the imagination of many Jews in the Soviet Union, as the story broke through the strict state control of news media.[16] In the USSR, the war drove a deeper Jewish identification with Israel and bolstered the confidence of those Soviet Jews who wanted to leave the country despite the USSR's fierce opposition to emigration. As one Soviet émigré told a British journalist:

> When we realised that there were Jews who were fighting a great battle and winning it, something came over us all, wherever we were living in the Soviet

Union. We had almost forgotten we were Jews. Now we wanted to be with the others and fight and work with them.[17]

The international campaign for Soviet Jewry, which sought to challenge the state's refusal to allow Jews to leave and to resist Soviet antisemitic discrimination, was similarly boosted by the conflict (although its origins long preceded it).

Jewish communities across the world became increasingly aware of the plight of Soviet Jews from the mid-1950s. In the aftermath of a series of antisemitic purges culminating in the Doctors' Plot in 1953,[18] and after the death of Stalin made engagement more possible, international Jewish and non-Jewish visitors to the Soviet Union began to 'inquire into the lot of Soviet Jewry'.[19] This interest was promoted and nurtured by the State of Israel, which, under the auspices of a Liaison Bureau, worked 'to rouse Western Jewish communities from their apathy about this issue'.[20] In 1960 a conference on Soviet Jewry was held in Paris, and in 1965 the Holocaust survivor and writer Elie Wiesel visited Jewish people in the Soviet Union on the High Holy Days, writing *The Jews of Silence* on his return. Wiesel's narrative called for immediate international action on behalf of Soviet Jews. He told his readers that the Ukrainian Jews he met had asked him, 'Why are the Jews outside so silent? Why aren't they doing something? Don't they know what is happening here? Or don't they want to know?'[21] In Britain, the silence perceived by the Ukrainian Jews did not so much represent a Jewish lack of interest as a reticence towards high-profile displays of political lobbying regarding Jewish causes and communities. In the post-war period, fault lines between this traditional caution and a more 'loud and proud' internationalist Jewish stance grew amid debates about how to support Jewish communities in the Soviet Union, epitomised by the challenge posed by a range of activist groups, keen to make their voices heard above and beyond diplomatic channels. Here, the traditional approach of the Board of Deputies, at least until the 1970s, was portrayed as ineffective and inappropriately cautious.[22]

British Jewish concern gathered pace in the face of the Soviet Union's many and sometimes extreme attempts to restrict both Jewish practice and culture, and in opposition to Soviet 'economic' trials which disproportionally targeted Jews. In the USSR, as the international community was increasingly aware, some aspects of the Jewish faith (such as circumcision) had been effectively banned and it was 'practically impossible' to fulfil others, such as having a bar mitzvah.[23] Campaigning reached a new pitch following the first Leningrad Trial of 1970, in which nine Soviet Jews (alongside two non-Jewish dissidents) were charged with high treason after an unsuccessful attempt to escape the Soviet Union by diverting a flight to Sweden.[24] The Leningrad case, and the international publicity it received, 'catapult[ed] the movement into high gear', bringing the plight of Soviet Jews to the attention of millions.[25] The severe sentences handed out to the would-be hijackers (including later-commuted death sentences in the cases of Eduard Kuznetsov and Mark Dymshits) led to substantial protest and outrage, and drove forward debates about the appropriate way to speak out on behalf of Soviet Jews.[26] Student outcry was immediate, with a protest held one day after the verdict was announced (on Christmas Day) outside the Soviet embassy.[27] One month after the trial, the Board of Deputies led a 10,000 strong protest march through London.[28] Attempting to head the British response, the deputies staged a major conference to bring together interested parties, evolving an umbrella organisation, the Soviet Jewry Actions Committee (SJAC), in 1971.[29] At Westminster, Greville Janner (MP for Leicester North West) established an All-Party Parliamentary Committee for the Release of Soviet Jewry in 1972, a lobby group which drew hundreds of parliamentarians under its scope. When, in the same year, the committee sent a *Siddur* (Jewish prayer book) to the son of a Soviet-Jewish refusenik who was celebrating his bar mitzvah, it was signed by over 200 MPs, including the Prime Minister.[30]

For some, however, what was needed was direct action, a challenge to those traditional approaches that had generally focused on high-level diplomatic interventions. One Jewish protest at the Soviet embassy in 1971 neatly illustrated this tension, signposting change in the way that British Jews were asserting both their own rights and those of Jewish people overseas. Unsurprisingly, Jewish students were at the forefront of the protest. The Universities' Committee for Soviet Jewry (UCSJ) had formed in 1965, organising its first public demonstration in the following year, striking out in directions that were more radical than had been traditional in British Jewry.[31] The presence of at least two senior Orthodox rabbis at the embassy protest, however, indicates a broader shift in the way that British Jews were feeling and acting.[32]

On the morning of 13 May, fifty Jewish Britons entered the Soviet embassy in London, ostensibly seeking entry visas to enable them to attend 'trials of Jewish dissidents in Leningrad and Riga'.[33] According to the diplomatic correspondent of *The Times*, what followed was a 'violent riot in the reception room' by a 'group of Jews', during which the leader of the UCSJ, Alan Freeman, 'kicked the First Secretary' before British police expelled the group from the building.[34] The demonstration was, according to a subsequent Soviet press release, a 'disgraceful anti-Soviet provocation' which had 'nothing to do with the "cause of defending" Soviet citizens of Jewish nationality'.[35] According to *The Times*, the British government was similarly unimpressed. The paper reported: 'Shortly after the incident, Sir Thomas Brimelow, Deputy Under-Secretary at the Foreign Office, telephoned to the Soviet embassy and apologized.'[36] For the Soviets, the incident provided evidence of the relationship between the students and the Israeli government. Freeman, in the melee, left behind a briefcase which contained correspondence 'implicating the Israeli embassy' in the funding of the student campaign.[37]

The narrative surrounding this disturbance, however, described from the perspective of British Jewish participants, was very different. In the week after the incident, Rabbi Saul Amias wrote a report alleging 'an anti-Semitic slant' in *The Times*'s coverage, arguing that a sincere request for visas had led the group (of which he was a part) to attend the embassy, where they were bullied and violently mistreated. According to Amias, while waiting in the embassy's reception room, Alan Freeman had found on display a copy of a 'virulently anti-Semitic' book and had started 'reading excerpts from it' aloud.[38] In the face of what was a vocal but peaceful protest about the presence of such literature in the embassy, 'suddenly eight giants of men' appeared and made a beeline for Freeman. Amias continued:

> At this point Alan Freeman began singing Havenu Shalom Aleichem [a traditional Jewish song literally translating as 'We bring peace upon you'], and when that ended he started the Hatikvah [the Israeli national anthem], and I should say this was the only occasion that our National Anthem was sung on Russian soil since the revolution. One of the giants then lifted up in his arms Alan Freeman, who naturally struggled, and the Russian gave him a bear's hug which could easily have driven the air out of that young man's body.[39]

Further Soviet violence, Amias explained, saw one of the women in the group receive 'a resounding wallop on the face' and another young man, who subsequently 'collapsed on the pavement outside the Consulate', 'pummelled … on the head' before British police removed the group.

In response to Soviet claims that the Jewish protestors had hurled 'curses and threats' at 'several British visitors' in the embassy, Amias was furious. 'Does it mean', he questioned, 'that our group, because we were Jews, were not British?' He was, he countered, 'born within the sound of Bow Bells … The only minister of any religious denomination in Edgware who volunteered for service.' Here, Amias and his group were setting out their stall as confident, angry citizens, not outsiders meekly begging for justice. Describing the Israeli national anthem as 'our anthem' cemented the point. These Jews did not feel that identifying with international Jewry jeopardised their own Britishness. As one respondent to Bernard Levin had put it, 'Any intelligent, mature man has dual, triple and more loyalties.'[40] Like Israel striking first in the Six-Day War, acting decisively to save Jews was now increasingly constructed as more important than playing by diplomatic rules which, after all, had in no way protected the previous generation. If radical actions helped Jews in the Soviet Union, then they were worth pursuing whatever other Britons, or anyone else, might think.

A longer-term illustration of this militant turn in Jewish protest can be seen in the work of the women's campaigning group, the 35s. This group of activists, Dave Rich has argued, 'changed the entire complexion of Soviet Jewry work in Britain', driving 'sister organisations across the world', and repeatedly pushing the traditional campaigning boundaries of the British Jewish establishment.[41] The group came into being in 1971, established to support Soviet Jews to live Jewish lives in the USSR or, if they wished, to leave the country. Again, support and encouragement was provided through the Israeli Liaison Bureau, which seemingly saw the women as more reliable advocates than the students after the briefcase incident at the embassy.[42] These campaigners were initially motivated to protest the plight of a Ukrainian dissident, Raiza Palatnik, who had been arrested and convicted of 'slandering the Soviet Union', having applied to emigrate to Israel.[43] Named after their initial number at a protest held for Palatnik at the Soviet embassy (and because Palatnik herself was 35 years old), the group gained prominence through publicity stunts across the country.[44]

The 35s, soon one of a few dedicated women's groups with similar goals, demonstrated at cultural and political events involving visitors from the Soviet Union, as well as at the doors of companies that did business with the USSR and at the Soviet embassy itself. In Leith, in 1972, members of Glasgow's 35s greeted passengers from a docking Soviet cruise liner, the *Mikhail Lermontov*, giving them each a 'flower wrapped in a leaflet' demanding the release of Palatnik.[45] In 1987 the 35s handed out flyers to spectators attending the Kirov Ballet in Manchester, asking them to remember the 'hundreds of musicians and artists now waiting for exit visas in the USSR'.[46] Ex-leader and group biographer Daphne Gerlis recalls how they 'dressed as prisoners weighed down with balls and chains, and when young mothers were separated from their babies they dressed in baby clothes, complete with nappies and dummies'.[47] For Doreen Gainsford, another of the 35s' leaders, the flamboyant and high-profile approach offered a crucial step change in contrast to the passivity of the community more broadly. She told the National Conference on Soviet Jewry in 1972, 'We as Jewish housewives do not intend to sit by and watch any Jew, ourselves, our brothers or sisters, hit for being a Jew. I did say our brothers and sisters, but it does not appear that in this country our brothers and sisters are quite so concerned.'[48]

As Gainsford's remarks here suggest, the approach of the 35s was not for everyone. Some British Jews saw the group's loud and confrontational style as counterproductive, likely to turn onlooking Britons against the cause of Soviet Jewry (possibly against British Jews too) and to antagonise the Soviets into even greater acts of hostility towards their Jewish population. A 35s activist in Glasgow remembers feeling this concern:

> I have a memory of trying to keep people on the right track as far as propaganda was concerned, because some people overdid it in the wrong direction ... I said, you mustn't say that, because that just puts the ordinary people's back up, you've got to be realistic.[49]

Gainsford recalled turning up at the Board of Deputies 'hot, sticky and not very clean' after the 35s first demonstration, only to be told by one representative, 'my dear you will just cause anti-Semitism; what are you doing?' This, Gainsford recalls, 'was the general attitude of the establishment'.[50] The 35s' penchant for memorable demonstrations at cultural and social events certainly made some Jews wary. One letter to the Board of Deputies expressed grave concern about a float that the 35s had contributed to a local carnival in Southgate. Amid a sea of happy exhibits, the 35s' float featured a caged man with his arms and legs tied, accompanied by a message to the Soviet Union asking for the 'release of innocent prisoners of conscience'. Such a stunt, the letter writer was concerned, might prove 'quite counter productive'.[51] There was particular anxiety about ruining sporting and cultural events for other British people, especially where this might be perceived as unpatriotic. After a 35s protest at an international athletics meeting at Crystal Palace, the chair of the SJAC shared his concern about 'adverse comments particularly from non-Jews of what was considered an interference in the enjoyment of the day and the successes of British athletes'.[52]

Community worries similarly focused on the decision of the 35s to demonstrate at international diplomatic gatherings, such as the Helsinki Accords in 1975. Against the traditionally quiet approach of the Board of Deputies, which would seek diplomatic discussion in such meetings, groups such as the

35s were dragging the community into more vocal and vociferous challenges on the outside. When the 35s shared their plans for protest at Helsinki with the SJAC, one member of the committee attacked the group for purporting 'to represent the women of the community. She – and she felt thousands like her – were not represented by them and did not wish to be so represented.'[53] Having heard the group's plan for protest at the summit, the SJAC voted 4–2 against participating in it.

Radical support for international Jewry was, though, increasingly seen as acceptable and desirable among British Jews. At the onset of the Six-Day War many offered to fight for Israel, and many more took part in high-profile campaigns to show their support. British Jews began to approach the Israeli embassy in London offering their services as the prospect of war grew in late May 1967.[54] By the time war was declared, more than 500 Britons were in transit to Israel, where it was intended that they would assume roles in the civilian economy vacated by enlisted Israelis.[55] For these volunteers, Israel's fate stood at the forefront of their identity as Jews. One young man told the Zionist newspaper, the *Jewish Observer and Middle East Review*, 'I feel vitally involved. The fate of Israel is our fate.'[56] In the end, as a result of the airport closure in Tel Aviv and the speedy Israeli victory, few Britons managed to arrive before the war's conclusion. Nonetheless, within two weeks of the beginning of the war, the Jewish Agency had sent 1,000 British volunteers to Israel, selected from over 8,000 candidates.[57]

Beyond volunteers trying to travel to Israel, British Jewry showed loud and proud solidarity through a massive effort of high-profile fundraising and lobbying. The heart of the British volunteer effort was the office of the Zionist Federation, Rex House, in London. Home to over 1,000 helpers processing the potential volunteers, stories of bravery and sacrifice in Rex House dominated the Jewish press. One article described the acceptance of a 23-year-old blind man who told the recruiters, 'Let me go. I'll sit on the floor for I can't stand, but I'll work.'[58] On 28 May 1967 10,000 people gathered in Hyde Park for a rally in support of Israel, a mass protest replicated a week later at the Royal Albert Hall.[59] Smaller-scale political action was similarly prominent. Jewish students organised street petitions, handed out car stickers and held campus events, while in the London suburb of Edgware, a Jewish business owner set up 'a display counter' in support of Israel 'in a prominent position in his hardware shop'.[60] Underpinning all of these activities were drives to raise funds, on the understanding that the conflict would inevitably damage Israeli infrastructure and its economy.[61] Two weeks prior to the war, the Joint

'We speak for them'

Palestine Appeal (JPA) would claim that 80% of British Jews had donated, in some form, to its fund.[62]

For British Jews, the Six-Day War and the campaign for Soviet Jewry revealed the extent of their shared sense of common cause with Jews abroad, and with the State of Israel in particular, even if there remained some uncertainties about how best to make voices heard. Military leaders from Israel's army and Soviet refuseniks were treated like celebrities in British Jewish communities, who eagerly brought them in for visits and staged events in their honour.[63] Understanding why British Jewry, once wary of putting its head above the parapet, now moved so publicly and decisively in support of international Jewish causes is the subject of the remainder of this chapter. It was change, I argue, rooted in a contradiction of increasing security and confidence on the one hand, and ongoing fear and trauma on the other. British Jews now felt sufficiently embedded in Britain to make their voices heard, but their determination to do so can also be understood as a trauma response, a need to ensure that they did not look on as another generation met the fate of European Jewry in the Holocaust. Support for causes of this nature in the end added up to a new way to be Jewish for some, replacing religious practice as people's primary manifestation of their Jewishness in an increasingly secular British environment.

'Never again' mentality

Many British Jews came from families that had fled Russia in the nineteenth and early twentieth century, a reality which made the plight of Soviet Jewry feel closer to home. 'We speak for them', Schneier Levenberg told a London conference in 1968, 'because many British Jews are of East-European origin; because of a deeply engraved feeling of solidarity.'[64] Addressing students at the Jewish boarding school Carmel College on the subject of twinning their bar mitzvahs with child refusenik Leonid Slepak, Greville Janner explained the essential similarity between Soviet Jews such as Slepak and the boys: 'They are our own – and most of us would be in Russia today, had our parents or grandparents or great grandparents not had the courage and initiative to emigrate.'[65] This shared past was still close enough to feel meaningful to many. In Sunderland, for example, the Jewish community adopted the refusenik Jews of Kaunas, 'where many of the Sunderland community originated'.[66] In Glasgow, the visiting Raiza Palatnik was introduced to an 84-year-old Jewish local, Sonia Granet, who (like Raiza) had fled Odessa in 1910.[67] All in all, many British Jews felt that they themselves had only been spared from sharing the plight of Soviet Jews by the smallest historical chance. Barbara Oberman, from the 35s, recalled her feeling: 'There but for the grace of God, go I.'[68]

The construction of Soviet Jewry as only arbitrarily separated from British Jews was underpinned by a similar construction of the Jewish victims of the Holocaust. Highlighting the extent of insecurity and trauma in the wake of the genocide, Jews across the world frequently perceived both the Six-Day War and the plight of Soviet Jewry as potential Holocaust continuations.[69] In Britain, this fear was felt acutely. In Glasgow's *Jewish Echo*, Arab leaders were drawn in cartoon form, taking direct advice from a deceased Hitler on how to complete his genocide against the Jews in 1967.[70] In these terms, the determined and substantial Jewish activism in this period can be seen as a Holocaust response, as British Jews worked through feelings of guilt and regret about what more could have been done for the previous generation, amid corresponding fears about what might now happen to the Jews of Israel and the Soviet Union. For Chaim Bermant, the British Jewish community suffered from 'the guilt feelings common among the survivors of a calamity', emotions that made them rally 'massively' to Israel's side.[71] Tim Cole argues in this context that the Six-Day War 'had a powerful impact on the Jewish community which had in many ways kept silent about the Holocaust for the last two decades'.[72]

The lesson seemingly taken above all others was that passivity was not an option, that Jews needed to fight to save themselves.[73] Jewish MP Leo Abse argued that 'Jews had learned the folly of passive resistance or no resistance at all, of literally digging their own graves'.[74] The struggle to support Soviet Jews was similarly underpinned by determination to act decisively this time. Jewish students, John Cooper noted, were 'ashamed of the passivity of their parents at the time of the Holocaust'.[75] A note from the Women's Campaign for Soviet Jewry described a 'cultural holocaust' facing Soviet Jews, and commented, 'In the thirties the world did not react, and the world has seen what resulted.'[76] In this way, the indefatigability and bravery of the 35s was seen as a new dawn in Jewish protest. 'I have no doubt', Israeli diplomat Ijo Rager argued, that the demonstrations of the 35s 'would have forced Britain to bomb Auschwitz'.[77]

The comparison to the Nazi era, in both cases, was compounded by the argument that the Jews of the Soviet Union, and many of the Jews in Israel, had themselves been Holocaust victims and were thus particularly deserving of protection. Preceding the Six-Day War, an editorial in the *Jewish Chronicle* linked the crisis directly to the Holocaust, presenting Israel as a nation of survivors: 'we remember the Nazi camps and crematoria and the miracle of the re-creation of the Jewish State which offered a home to the pitiful survivors. It is a harrowing thought that they should again be confronted with the threat of death and destruction.'[78] British Jews often framed their petitions to the Soviet Union in terms of reuniting families who, in the words of Board of Deputies president Solomon Teff, had been 'torn apart ... by the Nazi Holocaust'.[79] A 35s leaflet told Londoners that 'thousands of Jews whose families were decimated by the Nazis have had their religion and cultural heritage illegally suppressed by the KGB'.[80] Even for Elie Wiesel, who made clear his dislike of comparisons between the two experiences, it was 'impossible to escape the impression that the two communities have something in common', and the corresponding realisation that Jewish protest needed to be different this time. 'For the second time in a single generation', Wiesel concluded, 'we are committing the error of silence.'[81]

The horror of the Holocaust also shaped British Jewish reactions to the incarceration of dissident Soviet Jews. Press reports indicated that Jews were being held in prisons 'where guards armed with machine guns man tall turrets on the perimeter', an image that immediately evoked the concentration camps of the Holocaust.[82] The language of the concentration camp was employed by Soviet prisoners themselves, keen to alert Jews in the West to the horror that they were facing. One 35s handout contained a poem by dissident psychiatrist Semyon Gluzman describing his incarceration: 'In the smells, sounds, sights of the concentration camp I have felt and understood the sweetness of freedom.'[83] Particular outrage was caused by the repeated allegation that dissident Jews were imprisoned with ex-Nazi collaborators, 'from whom they suffer torment and indignities every day'.[84] These images bridged in the minds of many British Jews the short distance from the Holocaust to the Soviet gaol and redoubled efforts on behalf of Soviet Jewry. Never again, they asserted, would British Jews fail to act while their brethren were persecuted overseas. Here, the need to be perceived first and foremost as good Britons receded in a confident community determined to put to bed the traumas of the previous generation.

Politics is the new prayer

Beyond Holocaust trauma, however, the way that Jewish people responded to international Jewish causes also reflected evolving cultures of religious and ethnic identification in this period. Put simply, those who were not particularly religious sometimes found in political action another meaningful way to engage with their Jewishness. In the place of prayer and traditional religiosity, Zionism and international Jewish solidarity took centre stage in the Jewish lives of many, offering a 'readily accessible common denominator', an 'answer to the de-Judaization of Jewishness in the wake of secularization'.[85] As early as 1956, the honorary secretary of the World Jewish Congress (Britain branch) described how 'Zionism and the mere existence of Israel had applied a brake to assimilation throughout the Diaspora'.[86] Ethnographic research carried out in London and Glasgow confirmed this new state of affairs. Ernest Krausz's study of the north-west London Jewish community in Edgware argued that Jews were turning to Zionism 'in an effort to maintain their Jewishness', while Tova Benski in Glasgow explained how Israel was the 'new focal point of Jewish identity'.[87] In the Glasgow community, a letter to the local Jewish paper told of Jews 'who were hitherto unknown names in the community … coming forward to help' Israel in the Six-Day War.[88] One disgruntled congregant complained that while more than 1,000 Jews had turned out for a meeting 'about the crisis in Israel', only thirteen had attended synagogue service that evening.[89]

There is little doubt that international Jewish crises pulled Jews into self- and communal identification in a way that the traditional structures of Judaism, notably synagogal life, increasingly struggled to do. Maisie Mosco's novel *The Waiting Game* told the story of British Jews travelling to the Soviet Union to help beleaguered refuseniks. Here, the non-Jewish narrator 'had been surprised to learn that Howard and Barbara [the British Jewish activists] rarely attended synagogue services, but there were more ways of practising your religion than a formal way'.[90] In interview, Soviet Jewry campaigner Colin Shindler (who ran an information office in London between 1971 and 1975 and published a weekly bulletin on Soviet Jewry) explained activism in this period in similar terms, noting that there had developed 'parallel ways' to 'understand the odyssey of the Jewish people', and that Soviet Jewry activism had offered a 'different mode' of engagement both for himself and other Jewish people.[91] Put simply, the campaign had the power to draw in 'marginal Jews' who 'usually held aloof from anything to do with Anglo-Jewry or Israel'.[92] Similarly, at the time of the Six-Day War, a number of Jewish writers set up a pressure group, Writers for Israel, even though many, according to group member Chaim Bermant, had 'not thought of themselves as Jews, until this moment of crisis'.[93]

Religious Jews sometimes felt alienated by the extent to which political campaigning overran what was, for them, the key issue in the campaign for

Soviet Jewry, the need for Soviet Jews to be afforded full religious rights. For example, in 1967 the orthodox *Jewish Tribune* complained that a Board of Deputies delegation that met Soviet leaders did not include any rabbis, but only a set of 'bare-faced and bare-headed Jews'. In similar terms the newspaper criticised a World Jewish Congress and World Zionist Organisation visit to Eastern Europe: 'Could there have been a more disheartening and discouraging experience for them than to be met by five clean-shaven, hat-less "Jewish leaders" who seek no Shuls and require no Kashruth?'[94] Yet the division between the holy and the secular was not so clear-cut. By reminding British Jews how fortunate they were to be able to practise freely, and by highlighting the need to fight so that others might also enjoy the freedom of religion, such campaigns pulled back towards the faith many Jews who struggled otherwise to find meaning in the day-to-day rhythms of Jewish religious life.

For practising Jews, prayer could be heightened and made more meaningful by sharing with Soviet Jewry. Bournemouth's Reform rabbi David Soetendorp described his reading of the Torah in the USSR in terms that illustrated the potential power of this engagement on Jewish practice.

> We shared bibles between us, and I read aloud the first chapter of Genesis, whilst another translated the verses one by one into Russian. I could not say how often I have read this chapter of the Torah whether in synagogue, in shiurim or at home. But never did it mean so much to me. Relating as it does the story of Creation, it was to me as if I was created anew.[95]

In 1975 guidance from the SJAC advised that Jews would 'be carrying out a mitzvah [good deed in the Jewish religion] by obtaining the name and address of an individual or family in the USSR for the exchange of letters'.[96] In this way, work with Soviet Jewry could elevate the faith of British Jews. One visitor to Moscow recalled, on being thanked by Soviet Jews, that she felt that no gratitude was due, or rather that 'we thank you for the inspiration of your shining courage'.[97] As Daphne Gerlis put it, 'From discovering a long lost branch of her family, to discovering herself, every 35er has had her life enriched.'[98]

Similarly, the Six-Day War added meaning to the religious practice of many Jewish people. When an Israeli colonel spoke in the aftermath of the war to a fundraising event in London, he explained the Israeli victory in terms of the Bible-conscious soldier who understood that he was fighting in the 'land of his forefathers'. This, the colonel claimed, 'had spurred the people to victory'.[99] For its younger readers, the *Jewish Chronicle* stridently explained the war's outcome as 'the hand of God once again being outstretched towards

His people', and even posited the view that the victory might be 'the first steps towards the rebuilding of the Temple'.[100] While much in its international origins and history was fiercely secular, Zionism in Britain carried within it a strong spiritual root, allowing its appeal across a broad spectrum of Jewish religiosity. To those without meaningful faith, both Zionism and the Soviet Jewry campaign offered a new focal point of identification, which aligned them with a Jewish past and future; to some religious Jews, these causes were nothing less than the fulfilment of a historic religious destiny.

Changing cultures of activism

Aside from these specifically Jewish reasons for engaging with the Six-Day War and the campaign for Soviet Jewry, Jewish activism was both rooted in, and helped to shape, a changing culture of politics and protest in post-war Britain and beyond. The campaigning of the 35s offers a case in point. The group's initial style of protest, silent and dressed all in black, was seemingly inspired by the Black Sash women who stood in stoic opposition to the brutality of apartheid in South Africa. Focusing on a single political issue, forming women's groups and engaging in peaceful direct action, Soviet Jewry campaigners employed similar techniques to Britain's anti-apartheid protesters (who in this period staged numerous protests to disrupt sporting and cultural events that involved South Africa), and campaigners for nuclear disarmament. Rich has argued that the Soviet Jewry campaign offered Jewish students an 'outlet … to join in with this new liberationist politics', while Cooper has described Jewish activists as 'part of the wider international movement of student protest'.[101]

For some, Soviet Jewry was one of a series of international causes which sparked their activism. One 35 recalled previous involvement with Amnesty International and engaging with anti-apartheid groups in South Africa.[102] Soviet Jewry campaigning in the USA grew in the context of the Civil Rights struggle, a frame of reference that also trickled into the British scene.[103] For example, Colin Shindler attempted to secure the attendance of one of Angela Davis's lawyers (Professor Henry McGee) at the trial of Ruth Alexandrovich in Riga in May 1971, conscious that the parallels between people of colour in the USA and Soviet Jews bore emphasis and nurturing.[104] In this way, the issue of Soviet Jewry transcended British Jewish politics, interlinking with broader international human and civil rights causes. Amid the international meetings in Helsinki (which led to the Helsinki Accords of 1975), the cause of Soviet Jewry was increasingly presented as a human rights issue, aligned with the mood of the times.[105]

Similarly, activism in the Six-Day War, especially for many young Jewish people, fed from a broader countercultural urge to abandon capitalist society and build an ideological, new world. Israel's kibbutz movement was particularly well suited to receive such support, which could simultaneously feel for participants like an ideological countercultural act and a service to Judaism. As a result of the war, Chaim Bermant asserted, Israel became a 'floating youth international', a place for 'naïve romanticism'.[106] British youth thus constructed Israel in a similar manner to many other places and projects, as a cause that amplified their idealism. One kibbutz member remembers the impact of the war on youth volunteering in these terms: 'From then on, word got around all over the world: there were these great places to tune in and drop out for a few months … along with the trail to Katmandu and back, the kibbutzim were the "in" place.'[107] Here, British Zionism took its place among a range of political causes that came to represent the challenge of a generation.

Of course, this ideological framing could and did rub up against the realities of Israeli life. One member of the socialist Zionist youth movement *Habonim* outlined in his 'resignation' letter an ultimate jarring of values. He had joined the movement, he explained, out of 'a belief in the simple life' and an 'avowed tolerant and democratic attitude to one's fellow men'. In reality, however, things had turned out to be different. 'As a Socialist, and one who bases his Socialism on the broadest pacific and supra national grounds, I find life on a kibbutz good theoretically, but life in Israel abhorrent.'[108] Looking back, the centrality of nationalism in British Jewish support for Israel might seem obvious. At the time, however, Zionism could and did look to some like one of many radical international political causes.

In this atmosphere, the Soviet Jewry campaign increasingly departed from central authorities and became instead both local and personal, a reality supported by Israeli backers who knew that government-level pressure was better exercised from the USA.[109] One display of solidarity that was favoured by individual activists was letter writing, sometimes to political leaders in Britain and the Soviet Union, but most commonly to the Soviet Jews themselves, and often to Soviet Jewish prisoners. Aside from boosting the morale of the persecuted, campaigns of letter writing were designed to pressure and irritate the Soviet authorities. Such activism served to bring the personal nature of the campaign home to activists. In Glasgow, minutes of the 35s recorded how one member '"proudly" had a letter from a family to read to us. Her first ever.'[110] Getting close to Soviet Jews in this way was a core part of this kind of activism, enabling personal bonds across the Iron Curtain. Alongside letter writing, British activists increasingly tried to speak to Soviet Jews by telephone. Hearing the voices of Jews who had been denied the right to leave the Soviet Union brought an intimacy and immediacy to the campaign, enabling a seemingly distant struggle to feel much closer to home. As such, listening to telephone calls with Soviet Jews frequently became an activity for public meetings, as campaigners gathered to hear attempted contact with refuseniks and their families. The intimacy that was achieved through letters and phone calls served to create a sense of international Jewish community, entrenched by twinning and 'adoption' schemes that saw British Jewish families and communities take responsibility for specific refuseniks and prisoners of conscience in the Soviet Union.[111] Across Britain, Jewish children twinned their bar mitzvah ceremonies with Soviet children who had been denied them. The organiser of this scheme recalled how British youth 'were thrilled to feel that they were sharing their special day with a Russian youngster who had been so completely cut off from his or her Jewish roots'.[112]

In 1970 Chief Rabbi Jakobovits suggested that an 'empty chair' should be 'prominently situated' in local synagogues at 'every public function and gathering' so as 'to ensure that the burning issue of Soviet Jewry is constantly kept before the Jewish community'.[113] In Manchester's *Sha'arei Shalom* synagogue, just such a gesture was made in 1979 after the community adopted refuseniks Alec and Galina Zelichenok. The community left a chair and a tallit (prayer shawl) for Alec at the front of the synagogue, where it remained 'throughout the ten years of his refusal'. After receiving nearly 600 letters, Alec and Galina finally obtained permission to leave the Soviet Union in 1989. A few years later they visited the community that had campaigned for them for so long, an emotional scene described in the Reform Synagogues' newsletter:

> It was thrilling to accompany Alec and Galina into the synagogue hall while the whole congregation was standing. As we walked in we were greeted by one loud voice (almost as if it had been rehearsed) 'SHALOM'. Alec walked to his chair at the front and put on his tallit. There was not a dry eye in the hall. Alec recited the first blessing over the scroll and later gave an address. It was a most moving service and the culmination of ten years of hard work.[114]

Far from being a faceless and abstract mass of suffering, the empty chairs, letters and phone calls illustrated powerfully the common ground between the Jewish communities, facilitating a different kind of British Jewish lobbying and protest. Martin Gilbert has argued, in this context, that the 35s 'made brilliant use of the specific case and the specific name'.[115] This was the politics of the personal; vocal and confident, locally driven activism, harnessing the technology of the post-war period to strive for justice for Jews across the world. While high-level diplomatic channels remained important, British Jews felt increasingly able to speak for themselves, prepared to make their voices heard and put their heads above the parapet. In this way, Jewish campaigning in this period was very much British campaigning, reflecting broader change as party politics began to give way to personal, single-issue causes of rights and justice.[116]

* * *

Long after the Six-Day War, Zionism remains incredibly important to much of the British Jewish community. And while the peril facing Soviet Jews receded with the collapse of the USSR and mass migration to Israel and elsewhere, the need to speak out for Jews abroad has similarly remained a communal priority. In the end, what characterised political challenges in post-war British Jewry was a growing confidence to act publicly as Jews. Describing a busload of 35s making their way to a protest in London, Linda Grant painted a picture of 'middle-aged Jewish housewives who had been born in this country and weren't afraid of the police'.[117] Less concerned than previous generations about what other Britons thought, and better placed socially, educationally and financially to make their voices heard, British Jewish protest became a greater force, fuelled by the lingering trauma of the Holocaust, and specifically by the feeling that British Jews had failed to act decisively in the face of the genocide. It was a 'never again' mantra with a Jewish specificity, but also a style of campaigning that was very much British and of its time, personal, single-issue focused, often radical, and aligned with broader political challenges in the 1960s and 1970s. Through the Six-Day War and the campaign for Soviet Jewry, British Jews amplified their voices, speaking as confident and secure Britons, ready, willing and able to offer a strong hand of support to Jews in peril wherever they were. These campaigns empowered a new way to identify as Jews, particularly useful in an atmosphere where the decline of religious practice was a substantial cause of concern. Such campaigning, however, did not replace religiosity so much as give it a new urgency and inclusivity. Being a good Jew in post-war Britain meant acting in support of Jews abroad. Such activism was firmly ascribed as a mitzvah, a new path to God in a changing world.

4

'These wicked sons': Israel-critical Jews and the Zionist majority

In 1985 Antony Lerman published an editorial in the *Jewish Quarterly* on the 'politics of antisemitism'.[1] Lerman was a well-established figure in the British Jewish community, a researcher at the Institute of Jewish Affairs who had taken over as editor of the *Quarterly* after the death of its founder, Jacob Sonntag, in 1984. An ex-Zionist Youth Movement leader from *Habonim* who had previously lived in Israel and served in its army, Lerman had become more Israel-critical as he grew older. In his editorial, which was accompanied in the *Quarterly* by another article about antisemitism and racism by David Rosenberg of the Jewish Socialists' Group (JSG), he questioned contemporary thinking on the resurgence of antisemitism, arguing that excessive concern about Jewish vulnerability risked diverting funding from important educational and cultural work. Lerman's editorial observed, moreover, the impact of antisemitism anxieties on British Jewish thinking about the Jewish world. Constructing diaspora Jews as being in danger, he argued, positioned the Jewish state as the 'only secure future', thereby undermining important discussions about 'relations between what should be an independently-minded and assertive Diaspora and Israel'.[2] Putting too much emphasis on antisemitism, he concluded, added up to a 'failure of courage and imagination'.

Rosenberg's article, somewhat in contrast, emphasised the extent to which antisemitism remained a present danger.[3] The pieces converged, however, in the argument that diaspora Jewry should stand more independent from Israel. Highlighting steps by communal leaders to distance Jews from broader anti-fascist activity in Britain (because of worries that there were prominent anti-Zionists in such groups), Rosenberg complained that Zionism was 'increasingly being used as an instrument for centralising the authority of the communal leadership against pluralism'.

With hindsight, Lerman looks back on his broaching of the subject of antisemitism and Zionism as 'very naïve'.[4] 'I never thought for a minute', he told me, 'that anything I could write in the *Jewish Quarterly* could generate that kind of controversy.' Controversy, indeed, followed thick and fast. Eric Moonman, director of the Zionist Federation, complained about the *Quarterly* articles at the April meeting of the Board of Deputies, and Lerman was summoned (although he did not attend) to discuss the matter with the chairs of the Board's Israel and Defence committees. Such was the pressure generated from the Board that Lerman felt he had to resign the editorship, action which saw 'all hell [break] loose' as correspondence raged in the Jewish press for nearly two months.

While Moonman and others went out of their way to deny that they had demanded Lerman's resignation, clearly their actions had had that effect. As Bryan Cheyette and David Cesarani noted, in one of many letters to the *Jewish Chronicle* about the case, there was 'no doubt that intolerable pressure was placed on the editor … which contributed, ultimately, to his resignation'.[5] Looking back, Lerman saw the matter in simple terms: 'Zionism and Israel had become so integral to the Jewish community's self-perception, no challenge could be tolerated.'[6] Even though he and Rosenberg had been cautious in their criticism, some British Jews were not happy to see Jewish communal leaders take an Israel-critical stance. As the *Jewish Chronicle* explained, regarding the challenge from the Board, 'It was felt that Mr Lerman should not have allowed the publication of views contrary to official communal policy while at the same time working for a communal organisation, the IJA.'[7]

Since this period, discussion of antisemitism and Zionism in the community has hardly become less fraught. Twenty years after the incident at the *Quarterly*, Lerman was again forced to resign a Jewish leadership position, this time as director of the JPR at the end of 2008, amid allegations of anti-Zionism and hostility towards his thinking on antisemitism. Indeed, from the moment of his return to the organisation in 2006 he had faced huge pressure. At the news of his appointment, three directors resigned in protest.[8] In the *Jewish Chronicle*, historian Geoffrey Alderman made his opinion clear.

> Lerman is entitled to hold whatever questionable views he pleases on the nature of anti-Jewish prejudice. He is entitled to believe the fantastic myth that such prejudice was never indigenous to the Arab world. He is entitled to proclaim that those – including those Jews – who deny the right of Jewish national self-determination are by no means to be judged anti-Jewish. The problem is (isn't it?) that as head of the JPR no one is going to take him, or it, seriously any more.[9]

Despite holding on for nearly three years, and the expression of considerable support from some quarters, the pressure on Lerman eventually told. 'The attacks never stopped', he recalls; the campaign against him felt 'deeply unpleasant'.[10] For sure, the tone of discussion about Israel in the community in this period was at fever pitch. In 2007 the founders of an Israel-critical campaigning group, Independent Jewish Voices (IJV), were ridiculed by Melanie Phillips in a blog as 'Jews for Genocide',[11] an argument drawn out in a *Jewish Chronicle* article where she explained:

> The deadly enemies of the Jewish people are beside themselves with joy over the IJV. For the terrible thing is that, far from being silenced, Jewish voices like these are in the very forefront of the hate-fest against Israel. Martyrs of dissent? Hardly. They are the British arm of the pincer of Jewish destruction.[12]

In a post-Holocaust atmosphere where many British Jews continued to feel vulnerable to antisemitism, Jewish criticism of Israel was frequently presented as unwise and naïve if not treasonous. As Lerman's case illustrated, by the 1980s (if not before) it had become all but impossible to combine Israel-critical views with a leadership role at the centre of the community. As another Israel-critical activist, Julia Bard, told me, 'if you step out of line in the Jewish community you get defamed ... people's jobs are at risk and all sorts of relationships with their families, you know it's all very vicious'.[13]

Israel-critical stances within British Jewry are, however, nothing new, and in many moments and places have been far from marginal. Jewish uncertainty and anxiety about Israel and its impact on British Jewish life preceded the establishment of the state and has never really gone away. For some British Jews, then and now, Israel was at best a mixed blessing, at worst a substantial threat to the Jewish world. Such concerns have hailed from many different parts of the community and cannot easily be pigeonholed. As the case of Antony Lerman illustrates, Israel-critical Jews have often been intimately connected with Israel, their views formed from direct experience, and held alongside relationships with family and friends in the Jewish state. The challenges faced by such Jews have increased over the post-war period. Support for Israel has grown into one of the core characteristics of British Jewry, informing the stances of many religious and communal institutions, and serving as something of a loyalty test. As Cesarani put it, 'Zionism became', for British Jewry, 'a way of determining who was an authentic or acceptable Jew'.[14] This chapter sets out to explore the history of Israel-critical thinking in this context, asking what Jewish debates about Israel tell us about the changing markers of Jewishness in Britain, and about communal expectations of Jewish people in an increasingly secular age.

The roots of Israel-critical thinking in Britain

As political cultures evolved in eighteenth- and nineteenth-century Europe, debates raged inside and outside Jewish communities about the extent to which Judaism could be understood in discrete terms as a religion, or whether Jews ultimately shared a nationality and culture which directed their loyalties beyond the states in which they lived.[15] Across international Jewish communities, intellectuals and lay and religious leaders argued about what the Jewish future should look like, discussions which increasingly questioned, from the late nineteenth century, whether Jews should aspire to a national home in Palestine or elsewhere, or instead identify as permanent citizens of their states, carrying their faith and traditions as 'a travelling homeland'.[16] Theologies which highlighted the universal relevance of Judaism were bolstered by a post-Enlightenment Jewish desire to embrace new possibilities in Christian societies, epitomised in the hopes espoused for Jewry by philosopher and theologian Moses Mendelssohn. For Mendelssohn, devotional Jews were well placed to participate in the development of the nations in which they lived, a view increasingly accepted in non-Jewish circles as Enlightenment values broke down at least some of the barriers of separation and discrimination that historically had kept European Jewry apart from their non-Jewish neighbours.[17]

In this atmosphere, for most of the Jews of western Europe and the United States, what was wanted was full equality in their countries of domicile. From its nineteenth-century origins, across disparate Jewish quarters, Zionism was thus attacked as an abandonment of the idea that Jews belonged where they lived in favour of a 'dangerously narrow version of Jewish particularism' in the form of nationalism.[18] In response to the Zionist message, Jewish universalists accentuated the idea of a global Jewish mission, often justified through prophetic writings on social justice.[19] Thus the Pittsburgh Platform of 1885, formulated in a meeting of leading Reform rabbis in America, constructed Judaism as 'the establishment of the kingdom of truth, justice, and peace among all men', rejecting the idea of a 'return to Palestine' or 'the restoration of any of the laws concerning the Jewish state'.[20] This articulation of Judaism might have resonated in Reform theology, but it had roots in Orthodox communities too. In Germany, opposition from both Reform and Orthodox rabbis at the end of the nineteenth century drove the First Zionist Congress beyond their disapproving gaze, forcing the meeting into Switzerland.[21]

Where Jews were newly empowered with rights in European states, they often responded by emphasising and championing the outward-facing social value of their faith, a reciprocation seemingly demanded by Christian societies that were wary of Jewish clannishness.[22] In Nicholas de Lange's words, 'the eighteenth-century Enlightenment led to deep embarrassment or impatience with Jewish particularism, and at that time the universalistic side of Judaism was seen as a useful counterbalance to it'.[23] In the twentieth century this often meant highlighting Jewish theological and historical traditions of resisting oppression and seeking justice for all. The lessons of Jewish history were seemingly obvious, applicable to people in all countries and times. As Mike Marqusee put it,

> our Jewish history was full of heroes who stood up for the truth, who defied the powerful. The civil rights movement in the South was our cause, not only because the Negroes were the latter-day Jews, slaves in Egypt land, but also because so many Jews were involved in the movement.[24]

On the flip side, with the continuation of European antisemitism and in a climate of rampant European nationalism, Zionism emerged as a forceful counter-view, seeking to secure Jewish futures in a national home where Jews would no longer seek toleration as a minority but would instead take an honourable place among the nations. As much as scripture and tradition could point to a universal trajectory for Jewish futures, it could just as well champion a historic return to Palestine, constructed as a long-awaited divine act of restorative justice and the logical culmination of Jewish history. Here the Jewish state not only offered security but could be painted as 'the beating heart of the Jewish people, its spiritual centre'.[25] After the Holocaust, the idea of a safe and permanent Jewish home gained traction among the majority of British Jews. Yet to others, Judaism's history and message could never be constricted in this way. Instead, in a universalist mind frame, the very essence of Judaism was its historically proven ability to be strong and purposeful from anywhere. Writing about his Jewish life in Britain, David Rosenberg told the *Jewish Socialist*: 'There are many centres. Here is my centre.'[26]

For Yehuda Bauer, Jewish Israel-critical thinking emanated from two primary intellectual positions that in different ways were both rooted in beliefs concerning the universal relevance of Judaism and the global belonging of Jews: 'Western or Communist assimilation and ultra-orthodoxy'.[27] Among British Jewry, the roots of challenges to Israel have been somewhat more diverse, yet the issues raised by Bauer remain highly significant. Certainly, for some of those British Jews who prioritised integration of their Jewish lives within British society, Zionism was a problematic and potentially dangerous distraction which threatened to signal their essential foreignness to non-Jewish Britons who had long suspected as much. It was amid such concerns that an infamous letter was sent to *The Times*, authored by Claude Montefiore and David Lindo Alexander on behalf of the Conjoint Foreign Committee (ostensibly representing the Board of Deputies and the Anglo-Jewish Association) in anticipation of the Balfour Declaration in 1917, expressing anxiety about the potential impact of Jewish nationhood on Jews living in other countries.[28] Jewish Britons, the authors asserted, regarded themselves primarily as 'a religious community' and had 'based their claims to political equality … on this assumption'. If Jews were to be seen instead as a distinct nation, they cautioned, it 'must have the effect throughout the world of stamping the Jews as strangers in their native lands, and of undermining their hard-won position as citizens and nationals of those lands'.[29] Such an undesirable construction of Jewish Britons would of necessity be based on 'some loose and obscure principle of race and ethnographic peculiarity', not a good idea given the time it had taken Europe's Jews to convince their neighbours of their essential similarity, and of the value of Jewish presence in their lands.

Wariness about seeing Jews as a separate group mirrored a broader and growing interwar intellectual distancing from the idea that European populations were racially or morally distinct from one another. Such thinking gathered pace in Britain amid political opposition to the Third Reich, exemplified by the arguments made in the popular book *We Europeans* in 1935. This study, ostensibly written by zoologist Julian Huxley and anthropologist A. C. Haddon, but substantially authored by Jewish scholars Charles Singer and Charles Seligman, railed against Hitler's idea that Jews were essentially different, arguing instead that Jewish people were racially inseparable from the non-Jewish Europeans among whom they lived, that 'in each country the Jewish population overlaps with the non-Jewish in every conceivable character'.[30] Facing Hitler's regime and traumatised by generations of antisemitism, it is perhaps unsurprising that many British Jews saw things this way, and that such thinking had an impact on attitudes towards Zionism. Having fought long and hard for their place at the table in British society, it was easy to be troubled by a doctrine of Jewish nationalism which seemed to suggest that Jews had really belonged somewhere else all along. Zionism, as the *Jewish Guardian* newspaper explained in 1920, risked an antisemite complaining, 'The Jews asked for Palestine and have accepted it, so the least the Jews can do is to go there.'[31] Instead, the newspaper asserted, it was important to make clear that an 'English Jew is an Englishman of the Jewish faith, and not an alien residing in England'.[32]

While, no doubt, the popularity of Zionism in Britain increased in the face of the Third Reich, and was a dominant force by the time of the Declaration of the State of Israel in 1948, there remained a significant body of British Jews who were unconvinced of the sagacity of Jewish nationalism in these terms.[33] This disaffection was exemplified during and after the Second World War by the actions of the Jewish Fellowship, which was formed in the early 1940s to try to protect British Jewry from what it perceived as the 'false and dangerous claims of political Zionism'.[34] The Jewish Fellowship set out to articulate the place of British Jews firmly and unequivocally as Britons, striving to make clear that 'the Jews of Britain belong to the British nation'.[35] Explaining why he had written to *The Times* about the Fellowship's work prior to its official launch, its president, Brunel Cohen, highlighted the pressing need to avoid 'the growth of the idea that the Jews of Britain are different from their fellow citizens in anything more than religion'.[36] While the horrors of Nazism and the Holocaust spurred British Jews generally to support Zionism, the Fellowship represented an alternative view, arguing that the war showed that Jews could depend on Britain. 'For the past three hundred years', the Fellowship's newspaper *The Jewish Outlook* argued, 'when a Jew wanted to be safe he came to Britain – he didn't leave it.'[37] If such positions were driven by commitment to Britain, they were also underwritten by Jewish anxiety. The idea of losing 'hard won British identity' because of Zionism, Omer-Jackaman has argued, was, for some British Jews, a 'barely concealed terror'.[38]

Jewish assertions of Britishness, however, did not necessarily undermine the idea of Palestine being open for the migration and settlement of other Jews. Indeed, the Fellowship firmly supported Jewish immigration to Palestine as part of the solution to the post-Holocaust refugee crisis.[39] What was objection-able to these Jews was political Zionism, the idea that Judaism correlated with race or nationality, and the corresponding implication that British Jews belonged somewhere other than Britain. To both the Fellowship and the Anglo-Jewish Association (AJA), which held views that were more moderate but frequently similar, Britain's mandate role in Palestine provided evidence of the long-standing centrality of Jews in Britain's sense of self. In a statement that underplayed substantial Jewish anger with Britain's management of the mandate, the AJA's president Leonard Stein argued:

Thirty years of British rule have left an indelible impress on Palestine and made an enduring contribution to its welfare. History will not fail to do justice to the British achievement, nor is there a Jew in the world who does not know and will not gratefully acknowledge that it was by British exertions that the Jewish National Home in Palestine was brought into being and shielded while it struggled to its feet.[40]

On these grounds, to the Jewish Fellowship, an ongoing role for Britain in Palestine was seen as highly desirable, 'a very happy solution' to the end of the mandate, a view echoed by the AJA, which felt that 'If any arrangement can be reached which would allow Britain to remain in certain parts of Palestine (possibly in Jerusalem) and to be the protecting power, even without being the mandatory power, it should be made.'[41]

Believing religion to be the central plank of Jewish identity, the Fellowship worked to ensure its reinvigoration among British Jews, arguing that there could be no 'substitute for Judaism in the life of the Jewish people', and expressing a desire 'to revive the Jewish religious spirit among Jews and place Torah, the Synagogue and the ethics of Judaism at the heart of Jewish life'.[42] To Jews such as these, Zionism was a 'new paganism', diverting Jewish attention from faith and spreading the false doctrine that 'Jews can be Jews without religion'.[43] Fellowship leader Basil Henriques recalled with dismay a trip to Manchester where the extent of Zionist secularism, as a challenge to traditional Judaism, became clear to him:

I am absolutely horrified as I go about the country to find how deep rooted is national political Zionism. For example, in Manchester when I was addressing the Jewish Forum, a young fellow got up and said, 'I am proud to be an atheist, but prouder still to be a Jew.'[44]

While it claimed to represent a broad constituency of British Jews, the Fellowship was dogged by allegations that its religious heart resided in Progressive Judaism.[45] Most leading members emanated from Reform and Liberal communities, and although considerable efforts were made to present a united front with the Orthodox, this was a position that was hard to maintain amid broader traditional hostility towards Progressive Judaism.[46] As one Orthodox Jew explained in the *Outlook*, 'We find it difficult to cooperate with you because we do not consider most of your members to be Jews.'[47] That there was any potential for cooperation was rooted in the fact that some Orthodox Jews similarly viewed Zionism with suspicion and hostility. While such Jews less frequently prioritised the kinds of British nationalism that underpinned the religious stance of the Fellowship and its bedfellows, some Orthodox Jews were deeply uncomfortable about the Zionist turn in the community, which they were apt to see as a threat to the foundations of their faith.

While centrist Orthodoxy in Britain, characterised by the United Synagogue and the Chief Rabbi, generally accommodated their beliefs to Zionism with varying degrees of enthusiasm (and often became very supportive of it), to some Orthodox Jews it remained a 'heresy ... a denial of fundamental messianic beliefs and a violation of the promise made to God not to acquire the Holy Land by human effort'.[48] In these terms, Alderman has noted that the Orthodox luminary the Kamenitzer Maggid, who had come to Britain in 1890 and supported Jewish settlement in Palestine (but not the creation of a political state), regarded Theodor Herzl 'as a false messiah, and his movement as a threat to the preservation of Orthodox Jewish values'.[49] To varying degrees, this kind of thinking remained influential in Orthodox British communities throughout the century.[50] Members of the *Machzikei Hadass* community in Manchester recalled their fathers not regarding Zionists as 'frummer Yiden', and dismissing Zionist ideology as 'an aberration'.[51] While these views receded somewhat after the creation of the State of Israel, they certainly did not disappear. Facing a decline of religious practice in post-war Britain, some Orthodox people feared that Zionist Jews were increasingly 'putting the "religion" of statehood above their commitment to authentic Judaism'.[52] Articles in the *Jewish Tribune* accused the Zionist movement of 'brainwashing the youth' and altering for good the meaning of being Jewish.[53] 'They', one writer complained,

> want the future generation of Jews to be 'good Zionists' rather than good Jews! They will not worry if the ZF [Zionist Federation]-educated boy will never be able to daven [pray] properly – or even say a kaddish after a hundred-and-twenty-years. Their task is to make sure that when he grows up he will be able to understand some Hebrew – enough to make him Israel-minded and Israel-conscious.[54]

On the idea that Zionism risked diverting Jews from their religion, if on little else, Progressive and Orthodox critics of Israel could agree. Combined with the tendency among patriotic Jewish Britons to eschew the idea of a Jewish nation and instead seek their place in the bosom of Britishness, faith created grounds to resist Zionism (among a religious minority) and ensured that there remained Jews across the devotional spectrum who were not swept up in its post-war popularity. From the 1960s, moreover, a further body of Jews took up Israel-critical positions. These Jews were frequently neither particularly patriotic nor religious, but instead motivated by leftist and countercultural ideologies.

Such Jews often approached Israeli politics with 'an anti-colonial mindset', which led them down different paths when it came to understanding Israel/ Palestine.[55] Engagement with broader cultures of activism, as we have seen in the previous chapter, could lead back to conventionally Jewish causes such as the campaign for Soviet Jews and supporting Israel in the Six-Day War. But sometimes the evolution of Jewish identities within broader countercultural struggles against racism, capitalism and colonialism led to non- or anti-Zionist politics.[56]

This kind of thinking was often motivated by, and fuelled, a commitment to life in the diaspora, which linked these very different activists, in some ways, back to the patriotic Jews of the Fellowship and to Orthodox Israel critics. David Rosenberg recalled how the anti-Nazi slogan, 'Here to stay, Here to fight', made 'a profound impact' on him as he came to understand his place as a Jew in Britain.[57] For Jewish people such as Rosenberg and Julia Bard, the diaspora was something to be cherished, nurtured and defended, highlighting as it did the Jewish 'exemplary ability to adapt and to survive in diverse circumstances'.[58] For Rabbi David Goldberg, the diaspora was where 'the Jewish genius has flowered most productively', an environment to be protected, not abandoned.[59] Diaspora, in these terms, was essential for the survival of Jewish civilisation, the 'most important contribution that Judaism has to make to the world'.[60] This case had been made forcefully at the time of the Jewish Fellowship. Charles Singer argued, regarding the group's mission, 'We believe that this faith is necessary to the world; that it aids the religious life of this nation; that it flourishes most where men are free; and that the Jewish ideals of social justice are now, as ever, the sign-posts to freedom.'[61]

As the JSG became home to a significant number of Jewish Bundists at the start of the 1980s, Rosenberg recalled its growing focus on diaspora history.[62] Amid a broader Jewish community that was placing ever greater emphasis on Israel, engaging with the richness of the diaspora promoted an alternative political perspective, one in which Israel could be seen as diverting valuable resources, as well Jewish energy and imagination, from the historical and cultural centres of the Jewish world. Moreover, Israel was increasingly seen, in such circles, as being on the wrong side of global struggles against oppression and racism. Leftist Jewish activists, many of whom had previously supported the state to a significant degree, became alienated as they came to view Israel as a violator of human rights and/or as racist. Such anxieties grew during the Lebanon War of 1982, particularly as a consequence of massacres at the Sabra and Shatila refugee camps, in which Israel was criticised for complicity.[63]

Faced with this situation, some Jews felt that the broader community was neglecting its moral obligation to speak out, undermining Jewish values by prioritising support for Israel over social justice. Such concerns were exacerbated by the state's engagement with the military junta in Argentina and with apartheid South Africa. For Jews who were frequently involved in campaigns against such oppressive regimes, Israeli indifference left them feeling alienated. For Clive Gilbert, writing in the *Jewish Socialist* in 1985, right-wing Israeli governments 'stood in stark contrast to the honourable tradition of Jewish involvement in liberation struggles'.[64] The JSG, against the wishes of most of the communal leadership, began in this period to meet for talks with the PLO alongside other international and Israeli peace activists.[65]

Israel-critical views in the twenty-first century

Just as the Lebanon War drove more Jews to Israel-critical positions, so the Israeli response to the Second Intifada (2000–2005) motivated similar activism. After a study trip in Israel/Palestine, Irene Bruegel established Jews for Justice for Palestinians (JfJfP) in 2002. This organisation was conceived, Bruegel told the *Jewish Chronicle*, 'on the road block at Haris, on the West Bank' when her party was 'physically assaulted' by settlers for protesting against the occupation.[66] Launching at Passover with an advertisement in the *Jewish Chronicle*, JfJfP set out its stall by emphasising the Jewish commitment to human rights embodied in the festival, setting these against the actions of the Israeli government, which was cast as a disruptor of traditional Jewish values.

> As we celebrate Pesach, the festival of our freedom, we remember the oppression Jews have suffered throughout our history.
>
> We must also make a stand against the occupation of the West Bank and Gaza strip, which is generating horrendous terrorism and poses a very real threat to that freedom, as well as destroying Israel from within.
>
> Israeli policies that undermine the livelihoods, human, civil and political rights of the Palestinian people are utterly out of keeping with the humanitarian traditions of the Jewish people.[67]

Highlighting that their message was shared by at least some Jewish Israelis, JfJfP (alongside Just Peace UK) raised funds to bring two Israeli 'refusenik' soldiers, who had declined to serve in the West Bank or Gaza Strip, to speak at British universities.[68]

That year also saw a number of prominent Jewish people (including Bruegel) write an open letter to the *Guardian* renouncing their right to live in Israel as Jews under the Law of Return.[69] Very much in line with long-standing positions taken by Israel-critical Jews, the letter argued that the idea of Jewish 'return' to Israel was no 'kind of "solution"' for diaspora Jews, questioning the notion of Jewish racial belonging in the land. The letter writers looked forward, they asserted, to a time when people could live in Israel without 'any restrictions based on so-called racial, cultural, or ethnic origins', and demanded that the rights of Palestinians be upheld. Among the forty-five signatories were academics, performers and writers, whose prominence helped to secure national media coverage. In 2007 a similarly impressive array of Jewish luminaries emerged as IJV.[70]

Continuing violence in Israel, and a belief that the state was overstepping its right to speak on behalf of the global Jewish community, led to the IJV Declaration of 2007. These Jews, in their own words, 'were united in affirming certain fundamental principles. These included: putting human rights first, rejecting all forms of racism (whether aimed at Jews, Arabs, Muslims or whomever), respecting international law, and treating as equally legitimate the Palestinian and Israeli quests for a better – a peaceful, just and secure – future.'[71] In their Declaration, IJV railed against communal leaders who 'consistently put support for the policies of an occupying power above the human rights of an occupied people'. In contrast, IJV sought to voice an alternative Jewish opinion on Israel/Palestine, and in so doing reassert human rights at the centre of Jewish values.[72] This emphasis on universal human rights linked IJV and JfJfP with the ostensibly very different Israel-critical politics of previous generations of Jewish Britons.

Early and more recent critics of Zionism also shared the view that Jews did not primarily belong in Israel, but instead alongside the populations among whom they had always lived. The Jewish Fellowship had called on the United Nations to affirm 'the fundamental principle that the Jewish citizens of every land, fulfilling their obligation of complete loyalty to their respective countries, shall be guaranteed the correlative right of complete equality in every respect'.[73] Speaking after the Second World War, MP Daniel Lipson expressed his hope that many Jewish refugees would 'in spite of everything, be willing to return to their former homes and help to rebuild them on better and juster foundations'.[74] Here, as in later Israel-critical thinking, a strong case was made for Jewish presence in the diaspora as positive both for Jews and non-Jews. Ultimately, both for early and more recent Israel-critical Jews, the idea that Judaism (and thus Jews) belonged to the world, not to one state, was paramount.

Interacting with the Zionist majority

In a post-Holocaust atmosphere wherein many Jews saw the birth of Israel as offering essential protection against future global antisemitism, this kind of diasporism, and Jewish criticism of the Jewish state, was often seen as threatening and even heretical. Writing in the *Jewish Socialist*, Roberto Sussman explained that Israel criticism had become an 'ideological taboo', while another article articulated the view that expressing criticism, 'however mild, left such Jews ostracised by the institutions of the Jewish community and abused in the Jewish press'.[75] Jews who took up Israel-critical positions often felt that their very Jewishness was being questioned, that being an uncritical Zionist had become a proxy for being a good Jew in a way that left them unfairly cast aside. As one IJV activist put it:

> you might love to eat pork and hate chicken soup, never have seen the interior of a synagogue and never have celebrated a single Jewish festival in your life, but if you are prepared to justify the occupation of Palestinian territory and the erection of Israel's wall, you may rest assured that no one will question your Jewish identity.[76]

According to Yakov Rabkin, Israel-critical Jews were labelled 'as collaborators' and 'traitor[s]', and assigned, to David Landy's thinking, a 'semi-Pariah status' in the community.[77] Perhaps more than any other rebuke, the label 'self-hater' has been attached to Israel-critical Jews, a slur that has caused pain and offence over generations, described by one activist as 'farfetched, yet so personal. And so bitterly unfair.'[78] Such criticism felt stifling as well as hurtful. Another activist explained, 'accuse someone of self-hatred and the label sticks, the story ends'.[79] As tensions boiled over in friendship groups and families, Israel-critical Jews often paid a heavy price for their opinions, seen even by those close to them as 'strange and bizarre subjects who reject, hate and even fear their own Jewishness'.[80] To others in the community, Israel-critical Jews could easily appear 'disingenuous', designating themselves as Jewish 'merely with a view to strengthen or embolden their attacks on Israel'. In this way, such Jews were often pigeonholed as 'either bad Jews or Jews in bad faith'.[81]

For some, the prevalence of high-profile, 'celebrity' Jewish people among groups of Israel critics signalled a politics that was out of touch with the real

Jewish community, comprehensible as distasteful publicity seeking. In a blistering attack on IJV in the *Independent*, novelist Howard Jacobson described the Declaration as a 'self-indulgent fantasy'.[82] Highlighting the limitations of creative Jews (such as himself) in the political sphere, Jacobson commented, 'in play we can go where politicians and soldiers cannot. In play we hypothesise the world. But we shouldn't go confusing it with the real thing.' Here, Israel-critical Jews were accused of naivety and elitism (themes to which Jacobson returned at length in his novel *The Finkler Question*). IJV, he complained, was 'a group talking only to itself', a narcissistic project which espoused 'a narrow political sectarianism uninterested in conversation or the subtleties to which conversation might expose them'.

Taking such allegations to their ultimate (comic) conclusion, one of the ASHamed (Israel-critical) Jews of the *Finkler Question* is described in the process of trying unsuccessfully to regrow his foreskin in what can only be seen as the ultimate attempt to negate one's Jewishness.[83] In this story, Israel-critical Jews remembered their faith only so that they could criticise Israel from within. An ASHamed Jew, who didn't even know he was Jewish until a revelation on a TV ancestry show, was thus described: 'Born a Jew on Monday, he had signed up to be an ASHamed Jew by Wednesday and was seen chanting "We are all Hezbollah" outside the Israeli Embassy on the following Saturday.'[84] Ultimately, these ASHamed Jews embodied the ash of the Nazi crematoria. These were Jews who hadn't learned their lesson about trusting non-Jewish societies, and who did not appreciate the urgency of Jewish solidarity with Israel. Comic as it might have been, similar allegations were made in real life about members of IJV. Writing in response to the group's Declaration, Gerald Steinberg dismissed the Jews involved in just these terms. He told his readers, 'The British and Australian individuals who recently referred to themselves as "independent Jewish voices," such as the playwright Harold Pinter, have no Jewish identity other than denouncing Israel.'[85] Back in the novel, Finkler's Jewish-convert wife, coming fresh to the community, expressed her (and I think Jacobson's own) incredulity about the motivations behind Jewish Israel criticism: 'I don't get it. It makes no sense. Becoming an enthusiastic Jew again in order to turn on Judaism.'[86]

And yet, despite sharp rebukes from other Jews, being proudly Jewish in their activism has, over a long period, been important to many Israel-critical Jewish people. Such activists have emphasised their faith and ethnicity as part of what they and their adversaries have perceived as a battle for the essence of Judaism. Standing proud (and not ASHamed), Israel-critical Jews have refused to cede ground to dominant Zionism in Jewish communities. Jewish critics of Israel have perceived themselves to be acting Jewish in a way that Zionists have not, adopting the role of defenders of authentic Judaism. At the Jewish Fellowship it was repeatedly suggested that the time might come for a formal division between Jews and those whose interests were primarily related to Palestine/Zionism. An editorial in the *Jewish Outlook* asserted that 'it would seem as though the time were near when either those who profess Judaism should call themselves by another name, or those who have allowed political Zionism to supersede Judaism in their lives should do so, and call themselves candidly Zionists or Palestinians or anything else – saving the precious word "Jew"'.[87] On these terms, Orthodox critics of Zionism and those in movements such as the Fellowship worked hard to promote Jewish education that aligned with what they saw as authentic Jewish tradition, away from Zionist distraction. Zionists, they felt, were sacrificing Jewish knowledge in favour of spreading a tangential political message. As the *Jewish Tribune* put it, 'What they want is not education. It is Zionisation at which they aim, and Zionisation can only be realised on the elimination of Torah.'[88]

At another level, however, post-war Israel-critical Jews fought their case under a specifically Jewish banner because non-Jewish Israel-critical groups have not always felt like a comfortable space for Jewish people to be. Socialist and feminist groups, often the natural political homes of many of the Jewish Israel critics, were apt to broach the issue of Israel/Palestine in ways that could leave Jewish members and allies feeling attacked, misunderstood or ignored. The iconic feminist magazine *Spare Rib*, for example, infuriated some Jewish readers and supporters in 1982 when it published an article which incorporated the view that 'if a woman calls herself feminist she should consciously call herself anti-Zionist', a position repeated in subsequent issues.[89]

While *Spare Rib* published a response by a group of Jewish women, who dismissed its position as 'anti-semitic and hardly feminist', the magazine declined to publish letters from readers that it considered to be Zionists, arguing that giving voice to such views was 'an insult to all the Palestinian women and men who had suffered and died as a result of US-backed Zionist policies'.[90] A similar stance was taken by *Outwrite*, the magazine of an internationalist feminist collective that focused specifically on 'Black, "Third World" and working class women'.[91] This publication, Natalie Thomlinson has argued, 'regularly printed allegations about Israel that were inflammatory and unfounded'.[92] Like *Spare Rib*, *Outwrite* was not inclined to allow a right of reply on Israel and Zionism on the grounds that they would 'never publish any letter that tries to defend apartheid'. For them, any type of Zionism added up to 'the same ideology and racist practice'.[93] In language reminiscent of age-old antisemitic canards, *Outwrite* accused the Israelis of deliberately poisoning Palestinian school girls, 'intentionally' murdering Palestinian doctors and nurses, and, ultimately, being in the process of 'eliminating the Palestinians, mainly by means of mass murder'.[94] For many Jewish feminists, this stance felt intimidating and smelt of prejudice. A group of Jewish letter writers told *Outwrite*, 'It is dangerous to be naïve about anti-semitism in the fight for Palestinian liberation. And as Jews we feel the danger.'[95]

In the feminist movement, it too often seemed, Jews 'were being attacked personally because, by attacking Israel and Zionism, their Jewish subjectivity, collectively represented by Israel, was wounded'.[96] In this atmosphere, some Jewish feminists sought out new, specifically Jewish channels for their political activism. The emergence of *Shifra: A Jewish Feminist Magazine* in 1984 reflected a broader hunger among Jewish feminists to find new spaces where Israel-critical credentials would not be a condition of their presence, and where they would not feel marginalised or attacked.[97] In its first edition, *Shifra*'s editorial outlined a position more comfortable for Jewish Israel critics. It explained, 'As Jewish feminists we have a particular relationship to Israel. We understand why Israel exists and we defend the right of Jews to a homeland. We do not believe that this should be at the expense of the Palestinian people.'[98]

A similar moment of estrangement between Israel-critical Jews and the radical left came with the (non-) performance of Jim Allen's play *Perdition* at the Royal Court Theatre in 1987, after a last-minute decision to cancel performances amid concerns about antisemitism. *Perdition* was a 'court-room drama based on the libel case brought by Rudolf Kastner against Malkiel Grunwald in Israel in 1953–54', after Grunwald had accused Kastner of saving his own family and prominent Zionists at the expense of Hungarian Jewry during the Holocaust.[99] Allen's play leaned heavily on Lenni Brenner's *Zionism in the Age of the Dictators*, which had built a 'well-established anti-Zionist argument' wherein Israel was cast as a '"racist" state' amid 'reference to parallels between Nazi and Zionist ideology and instances of concrete collaboration'.[100] In Allen's rendering of this case, as at *Spare Rib*, many Jewish socialists smelled antisemitism amid the sound and fury of leftist anti-Zionism. As Roberto Sussman argued in the *Jewish Socialist*: 'An examination of events in the European context without due sensitivity, and with the ultimate purpose of scoring points in the ideological debate against Zionism, does not further the Palestinian cause and trivialises the oppression of European Jews.'[101] To many, *Perdition* was insensitive to Jewish suffering, engaging in what David Rosenberg described as 'classic fantasies of Jewish conspiracy'.[102] Rosenberg reminded the *Jewish Socialist*'s readers, 'Let's be clear – all Jews, whether Zionist or not, were the prime targets and victims of Nazism.'

These arguments about *Perdition*, and debates in the feminist press, highlight the complexity of the political space held by Israel-critical Jews. Often retaining deep emotional bonds to Israel and Israelis, and conscious of continuing antisemitism, such Jews were frequently not content to see Israel and Zionism portrayed as a cut and dried example of colonialism or racism, at least not without recognition that it was Europe's failure to protect Jewish communities that had brought Zionism into the centre of Jewish consciousness in the first instance. Such Jews knew, from personal experience, that Zionists were not necessarily racist, that there were complex and valid reasons for Jewish engagement with Israel. Gail Chester, in a collection of Jewish feminist voices which emerged in response to another set of claims about the incompatibility of feminism and Zionism, pointed out:

> While being an ardent feminist, anti-capitalist and anti-Zionist (whatever these things mean), I remain a person – a Jewish person whose family still live in the heart of the Jewish community, and whose oldest friends live in Israel. I can't stand by and pretend I don't mind what happens to any of them.[103]

On these terms, Israel-critical Jews frequently did not want to be forced into declaring their position as a kind of loyalty test, and baulked at the crude anti-Zionism of *Perdition* and *Spare Rib*. It needed to be recognised, Sussman argued in the *Jewish Socialist*, that it was 'perfectly legitimate … to both support Palestinian national rights and be concerned about the fate of the Israeli Jews'.[104]

Looking back on the *Spare Rib* fallout, Rabbi Sheila Shulman explained how she and others were not prepared to have their inclusion in feminist groups made conditional on a declared anti-Zionism, whatever their personal views: 'they said you can't have a right of reply unless you say you are not Zionists. No. I am not a Zionist but I'll be fucked if I say I'm not.'[105] At the National Union of Students conference in 1985, one Jewish student leader expressed similar exasperation at socialist attempts 'to tell us how to define our identity … [and] … place conditions on Jewish autonomy and Jewish participation in politics in general'.[106] The tiresome need to monitor and confront antisemitism in such circles detracted for many from the reasons why they engaged with Israel-critical political activism in the first place. As Rabbi Elizabeth Sarah put it, 'critiquing the Israeli government was one thing but the kind of stuff that was coming out was antisemitism and to spend one's time just reacting to antisemitism was just not my way'.[107] Looking for a political space where they could be themselves, Israel-critical Jews thus often sought solidarity and security in Jewish groups. In such spaces, criticism of Israel could live more easily alongside Jewish identities, and better navigate the complex challenges posed by being part of a community that frequently held sharply different views on Zionism and Israel.[108] Here, groups such as the JSG, and later JfJfP and IJV, offered a home for Israel-critical Jews, facilitating a space between socialism, anti-Zionism and the mainstream (Zionist) Jewish community.

* * *

Landy has described a 'tug of war' as Israel-critical Jews pulled towards and pushed away from the community. 'On the one hand', he argues, 'there is the wish to bring along other Jews and remain within the Jewish fold, and on the other the wish to remain attached (however autonomously) to mainstream criticism of Israel.'[109] This state of affairs is perhaps comprehensible only when one understands just how challenging many Jews find criticism of Israel. Without question, support for Israel has become one of the core foundations of British Jewishness in a way that has exasperated and pushed away Israel-critical Jews. IJV activist Brian Klug, for example, described his shock at seeing, on a visit to the London Beth Din, 'the centrality of Israel in Jewish life' listed on the wall as one of the 'six core "values"' of the United Synagogue. 'Evidently', he complained, 'the United Synagogue saw no tension between this item and the first on the list − "the welcoming of every Jew" into the synagogal community.'[110] Israel-critical Jews, in this context, seemingly didn't exist for the United Synagogue, or at least resided only outside the normal parameters of Judaism.

In the end, whether or not the United Synagogue was correct to see Israel as so central to Jewish life raises a question about the very meanings of Jewishness in post-war Britain. Was Judaism well understood as a diasporic free-standing global faith? Or was support for the world's only Jewish state a key part of Judaism's essence? After the Holocaust, Israel − macho, resilient, undaunted by international criticism − afforded a shot in the arm to a traumatised community that was mostly not inclined to cast aside its right to return, its insurance of future safety, as per the 2002 Israel-critical letter writers. Jewish communities, generally, bought into Israeli ambitions, fundraising, campaigning and visiting.

In the main, Zionism has proved irresistible to most British Jews, notwithstanding any concerns they might have about Israeli policies or specific governments.

For Israel-critical Jews, however, the state offers imperfect, even dangerous, solutions to real problems. For such Jews, ultimate safety and security does not reside in one small state, well-armed as it might be, but instead in deep integration in global communities and/or in the fastidious maintenance of Jewish religious traditions. Zionism, to many Israel-critical Jews, has in a moment of crisis diverted Judaism from its core mission, its commitment to global, ethical values. As one writer in the *Jewish Socialist* put it, 'Our political orientation should be to integrate Jewish emancipatory aspirations into a more general liberation struggle and to work against the illusion that the Jews could retreat to one corner of the earth.'[111] To some religious Jews, Israel has, moreover, usurped the promise of God to return the home of His people, imposing on the Middle East a fumbled and un-holy political project which could only ever be a distraction. The centrality of Zionists in British Jewish establishments, such Jews have felt, has caused 'untold devastation wherever they have been able to get a stranglehold'.[112]

Mostly, Jews with views of this nature have been seen at best as deviant and at worst as treacherous in a community that has taken Israel to its heart. Israel criticism has cost some Jewish leaders their jobs and damaged personal and professional relationships, which have often failed to navigate the strength of feeling on both sides. Nonetheless, the idea that Israel does not represent British Jews, or their faith, has always featured in British Jewry and is likely to continue to do so. Such thinking in the past was mainstream in the community, and while at present it is marginal, it seems certain that arguments about Israel will continue to rage, that the place of Zionism in British Jewish identity is unlikely to go unchallenged in the future. For those Jews who take an Israel-critical stance, new communities and groups have offered space to thrive or at least to support each other.[113] Such communities are, to Dashiel Lawrence, a 'by-product of a detraditionalized and globalized world', seemingly likely to grow and spread in an era of widening Jewish diversity.[114] For sure, Jewish worlds are changing, and yet there have always been Jews critical of the idea of Jewish nationalism. The debates that rage speak to the essence of what Judaism was, is and will be in the future, to what it means to live ethically and proudly as a Jew in the modern world.

1 Rudi Leavor at *Kehillah* in Bradford in front of his photograph. MW Photography.

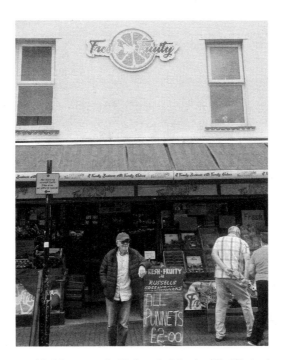

2 Steve Shipman outside his parents' old shop in Merthyr Tydfil. Author's photograph.

3 Synagogue open day in Merthyr Tydfil, 2024. Author's photograph.

4 Students' Soviet Jewry demonstration, Central Station, Glasgow, 1984. Scottish Jewish Archives Centre.

5 Jewish Gay Group contingent at London Pride, Kennington Park, 1987. Courtesy of Russell Van Dyk and Rainbow Jews.

You don't have to be Jewish to celebrate Christmas...

but it helps.

6 The Jews for Jesus advertisement that appeared in *The Times* on 17 December 1991. Courtesy of Jews for Jesus, UK.

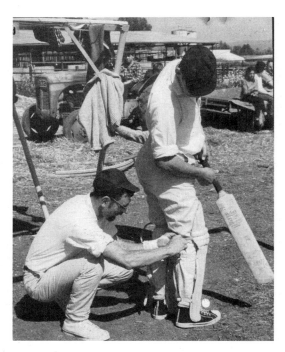

7 Geoff Bercovitch and Basil Levinson, Amiad, 1970. Yad Tabenkin Archive.

8 St George and the Dragon statue at kibbutz Kfar Hanassi. Author's photograph.

5

Oi vay – I'm Jewish and gay: queer Jewish lives and the struggle for recognition

On 12 July 1992 the new Chief Rabbi, Jonathan Sacks, led a high-profile march in Hyde Park. Billed as 'the first national Jewish community event to be held in the UK', Walkabout 1992 was conceived as an opportunity 'to bring the community together, while raising funds for charity'.[1] Stressing the event's inclusivity, John Corre, chair of the Walkabout's steering committee, told the press that the event was 'suitable for everyone from babies in pushchairs to great-grandparents'.[2] The idea of national Jewish unity, in this instance, meant in practice an opening of arms by the Chief Rabbi to non-Orthodox Jewish groups. Through Walkabout, Sacks reached out to Progressive and secular Jews whose day-to-day activities normally lay beyond his, and the United Synagogue's, purview. The event would be, Sacks explained, 'about unity, about community, and about charity'.[3] Unity, however, only stretched so far in the imaginations of Rabbi Sacks and his Walkabout team. When an application to participate was received from the Jewish Lesbian and Gay Helpline (JLGH) it was rejected.[4] Corre explained that while no individuals had been banned from the march, it was not appropriate to offer affiliation to the JLGH because it was 'not one of our registered charities'.[5] Members of the organisation were advised instead to join 'the Walkabout on behalf of one such charity'.

Given that in the run-up to the event all registered Jewish charities were 'invited to participate', and that the premise of Walkabout was a drive for Jewish unity, the rationale for rejecting JLGH (that it was not one of 'our' charities) did not, to many, ring true.[6] And indeed, in response to criticism, event organisers began to offer a different set of reasons as to why the JLGH had not been supported to take its place within the tapestry of Jewish groups involved. Speaking on behalf of the Walkabout team, Rabbi Pinchas Rosenstein argued that the group 'presented a lifestyle which we don't accept. We know that some people feel that they are inclined that way but we draw the line at institutionalising it.'[7] Meanwhile, in an interview on BBC radio in advance of the event, Sacks himself presented Jewish opposition to homosexuality as age-old and theologically consistent. Judaism could 'never accept', he said, 'any kind of sexual relationship that does not have bringing children into the world as part of its logic'. In the last days of Rome and Greece, Jews lived 'in a society where homosexuality was the norm in certain sectors and we stood out against it then, and we stand out against it now'.[8]

To gay Jewish people and their allies, the Walkabout decision exposed the ongoing presence of homophobia in Orthodox communal administration and the broader exclusion of gay people from Jewish life. Writing directly to the Chief Rabbi, one 'young Jewish gay man' urged Sacks to reflect on whether 'this effective driving away of individuals (intentional or otherwise) [was] morally justifiable'.[9] A leaflet from the JLGH itself argued that the Walkabout exclusion would 'serve both to reinforce socially acceptable homophobia and strengthen the feeling of rejection that many lesbian and gay Jews experienced; pushing them further away from their family, their community, and their heritage'.[10] Representatives of Jewish students and youth organisations spoke out against JLGH's exclusion, as did numerous rabbis from Reform and Liberal synagogues.[11] Indeed, the decision nearly prevented the participation of the non-Orthodox rabbinate in the event. A collective of Liberal and Reform rabbis sought a meeting with Sacks, while the convenor of the Reform Beth Din argued that he found it 'particularly difficult to justify [Reform participation] in the face of clear discrimination against one section of the community'.[12]

In the end, representatives of Progressive Jews restricted their challenge to a threat that they would 'have to seriously consider ... endorsement of such an event' in the future, if it was not clear that 'the whole community can participate'.[13] Ultimately, JLGH activists did take part in the Walkabout. Without any mandate from the Chief Rabbi's office, they 'joined walkers, distributing pink ribbons and leaflets'. The JLGH chair, Michael Lee, explained that they wanted 'to show that we are part of the community. We won't be defined as outsiders.' According to the JLGH secretary, 'No more than 20 per cent [of other attendees] voiced opposition. The majority were openly supportive, or bemused that we had been excluded.'[14]

In the aftermath, Rabbi Sacks claimed that Walkabout had seen British Jewry 'able to demonstrate goodwill as a total community without any tensions'. In reality, the event had exposed a fault line that went deeper than any division between Orthodox and Progressive Jewish communities.[15] Nowhere was this exposed more clearly than in the ire of one Jewish mother. Myra Julius had been a member of the United Synagogue for nearly forty years by the time of the Walkabout. But, as the proud mother of a gay son, she wrote to the *Jewish Chronicle* to renounce her synagogue membership so as not to 'be associated with any form of prejudice' after JLGH's exclusion. As a result of the Chief Rabbi's stance, Julius felt that her son had 'been humiliated, if not as an individual, then as part of the gay and lesbian community'. And as a Jew who knew 'what it was like to be made to feel different', she asked other parents to stand by her and call out the bigotry of the United Synagogue.[16]

Mrs Julius was not the only dissenting voice within the fold of Orthodox Judaism, although criticism of the Chief Rabbi's stance was heard most loudly beyond his United Synagogue community. Orthodox challenges were often rooted (as Julius's had been) in personal experience. One letter writer told the Chief Rabbi that she 'vociferously' dissented from his views about gay Jews and had supported a female friend who had come out. 'Surely', she said, 'the appropriate response for us, as observant Orthodox Jews, is to make sure that there is some helpline where people are not simply condemned, or told to go away with their Jewishness, but where they are listened to and supported in resolving their conflict.'[17] Another letter writer, himself a gay Jew who had wanted to study to be a rabbi, argued that Sacks's position was driving Jews away from their faith. 'At a time when a number of gay people are turning against all religious forms as oppressive bigotry, it distresses me that a narrow concept of what it means to be part of a family is alienating those people who desperately care about tradition and about loving.'[18]

These challenges hinted at the slow change that was afoot in British Jewish life as regards attitudes to homosexuality. Of course, such changes did not take place in social isolation but sat amid similar conversations taking place in other religious communities. The criticism of Sacks even among some of his Orthodox flock spoke to a broader religious climate in which moral values were increasingly seen as a matter of individual conscience. As Steve Bruce has put it, religious culture in post-war Britain saw people 'become more assertive in deciding what they … believe', driving an atmosphere wherein 'therapeutic improvement in the lives of believers' was seen as more important than doctrinal conformity.[19] On these terms, gay Jewish Britons and their allies increasingly asserted their rights and demanded recognition within Jewish devotional life. This changing terrain piled pressure on rabbis and community leaders to respond, sometimes to defend the traditional values of conservative parishioners, but increasingly to accommodate gay people who could not so easily be cast beyond the pale. Ultimately, these changes reflected a slow, often painful, but truly substantial opening up of Jewish life, a shift towards inclusion that was 'extraordinary from the perspective of the 1960s, never mind pre-World War Two European and immigrant communities'.[20]

Being gay and Jewish in post-war Britain

The possibilities and perils of gay living and loving changed slowly in post-war Britain. For the first generation of post-war Jews, being gay often meant living sexual lives that were illegal, where acting on homosexual desire could make you a social pariah and lead to prosecution and prison. In this respect, the Sexual Offences Act 1967 (SOA) was a major moment of change. While the SOA left many problems unsolved for gay people, not least the continuing criminalisation of gay sexual activity for those under 21 years of age, it nonetheless was something of a watershed.[21] In England and Wales, from that point onwards, gay people no longer needed to fear prosecution for same-sex sexual activity in private, a shift which removed (at least in terms of legal consequences) the terrible threat of blackmail and outing as 'the stigma against homosexuality gradually changed'.[22]

The Wolfenden Report in 1957 had advised that homosexuality should no longer be classified as a criminal offence, but even the partial change afforded by the SOA took a further ten years. Key here was the determination of MP and lawyer Leo Abse, whose Jewishness played a role in driving him to push for legislation to make Wolfenden's recommendations into law. As a Jew from Wales, Abse told the *Gay Times*, he knew how it felt to be 'a minority within a minority. Therefore it was natural that I was much more ready to empathise.'[23] Abse's argument, that Jews in particular should understand the sting of discrimination, became something of a recurring theme among those Jews who wished to take up cudgels for gay rights. A generation later, Jewish objections to Section 28 (a series of laws designed to prevent local government from 'promoting' homosexuality) again highlighted the commonalities of oppression. 'As Jews we feel for many reasons – not least the testament of history – a need to be vigilant in defending the needs of threatened minorities.'[24]

The slow and reluctant political acceptance of gay relationships says much about the depths of homophobia in Britain, which left a post-war generation of gay people to face the fear of sanction and humiliation. Indeed, for much of the 1950s, a seemingly growing enthusiasm for prosecuting homosexual offences among the public and the police led to an increased number of imprisonments.[25] Coming to adulthood in this period, Rabbi Lionel Blue recalled the dysfunction created by the illegality of gay sex, an atmosphere that drove self-loathing, anxiety and anger. 'Relationships didn't exist … You had to be terribly certain of someone you had a relationship with … and you had to be very careful you covered it up.'[26] In this climate, for Blue and many others, the realisation of homosexual desire dawned like a disaster. 'I cursed the world around me', he recalled, 'for locking me into a private hell.'[27]

Similarly, Rabbi Sheila Shulman, who went on to establish *Beit Klal Yisrael* (an inclusive synagogue in central London), recalled her initial awakening as a gay woman as 'a source of terror – not anything else'.[28] Of course, these feelings did not vanish with the passing of the SOA, as the taboo surrounding homosexuality endured in Jewish life and broader society. Many Jewish gay people, the secretary of the JLGH explained, continued to be 'forced to live a life of deceit, disguising the true nature of their feelings and relationships, and living in constant fear of discovery'.[29] To tackle the deeply ingrained social and political prejudices against homosexuality, which had inexorably leaked into the self-identities of gay people, the Gay Liberation movement in the United States began to promote new approaches both to gay living and to challenging those forces that sought to restrict and oppose it.

The Gay Liberation Front (GLF) began in New York in 1969, following rioting and resistance in response to a police raid on the Stonewall Inn in Greenwich Village. Shaped by 'all the radical social and political movements of the decade', the GLF called for both the immediate recognition of gay rights and for gay people themselves to come out and fight for them.[30] The emergence of the GLF in the UK, in October 1970, soon incorporated within its scope a Jewish Research Group, which met weekly in the Students Union of University College London from 1971.[31] The group was made viable by the 'large number' of Jewish gay people in the nascent GLF and was created, according to an early leaflet, 'in order to discuss and research on [Jewish] biblical and sociological views' and to 'approach our clergy and Jewish societies and arrange inter-meetings'.[32]

Group leaders saw Jewishness and Judaism as adding layers of complexity to gay life, arguing that Jewish homosexuals suffered 'even more' than other gay people because 'Judaism and the Jewish community discriminate and oppress us'.[33] Of course, Judaism was far from the only religion with strictures against homosexuality and traditions of homophobia. Being religious and gay, Peter Sweasey argued, often meant 'opposition from all sides'.[34] For many gay Jews, however, the idea of navigating two sets of minority statuses, especially where one status was overtly hostile to the other, was a particularly heavy burden to carry. Playfully broadcasting his own obituary, Blue recalled his initial feeling that being gay and Jewish was 'a kind of crucifixion'.[35] Armed with an awareness of the particular challenges posed by this double marginalisation, an increasing number of Jewish gay people began to organise.

Under the name of the Jewish Homophile Liaison Group, a public symposium was held at the Students Union on 10 February 1972 to discuss 'The Jewish Homosexual in Society'.[36] True to their word, the group attempted to engage with Jewish clergy, though with limited success. They wrote to Saul Amias, rabbi of the United synagogue in Edgware, who explained in his reply that he could not speak at an event of this nature. Given the theological proscription of homosexuality, Amias replied, the group could not expect 'any Rabbi or Minister openly to express any support'. Nonetheless, he confided, he did 'understand and sympathise' and wished the letter writer and his friends 'strength to resist the attacks still made upon something ... not yet well understood'.[37] In contrast, Rabbi Leslie Hardman (from Hendon United synagogue) was less conciliatory when the group approached him. 'Whether homosexuality is a SIN or a sickness', he asserted, no such group could expect 'communal or organisational status'. To Hardman, any engagement was tantamount to encouragement. 'Many who might be on the fringe of homosexuality might never be saved from that sort of life if your group were given "status" within the Jewish community.' 'The more you stress its "naturalness"', Hardman argued, 'the worse it will become.'[38]

Despite the refusal of these rabbis to engage, the event went ahead, with speakers including a Jewish social worker and the Student Director of Hillel House, who explained that he had spoken personally to the Chief Rabbi and 'found him very concerned and sympathetic (but nothing more)'.[39] By the end of the year, a further 'Teach In' had been organised after a Jewish youth group wrote to the Albany Trust (which had provided some early funding to the Jewish group in the GLF) to ask if they could provide information on the subject.[40] This event was attended by Orthodox Jewish chaplain Alan Unterman, although he requested that the *Jewish Chronicle* not report his presence, listing what *Gay News* recorded as 'a string of implausible terrors that could befall Jewish teachers who step out of line'.[41]

The Teach In was publicised in *Gay News*, which subsequently ran frequent advertisements inviting gay Jewish people to join the Jewish Homophile Liaison Group in London.[42] In the following years, the group evolved into the Jewish Gay Group (JGG, later the Jewish Gay and Lesbian Group or

JGLG), meeting regularly in members' homes, creating a grassroots social and support infrastructure for Jewish gay people. As one organiser outlined in *Gay News*, the group offered 'a meeting place … in which all gay Jews may meet without the tensions that would arise in a more conventional Jewish atmosphere'.[43] As well as providing a safe space for Jewish gay people, the JGG began to stake a claim in the community, serving (through its very existence) to illustrate the possibility of being both gay and Jewish. As one later article put it, 'The most obvious and simple function of the Group is to say: we are here.'[44]

Existing as a gay Jewish group, however, posed a series of challenges. Most obviously, the nascent JGG, while ostensibly for all gay Jewish people, provided a better home for gay Jewish men than it did for women or for trans Jews. In the early years of the JGG, Russell Van Dyk recalled, outreach to lesbian Jews 'hadn't even been considered', so that male dominance was almost total.[45] Writing his report as chair in 1978, Bernard Davis conceded that the group had 'regrettably failed to attract many women members'.[46] This under-representation left women who did attend feeling as though they didn't belong, 'victims of a triple oppression – as Jews, as women, and as Lesbians'. One young woman from north-west London told the *Jewish Chronicle* how 'lots of girls come once or twice and then don't return'.[47] On these terms it is unsurprising that separate efforts were made to form a Jewish Lesbian Feminist Group in 1974, while firm unity with the men (in the form of the JGLG) took far longer.[48] Similarly, although it was pointed out at the outset in 1972 that 50% of attendees in one London trans club were Jewish, trans issues and representation were not embraced by the JGG, which placed their focus firmly on the needs of Jewish gay men.[49]

Another problem was that JGG members remained fearful of public exposure and being outed to their families and colleagues, which limited the group in terms of what it could do and where. Ex-leaders and activists from the early years recalled the preference of members for meeting in private homes, the addresses of which could be kept quiet, ensuring that the risk of exposure was low.[50] In 1976 the annual report of group chair Peter Golds highlighted the problem: 'The one attempt at a function not held in a private house was a complete failure and therefore meetings have only been held when accommodation has been offered.'[51] Feelings of shame were increased by the refusal of some mainstream communal organs (most notably the *Jewish Chronicle*) to place advertisements for the group in its early days. Writing in advance of the Teach In in 1972, William Frankel, editor of the *Chronicle*, outlined the newspaper's stance in a letter to Francis Treuherz: 'We do not publish any advertisements which are contrary to Jewish law and for that reason we were unable to accept an advertisement promoting a homosexual society since homosexuality is condemned by all Jewish groupings.'[52] This position exasperated activists. At the Teach In, Simon Benson distributed 'samples of ads' from the *Chronicle* which had been published although they 'equally contravened Jewish law'. By the end of the event 'a strongly worded petition to the Editor had been produced'.[53] From 1983 the *Chronicle* did post JGG's adverts, an indication of change that was similarly reflected in Progressive Jewish support for JGG synagogue services from 1982.

Sabbath services (on Friday nights) were made possible after Dow Marmur, rabbi at the North Western Reform synagogue in Alyth Gardens, allowed JGG to use the synagogue's youth and community centre.[54] Marmur had for some time been active in supporting gay Jewish people. In 1973 he visited Integroup in Golders Green, a community of straight and gay people seeking 'to promote integration and a better understanding of human relationships'. Here he told the audience that 'despite' its theological proscription of homosexuality, Judaism owed 'a special feeling for and sympathy with persecuted or misunderstood minorities', an attitude that would later drive him to support gay Jewish participation at the North Western.[55] Although the services were held in a room within the synagogue complex, not in the synagogue itself, it nonetheless marked a significant breakthrough, reflecting growing engagement with gay Jewish life at least among Progressive Jewish groups. Being able to come together in Alyth Gardens, one activist recalled, 'made us come out more openly in the Jewish world'.[56]

Within the leadership of the Orthodox community, the idea of accepting, never mind embracing, Jewish gay identities remained challenging to say the least.[57] For many Orthodox Jews, the very idea of gay Jewishness seemed extraordinary and unfeasible. Responding to a letter in the *Jewish Chronicle* in 1977, Isaac Nodel (rabbi of Ilford Federation synagogue) claimed that he was 'astounded and shocked to read that Gay organisations exist among our people'.[58] Was the letter writer not aware, Nodel asked, 'that the Torah strictly condemns such vile conduct and pronounces severe penalties for these malpractices?' For commentator Chaim Bermant, writing about the concept of same-sex marriage in 1996, the idea of bringing together gay and Jewish identity remained untenable. Why, he questioned, would gay people 'want the blessing of a faith which regards their way of life with abhorrence'?[59] This kind of thinking, Alan Unterman argued, meant that gay–Jewish conversations often took place 'across the gap between two completely different emotional and cultural spaces'.[60] Indeed, this space has remained difficult, if not impossible, to bridge.

Orthodox and Progressive approaches

Orthodox objections to gay relationships were frequently articulated in terms of the challenge that homosexuality was seen to pose to Jewish reproduction. Explaining the prohibition of homosexuality in 1972, the *Jewish Telegraph* outlined that Judaism could not sanction 'sexual relations which do not contribute to procreation'.[61] 'The failure to marry and reproduce', Unterman explained, could be seen as 'akin to communal treason' in a minority group where procreation was 'the foremost weapon of Jewish demography'.[62] Such expectations weighed heavily on Jewish gay communities. The Jewish home, Laurence Brown explained in *Gay News*, was a 'world of luxuriant procreation' which 'the homosexual stands outside'.[63] Describing his experience in gay groups, Rabbi Mark Solomon told the *Pink Paper* that the Jews he met 'had strong feelings about the prospect of never having kids', while 'hardly any non-Jews expressed the same concerns'.[64]

In Orthodox Jewish thinking, however, the impact of gay lives on Jewish demography was not so much the key issue as a way to rationalise a deeper, theological hostility. For many, the biblical proscription of homosexuality was clear, unambiguous and the end of the conversation. Or at least, any ensuing conversation illuminated the religious view that nothing good, and much bad, would come from breaching biblical injunctions. This position was laid out clearly by Chief Rabbi Jakobovits, who explained the unequivocal nature of his own objections in an article in *The Times* in 1987.

> The Jewish view is plain and uncompromising. All the authentic sources of Judaism condemn homosexual relations as a heinous offence. No verbal acrobatics, no feats of casuistry, no attempts at rationalisation, and no outpouring of sympathy, can modify this verdict, harsh as it may be. [65]

For Jakobovits, the idea that gay desire might be natural was an irrelevance. If natural desires legitimised behaviour, he asserted, 'any act of adultery, or incest, or polygamy should be condoned as acceptable'. Ultimately, Jakobovits thought that homosexuality needed to be resisted if people were to live safely in the bosom of Jewish law. He concluded in dramatic terms, 'neither the moral nor the natural law can for long be violated without consequences'.

Of course, from the 1980s consequences could easily be pointed at, in terms of the terrifying spread of HIV and AIDS. Jakobovits was clear that contracting AIDS could not be seen as divine punishment. But there was a fine line, in his words, 'between ascribing massive suffering to personal or social depravity as a divine visitation, and warning that such depravity may lead to terrible consequences'.[66] With a tin ear for the suffering of gay communities in the context of the AIDS crisis, the Chief Rabbi even went so far as to state that gay people might 'deliberately' spread the disease in order to escape 'discrimination', a position which generated furious responses and was described as a 'wicked statement in the strictest sense of the word' by the Albany Trust's Antony Grey.[67] Unsurprisingly, in this period, for many gay Jewish people the Orthodox rabbinate felt totally out of bounds. One gay Jewish activist spoke bitterly of the lack of sympathy and pastoral support offered to those gay Jews who fell victim to AIDS, recalling that his childhood rabbi 'refused to shake [his] hand'.[68] Another complained that the Orthodox reticence to support such sick gay people was unethical in Jewish terms. Exasperated by the lack of help on offer, the chair of the Jewish AIDS Trust Michael Brown argued that 'HIV is an illness. Compassion towards the ill is a mitzvah.'[69]

And yet, while change was not obvious or fast, the Orthodox position on homosexuality was far from static. Evolving Orthodox thinking reflected broader currents of religious change in post-war Britain and beyond. Across many faith communities there was a growing awareness that religion needed to modernise to stay relevant in increasingly secular and diverse societies. While the Jacobs Affair highlighted the limits to which British Orthodox Judaism would tolerate the encroachment of such introspection, space did increasingly grow (even in some Orthodox circles) for discussion about the appropriateness of certain texts for present-day situations and consideration of how traditional rules impacted on the modern lives of the faithful. In this atmosphere, some Orthodox Jews began to seek out a new response to Jewish homosexuality, a journey that sometimes led out of the Orthodox world, but sometimes did not.

The departure from Watford United synagogue in 1992 of its rabbi, Mark Solomon, offers one illustration of this slowly changing terrain. Having been raised in Australia, Solomon had undertaken rabbinical training at Jews' College and became minister of the growing Watford community in 1990. Coming to terms with his sexuality as a gay man, however, Solomon decided that he could not continue in the post. He resigned, was 'reluctantly outed' by the *Jewish Chronicle* in 1992, and went on to teach Talmud at the Progressive Leo

Baeck College.[70] In the wake of his resignation, Solomon explained that he could not subscribe to the Orthodox position on homosexuality, which he labelled 'unrealistic and inhumane'.[71] For him, and a growing number of Orthodox people, recognition was needed that homosexuality was not a transgression so much as a manifestation of a person's true nature. At the heart of this challenge was the idea that God made people as they were, and thus that homosexuality needed to be reconceptualised as part of His work. Solomon explained: 'I believe that God made me gay and therefore wanted me to be gay – and to use my sexuality in a joyous, creative and holy way.' In these terms, a gay Orthodox person could more easily make peace with their sexuality as part of God's unknowable plan. One interviewee, Mark, from the 2001 documentary about Orthodox homosexuality *Trembling Before G-d*, explained, 'It's not a bad thing to be gay. It's a good thing. It's a chesed. It's a kindness from Hashem.'[72]

This kind of thinking did not lead automatically to a radical change of direction in Orthodox theology, but it did begin to crack open a conversation wherein an increasing number of Orthodox thinkers conceptualised homosexual living not as egregious sin, but rather as the lot of honest Jews who were struggling to play the hand dealt to them by the Almighty. This evolving position was not entirely new. Discreetly, some Orthodox ministers had for many years been giving advice and support to gay people which reflected a more liberal position than they publicly espoused. Remember, for example, Saul Amias's quietly expressed personal sympathy for the nascent JGG. From the 1990s, however, a more consistent and widespread change occurred. In this period, no doubt spurred on by both Progressive Judaism and the pressures of broader society, new Orthodox positions on being gay and Jewish increasingly came to the fore. The most substantial contribution to this evolving Orthodox stance came in the form of a 2004 book by Chaim Rapoport, rabbi of Ilford synagogue and member of the Chief Rabbi's cabinet.[73] Subtitled 'An Authentic Orthodox View', the book cemented its religious credentials by incorporating a foreword from Chief Rabbi Jonathan Sacks and a preface from Dayan Berel Berkovits from the Beth Din of the Federation of Synagogues. Rapoport's argument was characterised by a number of features, none of which served to present homosexuality as unproblematic for Orthodox Jewry, but which together combined to offer a path for gay people to remain within Judaism and reconcile homosexuality with their faith.

The starting point of Rapoport's analysis was a recognition that gay people, like Jews, had suffered discrimination and persecution, and merited solidarity in this context. Writing in his foreword, Jonathan Sacks noted that 'lesbians, gay men and bisexuals as well as Jews, were the victims of Nazi Germany and remain the object of prejudice and misunderstanding today'. On these grounds, Sacks cautioned that 'stereotyping, homophobia and verbal or other abuse [were] absolutely forbidden'.[74] This focus on homophobia has remained central in subsequent modern Orthodox approaches to Jewish homosexuality. A generation later, Chief Rabbi Ephraim Mirvis, in a publication designed to support LGBT+ children in Jewish schools, reminded Jewish readers that bullying or humiliating people was forbidden. While guidance on LGBT+, he noted, needed to be given 'in a Torah framework' (so that there could be no simple accommodation of gay sexual practice), it was of paramount importance to 'see the humanity in others and truly care about one another'.[75]

Rapoport's analysis highlighted the enduring Jewishness of gay Jews. Alan Unterman, in a 1993 article, had made a similar case when he pointed out that while the practice of homosexuality was sinful, it did 'not affect [gay Jews'] status as Jews'.[76] Hence, Unterman argued, gay Jews needed to live Jewish lives and repent their transgressions on the same terms as everyone else. 'Does God forgive gays for their sins when they repent, as He forgives straights for their sins when they repent? He does.' In the same vein, Rapoport made it clear that homosexuality hardly constituted a sin without parallel in Jewish life, and thus did not merit exceptional sanction. In his words:

> for a synagogue to welcome open-handedly known Sabbath-breakers, non-believers, eaters of forbidden foods, and violators of other aspects of the sexual code in Leviticus, while at the same time treating a person who is known to be a practising gay or lesbian as an unwelcome intruder, smacks of sheer hypocrisy.[77]

In this analysis, gay Jews were understood to be struggling against sinful tendencies, much the same as everyone else in the community, and merited the same kind of sympathy, support and inclusion. After all, Rapoport explained, 'our sexuality and the challenges it entails are not the be all and end all in life'.[78]

Struggling on as a homosexual Jew could be constructed in this way as brave and noble, fighting a terrible temptation. Sacks's foreword made clear that living by the Torah entailed a struggle which was 'little short of heroic … particularly so for those with a homosexual orientation'.[79] What was emerging here was something of a special path for gay people in Orthodox thinking, underpinned by the slowly acknowledged principle that gay Jewish people existed and could not remedy their sexuality. In what was a significant shift from earlier positions, Rapoport was clear that gay people should not be encouraged to engage in heterosexual marriage. In an article in 2000 he explained that instead, 'not being restricted to the rigours of family life, the homosexual can undertake many projects to which a married person could not commit himself'.[80] In this way, homosexuality was constructed as a calling to abstinence and service, a tough hand to play, but only similarly tough to the various challenges facing other congregants.

While falling some way short of accepting gay relationships, this kind of thinking facilitated a practical path for the participation of gay people in Orthodox communities, while maintaining adherence to the idea that homosexual practice was sinful. Mitigations were increasingly offered (Rapoport argued that Jews fell victim to homosexuality as a by-product of contemporary secularism) along with sympathy and a growing level of tolerance in some quarters at least. And yet for most Orthodox theologians, the biblical proscription of homosexual sex only left so much wriggle room. For Progressives, however, the position was somewhat different. Progressive theology supported the evolution of Jewish doctrine and practice for contemporary society, potentially enabling the inclusion of gay people on a different scale. While there were still many hurdles to overcome in terms of homophobic and uncertain congregants and leaders, gay participation and leadership in Progressive communities became so extensive that the fight for gay liberation has been described by Steven Greenberg as part of the 'religious mission' of Progressive Judaism.[81]

In 1976 a working group of 'Reform Rabbis and other interested people' was set up under the auspices of RSGB by Edgware rabbi Rodney Mariner 'to look at the problems and difficulties in the community which were apparently associated with homosexuality'.[82] Mariner, for his part, felt that if Progressive Judaism was 'worth its salt, it ought to be able to accommodate homosexuals'.[83] These meetings led, in 1980, to the publication of *Jewish and Homosexual* by doctor and counsellor Wendy Greengross, who had, with esteemed therapist Irene Bloomfield, been teaching pastoral care and counselling at Leo Baeck College.[84] Greengross's long pamphlet was something of a watershed. Looking back, Lionel Blue credited the work as offering 'the best things about gay life I know'.[85]

Greengross's study focused on providing support for the families of gay people. She explained: 'Parents, families and friends need help at these times, but unfortunately, many do not have the help and support that previous generations received from an extended family, and they are left to cope alone with their fears, their anxieties and their uncertainties.'[86] This focus on the families of gay people, rather than gay people themselves, might have made the study more palatable to some within RSGB, which as a community was far from exempt from the homophobic prejudices of broader Jewish (and non-Jewish) society. Nonetheless, the pamphlet offered a practical path for the incorporation of gay Jews into Jewish communities and laid down some different ways of thinking about homosexuality. Greengross argued that people were not gay as a matter of choice. While she was reluctant to offer firm conclusions as to the 'cause' of homosexuality, she was clear about the need to accept it as being 'as natural and normal for some people as heterosexuality is for others'.[87] Sexual feelings were, she explained, 'part of our essential, biological nature'.[88] From here, Greengross's analysis held that while she understood Jewish anxieties about homosexuality, especially in the context of the desire for procreation (and thus continuity), 'a ghetto mentality and isolationism' could no longer be relied on to keep the community together.[89] Instead, she argued, gay people should be welcomed because it was 'unnecessarily destructive', amid concerns about Jewish decline, 'to exclude quite arbitrarily many who have deep religious faith and deep religious conviction'.[90]

More than anything, the aim of Greengross's study was to open discussion. It was no good, she argued, to 'sweep problems under the carpet and pretend they don't exist'.[91] As a remedy, *Jewish and Homosexual* provided terms and concepts which supported the working through of some of the challenges that were seemingly posed by Jewish homosexuality, offering a framework which empowered Progressive Judaism to take new strides towards inclusion in the following years. This change, however, was often controversial among Progressive leaders and their congregants, reflecting Adrian Coyle and Deborah Rafalin's argument that 'lesbian and gay sexuality' remained 'a deeply contentious issue and a matter of some debate within Progressive Judaism'.[92] In the wake of *Jewish and Homosexual*, Dow Marmur allowed the JGG to hold Friday night services in his community buildings and, soon after, Leo Baeck College began to train openly gay rabbis. And yet the training and placement process for these early recruits was far from straightforward. Rabbis Elizabeth Sarah and Sheila Shulman graduated from Leo Baeck in 1989, having both completed the programme as 'out' gay women.[93] Both, however, were subjected (seemingly because of their sexuality) to tighter scrutiny than other candidates, and experienced significant difficulties in making rabbinical careers in RSGB. Rabbi Sarah recalls that she and Shulman were accepted at Leo Baeck only after two psychological interviews (other students underwent one) and assigned a five-year probationary period. When they both graduated, the movement's

Rabbinic Assembly 'put aside a whole day of its time to decide whether or not they were prepared to have us join'.[94]

RSGB, it seems, was worried about whether communities would accept a gay rabbi, and indeed homophobia in Reform communities remained commonplace. Rabbi Sarah was forced to leave her Buckhurst Hill congregation when certain members expressed fears that she might 'molest their daughters'.[95] The issue of Sarah working as an RSGB rabbi came to a head in the Hertfordshire community of Radlett in 1996, when she gave a sermon on *Kol Nidre* (the evening service of Yom Kippur), revealing her intention to officiate at an improvised wedding (covenant of love) ceremony for two Jewish women. Rabbi Sarah told the congregation that while there was not 'yet' any 'official liturgy' for such a service, she felt it was the right thing to do:

> The example of two women consciously devising a ceremony to mark their covenant of love reminds us what we already know about heterosexual marriage but perhaps take for granted because it is more familiar. The point is that the covenant made between two people is the key to what the covenant with God involves; the loving commitment of two individuals for one another is a model for our relationship with God.[96]

In interview, Rabbi Sarah recalled what happened next: 'a man stood up in the congregation which was about 700 strong in a sports centre, said that it's an abomination – direct quotation from Leviticus chapter eighteen – and then three other people stood up and they all walked out'.[97] After accounts of the incident leaked into the press, the rabbi was cajoled into a 'very humiliating' public apology and forced to retract her offer to officiate at the 'covenant of love'. RSGB, meanwhile, distanced itself from her position, asserting that it had made no decision on whether to allow same-sex ceremonies. Unsurprisingly, Rabbi Sarah soon decided to leave her role as Programmes Director of RSGB.[98] In similar terms, Sheila Shulman recalled being 'sickened' by discussions of same-sex relationships in Reform congregations and 'running back' to the inclusive community that she had created, *Beit Klal Yisrael* in central London, where she could 'shelter' from the bigotry of the wider movement.[99] Ultimately, both Shulman and Sarah found homes in the Liberal Synagogue, which was further along the road to integrating openly gay Jewish people within its leadership.

Notwithstanding these significant challenges, Progressive Judaism was making strides towards the inclusion of gay people which outpaced Orthodox congregations. Underpinning change was Progressive Judaism's willingness to reinterpret and even set aside parts of the biblical text. Because Progressive theology allowed for the idea that the Torah was not literally the word of God, there was space, at least to some extent, to dismiss the biblical proscription of homosexuality as a relic of times long past. Writing in response to Chief Rabbi Jakobovits in 1993, Liberal rabbi John Rayner argued, 'The fact that the Bible calls homosexual conduct an "abomination" (Lev 18:22) does not prove that it is an abomination, but only that the biblical writers believed so.'[100] For many Progressive theologians, it was essential for Judaism to align itself with the knowledge and wisdom of the present, and depart from ideas that were meaningful in earlier societies but now outdated. Rabbi Sarah thus opined that: 'The time has come for new Jewish teaching which acknowledges the limitations of legal enactments framed in different times and according to imperatives – such as the need to forge a separate identity in an "alien" environment – which are no longer relevant or appropriate in the 1990s.'[101] In this way, the proscription of homosexuality could seem, as Tony Bayfield put it in his introduction to the Greengross study, as belonging 'to another world'.[102] Instead of pandering to what it considered outdated rules, Progressive Judaism thus began to generate its own approach, often led by the experiences of rabbis and their congregations, and specifically by what felt Godly and right in the context of the present.

For Mark Solomon, the traditional prohibition of homosexuality could not align with the God he knew. To create gay people, only then to prohibit them from living according to their true nature, would have been 'a cruel and pointless command', behaviour incompatible with 'the very nature of God'.[103] This confidence that God was with gay people, and that they were living active gay lives according to His will, was shared by Lionel Blue, who held the belief that 'God has no prejudices. He speaks in a sauna as well as in a chapel.'[104] It was possible, in this mind frame, to comprehend the personal challenges of gay lives within a specifically Jewish worldview, and to ascribe a holiness to coming out. After all, the idea of liberation, Shulman argued, was 'at the core of Judaism', with obvious lessons as regards personal freedom. She explained: 'It is the first of our commandments. It is how Jews understand our relation to God … a God who is passionate about the people's particularity, their uniqueness, and is engaged with them in their struggle for the freedom to realise their liberation.'[105]

In this context, the Jewish festival of Passover took on an 'added significance' for gay Jewish people, some of whom gathered for communal Seder services from the early 1970s.[106] In interview, Jewish lesbian Clem Herman explained how the festival had a specific 'resonance … the whole idea of coming out of Egypt'.[107] Ultimately, amid growing Progressive confidence about the compatibility of gay lives with the true nature of the Almighty, same-sex relationships could be reimagined as positive drivers of Jewish communal life. Greengross argued in this context that 'many Rabbis and scholars now believe that the voluntary and mutual loving and caring of two adults who are free to commit themselves to each other, is good and brings happiness to the whole community'.[108]

Queering Jewish life?

While the more flexible theological parameters of Progressive Judaism enabled the incorporation of gay people and identities on a different scale to Orthodox theology, Judaism across the religious spectrum in post-war Britain was challenged by changing social attitudes towards homosexuality and the corresponding need to minister to 'out' and active gay Jews and their families. What was taboo and illegal in earlier decades now needed to be discussed and dealt with, in a period of rising secularism where homophobia was gradually becoming a broader social taboo. In this atmosphere, Jewish policy and attitudes towards gay people can be seen as something of an access point to broader tensions and pressures in post-war Jewish life writ large, amid the rise of new Jewish identities. As David Shneer and Caryn Aviv argued, queer Jews played a key role in 'redefining what it means to be Jewish, and what the role of Jewish institutions are and should be', exposing uncertainties about who was, and was not, part of Jewish communal life and who got to decide.[109] Amid rising individualism, Jewish people increasingly made their own models of faith without seeking communal approval, 'queering' Jewish religious practice and identity. As Naomi Braine put it:

> The process and moment of skewing cultural and ritual practices from a religious to a secular – particularly a secular-political – context requires maintaining a recognisable ritual framework while stripping out a central element. Both process and result fall within the essential meaning of 'queer' as peculiar, bent, recognisable but irrevocably changed.[110]

Coyle and Rafalin argued that the Progressive 'dismissal of the Leviticus injunction … [was] … not part of mainstream understandings'.[111] But if the majority of British Jews increasingly agreed with the Progressive view on homosexuality and its potential place in Jewish life, it seems arguable that the mainstream itself was on the move. The fallout surrounding the Chief Rabbi's

Walkabout, where this chapter began, highlights the change and reinvention at play. The exclusion of the JLGH, and the protest it caused, showed shifting Jewish values and the extent to which the United Synagogue (and the Chief Rabbi) were left floundering for a response. Social mores were changing and, one way or another, Judaism was changing too. Tellingly, representatives of the Zionist youth group *Hanoar Hatzioni* argued that the banning of the JLGH needed to 'be rejected in the interests of the wider community'.[112] To *Hanoar*, it wasn't a matter of making concessions for people at the fringes but one of recognising that the 'wider community' had moved in terms of what it wanted, needed and believed.

So much is evident from the changing dynamics of Jewish family life in Britain, especially as regards relationships between parents and queer children. For while Greengross's study among others highlighted the rifts and damage that children 'coming out' could cause within Jewish families, there was in this period a growing pattern of acceptance and accommodation, which challenges us to rethink, at least to an extent, the nature of Jewish family relationships in post-war Britain. Put simply, many of those Jews who 'came out' in this period were not met with unequivocal opposition, but more commonly with a blend of support, ambivalence and uncertainty. Not all parents were as openly supportive as Myra Julius, but many were ready to make peace with gay relationships in their families, albeit sometimes grudgingly. Lionel Blue, for example, described how his mother initially told him that his queerness was 'killing her', before coming to terms to the extent that she 'couldn't give a damn'.[113] When Beatles manager Brian Epstein came out to his family at their Friday night dinner, his mum 'went right up to him and hugged him'.[114] Sometimes parents were worried about the judgement of friends and neighbours in a way that complicated their personal responses. JGLG chair Peggy Sherwood remembered that her mother was 'fantastic' when she came out, but requested that she didn't write publicly about her sexuality in the *Jewish Chronicle* in case her friends did 'not understand'.[115] Slowly, inconsistently, times were changing. As Ruth Gilbert has argued, concerning her own family gatherings, 'what constitute[d] typical [was] now increasingly open to interpretation'.[116] Such analysis is not intended to diminish the very real struggles of gay Jewish people in post-war Britain. Coming out to their families, Greengross explained, frequently left gay Jewish people 'fearful of permanent and complete rejection', fears that were 'unfortunately often fully justified' by the reactions of unsure and sometimes hostile families.[117] But change was nonetheless real and reflected something altogether bigger in terms of post-war British society.

As they strove to entwine their faith and their sexuality, gay Jewish people struck out a path that queered British Judaism. They created new Jewish spaces where they could practise their faith and engage with other Jewish people without the need for anyone's approval. Many gay Jews were simply not content to live without their Judaism. Partly this reluctance was rooted in an awareness that gay British society was not unequivocally friendly towards Jews, Jewishness and religion more broadly. It was not, however, predominantly a desire for safety or understanding that drove gay Jewish people into specifically gay Jewish spaces so much as a hunger to live authentic lives across the spectrum of their identities. In these terms, growing Jewish spaces for gay people facilitated well-being and happiness, empowering gay Jews to build a home where they could more fully be themselves. As one article in *Gay News* explained, 'to be gay is no longer to be excluded from the Jewish family. We gays are recreating the family atmosphere in our own liberated image.'[118] In spaces such as the JGG, at least some Jewish gay people could experience the familiarity of Jewish life without fear of judgement or hostility, a reality which restored to the Jewish community many people who otherwise 'would have had little or no contact with their Jewish roots'.[119] As Van Dyk recalled of an early event, 'it was really special to be able to go there and just completely relax'.[120] In similar terms, attending early gatherings of Jewish lesbians was remembered by Peggy Sherwood as 'just the most wonderful feeling in the world'.[121]

Jewish gay groups were one of many manifestations of changing Jewish traditions in this period, whereby people sought new ways to express and live their Judaism beyond the confines of traditional religious communities. Here, the greater ability and inclination to flex allowed Progressive Judaism to take advantage. It could offer a home to new Jewish gay groups and individuals in ways that Orthodox Judaism struggled to do. Nowhere was this flex more visible than in Shulman's *Beit Klal Yisrael*, which explained its existence in terms of offering a Jewish home to 'those who are distanced or estranged from many facets of contemporary Jewish community life' and to Jews who 'may not think of themselves as religious but who identify strongly as part of the Jewish people'.[122] Of course, gay and gay-friendly groups were not the only manifestation of this hunger for new ways to identify as Jewish. Gay Jewish groups provided an outlet to keep Jews within the fold in a similar way to Zionist groups, groups campaigning for Soviet Jewry, and cultural and educational organisations such as Limmud.

And yet it is arguable that the rise of an 'out' gay Jewish presence in post-war Britain played a specific role in changing the broader community.

For one thing, the marginalisation of gay Jewish groups (especially in their early days) led to an openness towards interfaith activity which outpaced what was happening across most Jewish communities. As was the case in British Jewry, gay Christians were similarly seeking out spaces and ways to engage both their faith and their sexuality, and to challenge prejudice and discrimination.[123] Recognising each other's struggle, a gay Christian group invited the JGG to attend their carol service in 1976, an invitation which was reciprocated by an invitation to a JGG coffee evening.[124] After a meeting at Sheffield's GayFest in 1982 with the secretary of the Gay Christian Movement, Revd Richard Kirker, the JGG expressed an aspiration to keep their groups 'in closer touch in future'.[125] Speaking at the Silver Jubilee celebration of the JGLG in 1992, Kirker explained his enthusiasm for what was now a long-term engagement. He told the group: 'We are among your encouragers, and we are more than a little interested in the outcome. In fact, a great deal depends upon it for the future credibility of Jewish and Christian faith. Let alone the sanity, stability and wellbeing of all lesbian and gay people.'[126] Here, unity was cemented through the shared struggle to claim space within traditionally hostile faith communities, a struggle which dimmed theological differences as well as long-held Jewish suspicions about Christian motives for seeking friendship with Jews. Lionel Blue, who made peace with his own Judaism while sharing worship with Quakers, ran an inclusive congregation which incorporated Jewish converts to Christianity, and *Beit Klal Yisrael* met initially in a venue provided by a Christian order, the Sisters of Sion.[127] All in all, through the common struggles of gay people, barriers between Christianity and Judaism receded, and a broader inclusive theology began to emerge. The JGG's Norman Goldner recalls organising interfaith worship in the midst of the AIDS crisis at St Martin in the Fields (incorporating elements from the United Synagogue funeral service and the *Kol Nidre* service), and writing leaflets to advise both faith communities about AIDS.[128] Through these kinds of activities, bonds deepened between Christian and Jewish communities in Britain, bonds that would transcend the gay support groups that built them.

*   *   *

Some Jews in post-war Britain tried to present homosexuality as inherently un-Jewish with the idea that 'only goyim did that sort of thing'.[129] Yet, as one 1979 article in the *Jewish Chronicle* confirmed, it was in this period 'increasingly apparent that the Jewish homosexual [was] no mere oddity'.[130] As in British society more broadly, British Jewry was forced to evolve its thinking and its behaviour from the 1960s, as culture wars raged between conservative forces of tradition and radical voices for change. While, for sure, some parts of the Jewish community went further than others to accommodate gay people, change was felt everywhere.

Amid pressure and prejudice, gay Jewish people increasingly staked out their place as contributors to British Jewish life, often creating new channels of Jewish community in the process. These new paths to God queered traditional Judaism. They reflected a society where people felt increasingly able to negotiate their own relationship with the divine, and 'interpreted the Bible according to their own needs and experience'.[131] In the face of the seeming certainty of Leviticus, gay Jews and their allies segued to other scripture and tradition, opening a space where they could be who they were. Sheila Shulman invoked in this context Jacob wrestling with the Angel, asserting his place in the divine plan by refusing to let go until he was blessed.[132] Here, the wrestling of man told of a refusal to be excluded, of a belief that gay Jews had the right to be loved by God and to show Him that their lives were also holy. In the novel *Disobedience*, Naomi Alderman's gay protagonist reminded readers that Judaism boasted a tradition of arguing 'with God, that we might disobey His direct commandments and yet delight Him with our actions'.[133] Shulman explained that she couldn't imagine worshipping a God 'with whom I could not be angry and struggle against'.[134]

For some, however, being Jewish and gay was not a matter of discord but a special and sacred part of the divine plan. Looking back, Lionel Blue saw his gayness in just these terms, as a core and God-given reflection of his humanity. 'Being a member of two ghettoes', he argued, 'released me from the constrictions of each.' Having walked out of rabbinic college, Blue rediscovered his faith while sojourning amid the gay clubs of Amsterdam. Far from falling outside the kingdom of God, here, he explained, he 'found a ladder to heaven, sturdy enough to take the weight of [his] body and soul'.[135]

6

The (un)forgivable sin: intimacy, love and interfaith marriage

Manny Cohen (played by John Bluthal), single Jewish tailor in his forties, lives under the thumb of his overbearing mother (Ellen Pollock) in the ITV situation comedy *Never Mind the Quality, Feel the Width*.[1] In one episode from 1971, Manny wants to date an old school friend, Mary, who, as her name suggests, is quintessentially non-Jewish, and the comedy is drawn from his Jewish mother's hysterical response. 'You let a shiksa put one foot on my linoleum', Manny's mother warns him, 'and I'll give you a wedding present you'll never forget … an invitation to my funeral.'[2] Here in a nutshell, illuminated through the lightest of genres, was the most common construction of Jewish interfaith relationships in post-war Britain. In such stories, Jewish children (even old children like Manny) sought romantic lives with non-Jewish peers at their peril, while their parents' generation moved heaven and earth to stop it happening.

In Bernice Rubens' *The Elected Member*, the rabbi and father of the family responds to his daughter's decision to marry a non-Jew by reading 'prayers for the dead', henceforth making her name 'a forbidden word in the house'.[3] In Maisie Mosco's *Between Two Worlds*, the Jewish father tells his son (who has decided to marry a non-Jew) 'never to return'.[4] In fictional constructions of post-war Jewish lives this is generally how the story went. Marriage with non-Jews (usually described as intermarriage or 'marrying out') meant the highest of drama. And yet, as the genre of *Never Mind the Quality* suggests, the 'sackcloth and ashes' reaction to interfaith relationships was in this period becoming something of a canard, a pastiche of Jewish parenthood and the Jewish past.[5]

The idea that Jewish parents 'sat shiva' for children who chose non-Jewish partners, acting as if they had died, was frequently present in renderings of Jewish/non-Jewish relationships in post-war Britain, but whether it was in any way common is highly questionable. Writing in 1989, Stephen Brook asserted that 'should a child marry out' it was 'not uncommon for Orthodox families to go through the formal process of mourning, as though there had been a death in the family'.[6] And yet this claim is not borne out by the admittedly limited research conducted in this area. In his survey of views of intermarriage in the London suburb of Wembley, Gerald Cromer recorded that 'only one of the parents' he had consulted had 'referred to the traditional practice of "sitting shiva" for a child who has married out, and then only to say that he did not intend to do so in such an eventuality'.[7]

Writing in 2020 in the *Jewish Chronicle*, Miriam Shaviv confirmed, 'No one talks any more about "sitting shiva" for their intermarried children. Instead you invite your United Synagogue friends to their weddings. The stigma of intermarriage is gone.'[8] For Britain's Jews in the post-war period, changing values relating to the parent/child relationship softened marriage expectations by promoting greater recognition of everyone's right to choose, in line with broader trends towards personal freedom, described by Rabbi Jonathan Romain as 'the cult of the individual'.[9] As Cromer put it, there was an increasing acceptance that 'the grown child is an autonomous individual who must be allowed to make his own decisions and, if necessary, learn from his own mistakes'.[10] In this atmosphere, researcher Marlena Schmool explained in 2009 that cutting-off from the community was no longer a mainstream response to marrying out, even for half of the strictly Orthodox respondents to her survey.[11]

For some Jewish parents, the matter no longer seemed like the biggest of deals. One interviewee told me that her father had responded to her desire to marry a non-Jewish boyfriend in terms which didn't focus much on the interfaith issue:

> My dad said, 'Are you happy?'
> I said, 'Yes.'
> And he said: 'Do you really think he's right for you?'
> I said, 'Yes.'
> 'So then you have our blessing.'[12]

As memories of immigration faded, and third and fourth generations of Jewish Britons made ever deeper inroads into post-war British society, sexual and relationship norms began to change, a reality which many parents understood, albeit with varying degrees of concern. In another of Maisie Mosco's novels, a friend advises a Jewish father (who is concerned that his son will marry a non-Jew), 'Listen, the lads today aren't like we were, with don't touch engraved on our brains... They don't think of God when they look at the sky, only how big the world is.'[13] For Jews and non-Jews, Britain was becoming more secular, spawning generations who did not see interfaith relationships in the same way as their predecessors.[14] For Jonathan Romain, such relationships were part and parcel of a multicultural society 'in which pluralism and tolerance are regarded as virtues'. In this atmosphere, he argued, 'the sheer humanity of each other has broken through the religious barriers'.[15]

The fact, however, that few Jewish parents were prepared to end relationships with their offspring over intermarriage, and that mixed-faith relationships were becoming more common, should not be taken to suggest widespread Jewish acceptance of the practice, especially at a communal level. For many Jews, and for most Jewish communal organisations, Jewish/non-Jewish marriage was a substantial concern in the post-war period, driving a raft of policies and interventions designed to stem the flow. Anxieties abounded about the decline and ultimate death of the Jewish community, which was often perceived as the logical conclusion of too much intermarriage. As one young person explained in a *Jewish Chronicle* survey in 1969, 'People who marry out are being selfish because they are threatening the survival of the Jewish people.'[16] Writing in 1978, Lionel Kochen described intermarriage as 'the greatest single threat to the future of British Jewry', while a generation later one Orthodox rabbi argued that the tendency 'could put an end to British Jewry full stop'.[17] No one was more focused on the issue than Chief Rabbi Jonathan Sacks. Launching a new organisation promoting Jewish continuity, Sacks confided that he 'trembled' when he considered the implications of assimilation. The Jewish people, he feared, were 'vanishing into oblivion' as intermarriage threatened 'the very basis of Jewish survival in one community after another'.[18] Given that the stakes were understood in such terms it is perhaps unsurprising that intermarriage was frequently presented in British Jewish culture as 'the greatest crime a Jew can commit', 'the unforgiveable sin'.[19]

Understanding Jewish worries

In 1967 Chief Rabbi Immanuel Jakobovits was invited to address the Jewish Marriage Education Council on the subject of intermarriage, describing the phenomenon as a disease that 'attacks the very vitals of our existence', one that merited a level of community response equivalent to that shown in British Jewish support for the State of Israel in the Six-Day War (which had concluded months before).[20] Research from this period asserted that intermarriage was now occurring among British Jewry at a rate somewhere between 25% and 30%, and there was a broad consensus that the community was in the midst of a 'marked increase'.[21] A study from the newly created Demographic Research Unit of the Board of Deputies recorded a 'drastic fall in the rate of synagogue marriages', a decline 'so substantial it must give concern to all sections of the community'.[22] Marriage outside the faith was clearly a significant factor in this fall, a reality substantiated by the rising number of non-Jews seeking Reform conversion so that they could marry their Jewish partners.[23] Eyeing the prevalence of intermarriage in the American Jewish community, British Jewish leaders and thinkers grew more and more worried that Britain would soon face an epidemic of interfaith relationships.[24] Sacks opined, 'Where American Jewry is today, Anglo-Jewry is in danger of being tomorrow.'[25]

Nearly all British Jewish communal leaders were against the practice of marrying out and made it their business to prevent it from happening. Commenting on the community in the USA, one analyst observed the 'strong group pressure reinforcing endogamy', a behaviour similarly evident in Britain.[26] Likewise, many Jewish parents stood firmly opposed to their children marrying outside the faith. Some, Todd Endelman noted, removed their children from certain schools and forbade their entry to certain professions in order to ward off situations where intimate relationships with non-Jews might occur.[27] In Cromer's survey, 89% of Jewish parents stated that they would be unhappy with their child marrying out, or at least would prefer them to marry within the faith. Only a small proportion, he concluded, 'had no reservations at all'.[28] The fear of upsetting parents and damaging family and community relationships was no doubt felt by children. Responding to a *Jewish Chronicle* investigation, one 19-year-old Jewish woman explained her worry that dating a non-Jew would 'offend her parents' and threaten her place in the community. 'I like being Jewish', she told the *Chronicle*. 'I like the atmosphere and the closeness of the Jewish family life. If I married out, I would lose all this.'[29] Entering an interfaith relationship, it was frequently assumed, could permanently undermine family bonds. Isaac Sutton, a consultant psychiatrist, explained in the *Chronicle*'s investigation that family relationships could be 'disrupted' by intermarriage and 'are never the same again'.[30]

Communal attention was focused in particular on the burgeoning affluent and educated sections of the community. Jewish students were seen as particularly vulnerable, living beyond Jewish structures and families in an environment which brought them into intimate day-to-day contact with non-Jewish peers.[31] Similarly, Jews who had 'made it' into largely non-Jewish suburban communities were perceived as being at greater risk of losing their children to intermarriage. As Wallach argued in the *Jewish Chronicle*, 'the latter-day tendency to scatter into ever greener pastures is without doubt a contributing factor in the increasing incidence of out-marriage'.[32] All in all, the slippage of British Jewry from tight-knit urban communities, bonded by poverty and antisemitism, into broader streams of British society was seen as posing an unprecedented challenge. Jews could withstand antisemitism, but could the community survive assimilation in secular post-war Britain? To many, the answer to this question was a firm negative. Even when parents did 'all the right things' in terms of Jewish education and practice, they could not prevent their children's everyday intimate associations with the non-Jewish world. As Romain explained, 'they meet someone at the bus stop or the office party and the gym, and fall in love'.[33] And yet many in the community were determined to stop, or at least slow down, the rates of such relationships.

That this matter came to assume a pivotal place in communal thinking tells us something about what it meant to be Jewish in an increasingly secular post-war Britain. Of course, Jewish practice could (and did) also decline in families where Jews married other Jews, but it was intermarried couples who took much of the blame for declining religiosity. In the context of America, Jennifer Thompson has argued that concerns about intermarriage served as 'a proxy for working out anxieties and meanings attached to assimilation and Jewishness for American Jews in general'.[34] In Britain, Karen Glaser explained in the *Jewish Chronicle*, there were all kinds of people who were '100 per cent Jewish' but had 'zero interest in either Judaism or Jewishness and no feelings of connection with their fellow Jews'.[35] Yet assimilation anxieties focused time and again specifically on those who had married out, whether or not they wanted to engage with their Judaism, amid fears that intermarriage drove decline on a new and irreversible scale, threatening the next generation of Jews. If Jews married non-Jews, certainly where Jewish fathers and non-Jewish mothers were concerned, the offspring of such relationships would not be Jewish according to the principle of matrilineal descendance.[36] Jewish law did, of course, allow for the possibility of conversion, but in traditional Orthodox synagogues this was a long and demanding process that could not be entered into simply to legitimise marriage with a Jew. On these terms, Jewish/non-Jewish marriage posed a risk to community numbers, perceived as especially regrettable in the context of the Holocaust and subsequent Jewish desires to rebuild and repair what had been lost. As Romain put it, 'The fear is that intermarriage could be the "kiss of death" and achieve in one generation what Hitler and other anti-Semites had failed to do in centuries of persecution.'[37]

Beneath such practical considerations lurked a world of feelings that were harder for Jewish people both to declare and defend. Many felt that they were intrinsically different in their very make-up from non-Jews not just in terms of religious practice and lifestyle but also race and ethnicity. Thus, as Progressive synagogue bodies attempted to foster a practice- and belief-based definition of Judaism, their platform 'conflicted with the lived reality of Jews who defined Jewishness as a hereditary identity shaped by tradition'.[38] In this atmosphere, even formally converted Jews often felt like outsiders, left incredulous that 'their children's identities were questioned based on descent' despite their Jewish education and home life.[39] Patrilineal Jews (Jews who had a Jewish father and a non-Jewish mother) were particularly vulnerable to this kind of exclusion. Such Jews, Mehta has observed, were often left 'shocked and dismayed' as they discovered that they were not considered Jewish beyond Progressive communities.[40] Writing in *Shifra*, Tanya Wesker vented her fury about Jews who did not accept her (patrilineal) status. 'Their bloody-minded insistence has, over the years, made me feel angry, hurt, uncertain, confused, inadequate, and at times, totally bewildered.'[41]

The lingering commitment to the idea of Jewish descent, however, sat uncomfortably with an ostensible post-war rejection of racial ideas in the wake of Nazism.[42] Belief in race remained socially mainstream and deeply felt, but to be seen as racially prejudiced, or to insist that there were inherent differences between ethnic groups, was increasingly beyond the pale, especially among Jewish people after the Holocaust. In this atmosphere, Jewish and non-Jewish concerns about race in post-war Britain were mostly articulated in a seemingly softer language of ethnic or cultural difference. This change in language (but not necessarily in belief) is important when it comes to understanding Jewish opposition to intermarriage. For while many, perhaps most, British Jews continued to feel that there were deep differences between them and their non-Jewish neighbours, it was increasingly understood as undesirable and problematic to vocalise such beliefs. The desire not to appear racist thus led to new languages of opposition to intermarriage and a degree of shame and reticence in Jewish approaches to the subject. In Marshall Sklare's analysis of intermarriage in the United States, he noted the extent to which Jewish people perceived a contradiction between their inclination to support 'equality for all people' and the 'ethnocentric impulse' that led them to insist on keeping apart. 'As strongly as American Jews oppose intermarriage',

Sklare explained, 'many are dimly aware that such unions after all represent the logical culmination of the quest for full equality.'[43] In Britain too, similar thinking led Jewish people to ensure that their opposition to intermarriage could not be misread as racism. Family opposition to mixed-faith relationships was thus not often articulated in terms of inherent difference, but instead through concerns relating to the likely social problems that might arise from such unions and the persistence of antisemitism, an approach generally known as 'the discord thesis'.[44] Thus, in Cromer's research, he found that parental objections to intermarriage generally did not represent the practice 'as wrong, merely unwise'.[45]

Intermarriage, it was commonly argued, more frequently led to divorce as differences in values came to the fore.[46] After all, as one respondent told Cromer, 'Married life has got enough problems without looking for more.' Young people often expressed their own worries about intermarriage in similar terms. One woman told the *Jewish Chronicle* that she wouldn't marry a non-Jew as she feared 'our lives and views would not be compatible'. She knew of mixed marriages, she continued, 'that have not worked out and I suppose it was because of this difference in religion and background'.[47] Even if the marriage were successful, opponents asserted, the practice could create difficulties for resulting children. One consultant psychiatrist told the *Jewish Chronicle*, 'Social and emotional problems inevitably arise not only for the young people, but also for their children, and these can be more worrying than any religious problems which do occur.'[48] And even if children were content in such families, this argument continued, they would probably be lost to Judaism. 'It is difficult enough to bring up children in the Jewish faith', Dow Marmur asserted, but 'when a child senses split loyalties … the chances of his remaining Jewish are much smaller'.[49] All in all, marrying beyond the faith was, for many Jewish people, understood and articulated as an unnecessary risk to family happiness, a practice best avoided for a host of reasons beyond race. And yet in many objections it is possible to see deeper-lying anxieties, an ongoing and persistent belief that Jews and non-Jews were inherently incompatible.

For one thing, there was a belief that the intimate lives of Jewish and non-Jewish people were different, that Jews and non-Jews engaged with each other as 'forbidden fruit' in search of erotic highs unavailable within their own communities.[50] Karen McGinity has described the 'mysterious allure' which drew Jewish men to non-Jewish women.[51] 'The "big blonde"', Marmur argued, was 'a frequent image of Jewish male fantasy … she seems to embody all the joys of the flesh which the well brought up Jewish girl cannot, or must not, offer'.[52] Here, 'the shiksa' took on the form of a Siren, a temptress who would 'ultimately cause the destruction of the Jewish people by turning them away from Jewish religion and culture'.[53] In contrast, the idea that Jewish women were sexually conservative and Jewish sexual life stifling resounded in the Jewish fiction of the period. In Maisie Mosco's *Almonds and Raisins*, the Jewish father in the story, Abraham, has never seen his wife naked, 'and did not expect to'.[54] In Brian Glanville's *The Bankrupts*, the disaffected Jewish youth Bernard rails against Jewish homes 'where babies came from heaven, and the dirty preliminaries were taboo'. It is a world, he asserts, that is 'hideously puritan'.[55] In this mind frame, non-Jewish women served a function for hungry Jewish males who knew they could not expect 'their' women to give in to such needs. Another character in Glanville's novel explains the difference:

> The nice little Jewish girls giggled and kissed and let you play with their breasts. Sometimes they even allowed you to put a hand under their dresses, but when they said, 'No! No!' you knew it meant no, and you did not really resent it. There were always the others.[56]

Constructions such as these most frequently focused on women and girls both as objects of desire and in terms of the risk of sexual infiltration. While Marmur did cite the appeal of the 'swarthy circumcised Jew' to non-Jewish women, intermarriage was most frequently constructed through the male gaze, as an anxiety about the corruption of Jewish women.[57] Intermarriage, for 'our' women, could not lead anywhere good, but only to a barren life of regret. Thus, in *The Elected Member*, Esther, the rabbi's daughter, cannot bring herself to have children with her non-Jewish husband and cannot see the relationship as permanent. 'She thought of her suitcases in their bedroom, which since their marriage she had not unpacked, and how each night, he stepped over them to the bed, without a word.'[58]

It is telling that these British Jewish anxieties about marrying out were so persistent in a period when most Jews (and most Britons) were becoming more secular. Even among those who had largely ceased to practise their faith, the idea that their child might marry a non-Jew was still able to cause considerable concern. My mother's recollection of her own not very Jewish childhood illustrates the point:

> I didn't know anything about anything. My parents didn't do anything at all ... [they were] ... totally irreligious, until it came to who I was going to marry. And then there was a different story altogether, you know, they made it quite clear that they wouldn't be happy if I married out, I thought that was a bit of a liberty really under the circumstances.[59]

For Brook, understanding Jewish parents who 'don't believe anything' but 'go beserk' when their child wishes to marry out of the faith meant recognising what he called 'a primeval desire to perpetuate the tribe'.[60] In an atmosphere of secularism, the rejection of intermarriage was perhaps needed more than ever for boundary maintenance, to enable a continuation of Jewish community in the absence of Judaism. As Emma Klein explained, 'Rejection of any non-Jewish partner remained the last bastion of their Jewish identification.'[61] In an age when Judaism was seldom practised by many Jewish people, marrying-in thus assumed a heightened importance, a proxy for deeper concerns about 'the central issue ... how to balance autonomy and obligation'.[62] 'Having forgotten, or ignored, most of the traditional 613 commandments', Dow Marmur quipped, 'we create the 614th. "Thou shalt not marry out."'[63]

Of course, for those people affected by this atmosphere of disapproval, family and community hostility could feel hypocritical, rooted in murky motives. As my mother's case made clear, frequently the fault lines lay between generations. While Marmur was adamant that 'very few parents' would be anything other than hostile to their children marrying non-Jews, among young Jewish people themselves, according to Cromer's research, more than 50% were prepared to consider interfaith marriage.[64] For these young people, parental objections didn't seem to make much sense in a climate of growing secularism, and simply exposed illogical and outdated values. Responding to a *Jewish Chronicle* investigation, one 20-year-old clerk explained that he would 'marry any girl, no matter what her religion, if I loved her. Religion is immaterial to me; it's man made. Judaism is archaic, out-of-date and needs modernising to be relevant to the present day.'[65]

The difference between the attitudes of children and their parents is perhaps best explained by the former's increasing levels of contact with the non-Jewish world. Cromer noted in his research that while 83% of the parents he interviewed had mainly Jewish friends, this was true of only 59% of their children.[66] Engagement with non-Jewish people grew as new generations of Jews, more confident in Britain, sought 'fulfilment on a broader social and cultural plane than did their parents ... in practice, outside the informal boundaries of the community'.[67] In this context, student life in particular became the focus of much Jewish anxiety, as universities enabled young people to meet prospective partners with whom they had much in common, beyond parental or communal disapproval. For Mark and Joyce, the experience of falling in love at Birmingham University saw their contrasting faith backgrounds recede in importance. 'We were so much in love', Mark recalled, 'that everything else was secondary', religion a 'minor part'.[68] Meeting on the neutral ground of a university campus, Mark and Joyce didn't primarily see each other in terms of their differing faiths. Until Mark visited her Jewish parents in Bradford, he remembers, 'I didn't really see Joyce as being Jewish.' Not only did university provide opportunities for interfaith fraternising, but it was also seen as inherently permissive, likely to open minds in a dangerous way. Henry Shaw, director of the Hillel Foundation (which offered kosher accommodation and a broad range of Jewish services to students across the country), warned parents of the 'danger spots' of university, which led to 'the encouragement of scepticism and inquiry', and of an arts world 'where conventions are less regarded than in more formal circles'.[69] Marmur saw the risk in similar terms: 'Because our intelligentsia is the first to succumb to the pressures of assimilation, the fabric of Jewish society is at stake.'[70] In response, Jewish bodies rolled out Jewish chaplaincy services to sit alongside Hillel houses. Nonetheless, it was feared that Jewish students were losing their faith at university. Writing to the Chief Rabbi in 1944, historian Cecil Roth dismissed the Jewish students he saw at Oxford as 'merely "non-Aryan" ... A wholly infinitesimal proportion of them show the slightest Jewish interest of any sort whatsoever.'[71] In this atmosphere, Endelman describes a 'massive defection of young people', fuelled by increasing assimilation and a growing 'indifferen[ce] to religious practice and belief'.[72]

What to do about intermarriage?

Armed with a set of conscious and perhaps less conscious objections, a raft of strategies were employed by British Jewish communities, determined to protect their flock. For more conservative and Orthodox community leaders, responding to intermarriage boiled down to a two-pronged attack. To avoid an increase in the practice, they asserted, it was necessary to ensure that the community was properly, that is, Jewishly, educated. Decent education, it was hoped, would enable Jewish young people to 'love their Judaism' and resist intermarriage.[73] Carrot was to be combined with stick, as leaders proposed that barriers to the acceptance of intermarried couples and their families needed to be firmly maintained as a deterrent to others. Writing in 1945, Chief Rabbi Joseph Hertz published a 'pronouncement' on the subject, outlining the hard line that was to be taken to head off intermarriage. The children of non-Jewish mothers, Hertz asserted, were to be considered as 'non-Jews in every respect' and excluded from Jewish circumcision rites.[74] A Jewish man who had married a non-Jew, while not forbidden to pray in synagogue, was to be considered ineligible for 'membership in a congregation'. 'One whose wife and children are not part of the Jewish community', Hertz's pronouncement explained, should 'have no voice or influence in the direct or indirect administration of the religious life of that community'. While these rules were not consistently observed, a generation later Chief Rabbi Jakobovits made a similar statement in opposition to the acceptance of intermarriage in congregations. 'To belong to a community', Jakobovits argued, members needed to be fit to 'discharge certain responsibilities'.

> The moment that these responsibilities are renounced and an intermarriage occurs, then it may become necessary as a deterrent to exercise such sanctions as will prevent the situation from being accepted and taken for granted, from public honours being paid where, in fact, there had been responsibility for public dishonour and public disgrace.[75]

The idea that a hard line and firm dissuasion were needed to prevent the advance of marrying out was prominent in a 1988 campaign by 'Jet', a programme set up by Orthodox Jewish activists to 'arouse a sense of Jewish awareness and belonging … in the Jet age'.[76] Jet ran seminars, produced leaflets and advertised its message in the strongest terms in the *Jewish Chronicle*, describing its campaign as 'an urgent call to world Jewry'.[77] Intermarriage, Jet argued, was putting at risk 'millions of precious Jewish souls', leading to lives rife with 'unhappiness' and producing children with 'complexes and confusion'. At the heart of Jet's case were two ideas: the first, that intermarriage was a 'grave biblical sin'; the second that it would inevitably lead to unhappiness.[78] 70% of Jewish/non-Jewish marriages, Jet claimed, ended in divorce. 'Do not allow a temporary infatuation to ruin your life', its adverts cautioned Jewish young people.[79] To help, Jet launched a 'Jewish Safety Code', a guide to maintaining distance from situations which might result in intimate liaisons with non-Jews.

Jet's campaign caused considerable controversy and sparked furious rebuttals from Jews who had married non-Jews. In the *Jewish Chronicle*, one reader asserted that Jet's message put the Jewish community 'in danger of creating … inverted racism', while another dismissed Jet's argument as 'biased, hurtful and racist'.[80] These accusations of racism focused on Jet's analysis of the impact of intermarriage on children. One reader with a Jewish father and a Reform convert mother responded indignantly: 'Neither I or any other member of my family is confused in any way, nor do we have a divided outlook towards our religion. The only confusion lies within the Orthodox community and their hypocritical opinion of this so-called "mistake".'[81] Jet and its supporters countered that the advertisements were 'most definitely not racist'.[82] The accusation, one reader argued, was 'absurd' as anyone could convert to Orthodox Judaism if they so desired.[83] Surely it wasn't racist, Jet argued, to 'try to halt the diminution of our people'.[84] And yet the very notion that marrying non-Jews had this effect could be (and often was) seen as a racist stance, a concern about the decline of Jewish stock. Whether racist or not, the Jet campaign captured the tone of at least a section of the British Jewish community. One letter, defending Jet against the charge of being 'strident and offensive', justified the campaign by noting that intermarriage was, after all, 'a major sin of defection'.[85] For sure, most leaders of the British Jewish community shared Jet's desire to deal with the issue head on. But how?

The key weapon of Jewish defence against the threat of intermarriage, according to Jakobovits and many others, was the provision of substantial and high-quality Jewish education to the community's young people. In a sermon at Marble Arch synagogue in 1969, Jakobovits was clear:

> Only a thorough and profound understanding of Judaism, of Jewish ethics and philosophy, of Jewish law and theology, of Jewish literature and history, can counter the rebellion ... Without such understanding through education, especially at the post Bar Mitzvah level, many of our youth will be left defenceless against the allurements of defection and intermarriage.[86]

This approach was considered compelling beyond the Chief Rabbi's office. Concluding his research in Wembley, Cromer outlined the need to 'make education the community's primary concern' if intermarriage was to be avoided.[87] Similarly, statistician S. J. Prais told the Board of Deputies that Jewish education was the only way to stem the flow of people from the community. 'The number of schools that we succeed in establishing', Prais argued, 'will determine the size of the community of tomorrow.'[88]

The growing Reform movement in Britain was similarly focused on the need for education, and keen to state its opposition to intermarriage in line with the broader Jewish community. While, and perhaps because, the simpler and more accessible approach to conversion meant that it was considerably easier for non-Jews to join their Jewish partners in the Reform or Liberal Jewish flock, leading Reformers were keen to state that they shared Orthodox anxieties. Dow Marmur explained in his analysis of intermarriage that there was no need for a 'Reform view' on the subject as 'all sections of the community are equally appalled' by it.[89] Every part of British Jewry, he argued, was 'justifiably afraid of erosion through intermarriage'. On these grounds, Marmur claimed, it was impossible for a Reform rabbi to perform an interfaith marriage ceremony or for a Reform community to 'give its blessing to a marriage which constitutes a threat to Judaism'.[90] Writing a generation after Marmur, Reform leader Tony Bayfield was similarly unambiguous, asserting that it was his hope that 'every rabbi in every synagogue' would do 'everything they can to prevent marrying out taking place'.[91] While, as we shall see, the realities of Reform responses to intermarriage were very different to those of Orthodox communities, the desire of leading Reformers to state clearly their opposition was telling.

For a Reform movement that wished to avoid being seen as a diluted form of Judaism, taking a 'soft' stance on intermarriage was not an appetising option. In the 1970s some leaders in the Reform and Liberal movements had seemingly been hopeful of achieving a shared position with mainstream Orthodox communities on Jewish rites of passage. In 1975 and 1976 private meetings took place between the Chief Rabbi, the Haham (the religious head of the British Sephardi community) and leading Reform and Liberal rabbis to try to achieve some consistent cross-communal rules. In these meetings, Dow Marmur argued that 'ideally' Reform Judaism would 'like the kiddushin [marriages] of each of the movements to be accepted by all, and gittin [divorces] to be carried out by one Beth Din'.[92] Such unity would have facilitated easy movement between different congregations and warded off the growing feeling, as the Chief Rabbi put it, that 'there were two communities within our people gradually moving apart'.[93]

In the end, however, such a position could not be achieved, as Progressive Jewish communities asserted their own rules of membership. At the heart of the difference was a more accessible path to conversion, and the Liberal (and later Reform) policy that Jewish status could be conferred on the child of a Jewish father and non-Jewish mother. While these differences did not add up to Progressive acceptance of marriage beyond the faith, such policies signposted a greater potential for flexibility within Progressive Judaism. In post-war Britain, Progressive communities increasingly articulated a different approach towards interfaith families, encapsulated, as Marmur put it, in a Reform differentiation between 'acceptance' and 'approval'.[94]

From the Orthodox perspective, there was no easy way to incorporate into the community a family formed from an interfaith relationship, especially where it involved a Jewish man and a non-Jewish woman. Seeking advice from an Orthodox rabbi in Birmingham about the status of his soon-to-be-born son, David (whose pregnant wife was not Jewish) remembers being told, 'Your child won't be Jewish. Forget it. Have a good life, enjoy.'[95] This matter, however, did not look so bleak from a Progressive perspective, where additional theological wriggle room made a big difference. Having been distressed by the counsel he received, David sought out a second opinion from the Progressive rabbi, Curtis Cassell: '[He] gave the Progressive perspective or the Reform perspective that it can be patrilineal and as long as you committed to a Jewish lifestyle your child could be Jewish and I was so relieved at that. It really surprised me how much it meant to me.'[96] Armed with this advice, David and his non-Jewish partner (who later herself converted) raised their children in Birmingham's Progressive synagogue, highlighting the more flexible approach towards interfaith families in Reform and Liberal theology. This position, however, emerged slowly and inconsistently.

Reform theologians continued generally to hold to the idea that Jews should marry other Jews, but an increasing number began to focus on supporting (and thus retaining) those Jews who had already taken the decision to marry outside the faith. In the 1980s some Reform and Liberal ministers began to vocalise a concern that taking a hard line on intermarriage might be damaging to the future of British Judaism; specifically that such a position might drive away Jews (and their children) who would otherwise still want to be a part of the community. Rabbi Jonathan Romain argued in this context, 'should we tell these people to get lost, that they have betrayed their faith? Or do we say you are still Jewish and your children can be too?'[97] For Romain, the community's uncompromising stance on intermarriage had become counterproductive. He argued, 'people have been condemning intermarriage for years and it hasn't stopped it. It just succeeds in losing the Jewish partner to the community.'[98] If communities did not do more to accommodate such families, Romain cautioned, it would probably create 'a vacuum into which many vicars [would be] happy to step'.[99]

For at least some Progressive leaders, communal attitudes towards intermarriage needed to change so as to reflect the realities of modern life. Put simply, to Romain and others like him, the congregation was voting with its feet and the rabbinate needed to respond. Mixed-faith couples, he was aware, were increasingly refusing to accept '"no" for an answer' when it came to rabbis officiating at their wedding ceremonies, a reality which 'led a small but growing number to hold a Do-It-Yourself service', in Thompson's words, doing Jewish 'on their own terms'.[100] What was needed, Romain thought, was a 'new theological paradigm' which recognised with 'equal validity' the decisions of those Jews who had chosen partners outside the Jewish faith.[101]

In this context, in December 1988 the first of several seminars was held at the Reform movement's Sternberg Centre in London, aiming to draw interfaith couples back into a discussion about their Judaism. The seminars were the brainchild of Romain, who had hosted similar events for his community in Maidenhead.

Romain had the idea of running themed sessions in his home for Jewish people who were struggling with specific issues such as bereavement, unemployment and divorce, and decided to hold one such event for mixed-faith couples. All the other sessions, he recalled, 'had about fifteen people', but the intermarriage session 'had fifty five and people were ringing up from all over London and saying we've heard about this thing'. As a result, the rabbi realised, the potential for engagement 'was actually much bigger than just Maidenhead'.[102] In response, Romain organised a team of rabbis and counsellors to host the event at the Sternberg Centre, which was 'inundated' with interest. In the press at the time he described how 250 people came from 'all over the country' to take part, and he recalled in interview his own emotional reaction to those who flocked to the event.

> It was just wonderful to see these couples who had felt so isolated and they weren't just in their 20s, some of them in their 50s and 60s, who felt marginalised and isolated for years and years and years, rejected by their family, turned away by their synagogue.[103]

While organisers were quick to state that all eight of the rabbis who participated in the Sternberg seminar regarded 'mixed marriages as undesirable', the gathering signalled a new era of acceptance for those Jews who had chosen non-Jewish partners yet still felt a desire to be a part of the Jewish community.[104] This and subsequent events enabled rabbis such as Romain to explain the options open to such couples around Jewish rites of passage (circumcisions, marriages, funerals) and to discuss their, and crucially their children's, potential participation in the community. Through the Sternberg seminars, interfaith couples realised that they were far from alone. Romain recalls, 'As they came through the doors their mouths dropped open. They suddenly saw a hundred other people and they all thought they were the only one.' As two of the participants explained, while it was made clear that Progressive Judaism did not 'support or condone interfaith marriage, the framework for discussion had given hope'.[105] The seminars thus began to facilitate a restoration of Jewish community to many who had hitherto felt alienated because of their marriage. In the wake of the initial events, couples were brought back together for additional meetings. 'Social arrangements were made and couples met outside the group; on one occasion, a Passover meal was shared.'[106]

For Romain, the key aim was to help such Jews to understand that they were welcome in the community and could play a role in it, that 'just because you married somebody not Jewish it doesn't mean to say that you're any less Jewish'. This was not just a matter of goodwill but crucial to the future of Judaism as Romain saw it. Engagement with interfaith couples, he recalls, had the potential to 'bring back Jews' into the fold. It offered a way to keep 'the Jew Jewish and it also meant we often kept the next generation as well'. At the Sternberg seminars intermarriage was not presented as optimal, but neither was it understood as the end of the road. Instead, recognising the realities of life choices for British Jews, the programme began to work through the challenges of interfaith relationships in a new and more optimistic way, mindful of the need to draw such Jews back towards the faith, not least to ensure that their children understood and could partake in their Jewish parent's heritage. The Sternberg seminars ran, after 1988, for twenty-five years, and similar events were held around the country.

Even within Progressive Judaism, however, some people were 'nervous' about the seminars. Traditionally conservative, and keen not to give ammunition to those in Orthodox circles who readily questioned the credibility of Progressive theology and practice, some Reformers didn't want to put their heads 'above the parapet' on this issue.[107] Certainly, the seminars established a clearer distance between Orthodox and Progressive approaches. For while many participants in the Sternberg seminars came from Orthodox backgrounds (and while there would have been support for the events among many members of Orthodox synagogues), most leadership figures in the Orthodox community dismissed the Sternberg approach as ill-advised and potentially dangerous.[108] The director of the Jewish Marriage Council argued that the seminars sent 'a double message. It is not OK to intermarry, but if you do you will be all right afterwards.'[109] Underpinning such reactions was a worry that the acceptance offered by Progressive Judaism would encourage more Jews to take this path, 'just the opposite of what our position should be'. The line being held by Romain and other organisers (that they disapproved of intermarriage but wished to support Jews after it had happened) was attacked in some circles as dishonest; indeed Romain recalls being 'lacerated for doing it'.[110] The rabbi of Reading's Hebrew Congregation accused him of dealing not only with married, but also with engaged couples, who 'took considerable reassurance simply from the prospect of attending'. 'I am stunned beyond words', Rabbi Goodhardt asserted, 'how people who claim to have the interests of Jewry at heart, who claim the title of "rabbi", can even associate themselves with such a course, let alone plan and run it.'[111]

Responses to intermarriage exposed, at this moment, a fault line in the British Jewish community between pragmatists and Progressives on one hand, and the Orthodox and conservative on the other. What was at stake, to all involved, was nothing less than the future of British Jewry, as argument raged about the extent to which a more inclusive Progressive Judaism (which would welcome and nurture interfaith couples) might be part of a solution. In the meantime, new opportunities were seized upon by many intermarried Jews, who embraced growing Progressive acceptance and often joined these kinds of communities.[112] In Birmingham, mixed-faith couples drew strength from the welcome that they (and their non-Jewish partners) received in the Progressive synagogue, from the inclusion of their children, and the presence of each other. It was great, one interviewee told me, to meet 'other people like us'. It was 'reassuring', said another, to see in the Progressive community 'that other people were producing these loving, happy, highly successful families'.[113]

*   *   *

While RSGB (unlike the Liberal Jewish Synagogue) did not formally accept the legitimacy of patrilineal Jews until a rabbinical working group addressed the issue in 2013, it is clear that many Orthodox thinkers in post-war Britain saw the policies of Progressive Judaism across the board as a threat to the traditional boundaries of the community, boundaries that were becoming ever more porous as interfaith marriage became more common.[114] Rabbi Goodhardt's attack on Jonathan Romain's status as a rabbi highlights the stakes of this argument; how, to some, the acceptance or accommodation of intermarriage invalidated any claim to be working in the religious interests of the Jewish community. All the while, intermarriage continued in post-war Britain. While mainstream Jewish bodies fought to prevent it, or at least mitigate its effects, for other Jews the practice was increasingly understood as an unavoidable opportunity, not as the end of the line for the old faith. If Jews who had married out were embraced, Romain argued in 2005, 'we will gain not only them but their non-Jewish partners as well'.[115] Observing practice in the United States, Cromer noted that 'reluctant acceptance turned into a warm embrace'

146

as US Jewish bodies realised that intermarriage 'may lead to a net gain rather than a loss of American Jewry'.[116]

For this to be the case, Jewish communities needed to be accessible to non-Jewish partners. Progressive Jewish practice had, Dow Marmur argued, 'saved thousands and thousands of families for Judaism' in this context.[117] Of course, the type of Judaism that grew from the Progressive approach was not easy to swallow in Orthodox communities. Here, resistance was significant and enduring. The Orthodox would accept patrilineal Jews, Romain quipped, 'on the same day the Pope gets married'.[118] Whether, in the end, intermarriage was to be loathed and resisted, or accepted and even embraced, ultimately depended on what constituted a Jew in the eye of the beholder. As such, to a significant extent, attitudes towards intermarriage continue to differ between Orthodox and Progressive theologians. Among the latter, where Jewish law is understood as adaptable and responsive to broader society, allowing the participation of mixed-faith families (and embracing patrilineal Jews) has been considerably easier.

Meanwhile, as Karen Glaser recently put it in the *Jewish Chronicle*, 'real life can get in the way of theory', so that neither Progressive nor Orthodox responses to intermarriage have been consistent or clear-cut.[119] Despite the objections of rabbinical bodies, in a significant number of traditional Orthodox families non-Jewish partners have been accepted and welcomed. Even where synagogal participation has not been an option, non-Jewish partners and the children of mixed marriages have been incorporated into traditions and rituals in the Jewish home, where the arbiters have been parents and other family members (and not rabbis). In Progressive communities, moreover, as ideas about inherent differences between Jews and non-Jews persisted, it would be a mistake to say that families have always supported interfaith relationships. Anxieties that intermarriage spelled the end of truly Jewish people were more common in Orthodox communities, but they did not end there by any means. Indeed, for many Jewish people of all hues, the idea of racial or ethnic dilution remained a concern in the post-war period. To many, Judaism was a birthright, a matter of ethnicity and not negotiation. On these terms, intermarriage was a threat to Jewish integrity, to an ancient ethnic stream.

In the face of divided, uncertain, yet increasingly accepting Jewish stances towards intermarriage, the practice has continued to grow, an inevitable consequence of religious decline and assimilation. While its prevalence has not reached the same level as in the USA, recent research confirmed that the 'rate has been steadily rising' since 'at least the early 1970s'.[120] Many Jewish bodies continue to work to stem the flow, but it seems unlikely that this pattern will reverse. For most Jewish young people intermarriage is a possibility, even if they are committed to living Jewish lives. For some, there is no contradiction between the two. Many mixed-faith families have come to navigate Jewish spaces and traditions in an autonomous spirit of confidence and determination. The idea that, as one of my Progressive interviewees suggested, 'You can make your own Judaism. You can define it in a way that you want to'[121] encapsulates a challenge that has faced traditional religious bodies across faiths in post-war Britain, wherein the needs, desires, expectations and beliefs of individuals have pushed against the rules and regulations of previous generations. Partly this growing confidence has stemmed from a wider social awareness that claims of ethnic purity are inherently problematic, that 'each of us is a part of the other, that we are so unalterably tainted by a messy and heartbreaking history that any claim to purity or separation becomes insupportably fragile'.[122]

On these terms, individuals and families in post-war Britain have increasingly taken it upon themselves to decide what they are and will be. Here, the lived religion of Judaism has evolved away from the agreed rules of synagogal communities in a myriad of idiosyncratic and personal ways. After all, as Meredith McGuire has explained, 'at the level of the individual, religion is not fixed, unitary, or even coherent'.[123] Seeking out communities and rabbinic authorities that were prepared to engage on their terms (or simply managing without this support and validation), mixed-faith families have 'reshaped and reformed, sometimes creating new, blended forms of their traditions'.[124] In this atmosphere, religious roles and drivers can take unexpected turns, which have confounded traditional expectations about mixed-faith partnerships. Often it has ended up being non-Jewish mothers (supporting apathetic Jewish fathers) who have been the 'catalysts for Jewish practice' in mixed-faith homes.[125] Feeling that it is the right thing to do, or wanting to support their adopted community, such parents have commonly been the ones who have 'enrolled children in Jewish religious education and practiced rituals with them at home'.[126] Such mothers may or may not choose to become Jews themselves. There are numerous shades of messy compromise and accommodation, many levels of acceptance and inclusion.

For some in the community, intermarriage remains the number one concern and challenge of living in modern Britain. As Dow Marmur put it, 'Our long history of Diaspora has taught us how to be Jewish in the face of persecution. But we have not yet learnt how to remain loyal to our Jewish heritage in the open society.'[127] Yet many British Jews are coming to understand the concept of Jewish loyalty in different terms, whereby interfaith marriage and relationships can be a part of a new (perhaps different) Jewish tradition.

Back in 1932, the novelist Louis Golding used one of his characters, Mr Emmanuel, to imagine a future where distinctions of faith and background would blur into insignificance in the face of young love. Mr Emmanuel dreams of a world in which, 'like the dawn of a brighter day … All races and peoples will go hand in hand together along the road of universal love and the crowds on both sides of the road will throw flowers at them.'[128] In post-war multicultural Britain, characterised by theological softening and rising secularism, the path of interfaith couples is now much easier to tread. And yet, amid ongoing anxiety and uncertainty, Mr Emmanuel's vision of the future remains some way off on the horizon.

7

The nice Jewish boy (who believes in Jesus): Jews, Christianity and the challenge of Messianic Judaism

In July 2019 the *Jewish Chronicle* reported that the Jews for Jesus 'shop' in Hendon was to close its doors. Sited in a prominent position in the heart of one of London's most Jewish neighbourhoods, the premises had served as the public-facing headquarters of Jews for Jesus in London since 2013. Now, however, the newspaper reported, a 'To Let' sign indicated the end of operations, a departure that it felt it 'unlikely that anyone in the local Jewish community will mourn'. While the reasons for the closure were not known to the *Chronicle*, the article gloated that a 'lack of customers perhaps?' might have driven the decision.[1] The first UK director of Jews for Jesus was Richard Harvey. Brought up as a Liberal Jew in South London, Harvey was the organisation's director when it came to Britain in 1991, having previously worked for the Church's Ministry among Jewish People (CMJ). The reason for the Hendon centre closing, Harvey told me, was simply that it was time to try a different approach. Perhaps, he joked, he'd open a hummus bar instead.

That the changing strategy of this small religious movement was considered newsworthy to the *Jewish Chronicle*, as well as the tone of its reporting, highlights something of the feelings that Jews for Jesus can evoke among British Jewry. Often loathed and ridiculed, generations of Jews have been raised to understand Messianic Judaism as a serious threat. As a minority community keen to protect its integrity amid a historically Christian majority, pushing Jesus on to Jews has been constructed as 'a bit like bullying', an insult to Jewish history. Writing tongue-in-cheek in the *Chronicle*, David Aaronovitch categorised the efforts of today's Messianic Jews alongside 'past Jews for Jesus initiatives, such as the Spanish Inquisition'.[2]

Within British Jewish communities that are increasingly tolerant of Jewish people with no belief at all, as well as those who dabble in other religions such as Buddhism or live between faiths and cultures (perhaps because they have married non-Jews), the strong reactions provoked by Jews for Jesus are revealing. They reflect a community traumatised by a long history of subaltern status and persecution in the Christian world, but also one that remains largely united behind a basic belief structure, made visible by the threat of Christian incursion. Yet the continuing presence of Messianic Jews also tells a slightly different story, suggesting that the lines of demarcation between Jews and their Christian neighbours might have become less clearly drawn. This chapter explores Jewish–Christian relations in this context, with a specific focus on Messianic Jewish history. Such communities, and the strong feelings they evoke among many, tell us much about the boundaries of British Jewry and their maintenance. Understanding when and why people are perceived as beyond the pale, and if and how such feelings might change, opens a window into Jewish consciousness, identity and belief.

Jewish–Christian relations in modern Britain

In 1809 Joseph Frey, a Christian preacher who had been born an Orthodox Jew in Posen in 1771, founded the London Society for the Promotion of Christianity among the Jews, colloquially known as the London Jews' Society, the organisation to which CMJ can trace its origins.[3] Frey's group originally put down roots in Bethnal Green, and the first congregation of Jewish believers in Christ met regularly, under his chairmanship, as the *Bnei Abraham* (Children of Abraham) from 1813.[4] At the end of the nineteenth century the Jews' Society operated from Whitechapel, the centre of Jewish migration, ministering to the local population and offering medical care to thousands of sick Jewish people.[5]

The twentieth century, however, slowly brought changes in Jewish–Christian relations that in some ways marginalised the work of CMJ and like-minded bodies. In contrast to the activities cited above, which aimed to draw Jews into the charitable purview of the Church and allow Jewish people ultimately to see a home within the theologies of Christianity, a different set of structures began to appear, designed, at least ostensibly, to bring the Jewish and Christian faiths into conversation as distinct theologies. The impetus behind this change was a Christian desire to do better as regards the treatment of Jewish people, and an aspiration, among some Jews, to enhance their social status and security by increasing broader social recognition of the theological value of Judaism and championing its moral similarities to Christianity.

The roots of these new relationships can be traced back to the London Society for the Study of Religion in 1904, which was set up 'as a Jewish–Christian scholarly club'.[6] This group often met in the home of Liberal Jewish scholar Claude Montefiore, who in this period published substantial theological reflections on Christianity such as *Judaism and St Paul* and the *Synoptic Gospels*, research through which, according to one contemporary review, he sought to 'serve as a mediator between the intelligent Jewish public and modern Christian commentators'.[7] Montefiore's thinking, that it was 'of great importance for Jews to understand and appreciate aright the life and teaching of Jesus', summed up this growing movement, as did his desire to move beyond acrimonious histories and seek out areas of similarity and potential agreement. 'What is positive', Montefiore argued, 'is so much more pleasant and useful than what is negative.'[8]

In the 1920s two further groups developed Jewish–Christian dialogue: a committee of the Presbyterian Church organised to support better understanding between Christians and Jews, and a group emanating from the Liberal Jewish Synagogue that evolved into a Society of Jews and Christians in 1927.[9] That such efforts emerged from Liberal Judaism, where Montefiore was a founder member, was not surprising. This group, very much a minority in British Jewry, felt a strong bond with non-Jewish Britons and was, in Anne Summers's words, 'the sect most inclined to seek rapprochement with the non-Jewish, or more specifically Christian world'.[10] The success of the Society of Jews and Christians was limited, however, by the refusal of the Orthodox Jewish leadership, epitomised in the figure of the Chief Rabbi, to take part, not least because of a (well-founded) belief that many Christians in the Society remained keen to convert Jews away from their faith.[11]

Interfaith dialogue accelerated in the 1930s as Jewish and Christian groups sought community and solidarity in the face of Hitler's attacks on both Jews and non-conforming Church leaders. Deeper ties were nurtured through the decade by some committed Christian theologians. At the centre of these efforts was Anglican clergyman James Parkes, who was to become the most significant and dedicated interlocutor between Jews and Christians in Britain for the next half century. Parkes had published *The Jew and his Neighbour*, a thesis on antisemitism, prior to Hitler's rise to power in 1930.[12] In a similar spirit to Parkes, Methodist William W. Simpson had established a Youth Council on Jewish–Christian Relations and published a book on *Youth and Antisemitism*.[13]

With Parkes pushing hard in the background, the Council of Christians and Jews (CCJ) was formed on the initiative of the Archbishop of York, William Temple, in 1941, while a conference on Jewish–Christian relations was held in London later that year. Temple, who was soon to become Archbishop of Canterbury, chaired the first formal meeting of CCJ in March 1942.[14] Standing together against intolerance and oppression, the evils of Nazism were front and centre of the new organisation's concerns. This atmosphere allowed for a degree of cooperation which had hitherto been difficult to achieve. While substantial worries remained among both Jewish and Christian partners that CCJ risked a dangerous blurring of religious integrities, the danger in Europe afforded, in Tony Kushner's parlance, 'just enough' wriggle room for such anxieties to 'be put aside'.[15]

The challenge of evangelism

For CCJ to be able to function at all, Jewish anxiety about the Christian desire for Jewish conversion needed to be addressed. CCJ, at the outset, confirmed that 'neither conversionist activities or hopes would be promoted' through the organisation.[16] The assurance that Christians would make no attempt to evangelise to Jews, however, was not simple to give. William Temple, urged by Parkes to refuse patronage of CMJ (which fell traditionally to the Archbishop of Canterbury as part of his office), felt unable to surrender the role and confirmed his commitment to evangelism, even as he accepted the sensitivities involved. He told Parkes:

> I do not think I could interpret my interest in promoting Christian–Jewish friendship as in any way precluding an equal interest in attempting to convert Jews, because that does appear to me to be a Christian obligation; and if I had to choose it would take precedence of the other.[17]

Yet as the full extent of the Holocaust became better known, the CCJ approach, wherein Christianity treated Judaism as a valid and relevant theological tradition and didn't evangelise in the manner of CMJ, did become stronger. As Patrick Rodger, former Bishop of Manchester, recalled, 'Certainly in the atmosphere of Manchester and its friendships between Christians and Jews the CMJ and its policy of conversion was very much frowned upon.'[18] Numerous Church figures cited the Holocaust as evidence that Christianity had lost any moral right to preach to Jews, and instead promoted the idea that Christians should seek Jewish forgiveness for the European antisemitism that had culminated in genocide. As David Sheppard, Bishop of Liverpool, told the Liverpool Diocesan Synod in 1989, 'our repentance from the terrible things Christians have done to Jews down the centuries should include renouncing such approaches as targeting Jewish people for evangelism'.[19] As far as Christians of the CCJ mould were concerned, Walter Barker explained, 'the missionary society [was seen as] an anachronism and its work a positive hindrance to better relationships between Christians and Jews'.[20]

This evolving relationship between Christianity and Judaism could not, however, entirely dispense with the theological and historical Christian commitment to spreading the word of Jesus to all non-believers, including Jews. As Temple's initial reticence indicated, even some of those Christian leaders who were active in CCJ did not feel able to abandon core principles of evangelism. Patrick Rodger, for example, conceded that despite his commitment to 'repent' and 'learn' from the Jewish community, he had 'never been able to deny that there is a place for the Church's ministry among the Jews'.[21] And like Rodger, local leaders often found evangelical activity in principle difficult to reject, even as they stood up against certain methods and practices. For example, the Rt Revd Professor R. P. C. Hanson, reporting for CCJ on a case where 'a Jewish lady' in Didsbury had complained about local Christian preaching, 'refused to accept that all attempts on the part of Christians to convert Jewish people were necessarily sinful'. Instead, he felt, both faith groups 'should be free to attempt to convert each other, though dishonest and unfair methods must be condemned'.[22]

On this tricky matter some Christians in CCJ hoped to eke out a middle ground that would be acceptable to Jewish partners, whereby it would be understood that missionary activities were not being prioritised, but would be pursued ethically and in a way that did not specifically target Jewish people. In this spirit, a CCJ statement from 1985 repudiated 'the selection of any particular groups for special missionary activity' and urged Christians instead to 'strengthen people within their own family, and not promote conversions'.[23] Jewish partners could be reassured, or so it was hoped, that Christians were on a journey away from the idea of Jewish conversion. Peter Jennings thus advised Moshe Davis, from the Chief Rabbi's office, 'Just for your comfort, seven-eighths of the Christian world does not believe in the proselytising of Jews. The remaining eighth is diminishing slowly.'[24]

In 1992 George Carey, the Archbishop of Canterbury, became the first archbishop since 1841 to decline to serve as the patron of CMJ, citing his need 'to nurture trust across the boundaries of the faith communities' and his recognition that 'many Jewish people do not believe that CMJ respects their integrity'.[25] For those involved in CMJ this decision felt like a betrayal of faith. As one active CMJ member put it, 'if the Bible instructs us to give the good news of the resurrection of Jesus to others and then we deny that, well if the Archbishop is denying that, where does that leave the rest of us?'[26] In the wake of Carey's decision, however, no subsequent Archbishop of Canterbury has acted as CMJ's patron. While the Anglican Church, then, has never formally surrendered its commitment to spreading the Good News to all, CMJ and others (who focus their efforts specifically on ministering to Jewish people) have seemingly been moved, if not out of the community of the Church, then certainly some distance from its theological centre.

Jews for Jesus comes to Britain

Although significant ambiguities in Christian attitudes towards mission persisted (and persist), many Christians baulked at the tactics and tone of certain evangelical groups and were willing to criticise them publicly. No group served the function of whipping boy in this way more than Jews for Jesus. CCJ's Jim Richardson, for example, railed against Jews for Jesus as an organisation that was not worthy of Christian defence. In his 1989 report to the CCJ executive, he argued: 'CCJ will do all it can to arouse Christian concern about the growth of this imported organisation, to encourage church leaders to publicly state their objections, and privately to use their influence where it matters.'[27] Here, the US-imported style of evangelism, open in intent and loud in volume, was perceived as totally unacceptable. To Catholic priest Gordian Marshall, such evangelists may have been 'young, charming and naïve', but they were 'deadly in the way they influence people, subjecting them to pressures similar to those exerted by salesmen from the Banks, Travel companies, etc.'[28]

Jews for Jesus began across the Atlantic in San Francisco in 1973.[29] Founded by the Jewish-born American Moishe Rosen, the organisation came into being after Rosen was dismissed by the American Board of Missions to the Jews, which did not appreciate his independent spirit or the mounting hostility from local Jewish communities.[30] In 1976 Rosen visited Northern Ireland to intercede in the Troubles, a visit that allowed Richard Harvey to meet him at a conference at the London Bible College, organised under the auspices of CMJ.[31] Harvey was impressed with Rosen's message and keen to learn more. A few years later, at the Greenbelt Christian Music Festival, he recalled being inspired by a Messianic Jewish band from Philadelphia called Lamb. 'They were singing the Shema in sort of Israeli folk rock and I thought, this is where I want to be.'[32] Subsequently attending a conference in Harrisburg Pennsylvania, Harvey remembers the impact of these meetings on his personal faith: 'I went out a

Christian, I came back a Messianic Jew.'[33] It was a religious epiphany that would soon bring Jews for Jesus to the United Kingdom.

Harvey's sojourn in the USA led him (alongside four colleagues who had also attended the conference in Harrisburg) to form a Messianic Fellowship in London, and, after training in the US, to open the British branch of Jews for Jesus in 1991.[34] Jews for Jesus burst on to the British scene with a full-page advertisement in *The Times*, foregrounding Harvey's leadership and emphasising his Jewishness. 'You don't have to be Jewish to celebrate Christmas', the advert quipped, 'but it helps.' In the centre of the page was a photograph of the smiling Harvey who, the advert explained, was very much a Jewish person. Richard loved 'borscht, gefilte fish and the occasional game of Kaluki'. He thought that his mother's chicken soup was 'the best in the world'. Having established his kosher credentials, the article then threw a curve ball. Jewish Richard, 'it might surprise you to discover ... is also a follow of Y'shua (the Jewish way to say Jesus)'.[35]

While the Chief Rabbi complained about Jewish 'targeting' in the advert, and the veteran journalist Bernard Levin dismissed the message as 'slop', Jews for Jesus had arrived on the UK stage in a memorable manner.[36] In its first year it had not only taken a full-page advert in one of the nation's prominent broadsheets, but it had also been profiled in an episode of the BBC's documentary series *Heart of the Matter*.[37] With its unapologetic style and catchy name, Jews for Jesus was difficult to ignore. As Harvey told me, 'I just think I was looking for a high-profile approach. I mean Jews for Jesus is like Drink Coca Cola. It's a slogan. But it's such a powerful statement.'[38] Certainly, Jews for Jesus was quick to attract the attention of Britain's Jewish communities, many of which felt an urgent need to stop it in its tracks.

Jewish responses to Jews for Jesus

Jewish objections to Messianic Jewish communities such as Jews for Jesus were rooted in a determined rejection of the theological contention that it was possible to be Jewish *and* believe in Jesus as the Messiah.[39] To Rabbi Shmuel Arkush (who went on to lead the Jewish community's campaign against missionary activities, Operation Judaism), a person could not 'be a practising Jew and a practising Christian at the same time'. The Jewish and Christian faiths were 'mutually exclusive'.[40] In day-to-day life, this firm rejection of Messianic Jewish theology meant that Messianic Jews would not be accepted as part of, or generally tolerated within, mainstream Jewish communities. One Messianic

Jew recalls the denial of his request to join a local Liberal synagogue in these terms. 'One of them said to me you've got to decide are you a Jew or are you a Christian. You can't be both.'[41]

At the heart of Messianic Jewish theology, however, was the contention that a person simultaneously could be Jewish and Christian, and indeed that being a Jewish believer in Christ was the divine will. As one Messianic Jewish interviewee explained, 'I don't feel that I have left my faith in any way because I'm a Jewish woman who believes in the Jewish anointed one of Israel.'[42] Richard Harvey's thinking echoes the point: 'If Y'shua really is the Messiah, I'm still Jewish, it's no sin to be Jewish, you don't have to stop being Jewish when you become a disciple of Jesus.'[43] This challenge posed substantial questions about what Jewishness meant at the most basic level, especially in an age when it was widely accepted that many British Jews did not understand or articulate their Judaism (or at least not predominantly) within theological parameters. Speaking to CCJ's Advisory Group on Missionary Activity in 1987, one participant highlighted the issue as follows:

> From the Jewish side it has largely been assumed that, once a Jew converts or once somebody in my position submits to baptism, he or she ceases totally to be a Jew. This is an understandable but naïve view, particularly as Judaism is so far from being solely a matter of religion … it never has been the case that a Jew who becomes a Christian ceases to be a Jew in his own self-perception.[44]

This view, however, was not in line with the thinking of many people in the Jewish community, who saw in Messianic Jewry an unequivocal departure from both Judaism and Jewish heritage. For Jewish faith leaders, Messianic beliefs entailed a 'desecration of two traditions' and were even dismissed as insane.[45] Harvey recalls sitting down with two prominent (Progressive) rabbis 'who, in the politest way possible', told him that he was 'crazy and should see a psychiatrist'.[46] Similarly, another rabbi denied to Harvey the very possibility of his being a Jewish Christian, telling him, 'I'm very sorry, you don't exist.'[47]

This Jewish rejection was not merely a matter of theological incredulity. Rather, much of the Jewish community saw the Messianic Jewish message as an existential threat and reacted with anger and hostility. In Los Angeles, the far-right Jewish Defense League stole a Sefer Torah from a Messianic community and 'hurled rocks through a window'.[48] In Toronto, David Rausch described Jewish intimidation of a local Messianic group as 'defy[ing] logic and even decency at times'.[49] In Britain, Richard Harvey recalls being 'spat at' and 'beaten up', while Shmuel Arkush remembers counselling 'young people who wanted to go out and thump them'.[50] When a Messianic Jew attempted to state his views at a meeting in Edgware United synagogue about 'How to Combat Missionaries', he was 'immediately surrounded by hats and harangued in a fashion that has probably never happened to him before'.[51] In an attempt to persuade the Jewish community to speak out against such violence, Robert Weissman asked Chief Rabbi Sacks to provide 'a clear statement that you disapprove of threats of violence being made to missionaries of the Jews'.[52]

The extent of this hostility is comprehensible in terms of a long-standing Jewish resistance to Christian influence, but also indicates a post-Holocaust, 'never again' mindset, whereby Jewish communities were quick to challenge anything or anyone that threatened Jewish recovery and continuity. Dan Cohn-Sherbok has argued that 'the history of Christian anti-Semitism' rendered Jews who followed Jesus 'traitors to the Jewish people ... as having committed the ultimate act of ethnic and religious betrayal'.[53] Links were frequently drawn between the actions of Messianic Jews, antisemitic violence and the Holocaust. For example, Rabbi Arye Forta told *The Times*, regarding Jews for Jesus, of his fear that 'the missionaries [wer]e trying to do what Hitler and Stalin failed to achieve'.[54] Having survived the Nazi onslaught, Arkush argued on *Heart of the Matter*, the space desperately needed by Jewish communities to recover from genocide was being threatened by the missionaries:

> Jewish people not so long ago fled from Europe because of persecution, of being singled out and targeted ... a very high percentage of our educational institutions, intelligentsia, were eradicated by the Germans, it takes many generations to rebuild this ... and we just want to get on with the job, be members of society and basically be left alone.[55]

Such Jewish responses to Messianic Judaism were articulated amid the widespread belief that groups such as Jews for Jesus employed dark and devious tactics to drag Jews away from the fold, so that, as one letter writer put it, 'sophisticated modern and insidious methods of mass communication and indoctrination might succeed where torture once failed'.[56] To Jewish opponents, Messianic Judaism was a cult, preying on the vulnerable, attacking the underbelly of an unsuspecting, traumatised community. Most Jewish leaders and activists argued that Messianic Judaism was merely a cloak for Christianity, an elaborate ruse to bring reticent Jews into the Christian fold. No one articulated this view more clearly than Arkush, who believed that the whole enterprise was a new American evangelical tactic to achieve Jewish conversions. 'What they are doing here', he explained, 'has been specially worked out there. They take Jews and convince them that they are remaining Jews, while in reality they are giving them a Christian faith.'[57]

On these terms, Moishe Rosen had simply put old wine in new bottles, offering floundering evangelical groups a new approach to get at Jews. 'He was able to persuade the failing Christian community in America that wanted to convert Jews ... that he had a new way of doing it.'[58] This 'way of doing it', to Arkush and many others, had deception at its heart. Jews were welcomed into spaces that looked Jewish, sounded Jewish, even tasted Jewish, and were then lured into the Christian world while their guard was down. Arkush told *Heart of the Matter*:

> It's all a front. It's a dressing up in order to get the Jews interest and then to convert him. If you look at all their periodicals, it's full of Jewish symbolism, the Menorah, the seven branched candelabra, eight branch candelabra, you know the wearing of Jewish style dress, singing of Hebrew songs, they've even now taken the New Testament and taken out all the anglicised phraseology and put in Hebrew words to make it look more Jewish. They don't even refer to Jesus by his more well-known name any more, they try and use a Hebrew word.[59]

No doubt, the style, practice and presentation of Messianic Judaism did blur into mainstream Judaism in a way that could be confusing. Anthropologist Francine Samuelson attended a Messianic Jewish service in 1998 and noted, 'If I did not know where I was and what I was participating in, I would have been very confused.'[60] But of course, Messianic Jews would argue, people who attended such services did know exactly where they were. Indeed, Samuelson concluded that she had never seen 'deceptive proselytising' in her 'ten years of observing the movement'.[61]

But to many Jewish leaders and thinkers, the theology of Messianic Judaism was specifically designed to cause confusion. It was, Arye Forta argued, a 'tactical masterpiece' that would 'leave most Jews bewildered'.[62] Messianic Jewish missionaries, Forta claimed, were trained 'to present themselves as a cross between stage performers and high-pressure salesmen', consciously targeting the vulnerable. Messianic Jews, he alleged, had followed his 9- and 11-year-old children home from school and given them balloons with slogans about 'loving Jesus'.[63] Rabbi Jacob Schochet warned that the Jewish elderly required special protection from such missionaries. In the US, he noted, 'there had been a great effort against senior citizens in old age homes in Miami and California'.[64] In Britain, a leaflet designed to counter missionary activity told the terrifying story of a lonely Jewish woman, about to have major heart surgery, who fell victim to 'staff of evangelical inclination, working within the hospital [who] recognised her as easy prey and arranged for her to be visited'. The woman ended up being 'ripped apart' by the Messianic message. 'At a low ebb the only way out for her was to kill herself, which she duly did.'[65]

Operation Judaism and the defence of Jewish students

Jewish concern about missionary activity focused on universities, where it was feared that Jewish students could easily fall prey to proselytising advances, far as they were from their normal support networks and families. Student chaplains such as Shmuel Arkush were convinced that missionaries were making it their business to target Jewish students with a vigour and resource that necessitated a strong response. 'Why were you a Christian clergyman on campus?', Arkush questioned. 'You were out there to get souls. And you were being told that one of the biggest souls you can get hold of is a Jewish one and you were given a whole range of material to do it.'[66] As missionaries cloaked their true intentions, young Jews could be tricked into accepting 'free kosher meals as an inducement to attend gatherings', only for 'evangelists then [to] try to interest ... [them] ... in "born again" Christianity'.[67] The Jewish press reported that vulnerable students were being 'lured to parties', falling into Christianity while their guard was down.[68] This worry became a panic after the suicide of Benjamin Lesser in December 1979.

Benjamin Lesser left his family home in the West Midlands to study at university in London. There he developed a relationship with an evangelical Christian community known as the 'Invisible Church'. This church met in Earls Court under the leadership of South African pastor Nelson Nurse. It was, in Richard Harvey's analysis, a group that 'today we would call a new religious movement but in those days we called something like a cult ... it was just a very powerful, high demand, Church'.[69] Under considerable psychological strain, Lesser took his own life, triggering a furious, grief-ridden response from the Jewish community, spearheaded by his parents. Discussing the case on Radio 4's *Sunday* in January 1980, Lesser's mother claimed that her son's interactions with Christianity had left him so confused that 'at one stage "he believed himself to be Jesus Christ"'.[70] On this programme, a representative from CMJ countered that while the Invisible Church might have been 'perhaps over-zealous', he believed that 'Christ is your saviour as well as ours'. Lesser's father interrupted him, asking the show's host, 'Why can't he leave us alone?'

In the wake of the tragedy, the Invisible Church denied responsibility for Lesser's mental state. Nurse told a London Weekend Television investigation that when he had last seen Lesser, 'his problem was not the Church. In fact he had just called to tell me the tremendous news of his "relationship with Jesus".'[71] Many within the Jewish community, however, took a sharply different view. For Shmuel Arkush, who had counselled Lesser and tried to support him, the death was traumatic. 'I'll not forget. They just ruined this boy, they ruined him. And he died because of it ... I was having dealings with him, I was trying to help, he was in a very very bad way ... Whatever I said, they came along and said the opposite.'[72] Seven years later Arkush set up Operation Judaism to lead the charge against missionary activities. A high-profile campaign, Operation Judaism brought concerns about missionaries to the front and centre of British Jewish consciousness, placing a particular focus on supporting Jewish students.

As a student, Arkush himself had felt forced to abandon a degree in dentistry because of his university's unwillingness to accommodate Jewish Orthodox lifestyles.[73] As a rabbi, feeling that there was still 'no provision whatsoever' to support Jewish students, he set up the Midlands Region Chaplaincy Board and employed himself as the part-time chaplain. Under these auspices, in 1982 Arkush put on an exhibition at Birmingham's King David Jewish primary school about the pressures faced by Jews at university. This exhibition drew attention to the prevalence of campus antisemitism and anti-Zionism, but 'also pinpointed the increasing missionary activities of so-called Christian Jewish sects among Jewish students'.[74] Still driven by the Lesser case, Arkush's campus work became more and more focused on the issue of missionaries. To this end, Lesser's parents appealed for greater support for the Chaplaincy Board.[75]

Money for this kind of work was, however, hard to sustain. With many calls on the community's resources, in 1985 the Chaplaincy fund suffered 'severe financial problems' and Arkush's contract was terminated.[76] This left only one rabbi, Fishel Cohen, responsible for Jewish students across a huge swathe of the country. Not to be put off, Arkush visited Chief Rabbi Jakobovits in London and proposed Operation Judaism as a nationwide anti-missionary campaign. He recalls the conversation:

> I said, you know, Lord Jakobovits, we have a problem. I said there's a big problem, I said, the missionaries. He says, is there a problem? We do? So I said yes, you know, you need to do something about this. He said, we do? So, I said yes, somebody needs to be put in charge, so he said, well done. I ended up coming out being ... in charge of Operation Judaism, that's how the whole thing formed.[77]

Operation Judaism was provided with start-up money from the Board of Deputies, the Office of the Chief Rabbi and the Lubavitch Foundation, a coalition that added weight, as well as badly needed resources, to the campaign. In terms of the idea, it seems likely that it was inspired by anti-missionary activity in America. There, in 1985, Rabbi Bentzion Kravitz had established 'Jews for Judaism', which worked to draw Jewish people away from missionary activity and was similarly focused on university campuses.[78] While training in New York, Arkush recalled his experience of working in this field, 'schlepping out' young Jews who had become involved with alternative religious practices in 'the time of the gurus'.[79]

Operation Judaism was launched at a press conference in Birmingham in May 1986. Arkush explained that over thirty missionary societies in Britain were presently working to convert Jews, with access to a battle fund in excess of a million pounds. Armed with missionary literature that he had gathered from university chaplaincies, Arkush outlined his campaign strategy. Operation Judaism would produce its own pamphlets as well as a video to counter missionary activities. These resources, it was hoped, would support local Jewish communities to organise and defend themselves.[80] Looking back, Arkush recalls the campaign in simple terms. Missionaries were 'chupping people left, right, middle and centre ... I said, this ain't gonna happen – we're gonna stop it.'[81] Soon he was working nationwide, 'appearing at Jewish Societies on almost every University campus'.[82] Reporting to Operation Judaism's management committee, Arkush explained that the campaign was monitoring eighteen situations across different universities, for example, supporting 'a brilliant girl from Oxford' who had had to 'discontinue her studies because of her infatuation with Jesus', and monitoring a student at Leicester, 'a pupil of Richard Harvey', who 'was quietly waiting to use his new position to convert others'.[83]

Operation Judaism set out to support Jewish students with theological and practical advice through its video, manual and fact pack. This material offered a raft of theological interventions explaining why, from a Jewish point of view, the idea that Jesus was the Messiah was simply not tenable. The conclusions and analysis left little to the reader's imagination. Messianic Judaism, the manual concluded, was idolatry and stood on flimsy theological foundations. To become a Messianic Jew, one would have to:

a. Accept a "messiah" who failed to fulfil the messianic prophecies,
b. Believe that you are fulfilling Judaism by violating most of the commandments that G-d gave us,

c. Maintain that the written traditions of an ancient Jewish messianic sect are equivalent (and even superior to) the word of G-d conveyed to us by the Bible,

d. Bring yourself to view Torah-true, living Judaism as a distortion of Truth,

e. And participate in the worship of a being other than G-d.[84]

Looking at the matter as laid out by Operation Judaism could only lead the Jewish reader to one sensible conclusion, specifically that Messianic Judaism was flawed and meaningless. On these grounds, Messianic missionaries' only hope was to fool the vulnerable with dishonest and manipulative practices.

Presenting Messianic Jews as dangerous manipulators, Operation Judaism set out to help students fight them off in local situations. At Cambridge University in 1989, the campaign supported the local Jewish Society to engage with 'Cambridge Mission Week', which set out to bring students into the Christian fold and had invited Richard Harvey as one of its speakers 'in order to "target" as many Jewish students as possible'.[85] With the help of Operation Judaism, two Jewish student leaders conducted a substantial defensive campaign. They approached the local Christian Union (CU) and showed them Operation Judaism's video, leaving the CU 'genuinely shocked'.[86] While Harvey's invitation to speak was not rescinded, a set of ground rules were set out to minimise the risk to Jewish students and maximise their preparedness to withstand Messianic pressure. The CU agreed, Jewish students reported back to Operation Judaism, 'to suggest to any student thinking of conversion that they first approach the Jewish Society'.[87] Efforts were also made to ensure that the Jewish student community understood the challenge they were facing. One student leader wrote an article in the Jewish Society's weekly newsletter warning of missionary tactics that targeted 'the elderly, the sick, the lonely and the isolated', and Jewish students were sent a letter in advance of Mission Week which described Jews for Jesus as 'an insidious organisation' and Messianic Jewish theology as 'false and paradoxical'.[88] Jewish students were advised not to argue with missionaries who were 'trained to sidestep your objections' and were warned that their 'emotions and insecurities' would be targeted. Although 'no Jewish students converted' as a result of Mission Week, Cambridge's Jewish student leaders argued that the event had shown the 'burning need for increased awareness on this issue' and 'full support (both practical and financial)'.[89] This analysis resonated with that of Arkush and Operation Judaism, and was reflected in its campaign video, *Target Jews*.

Made by Tommy Schwarcz, *Target Jews* used a series of interviews to highlight the devious tactics of missionaries in Britain. In the film, a Jewish housewife from Birmingham, Caroline Grossman, explained that she had received unsolicited correspondence from a Hebrew Christian as she was grieving for her mother. A divorced, disabled, single parent, Grossman argued that she was an 'easy target' because of her vulnerability. The documentary's narrative told of pamphlets on Jewish themes that were 'often impossible' to distinguish from Jewish material, designed consciously to deceive and confuse Jewish people. This kind of literature, Arkush explained, was created using the 'very latest techniques in marketing and advertising'. 'Enormous amounts of money', *Target Jews* asserted, were 'being devoted to the conversion of Jews'.

At the centre of the production was the tragic story of Benjamin Lesser, who was introduced as a 'young student driven to suicide by the constant harassment he received'. In an emotional interview with Lesser's parents, his mother explained that missionaries had brainwashed her son, having initially invited him to a Chanukah party under the auspices of CMJ. They had refused to back away from their attempt at conversion, she asserted, even when Benjamin was admitted to hospital with depression, and had ultimately driven him to his death. Students, the video explained, were the 'prime targets'. One, Janet Evans, told of how she had been approached by an undercover evangelical Christian at her first Jewish Society Friday night meal at university. Overall, this powerful video pulled no punches. Missionary activity, according to *Target Jews*, added up to a new chapter of Christian antisemitism. 'Over the years', it explained, Jews had 'been attacked from many quarters'. This attack was 'still happening today' as Jewish souls, instead of Jewish bodies, assumed the focus of Christian attention.

Unsurprisingly, *Target Jews* made a considerable impact, bringing the issue to life for hitherto unaware Jewish audiences. At a meeting about missionary activity in Edgware, the *Jewish Chronicle* reported that watching *Target Jews* was 'by far the most realistic part of the evening'.[90] Arkush himself recalls that when he showed *Target Jews* to a meeting of the Board of Deputies, 'there was furore, the Board had never seen anything like this, this was bigger than the Second World War'.[91] Having watched the video, Shimon Cohen wrote to Arkush to pass on the Chief Rabbi's message that he and his wife 'were both extremely impressed with the documentary', were 'delighted in particular with the commentary', and wanted to 're-affirm [their] continued support for Operation Judaism'.[92] On the back of *Target Jews*, local groups were set up in conjunction with the national campaign. As the community's director of family education in the London suburb of Redbridge told the *Jewish Chronicle*, 'We were so impressed, and scared, by what Rabbi Arkush had to say that the audience was only too ready to set up the counter missionary group.'[93]

Messianic identities and the borders of Judaism

There is little doubt that Rabbi Arkush's response to Messianic Judaism aligned with the feelings of many in British Jewish communities who, like him, saw Messianic movements as a sinister threat to Judaism. Such perceptions were rooted in the idea that the kind of Christian-Jewish identities offered by Messianic Judaism were unobtainable, and that the missionaries knew this full well. As the mother of Benjamin Lesser explained in *Target Jews*,

> the whole idea of the missionaries to begin with was for him to keep his Judaism but to recognise Jesus as the messiah … This was the terrible part of it that they split him in two because you can't be Jewish and Christian at the same time. It just isn't possible.

The very notion, she concluded, was simply a tactic to 'brainwash … him so that he would become Christian'. Yet many Messianic Jews did not recognise this picture and rejected the binary division between Judaism and Christianity.

Perhaps Britain's most high-profile Messianic Jew, the singer Helen Shapiro was adamant that her faith journey had not entailed a passage from Judaism to Christianity. Preferring the moniker of 'Jewish believer', she told the *Jewish Chronicle*, 'I have not "converted" to a new religion, neither have I stopped being a Jew … I know more about why I am Jewish, I feel more Jewish and I identify with my people more than ever.'[94] This continuing identification with the Jewish community had been a feature of Hebrew Christianity since the nineteenth century, as Jews who found Jesus refused to acknowledge that their acceptance of Christ eroded their Jewishness.[95] As one believer told me, 'I hate hearing people say that Messianic Jews are no longer Jewish, that is so hurtful, that is a deep wound … I'm Jewish, I always will be.'[96]

The lack of understanding between Jewish and Messianic communities was not unidirectional. For their part, Messianic Jews often failed to realise the extent to which their faith alienated them from mainstream Jewish communities. One individual thus described the rejection of his membership application at a local synagogue after he confessed faith in Christ to the rabbi.

> I started to go to the Liberal synagogue … I was about to sign up when I had to fill in a form and it said where were you married so I told the truth – I said

I was married in the church and [the rabbi] said well what's your view of Jesus? And I said I've got a pretty high view of him. She said well would that view consider that Jesus is the messiah and I said yeah I think he's the messiah so she said well you've just compromised your membership, I hope you realise that...[97]

Incidents such as this indicate a discord between Jews and Messianic Jews regarding the core values of Judaism. Walter Barker, describing Messianic Jews in Israel, told of residents 'born of Jewish parents, living a Jewish life', who did not feel 'any less Jewish' because they believed in Jesus, while a vicar from Bromley, writing in *The Times*, argued that he was both a Jew and 'also a Christian'.[98] These kinds of identities simply sounded unreal to much of the Jewish community. Like the rabbi in the case above, to many Jews, hearing a person express faith in Christ served as an immediate signal that they were not Jewish and disqualified them from community membership.

That this was (and is) the case has made many Messianic Jews feel singled out for exclusion. Following his rejection from synagogue membership, my interviewee reflected, 'if I was gay and Jewish I would be cordially invited, that's nice, I think that's right and good, if I was an atheist they would accept me, or any other stripe really, but they draw the line at that'.[99] On these grounds, Dan Cohn-Sherbok has argued that the Jewish rejection of Messianic Judaism 'makes little sense'. Messianic belief, he asserts, 'is in principle not more radical than the Reconstructionist and Humanistic rejection of a supernatural deity'.[100] And yet for many Jews, bringing Christ to synagogue is perceived as more radical. Whether or not this makes sense, this Jewish stance tells us more than a little about the boundaries of Judaism; that to be accepted as a Jew in contemporary Britain you don't specifically have to believe anything, but there is at least one thing that you absolutely must not believe! Writing about mixed-faith families in the United States, Sylvia Fishman has thus concluded, 'Avoiding Christian activities in their homes still seems to be the bottom line for most American Jews.'[101] Howard Jacobson put it more comically: 'No problem about his not wanting to live a life demonstrably Hebraic, but Jesus, Jesus!'[102]

And yet, as Cohn-Sherbok's intervention suggests, the waters grow muddier. For some Jewish communities and families, forays into Christianity were not the end of the world and could be navigated within a Jewish landscape. While the acceptance of Christ could, and often did, cause ruptures in Jewish families, sometimes it was accepted. When Richard Harvey told his father that he was thinking of attending church as a teenager, his father responded that he was thinking about going too![103] In the end, Harvey's father, one brother and his grandfather all became followers of Jesus. While such a family response was not commonplace, neither, Harvey argues, was the extreme opposite: 'I tried to research the accusation that when Jewish people become Christians the family publish their obituary and have a funeral service for them – I never found any evidence so I think it's like many of the polemical myths that the other tells about the other.'[104]

In most cases, as one might expect, Jewish families found ways to work around the problem. One interviewee explained how her mother insisted on meeting her new Christian friends so that she could be assured that her daughter had not been brainwashed. This meeting allowed for an accommodation, albeit a grudging one. 'She wasn't happy with me, but it allayed her fears that I was in a cult.'[105] Subsequently, this mother maintained a relationship with her daughter, dealing with her Messianic faith from her own distance. When the interviewee was baptised, her mother and sister did not feel able to attend but did send flowers. Subsequently, when she asked her mother if she could pray with her, her mother replied, 'No. When you put the phone down, pray for me.' When, in the wake of the death of Benjamin Lesser, the *Jewish Chronicle* interviewed another young Jewish person who had joined the Invisible Church, they found that he was still living with his Jewish parents in the London suburb of Stanmore. Although the family was far from happy with the situation, an accommodation had been reached, the father even admitting that his newly converted son was 'now a nicer person'.[106]

Similarly, at a community level, dividing lines could sometimes blur. While, in the case above, my interviewee was told that he could not join the synagogue as a member, he was assured by the rabbi that he was 'welcome to worship' there as a visitor, a gesture that is increasingly commonplace across Jewish denominations.[107] Moreover, some members of this community accepted his participation in a way that transcended the grudging toleration of the synagogue. While attending, he explained to me, he made a Jewish friend who subsequently invited him to lead her family's Passover Seder despite knowing about the beliefs that he held in Jesus.[108]

Some Messianic Jews worship in synagogues simply by keeping their controversial opinions to themselves. One interviewee told me that since she had 'come out' as a Messianic Jew, a childhood Jewish friend had confided that she too was a secret believer, while another said that her father had been one.[109] In both cases, secrets were maintained so as not to jeopardise inclusion in the Jewish community and not to cause trouble. Richard Harvey explained that 'Jews come out of the woodwork' when they know they can confide in him, a case similarly made by the CMJ leaders that I have interviewed.[110] Given the potentially hostile attitudes of many Jews towards Messianic Judaism, it is not surprising that those Jews persuaded by or at least curious about Jesus sometimes keep their views to themselves in Jewish spaces, and it seems reasonable to speculate that there is at least a small community quietly keeping a foot in both camps.

For some Jewish people, the hard line taken by those such as Shmuel Arkush was perceived as undesirable and unnecessary. In the wake of the *Heart of the Matter* documentary, Gerald Jacobs, author and literary editor of the *Jewish Chronicle*, dismissed the work of Operation Judaism as hyperbolic and insensitive to the very real tragedies of the Jewish past. Complaining that Arkush was wrongheaded to suggested that missionaries constituted a similar threat to the Holocaust, he argued:

> If your son comes home wide-eyed over a stack of JFJ literature, why not show him how much more the genuine article – authentic Judaism – has to offer (which kicking him out of the home is hardly likely to do)? And if you're frightened that your daughter might succumb to proselytising patter, a warm, family talk might just equip her to say 'no' next time the Moonies or the Joonies come knocking at the door.[111]

*   *   *

As post-war multicultural Britain brought Jews and non-Jews into ever more intimate contact, the interplay between long-standing Jewish fears of Christianity and better day-to-day relations combined to enable what Yaakov Ariel has described as 'an avant garde form of postmodern realities' in the shape of Messianic Jewish movements.[112] These movements disturbed a great many within the Jewish community, but were tolerated by some others. For their small number of members they enabled a new way to be Jewish, albeit a way that has never been accepted by mainstream Jewish bodies of any denomination.

Far from being a mere front for the Church, Messianic communities allowed something of a safe space for those Jewish people who had come to believe in Jesus but retained similar uncertainties about Christianity to other Jewish people. Such Jews could feel, as a recent Anglican report on interfaith explained, 'doubly marginalised'.[113] One Messianic Jew told me that before she had found a Messianic congregation, she had felt isolated and angry about the stance taken towards Jews in the churches she attended. 'I would just feel so angry and I would hurt so much because I'm Jewish and all the things that they were saying … it would cut through me like a knife.'[114] Church communities, another Messianic Jew explained, could be 'hellishly antisemitic', an uncomfortable place for a Jewish believer to be.[115] For many Messianic Jews, it was not only the potentially hostile atmosphere which turned them off churches, it was also the belief that Christianity had appropriated Jesus from the Jewish community in the first instance.

Christ had not intended, one Messianic Jew told me, 'to start a new religion'.[116] The Church, another believer explained, had removed the central place of Judaism from Christ's theology, misappropriating his message by denying its Jewish core.

> The churches don't tell you, they have totally taken all Jewishness out of scripture .. It is called the Christian faith but for me its Judaism … it's an extended branch of Judaism because when … you read Y'shua's teaching, he never came away from the Torah … He stayed with the Jewish faith always.[117]

Jews such as this one needed a space to be able to reject 'the legacy of antisemitism that's been handed down by the Christian Church', but accept 'the truth that Jesus is the Jewish messiah'.[118] Messianic Jewish fellowships provided such a space, allowing Jews to maintain a Jewish life rhythm (celebrating the Jewish sabbath and Jewish festivals) but also to accept Christ. For such people, the rejection of the label Christian was not merely semantic.[119] As one Messianic Jew told me, it was a label that still made him 'bristle a bit'.[120]

Most Jews, however, did not recognise the validity of any such middle ground between the two faiths. Instead, Messianic Jewish activity was generally understood as the latest threat in the history of Christian antisemitism.[121] This was a history that left many Jews feeling safest when they were together, maintaining a substantial degree of communal separation from other faith communities. Arkush's recollection of his own school days in Birmingham offers a case in point. Having experienced antisemitism as an isolated Jewish student in his primary school, he felt safer at secondary school because there were more Jewish children:

> if there was any trouble, and there was every now and then, well you had 39 mates to get together in the playground and deal with the issue and we did, so I was forged in this sort of crucible if you like of how you live in England as a Jew.[122]

In this atmosphere, the Messianic Jewish desire to break down the lines between Jews and non-Jews was mostly perceived as an existential threat. For many, the Holocaust was the obvious point of reference. How, having survived the Nazi onslaught, could Jews allow themselves to fall victim to this new Christian attack? Groups such as Jews for Jesus were labelled as antisemitic because they targeted Jews. Arkush explained, 'I think by definition if you pick on Jews that's antisemitism.'[123]

While the history of antisemitism and the Holocaust loomed large in the articulation of Jewish opposition to Christian evangelism, it was broader anxieties about the decline of Jewish life in Britain that lay at the heart of Jewish concerns. Arkush, for example, had joined the Lubavitch movement, and ended up leading as a rabbi, because he had found post-war British Jewish practice lacking in passion and direction. 'I'd only ever seen people being Jewish because that's what had rubbed off at home, or this is what they were told they were meant to do, or they didn't have the nerve to break away from it.'[124] It was in the context of these kinds of concerns about Jewish communities not managing to inspire the next generation that evangelising Christians seemed so very dangerous. To Arye Forta, the Jewish failure to educate children was opening the door to desertion. With so many people not living an actively Jewish life, Forta argued, parents were 'actively educating their children that Judaism is not meaningful. It need not surprise these parents when their children seek meaning elsewhere.'[125]

In an atmosphere where Jewish religious leaders were struggling to maintain the attention of increasingly secular congregations, it is even arguable that missionary activity served a valuable function, offering a powerful reminder to Jewish parents of the need to maintain levels of devotion, and galvanising the Jewish community against a long-held and easily identifiable foe. This, presumably, was what the Jewish students at Cambridge had in mind when, in their report on Mission Week, they argued, 'Through facing this challenge together, we can strengthen our Jewish identity. If we are coordinated, coherent and united we can turn this threat to good.'[126]

The fear of missionary activities could bring people together in a way that was increasingly hard to achieve. In Stanmore in 1989, the United synagogue told members that it had invited a 'missionary from the "Jews for Jesus" movement to talk' to them. Of course, it had done no such thing. It was merely 'a ploy to pull in the crowds and educate them on the dangers'.[127] A leaflet advertising a subsequent gathering warned congregants, 'THE NEXT CONVERT COULD BE YOUR CHILD'. When Arkush was invited to Stanmore to show *Target Jews*, the event drew in over 400 people.[128] Here in a nutshell was the value of Jews for Jesus to the Jewish community. If they had not existed, perhaps they would have had to be invented.

As for the Jews who adopted Messianic Jewish theology, certainly they have been forced to live on the 'fringes of Judaism', as one of my interviewees explained.[129] In truth, though, it was largely from the fringes of Jewish life that Messianic Jews emerged in most instances. Generally, those Jews who found Jesus were not deserters from Jewish congregations but people who had never actively been Jewish in terms of practice.[130] Given the history of Jewish–Christian relations, many such people still did not want to be termed Christian and instead sought to locate Christ within a Jewish historical and cultural tradition. Looking back to the historical moment before the parting of the ways, Messianic Jewish communities question whether the division of the faiths wasn't a theological error, proposing instead a vision of unity which brings Jews to the front and centre of Christian practice. While in an increasingly secular age some Jewish people can accept, or at least tolerate, such a theology, the history of Christian antisemitism and broader fears of community decline have rendered Messianic Judaism beyond the pale for most Jewish people.

Cases such as that of Benjamin Lesser served to confirm a pre-existing fear of evangelical Christianity in any form, leading many Jews to construct Messianic Judaism as an extreme and cultish threat. While this construction is upsetting and offensive to many Messianic Jews, it has not been entirely unproductive. Community (over-) reaction to Messianic activities has allowed very small groups to achieve a substantial level of attention. When, in 2003, the Board of Deputies called for the banning of a Jews for Jesus advertisement featuring a 'doctored picture' of an Orthodox Jew at the Western Wall wearing a Jews for Jesus T-shirt, Joseph Steinberg, the UK director of Jews for Jesus, sent the Board 'a bouquet of roses in thanks for generating publicity'.[131] Jewish opposition, moreover, added something to the flavour of Messianic Jewish theology, confirming for believers the 'missionary motive' and tying them to a tradition of hostility towards those who set out to spread the Good News.[132]

Perhaps most of all, the reason that Messianic Jews have been so despised by many Jewish people is that their presence draws the eye to the elephant in the room of Jewish–Christian relations – the ongoing refusal of some Christian theologians to abandon their commitment to spreading the Gospel to Jews (and everyone else). Shmuel Arkush was uncertain of the sagacity of seeking friendships with Christian people for this reason. Christians, he worried, would ultimately have an ulterior motive. Writing in 1985, Arkush warned that, to his mind, any Christian 'who says he doesn't believe in missionary activities is a hypocrite or ignorant, or a fool'. On these grounds, Arkush asserted, Christian offers of friendship needed to be regarded with suspicion. 'In a way, if a Christian says, "Let's be friends", I find it sticks in the gullet.'[133]

Although the frankness of these comments drew sharp rebuke from both sides, similar tensions have simmered throughout post-war efforts to build bridges between Jewish and Christian communities. Writing an afterword to the Anglican Church's 2019 publication on Christian–Jewish relations, *God's Unfailing Word*, Chief Rabbi Ephraim Mirvis pointed out the extent to which Christian evangelism continued to pose an ongoing challenge. 'It is as though', Mirvis argued, 'we are jointly building an essential new structure, while simultaneously a small part of the construction team is deliberately destabilizing the building's very foundations.'[134]

The inconvenient truth, as Arkush had earlier pointed out, was that there was, at least for some Christians, no licence to surrender the part of their faith which called for evangelism, so that the message of *God's Unfailing Word* really hadn't changed much from the thinking of William Temple nearly eighty years earlier. The spreading of the missionary message could be managed within strict ethical parameters, it could recede within some Christian theological perspectives, it could be excluded from the operations of the likes of CCJ, but it could not easily vanish from Christianity. For Jews who felt it unwise to mix with those who would ultimately prefer them to be something else, however politely this was expressed, this was a very thorny problem indeed.

In such an atmosphere it is unsurprising that Messianic Jewish communities remain very small, not amounting even to 1% of British Jewish people. Since they follow a tradition that reaches back hundreds of years, it would be wrong to dismiss such groups as an American import. Instead, as Richard Harvey asserts, such communities are 'part of a subculture of British-Jewish or Anglo-Jewish history … even though it sounds like it's brash American in your face evangelism'.[135] Their continued existence speaks to the diversity of British Jewish life, then and now, and also to the pervasive influence of the majority faith on all those who live as minorities in Britain. Jewish opposition to such small groups tells us much about the community's concerns for the future. In an atmosphere where the decline of British Jewish life is ever feared, and past Christian violence far from forgotten, these kinds of groups are likely to remain unpopular in most Jewish circles. All the while, small bands of Messianic Jews continue to navigate the borders of British Jewish life. Often despised but occasionally tolerated, they provoke discussion about what is and isn't Jewish. In an increasingly secular society, where British Jews accept many kinds of diverse and divergent views, Messianic Judaism raises crucial questions. When does a Jew stop being a Jew? And who is in a position to judge?

8

The last outpost of the British Empire: youth movements and kibbutz *aliyah*

Myer Raines, along with twin sister Ena, was born in Manchester in 1923, although he was not to remain there. In many ways typical of his generation, he was the child of Lithuanian and Polish Jewish parents who had migrated to Ireland in 1881 to escape 'the burning Ghettos in Europe', and later moved on to join 'the large Jewish community in Manchester'.[1] For the Raines family, Britain became far more than a temporary refuge. Myer recalls his father feeling deeply proud of his adopted nation, 'the only country in the world that accepted him as a human being, without religious persecution or prejudice'.[2] Myer himself, however, from an early age held a different ideological perspective, believing that Jews would only be safe in their own nation and needed to build a Jewish state in Palestine. For British Jews, he recalled feeling, Zionism was the 'only way'.[3]

Myer Raines's Zionism, and the life he made in Israel, provokes questions. Why did he feel so different from his parents, and from other Jews, as regards remaining in Britain? What was the pull of Israel? And what does this migration tell us about post-war Jewish identities and belonging more broadly? As ever, such stories can't be understood in a vacuum, outside broader British and European history. For Jewish migration to Israel, or *aliyah* as it is generally described by those who did it (and by most of the British Jews who didn't), is invariably a story about pressures and beliefs that came into non-Jewish lives too, albeit in different ways. Migration to Israel speaks to cultures of nationalism, changing religiosities, political radicalism and counterculture. It also, however, speaks to the marginality of ethnic minorities in Britain, continuing cultures of racism and exclusion, and corresponding fears about personal safety and acceptance.

Myer Raines's Zionist education was moulded by his participation in the *Habonim* Jewish youth movement, in which his elder brother Cyril was a leader.

Habonim (literally 'The Builders') was established as a Zionist scouting group in 1929 by the assistant political secretary of the Zionist Executive in London, Wellesley Aron.[4] As a movement, it set out to 'combat assimilation and to introduce young Jews to the Jewish renaissance in Palestine'.[5] For Raines, echoing the words of Yehuda Halevi, *Habonim* would turn his heart 'towards the East' and shape him (as well as many others) into a committed lifelong Zionist.[6] By the mid-1930s *Habonim*'s ideology had crystallised as socialist and committed to *halutziut*, the idea of pioneering Zionist migration to Palestine, specifically to the development of socialist Jewish agriculture through kibbutzim (collective agricultural communities). To this end, *Habonim*, along with other similarly committed youth organisations across Europe, established training farms (*hachsharah*) in Britain to prepare their most committed members for life on kibbutz in Palestine. It was to such a camp, named Gorsey Leaze in Malmesbury, that Raines went to work in 1941. There he met his wife to be (a Jewish refugee from Nazism) and committed his adult life to kibbutz and Zionism.

Soon, however, Raines's Zionist education was interrupted by the Second World War. He was drafted into the British military, choosing the navy because he was advised by local Zionist leaders that Israel would need navy personnel 'when the state comes into existence'.[7] After a post-war period supporting the illegal immigration of Jewish survivors of the Holocaust (most notably crewing the *Exodus* on its ill-fated journey in 1947), Raines moved permanently to Palestine. He joined the ranks of his *Habonim* colleagues at a Jewish Agency camp in Hadera, before serving in the nascent Israeli navy in the Arab–Israeli War of 1948/49. After his release from military service he hitchhiked north to find his friends, who had by that point moved to establish a kibbutz of their own near the town of Rosh Pina in the Galilee. This kibbutz, soon named Kfar Hanassi (the president's village) after the first Israeli President Chaim Weizmann, was established in 1948 by *Habonim* members, bolstered by a small group of European survivors of the Holocaust. Raines, over seventy years later, continues to live there.

When one visits Kfar Hanassi it feels a little bit as though you have arrived at the end of the world. The road from Rosh Pina, which takes you past the Bedouin town of Tuba, literally ends at its gates. Finding the new kibbutz, in its infancy, was, as Raines recalls, no easy matter. Asking for directions, he was told in Rosh Pina to walk eastwards: 'lift your feet to there … go through a long avenue of pine trees, then pass by an abandoned air-field, and then you will get there – just keep going eastwards'.[8] Struggling to follow this cryptic advice, narrowly avoiding local Arab militia, Raines finally located the camp: 'quite suddenly', he remembers, 'I heard the holy tongue spoken with a strong English accent.' Unusual as it sounds, this British-made kibbutz community was far from unique. British migrants bolstered numerous similar kibbutzim in the post-war period, most notably Amiad, Bet Ha'Emek, Kfar Blum, Yasur and Zikim, and established the religious kibbutz of Lavi. But *Habonim*'s Kfar Hanassi, more than anywhere else, has come to represent the British footprint on kibbutz. A survey in 1966 showed that 170 of the kibbutz's adult members came from *Habonim* (nearly all from Britain, though some from Australia).[9]

This chapter reflects on the decision of those British Jews who, like Myer Raines, left the country of their birth to join Israeli kibbutzim. These stories, I argue, offer significant insights into the post-war British Jewish experience of which they remain a part, even in absentia. While only a very small minority of British Jews ultimately chose such a path, the journey to life on kibbutzim such as Kfar Hanassi tells us much about the working and practice of diaspora among British Jewry, Jewish identification and education, and the importance of Israel in the consciousness of many Jewish people. But to understand the life decisions that led to the kibbutz, one first needs to understand the very idea of ideological migration to Israel, or 'making *aliyah*' in Zionist parlance, and its place in post-war British Jewish thought.

Britain and *aliyah*

Aliyah historically described the ascent of Jews to the Temple to offer sacrifices, and in later times was used when Jews came up to the *bima* (raised platform) in synagogue to read from the Torah.[10] In Zionist ideology and historiography the term came to represent what was perceived as a similarly holy ascent, the movement to Palestine of ideologically committed Jewish migrants to restore and build up their ancient land. *Aliyah* as an idea and a practice has since been employed in Jewish and Israeli politics, society and academia to periodise pre-state Jewish immigration to Palestine, and to conceptualise some or all of post-state Jewish immigration as well.[11] As a concept, *aliyah* specifically separates Jewish immigration to Israel/Palestine from other global migrations. There is nothing ordinary about making *aliyah*, which is often understood as a commitment to a new way of Jewish living and the restoration of the Jewish people in Israel.[12] In the Zionist mind frame, ideologically driven Jews moving to the *Yishuv* (the pre-state Jewish community in Palestine) and to Israel were different from other migrants, who resettled out of necessity or a desire for economic advancement. Instead, Jews who had made *aliyah* were 'a unique phenomenon', an ancient diaspora coming home.[13] As Baruch Kimmerling explains, 'Zionist terminology incorporated the term for any kind of immigration to Eretz Israel or Israel, in order to present the act as ideological-Zionist immigration'.[14] Of course, such a lofty moniker could not easily describe all Jewish immigrants to Israel, so that those whose motives were perceived to fall short were sometimes labelled in baser terms as migrants, a differentiation which frequently ascribed the pioneering ideological spirit to western Jews and cast Mizrahi Israelis as lesser Zionists.[15] Nonetheless, as a blanket expression, to a great extent *aliyah* dominated Israeli, Jewish and broader constructions of all Jewish migration to Palestine and Israel, pre- and post-state, and in many ways continues to do so.[16]

The difference between reality and Zionist ideology, however, was substantial. For in sharp contrast to the idea of *aliyah*, the great majority of Jewish people who moved to live in Israel did so for similar reasons to those that drive migration worldwide; poverty, persecution, employment, retirement and family.[17] Most migrants to Israel came from countries where they were not safe, faced discrimination or poverty, or were not allowed to live as Jews. And even amid the smaller number of Jewish migrants from affluent and safe countries, motivations for moving to Israel have hardly been unique. Chaim Waxman's study of American *aliyah* has argued, for example, that there are 'distinct similarities in the patterns of emigration between American Jews who went on Aliyah and Americans who emigrated to Australia'.[18] The term *aliyah* thus does not best characterise the bulk of migration to Israel. Nonetheless, it better fits the British Jews under discussion in this chapter, who certainly would have used *aliyah* to describe their migration to Israel and would have been seen as ideological migrants both by the Israeli state and other British Jews. On these terms I want to question what exactly *aliyah* meant to those who did it, and understand why these British Jews decided that they belonged elsewhere.

The relationship between Britain's Jews and European Zionism was pushed into the limelight when Britain assumed the mandate for Palestine after the First World War. Coming in the wake of the Balfour Declaration, it seemed that Britain was on course to establish a Jewish national home in Palestine, making London 'the fulcrum of Zionist endeavour ... the nerve centre of the Zionist world'.[19] Yet while high-profile Zionist leaders operated in their midst, Britain's Jewish community were sharply divided over the sagacity of Zionist endeavour, where they were tuned in to it at all.[20] As we have seen in previous chapters, British Jews were frequently adamant that they were British through and through, and sceptical of an ideology that set them apart from other Britons, a situation that drove bitter infighting between Zionists and non-Zionists within Jewish communal leadership in the 1930s.[21] But after the State of Israel came into being in the wake of the Holocaust, opposition to the idea of a Jewish state increasingly became a thing of the past among the community's leadership. The Board of Deputies greeted the new nation by recording 'the joy of Anglo-Jewry at the re-establishment in Palestine of the State of Israel, after almost two thousand years wandering and homelessness', and by singing the Israeli national anthem, *Hatikvah*.[22]

In post-war Britain it became increasingly common for Jewish communal bodies to incorporate structures to support those who wanted to make *aliyah*. Local communities set up committees of people minded to migrate,[23] and national organisations, such as the Board of Deputies, held seminars on *aliyah* and adapted their infrastructure to help those who wished to go.[24] For most British Jews, however, a new (and uncertain) life in Israel was not on their personal agenda. While most were committed to the idea of Israel as a Jewish refuge, and often articulated its legitimacy in such terms, they did not perceive any likely personal need for it. Most British Jews became supporters of the Jewish state without accepting the idea that their lives in Britain were any kind of exile, an armchair Zionism which Omer-Jackaman argues left them in a 'Jewish identity hinterland'.[25] As such, for many, Israel became a much-needed home for other Jews, a 'place for Jews in crisis, rather than … a Jewish homeland for oneself'.[26] For most British Jews, Barry Kosmin and Caren Levy explained, support for Israel was thus 'viewed as payment on an insurance policy on which one never wants to collect'.[27]

A minority of British Jews, however, did migrate to Israel, and many more considered doing so or lived there for a period of their lives. As the state fought for its independence in the Arab–Israeli War of 1948–49, it was supported by at least 800 (mostly Jewish) British volunteers.[28] These people, like Myer Raines, were generally military men from the Second World War who elected to fight once again to support the creation of the Jewish state and protect Jewish lives under threat.[29] In the years after independence, hundreds and sometimes thousands of British Jews migrated every year, adding up to 32,594 people by 2011.[30] Aggregating out at roughly 500 migrants a year, this figure, as Chaim Bermant pointed out in 1969, 'hardly constitutes an exodus'.[31] Yet the number of British Jews moving to Israel has been sufficient for analysts to highlight this migration as a 'significant contributor to British Jewish population change'.[32] Certainly, the substantial difference between migration numbers among British and American Jews (the US has nineteen times the number of Jews but only three times the rate of migration to Israel) gives some pause for thought.[33]

For those who did decide to move, involvement with Zionism and *aliyah* often began, as it did for Myer Raines, in local Jewish youth organisations. Across a range of popular groups, such as the religious *Bnei Akiva* and socialist *Habonim*, Zionism played a central and substantial role in activities and ideology. Both movements aimed to encourage youthful attendees to relocate their lives to the Jewish state, and both, but especially *Habonim*, promoted the ultimate desirability of socialist life on kibbutz. This agenda was inscribed into *Habonim*'s core values from the 1930s. Its annual meeting in 1949 recorded that it was 'the duty of every conscious Jewish youth to choose the path of national recognition and join the ranks of chalutzic youth'.[34] For some ex-members, this approach was subsequently understood in terms of indoctrination. Looking back, *Habonim* member and one-time kibbutznik Tony Lerman opined, 'While no one was coerced into subscribing to socialist Zionist ideology, could it not be argued that the systematic effort to change basic beliefs and attitudes was a form of brainwashing?'[35]

Of course, youth movement participation generally did not begin with a commitment to Zionism or *aliyah* or to the values of a specific group. In most cases, motivations for joining groups such as *Habonim* were shaped by the desires of adolescence more than anything else. For many, such spaces offered the possibility of socialising and fun outside home and school, and an opportunity to engage with Jewish peers beyond the serious and formal atmosphere of synagogues. For most, at least at the outset, the Zionist ideology was very much a secondary matter. Chaim Bermant, for example, recalls his beginnings in *Bnei Akiva* in terms of meeting 'the dozen or so Glasgow youngsters of my age who did not go to football matches on Shabbat, and two or three good-looking girls'.[36] Another *Bnei Akiva* attendee, who ended up making *aliyah* with his family, recalled that he had no clue about the club's values when he first started attending. 'I didn't even know what BA meant. It was just two letters for me.'[37] For many such Jewish children, the youth club they attended was simply chosen because it was the nearest to their home. One interviewee who later made *aliyah* with *Habonim* explained that he first went because it was 'the only Jewish club there was in the area'.[38]

Although movements such as *Habonim* and *Bnei Akiva* were worlds apart in terms of their religiosity, Jewish children could and did attend both. One interviewee from Liverpool explained that he used to go 'to all sorts of youth groups' and decided 'which was the best to go to' on any given day.[39] Given that the high point of youth club attendance was one's teenage years, it is unsurprising that meeting possible romantic partners was often high on the agenda for many young people. One interviewee chose to attend the socialist *Hashomer Hatzair* club to 'play table tennis and pick up girls'.[40] A kibbutz migrant from South Africa explained that she had first attended *Habonim* after a friend told her there were 'nice boys' there.[41]

From these beginnings, engagement with youth movement values was incremental and felt natural to many participants. Having made friends and attended summer camps, members often graduated together to *hachsharah* training farms and leadership roles. 'All that', one member recalls, 'was cementing kibbutz, all the way down the line.'[42] Of course, members could and did step back at any point. Many, indeed most, dipped their toes into the world of Zionist youth movements and never came close to moving to kibbutz or Israel.[43] Parents mostly expected their children to engage with the youth clubs on these limited terms; to meet some Jewish people and learn some Jewish stuff, but not to go so far as to leave Britain for life on a distant kibbutz.[44] Recalling her family's 'sense of dismay' at her decision to make *aliyah*, one *Habonim* member remembers her mother saying to her, 'we never meant you to take it this seriously'.[45]

To some, however, *Habonim*, with its countercultural values and rhythms, offered a new way of living and a community to share it with. One member wrote that he only experienced 'true reality' when he was 'living with the movement'.[46] Another explained that *Habonim* had taught him 'what true friendship and cooperation really mean'.[47] For some, *Habonim* came to dominate their social world, so that moving to kibbutz with their peers was only logical. 'All the people I knew had been in *Habonim* and were now here … That was the people I had.'[48] By organising its devoted members into peer groups or *garin* in preparation for their collective migration to kibbutz, *Habonim* maximised this sense of family and obligation. The *garin* offered community as a core ingredient of the successful migration journey. The *Habonim* newsletter explained, 'It is easier for a Chevra to integrate rather than an individual, because of the mutual support and confidence that one can give the other.'[49] The presence of the *garin* also enforced a degree of peer pressure and influence. One member recollected, 'to be in the in crowd, you had to be in the *garin*'.[50]

The last outpost of the British Empire

From *hachsharah* to kibbutz

More than anywhere else, the place where *garin* formed and developed was the *hachsharah* camp. Joining such a community, one member recalls, made a person one of 'the elite' in *Habonim*'s culture.[51] *Hachsharah* training farms were first set up by Zionist movements in Eastern Europe in the 1920s, and operated in Britain from the 1930s.[52] During the Second World War *Habonim* ran three camps: the David Eder Farm, Gorsey Leaze (which Myer Raines attended) and Latton.[53] For religious Zionists, *Bachad* established its Farm Institute in Thaxted in September 1944.[54] By the time that the second Eder Farm in Horsham in Sussex closed its doors in 1970, *Habonim* alone had run seventeen such facilities in Britain.[55] Commonly, *hachsharah* farms hosted long-term residents making preparations for kibbutz life and also ran youth schemes for enthusiastic teens, which combined learning about agriculture (and agricultural labour) with Jewish and Zionist education. Among the youth movements committed to kibbutz, *hachsharah* was seen as a crucial stepping stone between youth club and *aliyah*. As one editorial explained, 'If we want more chalutzim or Aliyah tomorrow we must bring more youth into Hachsharah centres today.'[56]

In the run-up to the Second World War (and during the conflict) these communities, alongside youth-group-run hostels and summer camps, provided homes and support for both refugees from Nazism and British Jewish evacuees.[57] Writing about the pathway from *Bachad* to kibbutz Lavi, *Bnei Akiva* leader Aryeh Handler argued that it was the need to accommodate the refugees of the Kindertransport which 'resulted in the establishment of a considerable number of hachsharah centres'.[58] During the war *hachsharah* run by *Habonim* accommodated Jewish evacuees, and after the war they helped survivor children brought to Britain from Belsen and Buchenwald.[59] In Ireland, the Belfast and Dublin Jewish communities ran a farm at Millisle to support refugees from Nazism.[60] This mixing of British Jewish youth with European refugees ensured that the British participants were left in no doubt about the dangers of antisemitism in Europe. Chaim Bermant recalls a German *madrich* (leader) in his *hachsharah* community in Thaxted cautioning him that 'what happened in Germany could happen in Britain'. On these terms, he concluded, the 'real education' of *hachsharah* was 'in the company'.[61] Aside from highlighting the risks of life in Europe to British attendees, bringing these youth together naturally reinforced international Jewish solidarity as romances and friendships blossomed. Myer Raines, as we have seen, met his refugee wife Batya at Gorsey Leaze.

While many ended up in *hachsharah* centres as refugees, and some British Jews went there to avoid military service, in general these communities were driven by an ideological commitment to Zionism and *aliyah*.[62] The idea was to prepare Jewish young people for communal agricultural life and work in Israel; to ensure that members, in the words of one 1952 Zionist Federation report, 'become accustomed to physical work'.[63] Such a change required a transformative preparatory experience according to the thinking of the youth movements, so as to create 'the personal revolution necessary for the son of an urban bourgeois family to adapt himself not merely to a rural, but to kibbutz life'.[64] This rendering of Jewish types bought heavily into antisemitic tropes which had historically constructed Jews as urban, individualistic and unsuited to physical labour. In a racialised British society, the *hachsharah* experience was understood within and beyond the community as a stretch for Jewish people. Looking from the outside, a journalist reporting on *Bachad's* camp in Thaxsted was unsure whether the experiment could possibly work, 'whether they will succeed, with no farming tradition in their blood and with compulsion to take out rather than put back so long inbred in them'.[65]

In Zionist circles, the experience of *hachsharah* was romanticised as an abrupt *volte face* for Jewish youth, who could feel that they were rejecting the well-worn path of their ancestors and choosing a bold new one. Since the nineteenth century such thinking had been key to Zionist ideology, which frequently championed the creation of new, 'muscle' Jews in their own land.[66] Looking back from Kfar Hanassi, one member of the first Eder Farm waxed lyrical about his cohort:

> They were socialist-Zionists, born and bred in the British isles, the sons and daughters of middle class Jewry, educated to be doctors, lawyers, tailors, secretaries, merchants and housewives, who had revolted against their education and decided to form a society based on social equality, hard physical labour, and a desire to reunite with Jews from all over the world in their own land, Palestine … In order to achieve these aims a form of basic training was needed, not only in physical labour but for that form of communal living they had selected – the Kibbutz.[67]

In the testimonies of the migrants themselves, the idea that a new type of Jew was being created came through as a commitment to making Jewish lives more ordinary and similar to those of non-Jews. Working hard in agriculture, one Romanian Zionist told a British migrant, meant that 'here … in our own land. *We* are the "Goyim".'[68] For British Jews who had been pushed hard towards professional careers, meeting ordinary working-class Jews in Israel offered something of a rush. One *Bnei Akiva* member recalled the excitement of seeing a man cleaning the street with 'a kippa on his head', another the joy of being served by a waiter 'with a flowing black beard and peot ... a real "Hassidishe Yid"'.[69] Above and beyond theoretical Zionist ideology, British Jewish youth were inspired by the potential to live ordinary simple lives, a desire that cannot be separated from the perceived need to escape European antisemitism and its toxic impact on Jewish people. Here, *hachsharah* offered the first step.

Living together, discussing politics and ideology into the night, armed with 'a grand collection of records ... which were played constantly', *hachsharah* offered a highly romanticised, if austere and frequently sexist, introduction to Zionism.[70] This reflected the broader culture of British Zionist youth clubs, which were often saturated with varying brands of social radicalism, setting themselves in sharp contrast to the somewhat traditional and conservative world of Jewish parents. One *Habonim* member, who went on to migrate to Kfar Hanassi, remembers his attendance in terms of 'rebellion'. He told his father, who was a Zionist but also a capitalist, that he was 'not like you. All you think about is money.'[71] A member of *Habonim* in Glasgow recalled her participation in terms of the movement's 'sense of equality' and eradication of 'social barriers'. There was 'something exhilarating and a sense of importance' about *Habonim*. 'People found themselves. Found who they could be.'[72] A letter collectively signed by the *Habonim hachsharah* in 1959 explained that the movement was 'revolutionary', rooted in 'disillusionment with the structure of our parents' society and determination to create something which is more worthwhile to us'.[73] Living and working as part of their *garin*, members prepared for kibbutz life not only in terms of agricultural training but also communal living. One *Habonim* member recalled how his *hachsharah* 'lived like a kibbutz' with 'no money' and 'everybody equal'.[74] Under pressure, a *hachsharah* group could and did act collectively. For example, in the face of the Six-Day War, the training *Habonim garin* released a collective statement 'confirming' their 'immediate readiness to volunteer our services at the direction of the Government of Israel'.[75]

The last outpost of the British Empire

So intense was the *hachsharah* experience that the realities of life on kibbutz could seem something of a pale imitation. Despite their undoubted and sincere focus on Israel, the *hachsharah* centres were in the UK, and the experience they offered was one of British agriculture and labour. Thus, David Merron recalled his colleagues' construction of the camp as 'OUR land, our own ten acres of Bedfordshire'.[76] Chaim Bermant, describing the impact of his British *hachsharah*, noted, 'I had come to Thaxsted to prepare myself for a life in Israel and was left with a yearning to live in England.'[77] *Hachsharah* brought young people together, away from their parents and their rules. Such communities were often radical spaces which held the possibility of intellectual, political and sometimes sexual liberation. Even within the religious *Bachad*, one report of a visit to the *hachsharah* centre complained that the 'relationship between the chaverim and the chaverot was far beyond what it ought to have been'.[78] In the secular, socialist camps of *Habonim* and *Hashomer Hatzair* the 'romping around', as one member put it, went even further.[79] *Hashomer's hachsharah* centre, one attendee recalled, had 'mixed showers' and witnessed 'changing partners with amazing regularity'.[80]

When *hachsharah* graduates moved to kibbutzim they frequently found themselves in somewhat less radical (or differently radical) communities, which were not always receptive to the kind of countercultural politics that thrived in the British youth movements, or their members' permissive behaviour. One migrant recalls being criticised for coming armed with Beatles records into an environment where 'pure folk and classical [music]' were considered more acceptable.[81] Another remembers hiding English books under his bed on kibbutz, as older members would not accept non-Hebrew literature in the community.[82] While many graduates of *hachsharah* went to Israel in the hope of finding out 'where the revolution was', they often found the realities of kibbutz life staid and conservative.[83] Some of the British migrants felt that they had more in common with the volunteers passing through 'on their way to Kabul' than they did with the established kibbutz community.[84]

On these grounds, members could and sometimes did fall quickly out of love with living in Israel. Long-standing member Phil Moleman, as we saw above, had joined the kibbutz movement in search of 'the simple life, free from the artificial values of modern society in the European world', but found life in Israel 'abhorrent'.[85] What he had believed was a movement of 'revolutionary fervour' he feared was 'becoming the Scout movement of the Zionist Federation'.[86] Like Moleman, others too sometimes found that the realities of Israel and kibbutz jarred with their radical ambitions. But Zionist ideology was neither totalitarian nor static, so that the new immigrants could and did create, at least to some extent, an Israel in their own image. This image, at many levels, was frequently a recreation of Britain and Britishness, played out through a Zionist lens.

British Zionist migrants were far from alone in their tendency to (re)create old country cultures in their new home. In his study of ethnicity in Israel, Goldberg observed 'self-imposed homogeneity' in the way that most migrants chose to live.[87] Typically, British Jews in Israel displayed a strong instinct to stick together, leading one to joke with me that he had 'married out', because his Jewish-Israeli wife was not from Britain.[88] For all their zealotry and commitment to the Israeli state, many youth movement members made their life in Israel amid a network of fellow Britons. Staying together enabled migrants to continue, at least to some degree, to live and work in English. While the youth movements placed substantial emphasis on learning Hebrew, for many migrants English remained, from both necessity and desire, their primary language. In towns such as Netanya and Ra'anana close-knit migrant communities of English speakers grew in the post-war period. One such migrant confessed to a *Jewish Chronicle* interviewer in 1978, 'I often feel we're colonials because we mainly restrict our conversation to English-speaking people. Even with our Israeli neighbours, it's hard to get beyond simple pleasantries.'[89] At Kfar Hanassi, the possibility of operating in English made it easier for migrants to get on. One person told me that he had 'never really felt comfortable with Hebrew' and that 'there were quite a few people who never really mastered it .[90] Even the *ulpan* (Hebrew language school) run for prospective migrants at the kibbutz didn't necessarily solve the problem. 'They came to learn Hebrew but they all learnt English', one migrant recalled.

Although fiercely committed to supporting the development of Israel, British Zionist migrants often ended up recreating and generating forms of Britishness in their new home. Putting down roots in Palestine and later Israel in some ways meant putting down British roots. When, for example, Jewish communities back home paid for tree planting in Israel (one of the most popular forms of fundraising), forests were planted in the names of British figures: Winston Churchill, Queen Elizabeth, Harold Wilson.[91] British Jewish communities in Israel were often financially supported from home, a reality that 'enabled the British Jew to attach the benefits of Zionist success to his/her identity'.[92] At Kfar Hanassi, financial support took the form of substantial, and small personal, contributions. Keen Zionist and later Marks and Spencer chair Teddy Sieff paid for significant development of the kibbutz in the 1960s.[93] Fundraising by family and friends of kibbutz members played a similarly important role. An obituary of Leah Simon (whose sister and mother lived at Kfar Hanassi) celebrated her support work in the UK, which enabled the community 'to build the swimming pool, to buy a tractor and to supply us with gumboots and fans'.[94]

Links to Britain at Kfar Hanassi, however, went far beyond money. British culture was celebrated and valorised as part of the community's core identity so that it was sometimes seen, one migrant joked, as 'the last outpost of the British Empire'.[95] Beyond the ubiquitous use of English and the impressive statues of St George and the Dragon that a local artist built around the (now rarely used) dining hall, Britishness was celebrated as a key factor in the community's survival and success. Pomposity pricking and self-deprecating British humour in particular were important to Kfar Hanassi's identity, 'the glue that kept us together'.[96] British humour was, one report on the community claimed, 'the secret of Kfar Hanassi's stability and ability to weather storms'.[97] Specifically, the custom of zigging (performing satirical comedy sketches at communal events) was understood as a unique signifier of Britishness. Zigging, for migrants at Kfar Hanassi, highlighted the distance between themselves and non-British Israelis, and their unique dual identity. They, as Brits, stood apart from the rest, as they 'laughed at the same things … cried at the same things, because of our English background'.[98] As for the other Israelis, they weren't quite the same, 'they just couldn't understand why we were laughing'. The fact that others didn't get the joke was part of the fun, and a signifier of the group's cohesion. Describing the custom of zigging, *Habonim* member Norman Appelton recalled with glee the incomprehension of the group's *shaliach* (Israeli guide/mentor) when faced with the British zig.

> One shaliach earned long-lasting fame by sitting stolidly through an uproarious show and on being asked if he enjoyed it replying "ken ken, aval ze haya bli tochen" [yes yes but it was without content]. Naturally this became a catchphrase for years after, every time a joke was told or a zig rehearsed and performed.[99]

Zigs at Kfar Hanassi were rooted firmly in the history of British comedy. One, performed so frequently that it remains familiar to 'any child on the kibbutz today', offered a nod to Corporal Jones and the BBC's *Dad's Army*, a home-away-from-home humour that made immediate sense to expat Britons but, aside from a few military loan words from Hebrew, must have seemed somewhat bizarre to others in the northern Galilee.

> we had a zig we always did which was about the British in Africa … against what we called the fuzzy wuzzies … we done it about a 1000 times. The whole

kibbutz knows it … We said we fix bayonets … bifnim, in, turn it round, take it out, in Hebrew it's bifnim, mistadef, chutah … The fuzzy wuzzies don't like it…[100]

Through laughter, British culture was nurtured at Kfar Hanassi, and humour was far from the only way that such culture was made visible. The community boasted its own cricket and football teams, as well as an elaborate English-language lending library. This library, described by one member as 'the best English library in the north of the country', enabled the community to retain its cultural and linguistic roots.[101] In 1977 library statistics showed that nearly three times the number of books in English were borrowed compared to Hebrew.[102] British-style taking of tea also became a point of pride in the community. One non-British member recalled that tea brewing was 'a real ceremony' among the migrants. When a British government trade delegation came to visit, the Minister for Commerce and Trade 'wrote down Kfar Hanassi in his address book, as the best place for a cup of real English tea in Israel (and probably the entire Middle East!)', the kibbutz's weekly newsletter proudly noted.[103]

While this catalogue of Britishness might seem superficial, many British kibbutz members considered their hybrid culture to set them apart from the broader nation. For example, it was common for British migrants in Israel to assert a difference between themselves and other Israelis in terms of manners. Indeed, in my interviews this subject came up more than any other. Transitioning to Israeli life, for many, meant adopting a more aggressive and assertive persona, usually presented as an undesirable challenge. In an interview with the *Jewish Chronicle*, one migrant thus explained the personality changes she perceived to be necessary to embed her move: 'Only slowly did I become an Israeli. At first I was docile and demure. I acted as though I was still in England. Slowly I became aggressive, began shouting, began pushing in queues.'[104] Such a transition was seen as necessary at Kfar Hanassi too. One member described the experience of taking the kibbutz children on a day trip to Akko (Acre), how they learned to be 'more Israeli' as they went along: 'We had another lesson in civic responsibility in Akko. Trying to board the bus, we were shoved aside by a huge crowd, so by the time the second bus came, we had already taken up battle positions, and managed to get on first.'[105] Living in a community of Britons, the kibbutzniks of Kfar Hanassi could, and did, claim to have preserved some of their British manners in opposition to the communities surrounding them. On this kibbutz, one member explained, 'people would invite you to a cup of tea and they would speak to you in a way which is not Israeli'.[106]

Manners were highlighted by some as a surface manifestation of deeper, different values, characterised by a British tendency towards moderation and tolerance. Kfar Hanassi was seen by members as 'much more liberal', 'middle of the road, live and let live', than other kibbutzim which applied stricter socialist principles.[107] For example, the kibbutz was one of the first to allow children to live with their parents instead of in children's houses.[108] As far as its members were concerned it proffered an ideology which was 'untainted by extremism' and which managed to incorporate 'a deep concern of the community for the individual'.[109] Unlike other kibbutzim, one member recalled, Kfar Hanassi was characterised by a British 'feeling of acceptance ... even the people you don't like, you accept them'.[110]

Britishness, then, remained important to many migrants, who didn't leave behind their histories and cultures, but wedded them to Zionism in the Israeli landscape. *Aliyah* brought one into an 'imagined community' of like-minded people, nowhere more so than in kibbutzim such as Kfar Hanassi or Lavi. Stepped into as a 'fantasy of Jewish completeness', these new Jewish lives were constructed and nurtured in the minds of migrants.[111] Chaim Bermant remembers experiencing 'something like a vision. I saw myself as a shepherd in the hills of Galilee, with a typewriter on my knees, and a dainty shepherdess by my side.'[112] For the Zionist youth of Britain, Israel seemed to offer a Jewish home that could be shaped in their own image. In 1949, a year after the state's creation, *Bnei Akiva* attempted to motivate would-be migrants by warning that Israel risked being flooded by Jews who had 'no social or religious ideas'. It fell to them, candidates were told, to create communities that could serve as 'strongholds throughout the country'.[113] For *Habonim*, of course, there was the challenge of bringing socialism and the pioneering spirit, to create a society 'without the evils and injustices of that in which we live now'.[114] In both cases, what was at stake was little less than the creation of a new Jew, or at least a new way to be Jewish.

The meanings of *aliyah*

What, then, might this committed, ambitious, British-tinged Zionism tell us about British Jews in this period? Why, if the end result was a remaking of Britain in a corner of Israel, did such communities grow and thrive? For sure, places such as Lavi and Kfar Hanassi highlight the inspirational power of

Zionism, which was reshaping what it meant to be Jewish, at least for some Jewish Britons. Such communities also reflected the agency of affluent modern Europeans, who were able to get up and go, to build international lives aligned with their belief systems. For British Jews who desired it, Israel in this period was a land of opportunity, a place that offered a chance to live differently and better, not entirely unlike the migrant communities of previous centuries in America and Australasia.[115] Kibbutz *aliyah*, however, also tells another story, about young Jews in the wake of the Holocaust who felt that they did not belong in Britain and were not safe there.

For many of the migrants I interviewed, Israel seemed to offer the only way to live a safe and ordinary life as a Jewish person. Staying in Britain, in contrast, meant forever being an outsider, a tolerated guest who had to limit the visibility of their Jewishness to fit in. One migrant recalled how he had not been allowed to wear a skull cap in any of his British schools and had been warned that taking on an open persona of Jewishness was tantamount to 'causing trouble'.[116] In Britain, many felt that the conditional acceptance of Jews was open to reversal as old hostilities lingered dangerously close to the surface. Park your car badly, one migrant told me, and you could be told to 'go back to your own country'.[117] This idea, that Jews should be somewhere else, was also conveyed in terms of violence. One migrant remembered being beaten up in school and told to 'go back to Palestine, where you came from'.[118] For some, this kind of hostility led directly to their migration. Having had the 'hell' kicked out of him at university in Salford, one migrant recalled his reaction: 'That's it. Don't want to put up with that sort of thing.'[119] Israel offered refuge, a place where people could be Jewish without fear or explanation, where there was no need, as one migrant told the *Jewish Chronicle*, to 'defend [your] Jewishness'.[120] In Israel, if any violence was to be meted out, Jews would be able to defend themselves. One migrant recalled his inclination to come 'to a place where I would be trained in an army and would be able to fight if need be'.[121]

This desire to be able to defend oneself was often rooted in awareness of the Holocaust, and in an anxiety that European genocidal antisemitism was unfinished business. One migrant told me that he remained 'frightened' that the Holocaust 'will happen again'.[122] Myer Raines felt similarly that 'sooner or later it's going to come to England'. Ultimately, it was for this reason that Raines felt that Zionism was 'the only way'.[123] Jews, another migrant explained, 'need somewhere to live. Nobody particularly likes us.'[124] On these terms, British Jewish migrants to Israel sometimes perceived themselves as refugees, moving in search of the only possible safe and peaceful Jewish home. For later migrants, this fear was rooted in their understanding of the past, in the experiences of day-to-day post-war British antisemitism and feelings of exclusion. But for earlier migrants such as Raines, Zionism grew in company with the refugees from Nazism and Holocaust survivors who became his friends and family. To Jews such as these, the idea of investing one's lot in Britain was dangerous and delusional.[125] As one British Zionist put it in 1943 regarding the possibility of living as a Jewish Englishman, 'That way lies national suicide.'[126]

While anxieties about antisemitism might have led these Jews to leave Britain, the ongoing importance in their lives of British culture and identity indicates a deep and ongoing relationship with the country of their birth. Many migrants felt as though their move afforded them two complementary identities, so that feeling both Israeli and British became their natural way of being. 'When I talk English I feel English', one migrant told me. 'When I talk Hebrew I'm Israeli.'[127] 'I'm lucky', another joked, 'I've got two teams to support.'[128] Yet in both nations, these migrants frequently felt looked upon as outsiders. As one early migrant put it, 'in England I was a "bloody Jew" and here I had been transmogrified into an "Anglo-Saxon"'.[129] Feeling like a minority in both places, one migrant explained to me, 'In England I'm Jewish, that's my identity, and here I'm English.'[130] Moving to Israel, while retaining a good chunk of Britain as they went, resulted in some migrants feeling conflicted and confused. Chaim Bermant recalled how he was left wanting 'a conflicting mass of things' as he craved both British and Israeli/Jewish culture.[131] Another migrant said he felt as though he had a 'split personality', and that he understood himself as 'a strange creature, perpetually in the diaspora'.[132]

These kinds of feelings, however, of multiple identities, partial belonging, being an outsider, perhaps speak less of the specificities of these migrant journeys and more of the experience of post-war Jewishness, perhaps post-war life, writ large. As Devorah Baum argued in *Feeling Jewish*, 'None of us fit in. None of us belong. The world feels unnatural for everyone, now.'[133] Indeed, the histories of the British migrants to kibbutz, unusual and alternative as they are, reflect much of the international experience of living globally in the post-war world, at least among comparatively affluent communities. Gabriel Sheffer, for example, has noted the increasing ability of individuals to live in 'multidimensional global space', not to be restricted to living in one place or culture.[134] When early migrants arrived in economically stretched and ideologically stringent kibbutzim, returning to Britain for a visit was a privilege for which they might be asked to wait for many years. Those days, however, have long since passed, and migrants can and do live between places with increasing ease. This, of course, has not only been the experience of Britons in Israel. In similar research on Russian migrants, Tamar Horowitz has noted the prevalence of 'Jews who shuttle between the FSU and Israel without having resolved the question of their personal identity or at least their place of residence'.[135]

This analysis, which holds that migrants remain on the move, embrace diverse identities and feel only partially at home everywhere, makes the subjects of this chapter seem very ordinary. However, having undertaken frequently remarkable life journeys, that doesn't seem right. Eschewing British Jewish life, capitalism and traditional family structures; frequently alienating (or at least worrying) their families back home; and setting up kibbutzim while the state around them battled with its neighbours and itself – in many ways these are extraordinary tales. And yet, in the end, these migrant stories tell us so much about British Jewry in every sense. They highlight a Jewish Britain that remained traumatised by antisemitism and the Holocaust, where some Jews at least only felt conditionally welcome. They speak of a community that was grappling with the meanings of being Jewish in an increasingly secular age, in which radical solutions (such as moving to kibbutz in Israel) offered an answer for people who cared deeply about their Jewishness but did not primarily understand it in traditional terms. More than anything else, the lives of these migrants speak of a Jewish community that embraced Zionism but was unsure about what that meant. Parents sent their children to *Habonim*, *Bnei Akiva* and other similar Zionist youth groups, yet seemed surprised when they became enthusiastic believers. Almost as if an unspoken line had been crossed, the migrants in this chapter took the community's Zionism to its logical conclusion, creating lives that abandoned the very idea of diasporic Jewish community, only to create new diasporas in the process. The departure of these young people to Israel tells a broader story too, of a post-war Britain where youth were hungry for alternatives and adventure, where counterculture and global politics became an increasing part of young lives, and where the promise of capitalist comforts did not, to some, seem appealing.

For Myer Raines, whose story opened this chapter, Israel seemed to offer the only way forward for Jewish people. Committed to socialism and Zionism, he and his peers took extraordinary risks to find a home for the Holocaust survivors with whom they threw in their lot, risking their lives in what Raines described as the 'holy work' of illegal immigration.[136] Having fought so that Jewish refugees could live in Palestine/Israel, Raines's journey entailed a level of commitment that left England behind. As he put it, 'Jews were being shot by Arabs and Arabs were being shot by Jews, and every five years or so a war … And to me what happens in Coventry or in Kent or in Lanarkshire in Scotland, you know, it doesn't mean anything.'[137] Raines committed to speaking and living in Hebrew, building a new community on the kibbutz and raising a family of Israelis. His, though, was a zealotry of a particular period. As kibbutz life and Israel changed, Raines noted, 'materialism has taken the place of the cooperation and intimacy of the beginnings of the kibbutz'. For later migrants to Kfar Hanassi, the seriousness of Raines's generation seemed old fashioned. One such migrant laughed that he had only discovered that Raines spoke English, such was his dedication to Hebrew, after hearing him address his brother who was visiting the kibbutz. 'Two years I broke my teeth talking to Myer … one weekend I was in the dining room serving and his brother arrived and Myer says to him: "Pass the butter please."'[138] For those who came after, the journey had evolved from Raines's war-conditioned, radical Zionism. It is a journey best understood as a longing for a new way to be, a search for an alternative life which frequently and consistently looked back and engaged with British pasts, and fantasised new Jewish futures. While early migrants such as Raines aimed to transcend England and English, walking around Kfar Hanassi or Lavi today one firmly feels a foot in each nation. 'Colonial outposts' in the humour of their residents, they offer a window into contemporary western lives, and the challenge of maintaining Jewishness in a fast-changing world.

Conclusion:
ending, schmending

In the 'untidy workshop' of post-war Britain, British Jews built lives that evolved their faith and traditions. In some ways, the changes that emerged from this process of construction reflected the rhythms of British post-war life. In Jewish families as in non-Jewish families, the norms of relationships, sexualities, obligations and devotions changed amid growing prosperity, secularisation and technological innovation. And yet post-war British Jewish cultures were simultaneously shaped by international Jewish experiences, most obviously the Holocaust and its aftermath. Outside the Channel Islands, and beyond the experiences of the European Jews who managed to find refuge on these shores just in time, British Jews were spared the genocide. Nonetheless, compounding the trauma of antisemitic violence and prejudice in earlier generations, the Holocaust played a huge part in the collective endeavours of British Jews. Insecurity, guilt and grief shaped communal thinking about the importance of maintaining Jewish culture and tradition, drove campaigns for beleaguered Jews abroad, and turbocharged British Zionism. At its most stark, the memory of the Holocaust could make British Jewry seem anxious and ill. In Howard Jacobson's *The Mighty Walzer*, Aishky gives voice to a generation for whom it had all been too much to process. 'I've got some meshuggener illness. I say things that don't make sense. I'm tsemisht. I get a lot of headaches. The doctor says I probably do too much reading. I read all the time.'[1]

The steadfast determination to preserve Jewish life under this shadow could feel stifling and claustrophobic. Jews were tied by guilt to their traditions amid the idea that the old faith had been unchanging over thousands of years in the face of extreme persecution, so that it would be a betrayal to abandon it now. Louis Golding, in *Magnolia Street*, described old men in synagogue 'uttering those same words ... three centuries ago and ten centuries ago'. They would, he believed, 'pray so ten centuries hence'.[2] In the Polisher Shul in Manchester, one of Golding's young characters feels as though he is 'held captive' by this atmosphere, which seals off Jews from the outside world and anything it might have to offer. 'A current of the comparatively clean air … was declared with horror to be "A draught! A draught!" and with patriarchal fury the windows were closed.'[3] Here Judaism was morbid and stale, less a choice or celebration than a duty, meaningful only in terms of paying respects to the sacrifices of earlier generations, so that one rabbi complained of his Yom Kippur congregation, 'I think they have come to say memorial prayers for the religion of their forefathers which died.'[4] This was the feeling picked up in Nudrat Afza's *Kehillah*, Jews captured at the end of history, coming together, as Linda Grant put it, to link themselves 'with all the forgotten ones of the past who have nobody left to mourn them'.[5] To many, the stakes of breaking such a chain needed to be high to ward against unforgivable transgressions that seemed to threaten the future of Judaism. Campaigns against marrying out, the rejection of queer Jewish lives, opposition to missionaries and hostility towards Israel-critical Jews were all governed by a determination to stop those who would dare to open the windows.

In this book I have put a specific focus on such transgressors. I have afforded them pride of place, which was not offered to many narratives from the Jewish centre. This was a decision born from a professional instinct to fill in the gaps and explore the lives of at least some of those who have generally been left out of our history making or rendered peripheral to it. There was, however, a more urgent reason for such a focus. In the hustle and bustle of the communal centre, amid the determination to preserve our 'at-risk' faith and community, it has been too easy not to notice the rude health of Jewish Britain. The stories we have traditionally told, histories of our communal structures, political battles, our heroes and villains, fall back quickly on the community's caesurae, the Holocaust and Israel, driving stories of antisemitism, decline and the need for preservation. Such stories are important in helping us to understand communal and individual concerns, but they simultaneously obscure much of what has been going on in everyday post-war lives. The dominant constructions of Jewish Britain as vulnerable, traditional and rigid need to be kept in their place. After all, as Linda Grant's Evelyn explains in *When I Lived in Modern Times*, 'Tell someone your life story and what you have is exactly that, a story.'[6]

When you bypass, at least to an extent, the communal centre, an unorthodox set of narratives come to the fore which capture a more fluid and vibrant community, changing in alignment with broader British values. As discussions of the Jewish Gay and Lesbian Group, patrilineal Jews, Progressive Jews and

Jews who have 'married out' have laid bare, the communal centre has slowly shifted according to the changing demands of British Jews themselves. If and when synagogues and rabbis have not kept up with the expected pace of change, Jewish people have increasingly done their own thing, creating their own lived religion of communities and networks amid a broader social atmosphere that encouraged the devolution of religious and cultural practice to the level of the individual. In this way, the arbiters of who is and what is Jewish have been (and are) in flux, sparking a diversity of Jewishness that cannot easily be contained or represented by any communal or religious organisation. In an increasingly pluralistic atmosphere, alliances and networks have emerged that promote the possibility of new unities, not bonded by denomination or practice, but in a broader sharing of Jewish heritage and a passion for Jewish culture and history. Here, community centres such as London's JW3 and Brighton and Hove's BNJC, and the national and regional Limmud festivals, offer a case in point. The Jewish Genealogical Society is thriving, as is Jewish Book Week and the Jewish Film Festival. And of course, broad coalitions of Jews continue to come together in the face of challenge and threat.

Demonstrations of unity under pressure show the penetration of Jewishness into British life and the deep bonds between Jews and non-Jews who live, work and play together. At the Campaign Against Antisemitism's London march in November 2023 (held in the context of the war in Israel and Palestine), the prominent attendance of 'a huge number' of non-Jews was widely noted.[7] Such attendance reflects the complicated but increasingly close bonds between some Christian groups and Jewish people, but perhaps more centrally highlights the deep-rooted Jewish influence on the political, social and cultural landscape of modern multicultural Britain. Those on the march were brought together by a myriad of motives and international causes spanning numerous faiths and communities. That such diverse starting points all led back to a display of solidarity with Jewish Britons tells a story about the intermingling of Jewish activism and British multiculturalism more broadly. One non-Jewish attendee told the *Jewish Chronicle* that she had come to 'be in the middle of 105,000 people of all faiths and none, from all corners of the UK, in the middle of London, my city'.[8] Of course, for most Jewish attendees at the march the day was deeply unusual and born of crisis. Still traumatised by antisemitism and the Holocaust, still cautious about when and where to display public Jewishness, such large-scale activism remains exceptional, triggered only by the urgent need to respond to a sharp resurgence of antisemitism. Herein lies the contradiction of British Jewry in contemporary Britain; a safe and successful community dogged by the persistent feeling that it is unsafe and at risk.

There are good reasons for Jewish feelings of vulnerability, but this book has attempted to tell a more positive story, making the argument that Jewish history must not be reduced to a history of antisemitism. This approach is not intended to minimise or silence Jewish anxieties, nor to dispute the ongoing prevalence of the oldest hatred, but instead to illustrate the extent to which Jewish history and culture adds up to a great deal more. Historical traumas will sleep only slowly, but British Jews are nonetheless getting on with life, and have been doing so in Britain for hundreds of years. From mostly humble beginnings, with more hope than expectation that Britain would be a permanent settlement, that is exactly what the nation has become for its Jewish communities. Strong, successful and deeply embedded, Jews are in with the bricks in Britain, a core part of almost every aspect of what the nation has become. In this atmosphere Jewry is changing, sprawling outwards as some communities and traditions decline and synagogue attendance becomes less consistent. But 'Last Jew' narratives and weepy endings are way wide of the mark. Jewish Britain is an ongoing story, tightly interwoven into the fabric of the nation, so that even when British Jews leave to live elsewhere (like the kibbutzniks of the last chapter), they take their own brand of British Jewishness with them. For Louis Golding, Judaism was 'a radioactive core, which gives off countless particles of energy yet remains unexhausted and inexhaustible'.[9] Still energetic and meaningful to many, British Jewry is indeed unexhausted, sparking and shaping the multicultural nation that has become a home for good.

Acknowledgements

This book has been a long time in the making and I owe a debt of gratitude to a number of special people and organisations that have supported its completion. The project was born at the Frankel Center for Judaic Studies at the University of Michigan, where I was lucky enough to serve as a Fellow in 2016. Amid a group of wonderful colleagues, I had space and time to think through the project, and I am grateful especially to Shachar Pinsker, Todd Endelman and Jeff Veidlinger for affording me the opportunity. Back in Britain, the Jewish Historical Society of England gave me a small grant which kept the project moving, before the Leverhulme Trust awarded me a Major Research Fellowship to complete it. In an atmosphere where it is harder and harder for humanities academics to carve out the time to complete research projects, the space given to me by Leverhulme was game-changing. I would like to express my heartfelt thanks to the Trust for supporting me. I also owe thanks to my old employer, the University of Birmingham, where I was given support to grow as a scholar over fourteen years. Although I have now left to pursue a new challenge, the university will remain a big part of my life. As for the new challenge, I am grateful to Professor Malcolm Press and Manchester Metropolitan University for offering me such an exciting opportunity to take the next steps in my career. So far, so good!

Over the years I have benefited from the wisdom of many wonderful colleagues. First and foremost, without the friendship and support of Tony Kushner I would not have been able to write this book or indeed to have a career at all. In many ways this book is written for Tony, who has encouraged me for so long, and so consistently, to pursue Jewish history. Many colleagues, friends and interviewees have offered their wisdom along the way, reading drafts of chapters in various forms: Mo Moulton, Colin Shindler, Harvey Kaplan, Karen Skinazi, Jonathan Romain, Nudrat Afza, Panikos Panayi, Chris Clifford,

Acknowledgements

Margaret Jacobi, Antony Lerman, Dawn Waterman, Richard Harvey and Alex Cropper. I would like to pay tribute in particular to Anthony Joseph and Rudi Leavor, both lifelong servants of their Jewish communities, who passed away before this book was finished. At so many points I have been able to rely on the support of academic friends: Sadiah Qureshi, Michell Chresfield, Saima Nasar, Eliana Hadjisavvas, Amy Edwards, Brett Kaplan, Matthew Hilton, Julie Davies, Beth and Barnaby Parkes, Tim Grady and Courtney Campbell have all kept me believing in the value of this project.

My family have inspired this book in many ways. Going back to Merthyr to tell Jewish stories was such a personal decision. This was my grandma's shul, the place where my dad and his brother grew up. Interviewing my mum and dad felt both strange and important. Their unquestioning willingness and enthusiasm to help reflected the lifetime of support they have given me. As I wrote the book, the next generation were very much on my mind too. I wanted this history to be there for my boys, Joseph and Sam (and their cousins Max, Chloe and Holly). As usual, I am grateful to Christina for pretty much everything, but most of all for keeping the aforementioned children at a distance where they would not prevent the project's completion! Finally, I would like to express my gratitude to the British Jewish community in all its shades. From the most frum to the fiercely secular, the ardent activists to the merely Jew(ish), straight and queer, the Zionists, non-Zionists and anti-Zionists, there is no gang to which I would rather belong.

Figures

1 Rudi Leavor at *Kehillah* in Bradford in front of his photograph. MW Photography.
2 Steve Shipman outside his parents' old shop in Merthyr Tydfil. Author's photograph.
3 Synagogue open day in Merthyr Tydfil, 2024. Author's photograph.
4 Students' Soviet Jewry demonstration, Central Station, Glasgow, 1984. Scottish Jewish Archives Centre.
5 Jewish Gay Group contingent at London Pride, Kennington Park, 1987. Courtesy of Russell Van Dyk and Rainbow Jews.
6 The Jews for Jesus advertisement that appeared in *The Times* on 17 December 1991. Courtesy of Jews for Jesus, UK.
7 Geoff Bercovitch and Basil Levinson, Amiad, 1970. Yad Tabenkin Archive.
8 St George and the Dragon statue at kibbutz Kfar Hanassi. Author's photograph.

Abbreviations

AJA	Anglo-Jewish Association
ASGB	Associated Synagogues of Great Britain
CCJ	Council of Christians and Jews
CMJ	Church's Ministry among Jewish People
IJV	Independent Jewish Voices
JfJfP	Jews for Justice for Palestinians
JGG	Jewish Gay Group
JGLG	Jewish Gay and Lesbian Group
JGSGB	Jewish Genealogical Society of Great Britain
JLGH	Jewish Lesbian and Gay Helpline
JPR	Institute for Jewish Policy Research
JSG	Jewish Socialists' Group
RSGB	Reform Synagogues of Great Britain
SJAC	Soviet Jewry Actions Committee
UCSJ	Universities' Committee for Soviet Jewry
ULPS	Union of Liberal and Progressive Synagogues
UOHC	Union of Orthodox Hebrew Congregations

Notes

Introduction

1 Sharman Kadish, *The Synagogues of Britain and Ireland: An Architectural and Social History* (New Haven, CT: Yale University Press, 2011), p. 60.

2 '10 of England's Most Beautiful Synagogues', The Historic England Blog, https://heritagecalling.com/2015/08/07/top-synagogues/ (accessed 16 September 2024).

3 Todd Endelman, *Broadening Jewish History: Towards a Social History of Ordinary Jews* (Oxford: The Littman Library of Jewish Civilisation, 2011), p. 47.

4 Devorah Baum, *Feeling Jewish (A Book for Just about Anyone)* (New Haven, CT: Yale University Press, 2017), pp. 17–18.

5 Kate Maltby, 'My Parents Kept my Jewish Identity Secret', *Jewish Chronicle*, 28 July 2023.

6 Tony Kushner, *Anglo-Jewry since 1066: Place, Locality and Memory* (Manchester: Manchester University Press, 2009), p. 258.

7 The Jewish community's determination to present itself well to non-Jewish Britain is emphasised in Geoffrey Alderman, 'Introduction', in Geoffrey Alderman (ed.), *New Directions in Anglo-Jewish History* (Boston: Academic Studies Press, 2010), pp. vii–x.

8 See Tony Kushner and Hannah Ewence, 'Introduction', in Tony Kushner and Hannah Ewence (eds), *Whatever Happened to British Jewish Studies?* (London: Vallentine Mitchell, 2012), pp. 1–31 (p. 2).

9 Cecil Roth, *The Jewish Contribution to Civilization* (London: Macmillan, 1938), p. 16.

10 Scholars such as Tony Kushner, Anne Kershen, David Cesarani, Laura Marks, Geoffrey Alderman, Bryan Cheyette, Rickie Burman, Todd Endelman and David Feldman drove forward Jewish history, highlighting the complex racialised environment of British society, and the relationship between antisemitism and other racisms.

11 Endelman has argued that historians of British Jewry have neglected to frame their analysis in the context of global Jewish history, preferring instead to highlight the relevance of Jewish history to British history. See Todd Endelman, 'Anglo-Jewish Historiography', in Kushner and Ewence (eds), *Whatever Happened?*, p. 35.

12 See David Feldman, *Englishmen and Jews: Social Relations and Political Culture 1840–1914* (New Haven, CT: Yale University Press, 1994), pp. 14–15.

13 Board of Deputies MSS, London Metropolitan Archive, London, ACC/3121/C18/1/8, Conference on Jewish Life in Modern Britain held by the Institute of Jewish Affairs,

13 March 1977. Williams's paper was titled 'Local History: Where do we go from here?'

14 Ignaz Maybaum, 'Jewish Understanding of the Christian, Christian Understanding of the Jew', in Dow Marmur (ed.), *A Genuine Search: God – Torah – Israel: A Reform Perspective* (London: Reform Synagogues of Great Britain, 1979), pp. 221–5 (p. 224).

15 Gerda Charles, *The Crossing Point* (London: Eyre and Spottiswoode, 1961), p. 24.

16 Dianne Saunders and Philippa Lester, *From the Leylands to Leeds 17: Jewish Leeds in Words and Images* (Leeds: Leyland Books, 2014), p. 18.

17 See Gemma Romain, *Connecting Histories: A Comparative Exploration of African-Caribbean and Jewish History and Memory in Modern Britain* (London: Kegan Paul, 2006), and Anne Kershen, *Strangers, Aliens and Asians: Huguenots, Jews and Bangladeshis in Spitalfields, 1660–2000* (Abingdon: Routledge, 2005).

18 See Tony Kushner, *The Battle of Britishness: Migrant Journeys: 1685 to the Present* (Manchester: Manchester University Press, 2012).

19 See Todd Endelman, *The Jews of Britain, 1656 to 2000* (Berkeley, CA: University of California Press, 2002).

20 V. D. Lipman, *A History of the Jews in Britain since 1858* (Leicester: Leicester University Press, 1990), p. 229. Lipman notes that North African Jewish immigrants gave France Europe's biggest Jewish population from the 1960s.

21 Moshe Davis, 'The Theme of the Conference', in Julius Gould and Shaul Esh (eds), *Jewish Life in Modern Britain* (London: Routledge and Kegan Paul, 1964), p. xii.

22 See, for example, the highly critical writing of British Jewish novelist Louis Golding, who brought global attention to the plight of Jewish refugees at the hands of Britain through the final books in his *Doomington Saga*. Also note the conduct of the British army's Jewish Brigade in Italy, settling scores with members of the SS and helping Jewish refugees travel to Palestine. See Louis Golding, *To the Quayside* (London: Hutchinson, 1954), and Morris Beckman, *The Jewish Brigade: An Army with Two Masters 1944–45* (Stroud: Spellmount, 1998).

23 Callum Brown, *The Death of Christian Britain: Understanding Secularisation 1800–2000* (London: Routledge, 2001), p. 188.

24 Bernard Levin, 'Am I a Jew?', *New Statesman*, 23 July 1965.

25 Rabbi Lionel Blue argued that contemporary Jews felt 'guilty because they were not their grandparents' in his essay, 'European Jewry after the War', in Dow Marmur (ed.), *Reform Judaism: Essays on Reform Judaism in Britain* (Oxford: Reform Synagogues of Great Britain, 1973), pp. 215–27 (p. 218).

26 Reply by Mervyn Levy, *New Statesman*, 30 July 1965.

27 Patrick Marber, *Howard Katz* (London: Faber and Faber, 2001), p. 82.

28 Linda Grant, *Remind Me Who I Am, Again* (London: Granta, 1998), p. 33.

29 Caryn Aviv and David Shneer, *New Jews: The End of the Jewish Diaspora* (New York: New York University Press, 2005), p. 173.

30 Leonard Fein, *Where Are We? The Inner Life of American Jews* (New York: Harper and Row, 1998), p. 147.

31 'What it means', Fein concluded, was 'that when the winds die, the vessel will stall' (*Where Are We?*, pp. 145–6).

32 Simon Rawidowicz, *Israel: The Ever-Dying People and Other Essays* (Cranbury, NJ: Associated University Presses, 1986), p. 60.

33 Levin, 'Am I a Jew?', *New Statesman*, 23 July 1965.

Notes

34 Bernice Rubens, *The Elected Member* (London: Sphere, 1980 [1969]), p. 204.

35 Geoffrey Alderman, 'British Jewry: The Disintegration of a Community', in Sol Encel and Leslie Stein (eds), *Continuity, Commitment, and Survival: Jewish Communities in the Diaspora* (Westport, CT: Praeger, 2003), pp. 62–4.

36 Jonathan Sacks, *Future Tense* (London: Hodder and Stoughton, 2009), p. 2.

37 Institute of Jewish Policy Research, 'A Community of Communities: Report of the Commission on Representation of the Interests of the British Jewish Community', London, March 2000, p. 3, https://www.jpr.org.uk/reports/community-communities-full-report (accessed 8 October 2024).

38 Board of Deputies MSS, ACC/3121/C18/1/8, Conference on Jewish Life in Modern Britain, Institute of Jewish Affairs, 13 March 1977, paper given by Barry Kosmin, 'The Case for the Local Perspective in the Study of Contemporary British Jewry'. For a more recent staking out of the same argument, see Aviv and Shneer, *New Jews*, p. 20.

39 Sacks, *Future Tense*, p. 29.

40 Immanuel Jakobovits, '*If Only My People*': *Zionism in my Life* (London: Weidenfeld and Nicolson, 1984), p. 195.

41 British Jewish history, Rickie Burman rightly complained in 1984, had 'to a large extent been that of the Jewish male'. See Rickie Burman, 'Recovering Jewish Women's History', *Shifra: A Jewish Feminist Magazine*, 1 (December 1984). Ben-Ur has observed the absence of Ottoman and South Asian Jews from British Jewish history. See Aviva Ben-Ur, 'Identity Imperative: Ottoman Jews in Wartime and Interwar Britain', *Immigrants and Minorities*, 33:2 (2015), pp. 165–95 (p. 168).

42 Williams, 'Local History: Where do we go from here?'

43 Baum, *Feeling Jewish*, p. 41.

44 Board of Deputies MSS, ACC 3121/C18/1/4, notes from Schmool to Freedman, 16 February 1966.

45 Immanuel Jakobovits, *Jewish Review*, 18 July 1958, cited in Jakobovits, '*If Only My People*', p. 195.

46 Immanuel Jakobovits, *Journal of a Rabbi* (London: W.H. Allen, 1967), p. 8.

47 Martin Goodman, *A History of Judaism* (London: Allen Lane, 2017), pp. 477–8.

48 Cynthia Baker, *Jew* (New Brunswick, NJ: Rutgers University Press, 2017), p. 140.

49 Norman Cohen, 'Trends in Anglo-Jewish Jewish Religious Life', in Gould and Esh (eds), *Jewish Life in Modern Britain*, pp. 41–66 (p. 42).

50 David Vital, *The Future of Jews* (Cambridge, MA: Harvard University Press, 1990), p. 107. See also Bernard Wasserstein, *Vanishing Diaspora: The Jews in Europe since 1945* (London: Penguin, 1997), p. vii.

51 See Rachel B. Gross, *Beyond the Synagogue: Jewish Nostalgia and Religious Practice* (New York: New York University Press, 2021), p. 191.

52 This approach follows the scholarship of Juliet Steyn, *The Jew: Assumptions of Identity* (London: Cassell, 1999), p. 1, and Carolyn Steedman, *Landscape for a Good Woman* (London: Virago, 1986), p. 6.

53 Keith Kahn-Harris and Ben Gidley, *Turbulent Times: The British Jewish Community Today* (London: Continuum, 2010), p. 49.

54 Stephan Feuchtwang, 'Mythical Moments in National and Other Family Histories', *History Workshop Journal*, 59 (2005), pp. 179–93 (p. 180).

55 Alexander Baron, *The Lowlife* (London: Black Spring, 2021 [1963]), p. 114.

56 Howard Jacobson, *Kalooki Nights* (London: Vintage, 2006), p. 5.

Notes

57 Adam Andrusier, *Two Hitlers and a Marilyn* (London: Headline, 2021), p. 175.

58 Emil Fackenheim, 'The 614th Commandment', *Judaism*, 16:3 (1967), pp. 269–73.

59 Hanif Kureishi, *My Ear at His Heart: Reading My Father* (London: Faber and Faber, 2004), p. 7.

60 Alison Light, *Common People: The History of an English Family* (London: Penguin, 2015), p. 5.

61 Michael Frank, *The Mighty Franks: A Memoir* (London: 4th Estate, 2017), p. 171.

62 See Dara Horn, *People Love Dead Jews: Reports from a Haunted Present* (New York: W.W. Norton, 2021), pp. 88–90.

63 Ibid.

64 'Three Killed in Attic Fire Trap', *Evening Standard*, 5 May 1961.

65 'Three Die in Balham Blaze', *Tooting and Balham Gazette and Earlsfield Recorder*, 12 May 1961.

66 Ibid.

67 'Hordes of Sightseers Make Macabre Pilgrimage to Burnt Out Shell: Three Killed in Flat Blaze: Neighbours Rescued by Fireman', *Balham and Tooting News and Mercury*, 12 May 1961.

68 Coroner's Report into the Death of Bernard Clarke, London Metropolitan Archives, COR/LW/1961/135–9, 16 May 1961.

69 'Three Die in Balham Blaze: Hildreth Street Tragedy Inquest Adjourned', *Tooting and Balham Gazette and Earlsfield Recorder*, 12 May 1961.

70 'Balham Fire Tragedy: Inquest on Three Victims of Hildreth Street Blaze: Fire Brigade Officer Tells of Search for Bodies', *Tooting and Balham Gazette and Earlsfield Recorder*, 19 May 1961.

71 'Hordes of Sightseers Make Macabre Pilgrimage to Burnt Out Shell', *Balham and Tooting News and Mercury*, 12 May 1961.

72 Lionel Blue, *To Heaven, with Scribes and Pharisees: The Lord of Hosts in Suburbia, the Jewish Path to God* (London: Darton, Longman and Todd, 1975), p. 13.

1 The last Jew of Merthyr

1 *Bubbe meise*, Yiddish: a grandmother's fable, an apocryphal tale.

2 Interview with Nudrat Afza, 31 October 2019.

3 See Nigel Grizzard and Benjamin Dunn, *The Bradford Jewish Heritage Trail*, pamphlet produced as part of Making their Mark project, June 2013.

4 Interview with Rudi Leavor, 31 October 2019.

5 Leavor was speaking at *Kehillah*'s official opening at Cartwright Hall, 2 February 2020.

6 Interview with Nudrat Afza, 31 October 2019.

7 Helen Pidd, 'Say a Prayer: The Muslim Woman who Photographed Bradford's Last Synagogue', *The Guardian*, 8 September 2019. See also 'Focusing on Bradford's Struggle for Survival', *Jewish Chronicle*, 13 September 2019.

8 Rachel Lichtenstein, 'Shloimy Alman's Photographs of Jewish Manchester in the 1970s', in *Vanished Streets: 1970s Photographs of Jewish Manchester from the Shloimy Alman Archive* (exh. cat.) (Manchester: Manchester Metropolitan University, 2021), p. 6.

9 Henry Wadsworth Longfellow, 'The Jewish Cemetery at Newport', *Putnam's Monthly Magazine*, July 1854.

Notes

10 Josh Glancy, 'My Jewdar is so Good I Even Found One on the Falkland Islands', *Jewish Chronicle*, 20 May 2022. For another British example, see Mark Smith, 'The Last Jew in Greenock', *Jewish Chronicle*, 26 August 1994.

11 Horn, *People Love Dead Jews*.

12 Stephen Brook, *The Club: The Jews of Modern Britain* (London: Constable, 1989), p. 430. See also William Rubinstein, *A History of the Jews in the English-Speaking World: Great Britain* (Basingstoke: Macmillan, 1996), pp. 418, 425.

13 See, for example, Richard English and Michael Kenny, *Rethinking British Decline* (Basingstoke: Palgrave Macmillan, 1999), and Jim Tomlinson, 'The Decline of the Empire and the Economic "Decline" of Britain', *Twentieth Century British History*, 14:3 (2003), pp. 201–21.

14 Board of Deputies MSS, ACC3121/d/02/02, Aberdare, letter from Marriage Secretary, 1 December 1954.

15 Board of Deputies MSS, ACC3121/d/02/18, Brynmawr, Honorary Secretary to Clerk of the Board of Deputies, 21 November 1963.

16 Ursula Henriques, *The Jews of South Wales* (Cardiff: University of Wales Press, 2013), p. 216.

17 Noting that Jewish births had outpaced Jewish deaths in every year since 2006, Jonathan Boyd concluded, 'it's not all doom and gloom in British Jewry. On the contrary, we're blooming.' See 'Good News – We're Breeding and Blooming', *Jewish Chronicle*, 22 June 2018.

18 Chaim Bermant, 'Last Jews of the Valleys', *Jewish Chronicle* (Supplement), 25 November 1988.

19 Letter to the Editor from Gerald Baron Cohen, *Jewish Chronicle*, 9 December 1989.

20 Tony Scotland, 'The Last Jew in Merthyr', *Sunday Telegraph*, 6 July 1997.

21 Black, the *Jewish Chronicle* reported, died in 1999 aged 82. 'Welsh History Goes on Show', *Jewish Chronicle*, 14 June 2019.

22 Michael Mail, 'Preserving the Stories of Europe's Shuls', *Jewish Chronicle*, 11 October 2019.

23 Interview with Steve Shipman and Jackie Edwards, 15 December 2022.

24 Ibid.

25 See Todd Endelman, *Radical Assimilation in English Jewish History, 1645–1945* (Bloomington, IN: Indiana University Press, 1990), pp. 3–6. See also Brook, *The Club*, p. 430.

26 For analysis of broader currents of religious decline in this period, see Callum Brown, *Religion and Society in Twentieth-Century Britain* (Harlow: Pearson Longman, 2006).

27 Interview with Steve Shipman and Jackie Edwards, 15 December 2022.

28 Alderman, 'British Jewry: The Disintegration of a Community', pp. 62–4.

29 Interview with Steve Shipman and Jackie Edwards, 15 December 2022.

30 See, for example, S. J. Prais and Marlena Schmool, 'Statistics of Jewish Marriages in Great Britain: 1901–65', *Jewish Journal of Sociology*, 9:2 (1967), pp. 149–74; Maurice Freedman (ed.), *A Minority in Britain: Social Studies of the Anglo-Jewish Community* (London: Vallentine Mitchell, 1955); and, more recently, numerous studies from the Institute of Jewish Policy Research (JPR). The Chief Rabbi encouraged Orthodox mohels (religious performers of circumcision) to support the work of statisticians in 1970. See Office of the Chief Rabbi MSS, London Metropolitan Archive, London, ACC/2805/7/2/23, Clause 43, Chief Rabbi writes to senior Mohelim, 24 June 1970.

31 Fein, *Where Are We?*, p. 142. See also Aviv and Shneer, *New Jews*, p. xiv; Goodman, *A History of Judaism*, p. 534.

Notes

32 Rawidowicz, *Israel*, p. 61.

33 Kahn-Harris and Gidley, *Turbulent Times*, p. 39.

34 Grant, *Remind Me Who I Am, Again*, p. 68.

35 Tony Kushner, 'Heritage and Ethnicity: An Introduction', in Tony Kushner (ed.), *The Jewish Heritage in British History: Englishness and Jewishness* (London: Frank Cass, 1992), pp. 1–28 (p. 12).

36 Grace Paley, 'Goodbye and Goodluck', in *The Collected Stories* (London: Virago, 1988), p. 7.

37 Board of Deputies MSS, ACC/3121/C/7/1/8, Disused Cemeteries, Secretary to enquirer, 14 January 1963.

38 See Lloyd Gartner, *The Jewish Immigrant in England: 1870–1914*, 3rd edn (London: Vallentine Mitchell, 2001), p. xxviii.

39 Bill Williams, 'Heritage and Community: The Rescue of Manchester's Jewish Past', in Kushner (ed.), *The Jewish Heritage in British History*, pp. 128–46 (pp. 128, 136).

40 Kushner, 'Heritage and Ethnicity', p. 24.

41 Interview with Anthony Joseph, 15 April 2019.

42 Interview with Harvey Kaplan, 12 December 2019.

43 Kushner, 'Heritage and Ethnicity', p. 12.

44 Morris Beckman, *The Hackney Crucible* (London: Vallentine Mitchell, 1996), p. 1.

45 Interview with Anthony Joseph, 15 April 2019.

46 Interview with Harvey Kaplan, 12 December 2019.

47 Williams, 'Heritage and Community', p. 138.

48 Interview with Anthony Joseph, 15 April 2019. See also Williams, 'Heritage and Community', p. 133.

49 Beckman, *The Hackney Crucible*, p. 2.

50 Richard Rabinowitz, *Objects of Love and Regret: A Brooklyn Story* (Cambridge, MA: Belknap Press of Harvard University Press, 2022), p. 144.

51 Jacobson has sought to explain this generational change in post-war American society in Matthew Frye Jacobson, *Roots Too: White Ethnic Revival in Post-Civil Rights America* (Cambridge, MA: Harvard University Press, 2006), p. 2.

52 Andy Pearce, *Holocaust Consciousness in Contemporary Britain* (Abingdon: Routledge, 2014), p. 166. Pearce does not ascribe the same impact to the *Holocaust* series in Britain but argues that it helped 'to get people talking about "the Holocaust" in ways they previously hadn't' (p. 173).

53 See Alex Haley, *Roots: The Saga of an American Family* (New York: Doubleday, 1976). Having hit American screens in January, the *Roots* miniseries aired on BBC 1 in April 1977, and was repeated in 1978 and 1981. For analysis of the impact of the miniseries, see Martin Stollery, 'The Same, But a Step Removed: Aspects of the British Reception of Roots', in Erica Ball and Kellie Carter Jackson (eds), *Reconsidering Roots: Race, Politics, and Memory* (Athens, GA: University of Georgia Press, 2017), pp. 147–64. For the impact of *Roots* in the US, see Robert J. Norrell, *Alex Haley and the Books that Changed a Nation* (New York: St Martins Press, 2015). Norrell notes that Haley's book sold one million hardback copies in 1977 (p. 170).

54 Stollery, 'The Same, But a Step Removed', p. 149.

55 Interview with Anthony Joseph, 15 April 2019.

56 Michael Sharpe, *Family Matters: A History of Genealogy* (Barnsley: Pen and Sword, 2011), p. 179.

Notes

57 Gross has highlighted the US Jewish interest in *Roots* and contended that *Holocaust* 'was clearly intended to be a Jewish parallel to *Roots*' (*Beyond the Synagogue*, pp. 49–51).

58 Ibid., p. 51.

59 Interview with Harvey Kaplan, 12 December 2019.

60 T. R. Fyvel, 'Uprooted', *Jewish Chronicle*, 22 April 1977.

61 Michael Wallach, 'Roots? Who Really Needs Them', *Jewish Chronicle*, 20 May 1977.

62 '"Roots" Honour', *Jewish Chronicle*, 23 September 1977.

63 D. H. Akenson, *Some Family: The Mormons and How Humanity Keeps Track of Itself* (Montreal: McGill-Queen's University Press, 2007), pp. 7, 185. For analysis, see Gross, *Beyond the Synagogue*, p. 48.

64 Sharpe, *Family Matters*, p. 183.

65 Don Steel, *Discovering Your Family History* (London: BBC Books, 1980), p. 7.

66 Sharpe, *Family Matters*, p. 168.

67 Graham Jaffe, 'Editorial', *Shemot: The Jewish Genealogical Society of Great Britain*, 1:3 (1993).

68 Graham Jaffe, 'Editorial', *Shemot*, 1:4 (1993). Anthony Joseph asserted that the membership numbers stabilised at 1,000 in interview, 15 April 2019.

69 Kushner, 'Heritage and Ethnicity', p. 22.

70 Interview with Harvey Kaplan, 12 December 2019.

71 Brigit Grant, 'A Manor House Museum', *Jewish Chronicle*, 28 October 1983.

72 Williams, 'Heritage and Community', pp. 141–2.

73 See Tony Kushner, 'The End of the "Anglo-Jewish Progress Show": Representations of the Jewish East End, 1887–1987', in Kushner (ed.), *The Jewish Heritage in British History*, pp. 78–105 (p. 94). White published an iconic study of the Rothschild Buildings in the East End in 1980.

74 Williams, 'Heritage and Community', p. 140.

75 This research led to an exhibition in the Gorbals, and subsequently to the publication of Charlotte Hutt and Harvey Kaplan (eds), *A Scottish Shtetl: Jewish Life in the Gorbals, 1880–1974* (Glasgow: Gorbals Fair Society, 1984).

76 Tony Kushner, 'The Manchester Jewish Museum', *Bulletin – Society for the Study of Labour History*, 51:3 (1986), pp. 18–20. The Museum of the Jewish East End gave attention to the 'diverse roots and social history of Jewish people across London'. See https://jewishmuseum.org.uk/about-us/history/our-story/ (accessed 16 September 2024).

77 Kushner, 'Heritage and Ethnicity', p. 22.

78 Alderman, 'British Jewry', p. 63.

79 Chairman's Report by Graham Jaffe, *Shemot*, 3:2 (1995).

80 Richard Gilbert, 'You Are Never Too Young', *Shemot*, 1:3 (1993).

81 Board of Deputies MSS, ACC/3121/C/7/1/9, Meeting of the Law, Parliamentary and General Purposes Committee, February, 1974. On synagogues sharing the costs of maintenance, see ACC3121/C/7/1/10, Minutes of Meetings of Synagogal Organisations – Disused Cemeteries, 8 January 1976.

82 Simon Rocker, 'Battle is On to Save British Jewry's Historical Landmarks', *Jewish Chronicle*, 18 October 1991.

83 Bernice Rubens, *I, Dreyfus* (London: Little Brown, 1999), p. 68.

84 Ariel Segal, 'Jews of the Amazon: Voices from the Earthly Paradise', in Barbara Kirshenblatt-Gimblett (ed.), *Writing a Modern Jewish History: Essays in Honor of Salo Baron* (New York: Jewish Museum, 2006), p. 67.

Notes

85 Etan Vlessing talks to Alfred Dunitz, 'A New Lease of Life for Cemeteries', *Jewish Herald International*, 7 April 1989.

86 Board of Deputies MSS, ACC 3121/C/7/1/8, letter from de Lange to Board of Deputies, 3 August 1973.

87 Norman Levine, 'In a Jewish Cemetery', *Jewish Chronicle* (Supplement), 25 March 1983.

88 'A New Lease of Life for Cemeteries', *Jewish Herald International*, 7 April 1989.

89 Board of Deputies MSS, ACC 3121/C/7/1/8, Report on Great Yarmouth. ACC3121/C/7/1/11, letter from Lord Fisher of Camden to HA Halpern, 10 January 1979.

90 Reform Jewish Community of Manchester MSS, Manchester Central Library, M779, MRS40, President's Report, 1983.

91 'Forthcoming Events', *Shemot*, 3:1 (1995).

92 https://jewish-gilroes.org.uk/the-project/ (accessed 16 September 2024); https://www.willesdenjewishcemetery.org.uk (accessed 16 September 2024).

93 Board of Deputies MSS, ACC3121/C/7/1/10, Malcolm Slowe to Chief Rabbi, 'Vanishing History', 13 May 1977.

94 Harold Lewin, 'Genealogical Records – Prospects for Survival', *Shemot*, 1:2 (1993).

95 Rocker, 'Battle is On to Save British Jewry's Historical Landmarks', *Jewish Chronicle*, 18 October 1991.

96 Board of Deputies MSS, ACC3121/D2/33, Exeter, Circular on Exeter Synagogue (c. 1963).

97 Sharman Kadish, 'First National Survey of Jewish Built Heritage', *Context: Journal of the Institute of Historical Building Conservation*, 59 (September 1998), pp. 36–8.

98 Catherine Nash, *Of Irish Descent: Origin Stories, Genealogy, and the Politics of Belonging* (Syracuse, NY: Syracuse University Press, 2008), p. 18.

99 Eviatar Zerubavel, *Ancestors and Relatives: Genealogy, Identity, and Community* (Oxford: Oxford University Press, 2012), p. 10.

100 This list, 'Irreplaceable: A History of England in 100 Places', is published online and in book form. See https://historicengland.org.uk/campaigns/100-places/ (accessed 16 September 2024).

101 https://historicengland.org.uk/get-involved/100-places/faith-belief/fountains-abbey-and-jewish-cemetery-cornwall/ (accessed 16 September 2024).

102 Tony Kushner, 'Jewish Local Studies and Memory Work: A Case Study of Cornwall', *Journal of Jewish Studies*, 55:1 (2004), pp. 157–62.

103 Paul Kleiman and Jo Richler, 'Get Your Facts Straight', *Jewish Chronicle*, 3 June 2022.

104 Kushner, 'Jewish Local Studies and Memory Work', p. 161.

105 This is the analysis of David Ison, the Dean of St Paul's and judge in the 'Faith and Belief' category of the Top 100 list.

106 Interview with Rudi Leavor, 31 October 2019.

107 Gross, *Beyond the Synagogue*.

108 For analysis of the synagogue in architectural terms, see S. Kadish, 'Jewish Heritage in Scotland', *Jewish Historical Studies: Transactions of the Jewish Historical Society of England*, 47:1 (2015), pp. 179–216 (pp. 198–9).

109 'The Jewish anarchists fighting to save Langside synagogue', https://www.bbc.co.uk/news/uk-scotland-50808796 (accessed 16 September 2024).

110 Interview with Harvey Kaplan, 12 December 2019.

111 'The Jewish anarchists fighting to save Langside synagogue'.

112 Scholars of American Jewry have recently argued that 'decline and loss' and 'resilience and change' narratives are 'intertwined' and 'need each other'. See Alan Cooperman and Becka Alper, 'Introduction to the Special Issue', *Contemporary Jewry*, 43 (2023), pp. 193–200.

113 Interview with Steve Shipman and Jackie Edwards, 15 December 2022.

114 Scotland, 'The Last Jew in Merthyr', *Sunday Telegraph*, 6 July 1997.

115 Interview with Steve Shipman and Jackie Edwards, 15 December 2022.

116 Kleiman and Richler, 'Get Your Facts Straight', *Jewish Chronicle*, 3 June 2022.

2 Meshuga frum?

1 *Meshuga frum*, slang, from Yiddish, 'crazy religious'. A term used by a Jewish person, comedian Ashley Blaker quipped, to describe someone 'who is just slightly more observant' than themselves. 'Are You Meshuga Frum?', *Jewish Chronicle*, 23 January 2017.

2 *You Don't Have to Be Jewish*, BBC Radio London, 26 December 1982, https://www.bbc.co.uk/sounds/play/p09f5tmq (accessed 16 September 2024).

3 See Jonathan Sacks, *One People? Tradition, Modernity, and Jewish Unity* (London: The Littman Library of Jewish Civilisation, 1993), p. 183.

4 Letter to the Editor from Hanna Meyer, *Jewish Chronicle*, 7 January 1983. Meyer expressed her 'utter revulsion' at the way Gryn was addressed in the broadcast.

5 Chief Rabbi MSS, ACC/2805/7/16/10, Meeting of the Consultative Committee on Jewish/Christian Relations, 11 May 1983.

6 Ibid.

7 Ibid.

8 Rabbi Moshe Young, 'Reform: A Hybrid of Old Falsehoods', *Jewish Tribune*, 24 October 1996.

9 Research in 2017 showed that 66% of synagogue-attending Jews remained affiliated to Orthodox communities. See Donatella Casale Mashiah and Jonathan Boyd, *Synagogue Membership in the United Kingdom in 2016* (Institute of Jewish Policy Research and Board of Deputies, 2017). For the earlier statistics, see S. J. Prais, 'Synagogue Statistics and the Jewish Population of Great Britain, 1900–70', *Journal of Jewish Sociology*, 14:2 (1972), pp. 215–28 (p. 219).

10 Board of Deputies MSS, ACC3121/C18/1/8, Conference on Jewish Life in Modern Britain put on by the Board of Deputies and the Institute of Jewish Affairs (1977), paper given by Immanuel Jakobovits, 'An Analysis of Religious Versus Secular Trends on Anglo-Jewry, Especially During the Past Fifteen Years'.

11 Jonathan Wittenberg, 'Tributes to the "Rabbi's Rabbi"', *Jewish Chronicle*, 23 August 1996.

12 Ibid.

13 Letters to the Editor, Rabbi M. Bernstein, *Jewish Tribune*, 5 September 1996.

14 Ben Yitzchok, 'The Man Who Has Intermarriage on his Conscience', *Jewish Tribune*, 29 August 1996.

15 Chaim Bermant, 'Mean Minds Muddying the Mainstream', *Jewish Chronicle*, 30 August 1996.

16 Letter from David J. Goldberg, rabbi of the Liberal Jewish synagogue in St Johns Wood, *Jewish Chronicle*, 4 October 1996.

Notes

17 When he decided to attend a subsequent memorial service for Gryn, Dayan Chanoch Padwa of the UOHC leaked a letter sent to him by Sacks justifying his attendance (in which he had dismissed Gryn in 'harsh terms'), seemingly both to embarrass the Chief Rabbi and to highlight what Padwa would have seen as an unacceptable compromise in the Chief Rabbi's position. See Geoffrey Alderman, 'That Letter ... Rabbinical Politics and Jewish Management', *Judaism Today* (1997–98), cited from Geoffrey Alderman, *Controversies and Crisis: Studies in the History of the Jews in Modern Britain* (Boston: Academic Studies Press, 2008), pp. 337–46.

18 See, for example, Vivian Lipman, *A History of the Jews in Britain since 1858* (Leicester: Leicester University Press, 1990), p. 243; Benjamin Elton, 'British Orthodox Jewry 1945–90: Swing to the Right or Shift to the Centre?', *Journal of Modern Jewish Studies*, 13:2 (2014), pp. 264–83 (p. 270); Miri J. Freud-Kandel, *Orthodox Judaism in Britain since 1913: An Ideology Forsaken* (London: Vallentine Mitchell, 2006), p. 122; and Alderman, *Modern British Jewry*, pp. 321–78.

19 Alderman, 'British Jewry: The Disintegration of a Community', p. 50, and Endelman, *The Jews of Britain*, p. 229.

20 Board of Deputies MSS, ACC3121/C18/1/8, Conference on Jewish Life in Modern Britain, Immanuel Jakobovits, 'An Analysis of Religious Versus Secular Trends on Anglo-Jewry'.

21 Freud-Kandel, *Orthodox Judaism in Britain*, p. 110.

22 Manchester Jewish Museum, interview with Chaim Hailpern, MANJM: 2012.50.34, by Bill Williams, 14 November 2002.

23 Manchester Jewish Museum, interview with Jack Morgenstern, MANJM: J182, by Ros Livshin, September 1978.

24 Anne Kershen and Jonathan Romain, *Tradition and Change: A History of Reform Judaism in Britain, 1840–1995* (London: Vallentine Mitchell, 1995), p. 166. See also David Soetendorp, 'Confrontation or Cooperation? The Relationship between Orthodox and Progressive Judaism', in Jonathan Romain (ed.), *Renewing the Vision: Rabbis Speak Out on Modern Jewish Issues* (London: SCM Press, 1996), pp. 18–19.

25 Kershen and Romain, *Tradition and Change*, p. 167.

26 See David Miller, 'Traditionalism and Estrangement', in Philip Longworth (ed.), *Confrontations with Judaism* (London: Anthony Blond, 1967), pp. 197–231 (p. 197). For immigrants being put off by the anglicised appearance of British rabbis, see also Bernard Homa, *Orthodoxy in Anglo-Jewry 1880–1940* (London: Jewish Historical Society of England, 1969), p. 11, and Geoffrey Alderman, *The Federation of Synagogues: A New History* (London: Federation of Synagogues, 2018), p. 26.

27 Louis Jacobs, *Helping with Inquiries: An Autobiography* (London: Vallentine Mitchell, 1989), p. 32.

28 Interview with Chaim Hailpern, MANJM: 2012.50.34, by Bill Williams, 14 November 2002.

29 Manchester Jewish Museum, interview with Dayan Golditch, MANJM: J99, by Ros Livshin and Bill Williams, May/June 1978.

30 See Alderman, *Modern British Jewry*, pp. 142–5, and Homa, *Orthodoxy in Anglo-Jewry*, pp. 10–13.

31 See Joseph Finlay, 'Between Religion and Ethnicity: How Jews Navigated Race Relations in Postwar Britain', PhD thesis, University of Southampton, 2023, pp. 32–4, and Endelman, *The Jews of Britain*, p. 232. On the impact of these immigrants on the Sephardi community in Britain, see Stephen Bush, *Commission on Racial Inclusivity in the*

Jewish Community, Board of Deputies, April 2021, p. 30, https://bod.org.uk/wp-content/uploads/2021/04/Commission-on-Racial-Inclusivity-in-the-Jewish-Community.pdf (accessed 8 October 2024).

32 See Alderman, *The Federation*, pp. 38–40.

33 Ibid., p. 101.

34 See Bernard Homa, *A Fortress in Anglo-Jewry: The Story of the Machzike Hadath* (London: Shapiro, Vallentine and Co., 1953); Homa, *Orthodoxy in Anglo-Jewry*, pp. 19–21; Alderman, *Modern British Jewry*, pp. 145–50.

35 See Yaakov Wise, 'The Establishment of Ultra-Orthodoxy in Manchester', *Melilah: Manchester Journal of Jewish Studies (1759–1953)*, 7:1 (2012), pp. 1–33.

36 Freud-Kandel, *Orthodox Judaism in Britain*, pp. 80–1.

37 Homa, *Orthodoxy in Anglo-Jewry*, p. 28. See also Harry Rabinowicz, *A World Apart: The Story of the Chasidism in Britain* (London: Vallentine Mitchell, 1997), p. 73.

38 University of Southampton, Hartley Library, Archives and Special Collections, MS183/39/6, 'Constitutional Principles of the Union of Orthodox Hebrew Congregations', July 1974.

39 University of Southampton, Hartley Library, Archives and Special Collections, MS183/39/6, Solomon Schonfeld, 'The Right Wing of Anglo-Jewry', 1971.

40 Chasidic sects, Alderman has noted, 'naturally attached themselves to the UOHC, which could provide shechita and burial facilities of the required standard' (*Modern British Jewry*, p. 365).

41 Miriam Dansky, *Gateshead: Its Community, Its Personalities, Its Institutions* (Southfield, MI: Targum, 1992), pp. 49–50. Also see Freud-Kandel, *Orthodox Judaism in Britain*, p. 112.

42 Miller, 'Traditionalism and Estrangement', p. 204.

43 Ibid., p. 205.

44 University of Southampton, Hartley Library, Archives and Special Collections, MS183/39/6, Dr S. Schonfeld, 'The Union in Review', 1972.

45 Interview with Dayan Golditch, MANJM: J99, by Ros Livshin and Bill Williams, May/June 1978.

46 Interview with Chaim Hailpern, MANJM: 2012.50.34, by Bill Williams, 14 November 2002.

47 University of Southampton, Hartley Library, Archives and Special Collections, MS183/39/6, 'Constitutional Principles of the Union of Orthodox Hebrew Congregations', July 1974.

48 Separation, Freud-Kandel explains, was seen as 'necessary in order to preserve the Orthodox integrity of one's own community' (*Orthodox Judaism in Britain*, p. 112).

49 S. Ben Sheva, 'A Postscript to the Chief Rabbinate', *Jewish Tribune*, 11 June 1965.

50 Shlomit Flint Ashery, *Spatial Behavior in Haredi Communities in Great Britain* (Cham: Springer, 2020), pp. 100–1.

51 See Rabinowicz, *A World Apart*, p. xiii, and Christine Holman and Naomi Holman, *Torah, Worship and Acts of Loving Kindness: Baseline Indicators for the Charedi Community in Stamford Hill*, Interlink Foundation, November 2002, p. 13, https://www.fbrn.org.uk/sites/default/files/files/Holman%20Report.pdf (accessed 8 October 2024).

52 Flint Ashery, *Spatial Behavior in Haredi Communities*, p. 89.

53 *Volvo City*, directed by Susanna White, produced by Roy Ackerman, broadcast on Channel 4, 4 November 1991.

54 Louise Tallen, 'Jewish Identity Writ Small: The Everyday Experience of Baalot Teshuvah', in Howard Wettstein (ed.), *Diasporas and Exiles: Varieties of Jewish Identity*

Notes

(Berkeley, CA: University of California Press, 2002), p. 243. See also Rabinowicz, *A World Apart*.

55 Interview with Dayan Golditch, MANJM: J99, by Ros Livshin and Bill Williams, May/June 1978.

56 Rabinowicz, *A World Apart*, p. 32.

57 Interview with Chaim Hailpern, MANJM: 2012.50.34, by Bill Williams, 14 November 2002.

58 Interview with Dayan Golditch, MANJM: J99, by Ros Livshin and Bill Williams, May/June 1978.

59 Rabinowicz, *A World Apart*, p. 217.

60 Freud-Kandel, *Orthodox Judaism in Britain*, pp. 116–17

61 Samuel Heilman, *Defenders of the Faith: Inside Ultra-Orthodox Jewry* (New York: Schocken, 1992), p. 35.

62 Rabinowicz, *A World Apart*, p. 217.

63 University of Southampton, Hartley Library, Archives and Special Collections, MS183/357/3, Aubrey Rosen, 'What I Envisage for the Union', undated.

64 Bruce Mitchell, 'London's Haredi Publications in Yiddish: Language, Literature and Ultra-Orthodox Ideology', *European Judaism*, 32:2 (1999), pp. 51–66 (p. 55).

65 Interview with Dayan Golditch, MANJM: J99, by Ros Livshin and Bill Williams, May/June 1978.

66 Rabinowicz points out that no other section of British Jewry spends as much on education (*A World Apart*, p. xiv).

67 Jacobs, *Helping with Inquiries*, p. 13.

68 Heilman, *Defenders of the Faith*, p. 35.

69 Interview with Dayan Golditch, MANJM: J99, by Ros Livshin and Bill Williams, May/June 1978.

70 Endelman, *The Jews of Britain*, p. 251.

71 Homa, *Orthodoxy in Anglo-Jewry*, p. 51.

72 Endelman, *The Jews of Britain*, p. 251.

73 Interview with Chaim Hailpern, MANJM: 2012.50.34, by Bill Williams, 14 November 2002.

74 Manchester Jewish Museum, interview with Abraham Hailpern, MANJM: J324, by Ros Livshin (undated).

75 Interview with Chaim Hailpern, MANJM: 2012.50.34, by Bill Williams, 14 November 2002.

76 Michael Leigh, 'Reform Judaism in Britain (1840–1970)', in Dow Marmur (ed.), *Reform Judaism: Essays on Reform Judaism in Britain* (Oxford: Reform Synagogues of Great Britain, 1973), pp. 3–52 (p. 6).

77 Michael Meyer, *Response to Modernity: A History of the Reform Movement in Judaism* (Oxford: Oxford University Press, 1988), p. 41.

78 Ibid., pp. 75–99. See also Harvey Hill, 'The Science of Reform: Abraham Geiger and the Wissenschaft des Judentum', *Modern Judaism*, 27:3 (2007), pp. 329–49.

79 Leigh, 'Reform Judaism', pp. 7–11.

80 Meyer, *Response to Modernity*, p. 174.

81 Stephen Sharot, 'Reform and Liberal Judaism in London 1840–1940', *Jewish Social Studies* 41:3/4 (1979), pp. 211–28 (p. 212).

82 Kershen and Romain, *Tradition and Change*, p. 15.

83 Leigh, 'Reform Judaism', p. 26.

Notes

84 See ibid., p. 24, and Kershen and Romain, *Tradition and Change*, pp. 19–20. This religious caution was lifted in 1849. See Sharot, 'Reform and Liberal Judaism', p. 214.

85 Leigh, 'Reform Judaism', p. 20; Kershen and Romain, *Tradition and Change*, p. 14; Sharot, 'Reform and Liberal Judaism', p. 212.

86 Louis Jacobs, *Beyond Reasonable Doubt* (London: The Littman Library of Jewish Civilisation, 1999), p. 166, and Kershen and Romain, *Tradition and Change*, pp. 58–91.

87 Lily Montagu, 'Spiritual Possibilities of Judaism To-Day', *The Jewish Quarterly Review*, 11:2 (1899), pp. 216–31.

88 Lawrence Rigal and Rosita Rosenberg, *Liberal Judaism: The First Hundred Years* (London: Liberal Judaism, 2004), p. 40.

89 Ibid.

90 Montefiore, 'Outlines of Liberal Judaism', 1912, cited in Edward Kessler, *A Reader of Early Liberal Judaism: The Writings of Israel Abrahams, Claude Montefiore, Lily Montagu and Israel Mattuck* (London: Vallentine Mitchell, 2004), p. 20.

91 Meyer, *Response to Modernity*, p. 221.

92 Israel Mattuck, *Jewish Ethics* (London: Hutchinson, 1953), p. 16.

93 Kershen and Romain, *Tradition and Change*, p. 141.

94 Sharot, 'Reform and Liberal Judaism', p. 217, and Kershen and Romain, *Tradition and Change*, p. 158.

95 Kershen and Romain, *Tradition and Change*, p. 159.

96 Ibid., p. 164.

97 University of Southampton, Hartley Library, Archives and Special Collections, MS137/AJ436/27/4, statement by Stein at a meeting of the AJA Council, 25 May 1948.

98 University of Southampton, Hartley Library, Archives and Special Collections, MS302/A3069/1/24, speech by Hugo Gryn at RSGB Jubilee, 29 March 1992; Leigh, 'Reform Judaism', pp. 42–3.

99 University of Southampton, Hartley Library, Archives and Special Collections, MS302/1, Executive Minutes, Conference of Associated British Synagogues, 22 February 1945.

100 University of Southampton, Hartley Library, Archives and Special Collections, MS302/1, Minutes of the Conference of the Associated British Synagogues, 23–24 July 1946.

101 University of Southampton, Hartley Library, Archives and Special Collections, MS302/1, Minutes of Annual Conference, 13–15 April 1951.

102 Hill, 'The Science of Reform', p. 346.

103 In 2005 another rebadging saw RSGB evolve into the Movement for Reform Judaism.

104 University of Southampton, Hartley Library, Archives and Special Collections, MS302/1, Minutes of the Special Conference of the ASGB, 17–18 May 1958.

105 University of Southampton, Hartley Library, Archives and Special Collections, MS302/1, Executive Meeting, 16 December 1948.

106 Ignaz Maybaum, *The Jewish Mission* (London: James Clarke, 1951), p. 99.

107 Sheila Shulman, 'In the Beginning: Introduction', in Sybil Sheridan (ed.), *Hear Our Voice: Women Rabbis Tell Their Stories* (London: SCM Press, 1994), p. 39.

108 Interview with Rabbi Jonathan Romain by Gavin Schaffer, 24 September 2020.

109 University of Southampton, Hartley Library, Archives and Special Collections, MS302/1, Minutes of the Conference of the Associated British Synagogues, 23–24 July 1946. For the establishment of the college, see Kershen and Romain, *Tradition and Change*, pp. 203–4, and Michael Leigh, '1956 and All That', in Romain (ed.), *Renewing the Vision*, pp. 165–70.

110 Kershen and Romain, *Tradition and Change*, p. 204.
111 University of Southampton, Hartley Library, Archives and Special Collections, MS302/A3069/1/24, Raymond Goldman (Executive Director RSGB), 'Celebrating our Heritage: Building for the Future', 1992.
112 Simon Rocker, 'It took me a long time to realise I had this odd situation of being the first women rabbi, I had to live up to it', *Jewish Chronicle*, 12 January 2024.
113 See Jackie Tabick, 'I Never Really Wanted to be First', in Sheridan (ed.), *Hear Our Voice*, pp. 16–20 (p. 18).
114 Ibid., p. 19.
115 Having been passed over as Gryn's replacement at West London, Tabick became rabbi of the South-West Surrey Reform synagogue. See Rocker, 'It took me a long time', *Jewish Chronicle*, 12 January 2024.
116 See Lionel Blue, *Hitchhiking to Heaven: An Autobiography* (London: Hodder and Stoughton, 2004), pp. 307–8.
117 London Metropolitan Archives, Rainbow Jews, interview with Rabbi Sheila Shulman by Surat Knan, LMA-4653–PR-01–03–018–001, 23 October 2013.
118 Steven Greenberg has argued that 'Reform and Reconstructionist Jewish communities have formally taken on gay liberation as part of their religious tradition', in *Wrestling with God and Men: Homosexuality in the Jewish Tradition* (Madison, WI: University of Wisconsin Press, 2004), p. 30.
119 Dow Marmur, 'Introduction', in Marmur (ed.), *A Genuine Search*, p. 38.
120 University of Southampton, Hartley Library, Archives and Special Collections, MS302/1, ASGB Executive Minutes, 9 February 1948.
121 University of Southampton, Hartley Library, Archives and Special Collections, MS302/1, Minutes of the Special Conference of the Association of Synagogues of Great Britain, 9–11 November 1956.
122 University of Southampton, Hartley Library, Archives and Special Collections, MS302 A3069/2/1/1, Blackpool, notes on the Annual Conference of the Reform Synagogues of Great Britain, Buxton, 18–20 May 1973.
123 Interview with Rabbi Jonathan Romain by Gavin Schaffer, 24 September 2020.
124 University of Southampton, Hartley Library, Archives and Special Collections, MS302/1, Minutes of the Special Conference of the Association of Synagogues of Great Britain, 9–11 November 1956.
125 Ibid.
126 University of Southampton, Hartley Library, Archives and Special Collections, MS302/A3069/1/24, Hugo Gryn, 'Urgent New Tasks Face Britain's Reform Movement', Jubilee Article, 4 March 1992.
127 Manchester Central Library, MS 779 54, Papers of Manchester Reform Synagogue, President's Report by S. L. Goodman, 1983.
128 Jeffrey Newman, 'New Ways in Religious Thought', in Marmur (ed.), *A Genuine Search*, pp. 84–98 (p. 87).
129 Manchester Central Library, MS 779 54, Papers of Manchester Reform Synagogue, President's Report by Hans Kurer, 1967.
130 Lionel Blue, 'God and the Jewish Problem', *Inform*, 5 February 1975.
131 LMA, 4653, PR 01/03/001/001–4, interview with Rabbi Lionel Blue, Sharon Rappoport interviews, 12 April 2013.
132 Blue, *Hitchhiking to Heaven*, p. 87.
133 Sacks, *One People?*, p. 224.

Notes

134 University of Southampton, Hartley Library, Archives and Special Collections, MS302/1, Executive Minutes, note from Mr Barnett at the Conference of the Associated British Synagogues, 5 March 1944.

135 University of Southampton, Hartley Library, Archives and Special Collections, MS302/1, Executive Minutes, ASGB Executive Meeting, 1 December 1947.

136 University of Southampton, Hartley Library, Archives and Special Collections, MS302/1, Executive Minutes, ASGB Executive Meeting, 18 January 1949.

137 University of Southampton, Hartley Library, Archives and Special Collections, MS302/4, Reform Synagogues of Great Britain, Executive Minutes, 6 August 1967.

138 'Parting Company', *Jewish Tribune*, 30 July 1971.

139 University of Southampton, Hartley Library, Archives and Special Collections, MS302/1, ASGB Executive Committee Meeting, 27 November 1957.

140 'Combating Reformers', *Jewish Tribune*, 18 February 1972.

141 Letter to the Editor, *Jewish Tribune*, 4 May 1962.

142 Winston Held LLB, 'The Problem of the Jewish University Student', *Jewish Tribune*, 10 December 1965.

143 *Jewish Chronicle*, 23 April 1979.

144 Chief Rabbi MSS, ACC/2805/7/6/7, Jakobovits to letter writer, 30 April 1979.

145 Danny Weiner and Lucille Levi, 'Readers say "Orthodox Intolerance"', *Jewish Gazette*, 13 April 1979.

146 Ben Azai, 'Personal Opinion', *Jewish Chronicle*, 23 April 1979.

147 Chief Rabbi MSS, ACC/2805/7/6/7, Jakobovits to Marmur, 4 June 1979.

148 Sacks, *One People?*, p. 224.

149 Chief Rabbi MSS, ACC/2805/7/6/7, 'Two Kinds of Truth', sermon by John Rayner delivered at St Johns Wood, 2 June 1979.

150 University of Southampton, Hartley Library, Archives and Special Collections, MS302/A3069/2/3/2, Raymond Goldman (General Secretary of RSGB), RSGB Newsletter, July 1967.

151 Alderman, *Modern British Jewry*, p. 375.

152 University of Southampton, Hartley Library, Archives and Special Collections, MS302/A3069/2/3/2, Raymond Goldman (General Secretary of RSGB), RSGB Newsletter, July 1967.

153 Kershen and Romain, *Tradition and Change*, p. 280.

154 University of Southampton, Hartley Library, Archives and Special Collections, MS302/3/1, RSGB Standing Committee on Relationships with Anglo-Jewry, MAB King-Hamilton to Chief Rabbi Jakobovits, 6 February 1970.

155 *Jewish Tribune*, 7 August 1970.

156 Chief Rabbi MSS, ACC2805/7/2/24, Jakobovits to Sidney Hamburger, 30 September 1971.

157 Chief Rabbi MSS, ACC2805/7/2/24, Michael Fidler to Bernard Homa, 4 August 1971.

158 Chief Rabbi MSS, ACC2805/7/2/24, Jakobovits to Homa, 24 August 1971.

159 Chief Rabbi MSS, ACC2805/7/2/24, Homa to Jakobovits, 13 August 1971

160 Chief Rabbi MSS, ACC/2805/7/2/23, L. D. Brunner to Rabbi Gaon, 25 September 1970.

161 Kershen and Romain, *Tradition and Change*, p. 282, and Alderman, *Modern British Jewry*, p. 375.

Notes

162 Chief Rabbi MSS, ACC2805/7/2/24, Salmond Levin to Jakobovits, 3 November 1971.

163 Chief Rabbi MSS, ACC2805/7/2/24, Jakobovits to Levin, 5 November 1971.

164 Chief Rabbi MSS, ACC2805/7/2/24, statement to the Press by the Chief Rabbi and the Haham (undated).

165 Chief Rabbi MSS, ACC2805/7/2/24, Jakobovits to Homa, 28 October 1971.

166 Chief Rabbi MSS, ACC2805/7/2/24, Homa to Jakobovits, 2 November 1971.

167 Montefiore, *The Old Testament and After* (1923), cited from Kessler, *A Reader of Early Liberal Judaism*, p. 97.

168 Blue, *To Heaven, with Scribes and Pharisees*, p. 29.

169 For detailed analysis, see Meir Persoff, *Faith Against Reason: Religious Reform and the British Chief Rabbinate 1840–1990* (London: Vallentine Mitchell, 2008), pp. 283–317.

170 Alderman, *Modern British Jewry*, pp. 362–3.

171 Ibid., p. 364. For an in-depth account, see Jacobs, *Helping with Inquiries*, pp. 134–43, 159–78.

172 Jacobs, *Helping with Inquiries*, pp. 204–9.

173 Persoff, *Faith Against Reason*, p. 337.

174 Louis Jacobs, *We Have Reason to Believe: Some Aspects of Jewish Theology Examined in the Light of Modern Thought*, 4th edn (London: Vallentine Mitchell, 1995), p. 1.

175 Jacobs, *Beyond Reasonable Doubt*, p. 1.

176 'Chief Rabbi's Statement on Controversy', *Jewish Chronicle*, 8 May 1964.

177 James Parkes, 'Behind the Split: The Fear of Change', *Sunday Times*, 26 April 1964.

178 'Jews Divided', *Daily Telegraph*, 6 May 1964.

179 Jacobs, *We Have Reason to Believe*, p. 4.

180 Ibid., p. 1.

181 Persoff, *Faith Against Reason*, pp. 291–2, and Alderman, *Modern British Jewry*, p. 362.

182 'The Community's Future', *Jewish Chronicle*, 29 December 1961.

183 Jacobs, *Helping with Inquiries*, p. 134.

184 Alfred Sherman, 'Trial by Jewry', *Sunday Telegraph*, 26 April 1964.

185 'Jews' College Controversy: London Dayanim Issue Statement', *Jewish Chronicle*, 2 February 1962.

186 Jacobs, *Helping with Inquiries*, p. 181.

187 Chief Rabbi MSS, ACC/2805/7/2/24, Jakobovits to Levin, 5 November 1971.

188 'Priority Problems', *Jewish Tribune*, 3 March 1967.

189 Heilman, *Defenders of the Faith*, p. 13.

190 Chief Rabbi MSS, ACC/2805/7/2/24, Levin to Jakobovits, 3 November 1971.

191 Soetendorp, 'Confrontation or Cooperation?', p. 18.

192 Blue, *To Heaven, with Scribes and Pharisees*, p. 21.

193 Soetendorp, 'Confrontation or Cooperation?', pp. 23–4.

194 See Freud-Kandel, *Orthodox Judaism in Britain*, p. 111.

195 Emile Marmorstein, 'An Organ of Orthodox Jewry', *Jewish Tribune*, 30 May 1962.

196 University of Southampton, Hartley Library, Archives and Special Collections, MS302 A3069/1/24, Hugo Gryn, 'Urgent New Tasks Face Britain's Reform Movement', Jubilee Article, 4 March 1992.

197 University of Southampton, Hartley Library, Archives and Special Collections, MS302 A3069/1/24, message at Jubilee Service from Ruth Cohen, 29 March 1992.

198 Chief Rabbi MSS, ACC/2805/6/2/6, Gateshead, Kollel Ha-Rabbanim, Jubilee Report (1942–52).

199 'Rabbi Sir Israel Brodie at Anniversary Dinner', *Jewish Tribune*, 23 June 1972.

Notes

200 University of Southampton, Hartley Library, Archives and Special Collections, MS302 A3069/1/24, Hugo Gryn, 'Urgent New Tasks Face Britain's Reform Movement', Jubilee Article, 4 March 1992.

201 Maybaum, *The Jewish Mission*, p. 44.

202 Freud-Kandel, *Orthodox Judaism in Britain*, p. 118.

203 Barbara Myerhoff, *Number Our Days: A Triumph of Continuity and Culture Among Jewish Old People in an Urban Ghetto* (New York: Simon and Schuster, 1978), p. 184.

3 'We speak for them'

1 Bernard Levin, 'This Dangerous Talk about Jews Shirking their Duty', *Daily Mail*, 2 June 1967.

2 Jakobovits's position was outlined in 'Volunteers Rush to Serve', *Jewish Chronicle*, 2 June 1967.

3 Levin, 'This Dangerous Talk', *Daily Mail*, 2 June 1967.

4 See Schneier Levenberg, *The Board and Zion: An Historical Survey* (Hull: Rare Times, 1985), and Stuart Cohen, *English Zionists and British Jews: The Communal Politics of Anglo-Jewry, 1895–1920* (Princeton, NJ: Princeton University Press, 1982), pp. 232–9. Wendehorst notes that Zionism did not become 'a mass phenomenon' among British Jewry until the late 1930s, in Stephan Wendehorst, *British Jewry, Zionism, and the Jewish State, 1936–1956* (Oxford: Oxford University Press, 2012), p. 266.

5 See Gavin Schaffer, 'Unmasking the "Muscle Jew": The Jewish Soldier in British War Service, 1899–1945', *Patterns of Prejudice*, 46:3–4 (2012), pp. 375–96.

6 'Middle East Debates: How Jewish MPs Voted', *Jewish Chronicle*, 9 November 1956. For the vote of 'no confidence' in Janner, see 'Jewish MPs' Suez Vote', *Jewish Chronicle*, 23 November 1956. For analysis, see Alderman, *Modern British Jewry*, pp. 339–40, and Jack Omer-Jackaman, *The Impact of Zionism and Israel on Anglo-Jewry's Identity, 1948–82: Caught Somewhere between Zion and Galut* (London: Vallentine Mitchell, 2019), pp. 47–52.

7 'Middle East Debates: How Jewish MPs Voted', *Jewish Chronicle*, 9 November 1956.

8 Omer-Jackaman, *The Impact of Zionism*, p. 121.

9 Ibid.

10 Levin's remarks were described as contemptible by Ben Azai (Chaim Bermant), 'Personal Opinion', *Jewish Chronicle*, 9 June 1967. Support for Levin came from Sir Louis Gluckstein (President of the Liberal Jewish Synagogue), who argued that he could not believe Jakobovits 'was speaking for Anglo-Jewry'. '"Unwise" Views on Dual Loyalty', *Jewish Chronicle*, 16 June 1967.

11 Emmwood, *Daily Mail*, 9 June 1967.

12 Sara Yael Hirschhorn, *City on a Hilltop: American Jews and the Israeli Settler Movement* (Cambridge, MA: Harvard University Press, 2017), p. 36.

13 Tom Segev, *The Seventh Million: The Israelis and the Holocaust*, trans. Haim Watzman (New York: Hill and Wang, 1993), p. 137.

14 'Brown Attacked by Shinwell', *Jewish Chronicle*, 23 June 1967.

15 Antony Lerman, *The Making and Unmaking of a Zionist: A Personal and Political Journey* (London: Pluto, 2012), p. 30.

16 Colin Shindler, in email discussion with the author, noted that many Soviet Jews listened to Israeli-broadcast *Kol Yisrael* radio in secret. Shindler to the author, 11 February 2024.

Notes

17 'Russians against the Kremlin: Who Fights for What', *Sunday Telegraph*, 14 May 1972.

18 In 1953, amid a slew of antisemitic canards, a group of mostly Jewish high-level doctors were accused of deliberately accelerating the deaths of several of the Soviet leadership, a trumped-up nonsense which could have triggered a substantial purge (and possibly mass Jewish deportations) had it not been for the death of Stalin two months later. The 'Killer Doctors' conspiracy was the nadir of several years of accelerating Soviet antisemitism, during which Jews frequently faced allegations of disloyalty and anti-patriotism. See Yoram Gorlizki, 'Jews', in Graham Smith (ed.), *The Nationalities Question in the Soviet Union* (Harlow: Longman, 1990), pp. 339–59 (p. 343). For analysis of antisemitism in the Soviet Union prior to the plot, see John Cooper, *The British Campaign for Soviet Jewry 1966–1991: Human Rights and Exit Permits* (Manchester: i2i, 2023), pp. 34–41.

19 Yaacov Roi, *The Struggle for Soviet-Jewish Emigration, 1948–67* (Cambridge: Cambridge University Press, 1991), p. 7.

20 Cooper, *The British Campaign*, p. 13.

21 Elie Wiesel, *The Jews of Silence: A Personal Report on Soviet Jewry* (Philadelphia, PA: The Jewish Publication Society of America, 1967), p. 70.

22 Cooper, *The British Campaign*, pp. 63–4.

23 Benjamin Pinkus, *The Jews of the Soviet Union: The History of a National Minority* (Cambridge: Cambridge University Press, 1988), p. 291.

24 See Cooper, *The British Campaign*, pp. 212–23.

25 Roi, *The Struggle for Soviet-Jewish Emigration*, p. 6.

26 For details, see Wasserstein, *Vanishing Diaspora*, pp. 191–2.

27 This immediate protest was organised by Colin Shindler, email to author, 11 February 2024.

28 Daphne Gerlis, *Those Wonderful Women in Black: Story of the Women's Campaign for Soviet Jewry* (London: Minerva Press, 1996), p. 22.

29 This conference was held at the Piccadilly Hotel in London in June 1969. Speeches at the conference were subsequently published in David Carrington (ed.), *Light on Soviet Jewry* (London: Ranelagh Press, 1969).

30 Gerlis, *Those Wonderful Women*, pp. 115–16. 'Refusenik' became the primary descriptor of Jews who were refused the right to leave the Soviet Union. Cooper has argued that the term was coined by British campaigner Michael Sherbourne (*The British Campaign*, p. 94).

31 Dave Rich, 'The Activist Challenge: Women, Students, and the Board of Deputies of British Jews in the British Campaign for Soviet Jewry', *Jewish History*, 29 (2015), pp. 163–85 (pp. 167–8). Cooper has argued that the student campaign grew after the establishment of the Student Struggle for Soviet Jewry in the United States in 1964 (*The British Campaign*, p. 471).

32 In the embassy group were Cyril Harris (rabbi of Kenton synagogue) and Saul Amias (rabbi of Edgware synagogue). Harris recalls the incident in *For Heaven's Sake* (London: Vallentine Mitchell, 2000), p. 28.

33 Cooper, *The British Campaign*, p. 90.

34 A. M. Rendel, 'Apology over Embassy Invasion', *The Times*, 14 May 1971.

35 Board of Deputies MSS, ACC/3121/E/04/0053, statement from the Press Department of the Soviet Embassy, 14 May 1971.

36 Rendel, 'Apology over Embassy Invasion', *The Times*, 14 May 1971.

37 Cooper, *The British Campaign*, p. 81.

Notes

38 Board of Deputies MSS, ACC/3121/E/04/0053, Saul Amias, 'Report on Incident at Russian Embassy on Thursday, 13th May, 1971'.

39 Ibid.

40 Charles Spencer, 'A Reply to Bernard Levin', *Jewish Echo*, 9 June 1967.

41 Rich, 'The Activist Challenge', pp. 173–4.

42 Cooper, *The British Campaign*, p. 81, and Gerlis, *Those Wonderful Women*, p. 28.

43 University of Southampton, Hartley Library, Archives and Special Collections, MS254/1/3/2, Papers of Rita Eker and Margaret Rigal on 'Women's Campaign for Soviet Jewry Administration', History of the Group, c. 1991. For a history of Palatnik's case, see Gerlis, *Those Wonderful Women*, pp. 26–9.

44 Barbara Oberman recalls that there were not actually 35 women at the initial protest, in Gerlis, *Those Wonderful Women*, p. 30.

45 'Protest over Jailed Jew', *Glasgow Herald*, 24 July 1972.

46 University of Southampton, Hartley Library, Archives and Special Collections, MS254/1/3/107, leaflet for the Kirov ballet performance at the Palace Theatre Manchester, 10–15 August 1987.

47 Gerlis, *Those Wonderful Women*, pp. 64–5.

48 Board of Deputies MSS, ACC/3121/E/04/0810, National Conference on Soviet Jewry, 5 March 1972.

49 Scottish Jewish Archives Centre, Oral History Project, 'Reunion of 35s Group Members', group interview led by Harvey Kaplan, 29 January 2015.

50 Gerlis, *Those Wonderful Women*, p. 24. Cooper has argued that the Board of Deputies grew 'tired of the stunts and activism of the Women's Campaign' (*The British Campaign*, p. 474).

51 Board of Deputies MSS, ACC/3121/E/04/0902, letter to Avram Marks, 20 June 1975.

52 Board of Deputies MSS, ACC/3121/C/01/010, Minutes of Soviet Jewry Actions Committee, 22 July 1975.

53 Ibid.

54 'Volunteers by the Hundred', *Jewish Chronicle*, 26 May 1967.

55 'Volunteers Rush to Serve', *Jewish Chronicle*, 2 June 1967.

56 'Young Jews Fly to Israel', *Jewish Observer and Middle East Review*, 2 June 1967.

57 'Over 8000 Volunteers for Israel', *Jewish Chronicle*, 23 June 1967.

58 'The Unsung Heroes', *Jewish Chronicle*, 16 June 1967.

59 For coverage of the Hyde Park rally, see 'Volunteers Rush to Serve', *Jewish Chronicle*, 2 June 1967. For the Albert Hall rally, see 'Past Divisions and Differences Were Shelved', *Jewish Chronicle*, 9 June 1967. These rallies reflected the actions of Jewish communities across the world. In Melbourne 7,000 Jews attended a public rally, 45,000 marched in New York, and 7,000 in Rome. For details, see 'World Jewry on the March', *Jewish Observer and Middle East Review*, 2 June 1967. For details on the Australian response, see Ronald Taft, 'The Impact of the Middle East Crisis of June 1967 on Melbourne Jewry: An Empirical Study', *Jewish Journal of Sociology*, 9:2 (1967), pp. 243–62.

60 'Youth: Order out of Chaos' and 'Israel Campaign Hots Up', *Jewish Observer and Middle East Review*, 9 June 1967.

61 A report on the relationship between British Jews and Israel described fundraising, 'especially at times of crisis', as a 'phenomenal success'. See Barry Kosmin, Antony Lerman and Jacqueline Goldberg, 'The Attachment of British Jews to Israel', JPR

Report, 1997, p. 20, https://www.jpr.org.uk/reports/attachment-british-jews-israel (accessed 8 October 2024).

62 JPA News, *Jewish Observer and Middle East Review*, 14 July 1967.

63 Cooper, *The British Campaign*, p. 479.

64 Levenberg's speech published in Carrington (ed.), *Light on Soviet Jewry*, p. 41.

65 University of Southampton, Hartley Library, Archives and Special Collections, MS 254/1/2/50, press release 1971.

66 University of Southampton, Hartley Library, Archives and Special Collections, MS254/1/2/11, press release 1973.

67 'Raiza and Sonia Meet in Glasgow: with Barbara Scot', *Glasgow Herald*, 26 January 1973.

68 Gerlis, *Those Wonderful Women*, p. 30.

69 James E. Young, *The Texture of Memory: Holocaust Memorials and Meaning* (New Haven, CT: Yale University Press, 1993), p. 214.

70 The link between the Nazis and Israel's Arab enemies was repeatedly made in film and literature. See Peter Novick, *The Holocaust in American Life* (Boston: Houghton Mifflin, 1999), p. 157.

71 Chaim Bermant, *Troubled Eden: An Anatomy of British Jewry* (London: Vallentine Mitchell, 1969), p. 259. For analysis, see Pearce, *Holocaust Consciousness in Contemporary Britain*, p. 27.

72 Tim Cole, *Images of the Holocaust: The Myth of "Shoah Business"* (London: Duckworth, 1999), p. 10.

73 Novick, *The Holocaust in American Life*, p. 159.

74 'Hands off Middle East: Labour MPs Warn Government', *Jewish Observer and Middle East Review*, 30 June 1967.

75 Cooper, *The British Campaign*, p. 472.

76 University of Southampton, Hartley Library, Archives and Special Collections, MS254 1/3/2, 'Women's Campaign for Soviet Jewry Administration', 'Show Trials and Cultural Holocaust for Soviet Jewry', 22 October 1984.

77 Gerlis, *Those Wonderful Women*, p. 183.

78 'The Hour of Danger', *Jewish Chronicle*, 26 May 1967.

79 Board of Deputies MSS, ACC3121/E/04/0810, speech by Solomon Teff at Meeting of Foreign Affairs Committee, 8 April 1965.

80 University of Southampton, Hartley Library, Archives and Special Collections, MS 254/1/3/23, public handouts of the 35s, 40th Anniversary of the Soviet Weekly, 13 February 1982.

81 Wiesel, *The Jews of Silence*, pp. 73–4, 102. The original title of Wiesel's groundbreaking Holocaust memoir, *The Night*, was *And the World Remained Silent*.

82 Adella Lithman, 'Camp 19 – and the Price One Man Paid for Freedom', *Daily Express*, 20 November 1973.

83 University of Southampton, Hartley Library, Archives and Special Collections, MSS254/1/3/23, 'Public Handouts of the 35s', handout at a performance of musician Yevgeny Yevtushenko, 25 February 1979.

84 Board of Deputies MSS, ACC3121/E/4/0823, letter from Mike Whine to British rabbis about 'Prisoner of Conscience Shabbat', 29 November 1973.

85 Wendehorst, *British Jewry*, pp. 133, 286.

86 'The Problem of Assimilation: WJC Discussion', *Jewish Chronicle*, 12 October 1956.

Notes

87 See Ernest Krausz, 'The Edgware Survey: Factors in Jewish Identification', *Jewish Journal of Sociology*, 11:2 (1969), pp. 151–64 (p. 162), and Tova Benski, 'Identification, Group Survival and Inter-Group Relations: The Case of a Middle-Class Jewish Community in Scotland', *Ethnic and Racial Studies*, 4:3 (1981), pp. 307–20 (p. 313).

88 Carl Gordon, 'Synagogue and Rally', *Jewish Echo*, 9 June 1967.

89 Ibid.

90 Maisie Mosco, *The Waiting Game* (Sevenoaks: New English Library, 1987), p. 74.

91 Interview with Colin Shindler, 22 January 2021.

92 Cooper, *The British Campaign*, pp. 126, 487.

93 Chaim Bermant, *Coming Home* (London: George Allen and Unwin, 1976), p. 177.

94 'Jewish Leadership', *The Jewish Tribune*, 12 May 1967.

95 Papers of the Reform Jewish Community of Manchester, Manchester Central Library, MS779/4, 'Thank God we have not been forgotten: Bournemouth's Rabbi Soetendorp visits Russia', *Inform*, 5:2 (July 1975).

96 Board of Deputies MSS, ACC/3121/C/01/010, paper on 'Correspondence with Jews in the USSR', 19 February 1975 following meeting of SJAC, 17 February 1975.

97 Papers of the Reform Jewish Community of Manchester, Eva Mitchell, 'It Wasn't Cold in Moscow', *Inform*, 3:4 (May 1978).

98 Gerlis, *Those Wonderful Women*, p. 179.

99 'Chinn Appeal at Hendon', *Jewish Observer and Middle East Review*, 28 July 1967.

100 'Junior Chronicle', *Jewish Chronicle*, 16 June 1967.

101 Rich, 'The Activist Challenge', p. 167, and Cooper, *The British Campaign*, p. 472.

102 See Gerlis, *Those Wonderful Women*, pp. 89–90.

103 Rich, 'The Activist Challenge', p. 167.

104 Interview with Colin Shindler, 22 January 2021.

105 Cooper, *The British Campaign*, pp. 147–9.

106 Bermant, *Coming Home*, pp. 126, 166.

107 David Merron, *Collectively Yours: Tales from the Borderline* (Bakewell: Country Books, 1999), p. 130.

108 Habonim Archive at Yad Tabenkin, Box 11/1, 72308, *Habonim News Letter*, 23 December 1959.

109 Cooper, *The British Campaign*, p. 482.

110 Scottish Jewish Archives Centre, POL SOV 0003, Meetings of Glasgow Branch of the 35s, 13 December 1989.

111 Minutes of the SJAC recorded that 350 refuseniks had been 'assigned to Britain' in 1975. Board of Deputies MSS, ACC3121/C/01/010, 22 April 1975. Similarly, Jewish Prisoners Month was 'coordinated throughout the world' from 1973. Board of Deputies MSS, ACC/3121/E/04/0901, Report by Mike Whine, 25 October 1973.

112 Sue Usiskin in Gerlis, *Those Wonderful Women*, p. 91.

113 Board of Deputies MSS, ACC/2805/7/2/23, Clause 43, Immanuel Jakobovits to Alderman Fidler, 15 April 1970.

114 Helen Abendstern, 'Tallit Waiting', *Inform*, 72 (March 1992).

115 Gerlis, *Those Wonderful Women*, p. 46.

116 Matthew Hilton, 'Politics is Ordinary: Non-governmental Organizations and Political Participation in Contemporary Britain', *Twentieth Century British History*, 22:2 (2011), pp. 230–68.

117 Linda Grant, *The Story of the Forest* (London: Virago, 2023), p. 231.

Notes

4 'These wicked sons'

1 'Editorial: The Politics of Antisemitism', *Jewish Quarterly*, 32:1 (1985), pp. 1–2.
2 For Lerman's more recent thinking on antisemitism, see Antony Lerman, *Whatever Happened to Antisemitism? Definition and the Myth of the 'Collective Jew'* (London: Pluto, 2022).
3 David Rosenberg, 'Racism and Antisemitism in Contemporary Britain', *Jewish Quarterly*, 32:1 (1985).
4 Interview with Antony Lerman, 16 June 2022.
5 Letter to the Editor from Bryan Cheyette and David Cesarani, *Jewish Chronicle*, 23 August 1985.
6 Lerman, *The Making and Unmaking of a Zionist*, p. 81.
7 'Magazine Editor is Replaced', *Jewish Chronicle*, 19 July 1985.
8 'Directors Quit Over New JPR Appointment', *Jewish Chronicle*, 23 December 2005. The directors in question were Larry Levine, Adrian Cohen and Richard Bolchover.
9 Geoffrey Alderman, 'JPR Loses Mind in Choice of New Head', *Jewish Chronicle*, 13 January 2006.
10 Interview with Antony Lerman, 16 June 2022.
11 See Jonathan Freedland, 'The Danger of Melanie Phillips', *Jewish Chronicle*, 30 March 2007.
12 Melanie Phillips, 'IJV: Leaders of the Israel Hate Fest', *Jewish Chronicle*, 16 February 2007.
13 Interview with David Rosenberg and Julia Bard, 1 July 2022.
14 David Cesarani, 'One Hundred Years of Zionism in England', *European Judaism*, 25:1 (1992), pp. 40–7 (p. 45).
15 See Leora Batnitzky, *How Judaism Became a Religion: An Introduction to Modern Jewish Thought* (Princeton, NJ: Princeton University Press, 2011).
16 See Daniel Boyarin, *A Traveling Homeland: The Babylonian Talmud as Diaspora* (Philadelphia, PA: University of Pennsylvania Press, 2015). See also Daniel Boyarin and Jonathan Boyarin, 'Diaspora: Generation and the Ground of Jewish Identity', *Critical Inquiry*, 19:4 (1993), pp. 693–725.
17 For analysis, see Batnitzky, *How Judaism Became a Religion*, p. 20.
18 Lerman, *Whatever Happened to Antisemitism?*, p. 265.
19 That the universal impulse was often interpreted in terms of a specific Jewish history and destiny led Hughes to question whether it wasn't 'ultimately another form of particularizing', in Aaron Hughes, *Rethinking Jewish Philosophy: Beyond Particularism and Universalism* (Oxford: Oxford University Press, 2014), pp. 47–8.
20 For analysis, see Batnitzky, *How Judaism Became a Religion*, p. 168.
21 For analysis of opposition from rabbis in Berlin and Munich, see Lawrence Epstein, *The Dream of Zion: The Story of the First Zionist Congress* (Lanham, MD: Rowman and Littlefield, 2014), pp. 38–40.
22 David Feldman, 'Conceiving Difference: Religion, Race and the Jews in Britain, c. 1750–1900', *History Workshop Journal*, 76:1 (2013), pp. 160–86 (p. 173).
23 Nicholas de Lange, *An Introduction to Judaism*, 2nd edn (Cambridge: Cambridge University Press, 2010), p. 33.
24 Mark Marqusee, *If I Am Not for Myself: Journey of an Anti-Zionist Jew* (London: Verso, 2008), p. 50.
25 Lerman, *Whatever Happened to Antisemitism?*, p. 258

Notes

26 David Rosenberg, 'I Was a Teenage Zionist', *Jewish Socialist*, 8 (winter 1986/7).

27 Yehuda Bauer, 'Antisemitism and Anti-Zionism – New and Old', in Robert Wistrich (ed.), *Anti-Zionism and Antisemitism in the Contemporary World* (Basingstoke: Macmillan, 1990), p. 200.

28 For analysis, see Cohen, *English Zionists and British Jews*, pp. 232–9; Levenberg, *The Board and Zion*, pp. 50–7; Alderman, *Modern British Jewry*, pp. 246–7.

29 David Alexander and Claude Montefiore, 'The Future of the Jews. Palestine and Zionism. Views of Anglo-Jewry', *The Times*, 24 May 1917.

30 Julian Huxley and A. C. Haddon, *We Europeans: A Survey of Racial Problems* (London: Jonathan Cape, 1935), p. 96. For analysis of the writing of *We Europeans*, see Gavin Schaffer, *Racial Science and British Society, 1930–62* (Basingstoke: Palgrave, 2008), pp. 32–4.

31 *Jewish Guardian*, 4 June 1920.

32 Ibid.

33 For analysis of the rise of Zionism within the Board of Deputies, see Levenberg, *The Board and Zion*, pp. 61–2; Wendehorst, *British Jewry*, p. 48; Alderman, *Modern British Jewry*, pp. 265–320.

34 Rory Miller, *Divided Against Zion: Anti-Zionist Opposition in Britain to a Jewish State in Palestine, 1945–8* (London: Frank Cass, 2000), p. 249.

35 University of Southampton, Hartley Library, Archives and Special Collections, MS150/ AJ110/14, pamphlet, 'The Jewish Fellowship: a Challenge to All Jews'.

36 University of Southampton, Hartley Library, Archives and Special Collections, MS140 A2049/468/11, Council Meeting of the Jewish Fellowship, 23 May 1944.

37 'It Can't Happen Here', *Jewish Outlook*, April 1946.

38 Omer-Jackaman, *The Impact of Zionism*, p. 227.

39 Miller, *Divided Against Zion*, p. 249.

40 University of Southampton, Hartley Library, Archives and Special Collections, MS137/AJ436/27/4, statement by Stein at a Meeting of the AJA Council, 25 May 1948.

41 University of Southampton, Hartley Library, Archives and Special Collections, MS137/ AJ436/27/4, statement by the Jewish Fellowship Delegation at the Anglo-American Committee of Inquiry, 30 January 1946. The AJA statement is from MS137/6/1b/11, Robert Weltsch, 'Note on the Situation in Palestine by a Correspondent recently in the Country', 20 November 1947.

42 University of Southampton, Hartley Library, Archives and Special Collections, MS150 AJ110/14, pamphlet, 'The Jewish Fellowship: a Challenge to all Jews'.

43 University of Southampton, Hartley Library, Archives and Special Collections, MS140/ A2049/248/2, letter from Joseph Leftwich (Organising Secretary) to Chief Rabbi Hertz, 24 February 1944.

44 University of Southampton, Hartley Library, Archives and Special Collections, MS150/A3006/1/3/53, Basil Henriques to The Hon. Ewen Montagu, 18 October 1945.

45 Miller, *Divided Against Zion*, p. 90.

46 Rabkin notes how, historically, Reform Judaism had sought 'a weakening of the ethnic dimension of Judaism', in Yakov Rabkin, *A Threat from Within: A Century of Jewish Opposition to Zionism*, trans. Fred A. Reed (London: Zed Books, 2006), p. 20.

47 'Letters: An Agudist Writes', *Jewish Outlook*, 2 May 1946.

48 Rabin, *A Threat from Within*, p. 19.

Notes

49 Alderman, *The Federation of Synagogues*, pp. 64–6.

50 For the most obvious example of this Orthodox hostility to Zionism, see the views of Joel Teitelbaum and the Satmar Hasidic community as detailed in Batnitzky, *How Judaism Became a Religion*, p. 187.

51 Interviews held in the Manchester Jewish Museum, interviews of Abraham Heilpern (J324) and Dayan Golditch (J99). *Frummer Yiden* could be translated from Yiddish as 'religious Jews'.

52 Editorial by Hefkerus, *Jewish Tribune*, 25 May 1973.

53 Jacob Bentov, 'Threat to the Youth – More Teachers the Answer', *Jewish Tribune*, 11 December 1970.

54 A. B. Solomon, 'Education in Anglo-Jewry', *Jewish Tribune*, 24 December 1965.

55 David Landy, *Jewish Identity and Palestinian Rights: Diaspora Jewish Opposition to Israel* (London: Zed Books, 2011), p. 129.

56 Dashiel Lawrence, 'Pushing the Boundaries: Contemporary Jewish Critics of Israel and Zionism', in Maria Diemling and Larry Ray (eds), *Boundaries, Identity and Belonging in Modern Judaism* (Abingdon: Routledge, 2015), pp. 193–207 (p. 200).

57 Interview with David Rosenberg and Julia Bard, 1 July 2022.

58 Julia Bard, 'Self Determination in the Diaspora', in Anne Karpf, Brian Klug, Jacqueline Rose and Barbara Rosenbaum (eds), *A Time to Speak Out: Independent Jewish Voices on Israel, Zionism and Jewish Identity* (London: Verso, 2008), pp. 235–6.

59 David J. Goldberg, *This is Not the Way: Jews, Judaism and Israel* (London: Faber and Faber, 2012), p. 21

60 Boyarin and Boyarin, 'Diaspora: Generation and the Ground of Jewish Identity', p. 723.

61 University of Southampton, Hartley Library, Archives and Special Collections, MS140/A2049/248/2, Charles Singer, 'Supplementary Aims', Executive Meeting of the Jewish Fellowship, 28 April 1943.

62 Interview with David Rosenberg and Julia Bard, 1 July 2022. See also Finlay, 'Between Religion and Ethnicity', p. 116.

63 Omer-Jackaman, *The Impact of Zionism*, p. 215. See also Cesarani, 'One Hundred Years', p. 46.

64 Clive Gilbert, 'Israel and the Diaspora', *Jewish Socialist*, 1 (1985).

65 In interview, David Rosenberg recalled the establishment of channels of dialogue in this period. JSG members also joined meetings in Holland. See 'Dutch Doubles in the Peace Game', *Jewish Socialist*, 5 (spring 1986).

66 Letter from Irene Bruegel, *Jewish Chronicle*, 3 May 2002.

67 'The Occupation is Killing Us All', *Jewish Chronicle*, 5 April 2002.

68 Irene Bruegel and Tirza Waisel, 'Letter: Academic Liberty and Boycotts', *The Guardian*, 16 December 2002.

69 'We Renounce Israel Rights', *The Guardian*, 8 August 2002.

70 IJV grew partly from another Israel-critical group, the Jewish Forum for Justice and Human Rights. See Lerman, *The Making and Unmaking of a Zionist*, pp. 113–14. The primary driver of IJV was Jacqueline Rose, who set up the organisation with support from Tony Klug, Anne Karpf, Gillian Slovo, Brian Klug, David Goldberg, Ann Jungman, Anthony Isaacs and Edie Friedman (among others). For tactical reasons, Antony Lerman was not a signatory, but he wrote a sympathetic supporting article in the *Guardian*.

71 'Editors' Introduction', in Karpf et al. (eds), *A Time to Speak Out*, p. ix.

Notes

72 IJV Declaration, *The Times*, 5 February 2007. See also Goldberg, *This is Not the Way*, pp. 245–8.

73 University of Southampton, Hartley Library, Archives and Special Collections, MS140/A3006/1/3/53, statement adopted by the Executive Committee of the Jewish Fellowship, 14 April 1943.

74 University of Southampton, Hartley Library, Archives and Special Collections, MS140/A2049/468/11, Daniel Lipson to the Council of the Jewish Fellowship, 30 January 1946.

75 Roberto Sussman, 'Zionism and Anti-Zionism: Beyond the Slogans', *Jewish Socialist*, 8 (winter 1987), and Clive Gilbert, 'Israel and the Diaspora', *Jewish Socialist*, 1 (spring 1985).

76 Emma Clyne, 'A Student's Story', in Karpf et al. (eds), *A Time to Speak Out*, pp. 75–93 (p. 82).

77 Rabkin, *A Threat from Within*, p. 21, and Landy, *Jewish Identity*, p. 113.

78 Marqusee, *If I Am Not for Myself*, p. 61.

79 Jacqueline Rose, 'On the Myth of Self Hatred', in Karpf et al. (eds), *A Time to Speak Out*, pp. 84–95 (p. 84).

80 Lawrence, 'Pushing the Boundaries', p. 195.

81 Marqusee, *If I Am Not for Myself*, p. ix.

82 Howard Jacobson, 'Independent Jewish Voices can carry on talking to themselves. I don't want to know', *The Independent*, 10 February 2007.

83 Howard Jacobson, *The Finkler Question* (London: Bloomsbury, 2010), p. 220.

84 Ibid., p. 139.

85 Gerald Steinberg, 'These Wicked Sons Would Still be Slaves', *Canadian Jewish News*, 5 April 2007.

86 Jacobson, *The Finkler Question*, p. 115.

87 Editorial, *Jewish Outlook*, 9 (January 1947).

88 'Editorial: Mock Education', *Jewish Tribune*, 24 August 1962.

89 'Women Speak Out against Zionism: If a woman calls herself feminist she should consciously call herself anti-Zionist', *Spare Rib*, 121 (1982).

90 For a Jewish response, see Sheila Shulman, Elizabeth Sarah, Lilian Mohin, Bev Gold, Hannah Aziz, Lin Davidson, Linda Bellos and Jenny Lovell, 'About Anti-Semitism', *Spare Rib*, 123 (1982). For the letters policy in the wake of the incident, see Roisin Boyd, 'Sisterhood is Plain Sailing', *Spare Rib*, 132 (1983). For analysis of this incident, see Natalie Thomlinson, '"Sisterhood is plain sailing?" Multi-racial Feminist Collectives in 1980s Britain', in Kristina Schulz (ed.), *The Women's Liberation Movement: Impacts and Outcomes* (London: Berghahn, 2017), pp. 198–213 (pp. 207–8).

91 Statement from *Outwrite*, 5 (August 1982).

92 Natalie Thomlinson, *Race, Ethnicity and the Women's Movement in England, 1968–93* (Basingstoke: Palgrave, 2016), p. 126.

93 Statement from *Outwrite*, 5 (August 1982).

94 See 'Prisoners, Nurses and the War', *Outwrite*, 11 (February 1983); 'Poisoning Women', *Outwrite*, 14 (May 1983).

95 'Jewish Women Write', *Outwrite*, 4 (July 1982).

96 Nira Yuval-Davis, 'Introduction to "Antisemitism, Anti-Racism and Zionism: Old Debates, Contemporary Contestations": Reflecting Back on My Article "Zionism, Antisemitism and the Struggle Against Racism: Some Reflections on a Current Painful Debate Among Feminists", *Spare Rib*, September 1984', *Feminist Review*, 126:1 (2020), pp. 173–7.

97 For analysis of Jewish feminist responses, see Thomlinson, *Race, Ethnicity and the Women's Movement*, pp. 123–4.

98 Editorial, *Shifra: A Jewish Feminist Magazine*, 1 (December 1984).

99 See David Cesarani, 'The Perdition Affair', in Wistrich (ed.), *Anti-Zionism and Antisemitism in the Contemporary World*, pp. 53–62 (p. 54).

100 Ibid.

101 Roberto Sussman, 'Zionism in the Limelight', *Jewish Socialist*, 9 (spring 1987).

102 David Rosenberg, 'Raising the Curtain on History', *Jewish Socialist*, 9 (spring 1987).

103 Gail Chester, 'Notes on the Impossibility of Passing', in Danielle Harway, Ros Schwartz and Val Johnson (eds), *A Word in Edgeways* (London: JF Publications, 1988), pp. 10–14 (p. 12).

104 Sussman, 'Zionism in the Limelight'.

105 Interview with Rabbi Sheila Shulman by Surat Knan, 23 October 2013.

106 Michelle Carlisle, 'Israel, Palestine and Sunderland', *Jewish Socialist*, 2 (summer 1985).

107 London Metropolitan Archives, Rainbow Jews, interview with Rabbi Elizabeth Sarah by Suzanne Paginton, RJ201314A, 26 September 2013.

108 Carlisle, 'Israel, Palestine and Sunderland', *Jewish Socialist*, 2 (summer 1985).

109 Landy, *Jewish Identity*, p. 99.

110 Brian Klug, 'A Time to Move On', in Karpf et al. (eds), *A Time to Speak*, pp. 286–96 (p. 287).

111 John Bunzl, 'Zionism and Jewish Identity', *Jewish Socialist*, 3 (autumn 1985).

112 Bentov, 'Threat to the Youth', *Jewish Tribune*, 11 December 1970.

113 Lawrence, 'Pushing the Boundaries', p. 202.

114 Ibid., p. 204.

5 *Oi vay* – I'm Jewish and gay

1 Anne Sacks, 'Walkers take Giant Stride for Dr Sacks', *Jewish Chronicle (Community Chronicle* Supplement), 28 February 1992. See also the advertisement for the event in *Jewish Chronicle (Community Chronicle)*, 20 March 1992.

2 Sacks, 'Walkers take Giant Stride'.

3 Ibid.

4 Simon Rocker, 'Gay and Lesbian Group Banned from Chief's Charity Walkabout', *Jewish Chronicle*, 1 May 1992.

5 John Corre, 'No Individuals Banned from Walk', *Jewish Chronicle*, 4 September 1992.

6 The advertisement for the event in the *Jewish Chronicle* outlined that 'all registered Jewish charities are invited to participate', 20 March 1992.

7 Rocker, 'Gay and Lesbian Group Banned from Chief's Charity Walkabout', *Jewish Chronicle*, 1 May 1992.

8 Simon Rocker, 'Students Back Gay Helpline in Fight against Ban from Chief's Walkabout', *Jewish Chronicle*, 22 May 1992.

9 London Metropolitan Archives, Chief Rabbi MSS, ACC/2805/08/13/03/001, letter to Chief Rabbi, 25 June 1992.

10 London Metropolitan Archives, Rainbow Jews MSS, LMA/4653/PR/01/06/020, leaflet from the Jewish Lesbian and Gay Helpline (c. 1992).

11 Rocker, 'Students Back Gay Helpline', *Jewish Chronicle*, 22 May 1992.

Notes

12 Simon Rocker, 'Chief Puts off Meeting over Gay Controversy', *Jewish Chronicle*, 26 June 1992.

13 Simon Rocker, 'More than 4000 set to Walkabout', *Jewish Chronicle*, 10 July 1992.

14 Anna Maxsted, 'Peaceful Protest from Barred Gays', *Jewish Chronicle*, 17 July 1992.

15 Simon Rocker interviews Chief Rabbi Sacks on his first anniversary, 'Generally Good Marks in the End-of-Year Report', *Jewish Chronicle*, 11 September 1992.

16 'Mother's Dilemma over her Gay Son', *Jewish Chronicle*, 21 August 1992.

17 Chief Rabbi MSS, ACC/2805/08/13/03/001, letter writer to Sacks, 23 June 1992.

18 Chief Rabbi MSS, ACC/2805/08/13/03/001, letter writer to Sacks, 10 June 1992.

19 Steve Bruce, *British Gods: Religion in Modern Britain* (Oxford: Oxford University Press, 2020), p. 252.

20 Naomi Braine, 'Queering Secular Jewish Culture(s)', in Yvette Taylor and Ria Snowdon (eds), *Queering Religion, Religious Queers* (Abingdon: Routledge, 2014), p. 34.

21 Weeks notes that in the ten years following the legislation the number of convictions for indecency between males quadrupled, in Jeffrey Weeks, *Sex, Politics and Society: The Regulation of Sexuality since 1800* (London: Longman, 1989 [1981]), p. 274.

22 Ibid., p. 275.

23 Richard Smith, 'Against the Law', *Gay Times*, 347 (August 2007).

24 Declaration on Section 28, 'Jewish Celebrities Join Gay Rights Battle', *Gay Times*, 124 (January 1989).

25 See Weeks, *Sex, Politics and Society*, pp. 239–40, and Neil Miller, *Out of the Past: Gay and Lesbian History from 1869 to the Present* (London: Vintage, 1995), pp. 280–1.

26 Interview with Lionel Blue by Sharon Rappaport, LMA/4653/PR/01/03/001–4, Rainbow Jews, 12 April 2013.

27 Lionel Blue, *Hitchhiking to Heaven*, p. 42.

28 Interview with Rabbi Sheila Shulman by Surat Knan, LMA/4653/PR/01/03/018/001, Rainbow Jews, 23 October 2013.

29 Jack Gilbert, 'Not Labels but Lives', *Jewish Quarterly*, 151 (1993), pp. 15–19.

30 Miller, *Out of the Past*, pp. 365–9.

31 For the emergence of the GLF in Britain, see Sally Munt and Paula Kitching, 'The Origins and Development of the Lesbian, Gay, Bisexual and Transgender Civil Rights Movement in Britain from 1960 to the Present', *The Historian*, 136 (winter 2017/2018), pp. 14–17, and Weeks, *Sex, Politics and Society*, pp. 285–6.

32 Simon Benson, 'New Group Forming to Research Jewish Problem', *Lunch*, 7 (1 April 1972).

33 Board of Deputies MSS, ACC 3121/E/04/0393, Gay Liberation Front: Jewish Research Group, letter: 'Gay Liberation Front. Jewish Research Group: Shalom' (undated, c. 1972).

34 Peter Sweasey, *From Queer to Eternity: Spirituality in the Lives of Lesbian, Gay and Bisexual People* (London: Cassell, 1997), p. 5.

35 Lionel Blue, 'My Obituary', BBC Radio 4, 20 December 2016.

36 Around the same time, with help from Orthodox chaplain and academic Dr Alan Unterman, a similar group was started among Jewish students in Manchester. See 'Student Homosexuals', *Jewish Telegraph*, 4 February 1972.

37 London School of Economics [LSE] Library, HCA/Albany Trust/14/69, letter from Saul Amias to Simon Benson, 9 February 1972.

38 LSE Library, HCA/Albany Trust/14/69, letter from Leslie Hardman to Simon Benson, 7 February 1972.

39 Board of Deputies MSS, ACC 3121/E/04/0393, Gay Liberation Front: Jewish Research Group, letter on First Public Symposium (undated, February 1972). The conversation between Paul Shaw, student director of Hillel House, and the Chief Rabbi, was relayed in Benson, 'New Group Forming', *Lunch*, 7 (1 April 1972).

40 The advertisement for this event, which took place at the West Central Jewish Club on 19 November, appeared in *Gay News*, 1 November 1972. For an account of how the event came about, see Timothy Goldard, 'So you think that you have problems?', *Gay News*, 4 September 1974.

41 Jakov Geissman, 'National Jewish Talk In', *Gay News*, 1 December 1972.

42 LSE Library, HCA/Albany Trust/14/69, notice from the Jewish Homophile Liaison Group. The 'Teach In' on 'Judaism and the Jewish Homosexual' was held on 19 November 1972.

43 Goldard, 'So you think that you have problems?', *Gay News*, 4 September 1974.

44 LSE Library, HCA/LGCM/7/30, 'A Ghetto within a Ghetto', *Capital Gay*, 8 June 1984.

45 LMA 4653/PR01/02/006, Rainbow Jews, interview of Russell Van Dyk by Surat Knan, 19 June 2013.

46 LSE Library, HCA/LGCM/7/30, JGG Newsletter, Chairman's Report, 6 September 1978.

47 Gerald Jacobs, 'Young, Gay and Jewish', *Jewish Chronicle*, 29 June 1979.

48 Interview with Sheila Shulman, 23 October 2013.

49 Comment from 'an American Jewish transvestite called Rachel' in Benson, 'New Group Forming', *Lunch*, 7 (1 April 1972).

50 See interview with Norman Goldner by James Lesh, 26 August 2014, https://www.rainbowjews.com/norman-goldner-jewish-and-gay/ (accessed 16 September 2024), and interview with Russell van Dyk by Surat Knan, 19 June 2013.

51 LSE Library, HCA/LGCM/7/30, Peter Golds, Chairman's Annual Report (1975–6).

52 LSE Library, HCA/Albany Trust/14/69, letter from William Frankel to Francis Treuherz, 26 October 1972.

53 'Jewish Homophile Liaison Group Think-In', *Lunch*, 16 (January 1973).

54 Interview with Russell Van Dyk, 19 June 2013.

55 'Judaism and Gayness', *Gay News*, 7 March 1973.

56 LSE Library, HCA/LGCM/7/30, JGG Newsletter by Barry Crown, 22 November 1982.

57 Barry Dov Schwartz, 'The Jewish View of Homosexuality', in Harry Brod (ed.), *A Mensch Among Men: Explorations in Jewish Masculinity* (Freedom, CA: The Crossing Press, 1988), p. 133.

58 Isaac Nodel, 'Gay Practices', *Jewish Chronicle*, 15 July 1977.

59 Chaim Bermant, 'Same-Sex Spouses = non-Kosher Houses', *Jewish Chronicle*, 11 October 1996.

60 Alan Unterman, 'Judaism and Homosexuality: Some Orthodox Perspectives', *Jewish Quarterly*, 151 (autumn 1993), pp. 5–9 (p. 5).

61 'Homosexuality Almost Unknown Among Jews', *Jewish Telegraph*, 4 February 1972.

62 Unterman, 'Judaism and Homosexuality', p. 5.

63 Laurence Brown, 'Jewish and Gay: Comfort or Conflict?', *Gay News*, 7 April 1977.

64 Ryan Levitt, 'Keeping Kosher', *The Pink Paper*, 29 September 2000.

65 Immanuel Jakobovits, 'Compassion, but We Cannot Condone Evil', *The Times*, 9 November 1987.

66 Immanuel Jakobovits, 'Only a Moral Revolution Can Contain this Scourge', *The Times*, 27 December 1986.

67 Jakobovits made his comments in 'An Orthodox Morality: Sir Immanuel Jakobovits talks to Andrew Brown', *The Independent*, 24 November 1987. For Grey's response, see Chief Rabbi MSS, ACC/2805/07/18/007, Antony Grey to Jakobovits, 24 November 1987.

68 Interview with Norman Goldner, 26 August 2014.

69 LSE Library, HCA, Brown/2, Michael Brown, 'Why AIDS Presents Special Ethical Problems', 1988.

70 Levitt, 'Keeping Kosher'.

71 Anna Maxted and Simon Rocker, 'Minister Tells Why He Could Not Remain within Orthodoxy', *Jewish Chronicle*, 28 August 1992.

72 Sandi Simcha Dubowski (director), *Trembling Before G-d* (New York Films, 2001). Hashem (literally 'the name') is a common Jewish way to refer to God.

73 Chaim Rapoport, *Judaism and Homosexuality: An Authentic Orthodox View* (London: Vallentine Mitchell, 2004).

74 Ibid., p. ix.

75 Ephraim Mirvis, 'The Wellbeing of LGBT+ Pupils: a Guide for Orthodox Jewish Schools', September 2018, https://www.keshetuk.org/uploads/1/3/8/6/13861493/the_wellbeing_of_lgbt__pupils_a_guide_for_orthodox_jewish_schools.pdf (accessed 8 October 2024).

76 Unterman, 'Judaism and Homosexuality', p. 7.

77 Rapoport, *Judaism and Homosexuality*, p. 85.

78 Ibid., p. 129.

79 Ibid., p. viii.

80 Ibid., p. 102.

81 Greenberg, *Wrestling with God and Men*, p. 30.

82 Wendy Greengross, *Jewish and Homosexual* (London: Reform Synagogues of Great Britain, 1980).

83 Jacobs, 'Young, Gay and Jewish', *Jewish Chronicle*, 29 June 1979.

84 Tony Bayfield, *Being Jewish Today: Confronting the Real Issues* (London: Bloomsbury, 2019), p. 94

85 Interview with Lionel Blue by Sharon Rappaport, 12 April 2013.

86 Greengross, *Jewish and Homosexual*, p. 4.

87 Ibid., p. 11

88 Ibid., p. 12

89 Ibid., p. 39.

90 Ibid., p. 37.

91 Ibid., p. 4.

92 Adrian Coyle and Deborah Rafalin, 'Jewish Gay Men's Accounts of Negotiating Cultural, Religious, and Sexual Identity: A Qualitative Study', *Journal of Psychology & Human Sexuality*, 12:4 (2000), p. 23.

93 Shulman recalled that she had felt able to enter the college after explicitly defining herself in her application as both a lesbian and radical feminist. Interview with Rabbi Sheila Shulman by Surat Knan, 23 October 2013.

94 Interview with Rabbi Elizabeth Sarah by Suzanne Paginton, LMA 4653/PR/01/03/014, Rainbow Jews, 26 September 2013.

95 Ibid.

96 Speech archived as part of the Rainbow Jews project, https://www.rainbowjews.com/wp-content/uploads/2013/05/1996-Elli-Sarah-speech.pdf (accessed 16 September 2024).

97 Ibid.

98 Charlotte Seligman and Lorraine Kirk, '"Gay Weddings" Rabbi to Quit Top Reform Job', *Jewish Chronicle*, 28 March 1997.

99 Interview with Rabbi Sheila Shulman by Surat Knan, 23 October 2013.

100 John Rayner, 'Unnatural Reactions', *Jewish Chronicle*, 6 August 1993.

101 Elizabeth Sarah, 'Judaism and Lesbianism: A Tale of Life on the Margins of the Text', *Jewish Quarterly*, 151 (autumn 1993), pp. 20–3.

102 Greengross, *Jewish and Homosexual*, p. 1.

103 Mark Solomon, 'A Strange Conjunction', *Jewish Quarterly*, 151 (autumn 1993), pp. 10–14.

104 Blue, *Hitchhiking to Heaven*, pp. 147, 149.

105 Shulman cited in Sweasey, *From Queer to Eternity*, p. 33.

106 Sweasey, *From Queer to Eternity*, p. 33. The first seder of the nascent JGG took place in 1973. See 'First Gay Seder', *Gay News*, 16 May 1973.

107 Manchester Jewish Museum, MANJM 2019.55, Clem Herman interviewed by Alex Cropper, 8 July 2019.

108 Greengross, *Jewish and Homosexual*, p. 37.

109 David Shneer and Caryn Aviv, 'Introduction: Heeding Isaiah's Call', in David Shneer and Caryn Aviv (eds), *Queer Jews* (London: Routledge, 2002), pp. 13–34 (p. 23).

110 Braine, 'Queering Secular Jewish Culture(s)', p. 35.

111 Coyle and Rafalin, 'Jewish Gay Men's Accounts', p. 23.

112 Rocker, 'Students Back Gay Helpline', *Jewish Chronicle*, 22 May 1992.

113 Interview with Lionel Blue, 12 April 2013.

114 Ray Coleman, *Brian Epstein: The Man who Made the Beatles* (London: Penguin, 1990), p. 35.

115 Interview with Peggy Sherwood by Anna Barker, LMA/4653/PR/01/03/022, Rainbow Jews, 11 November 2013.

116 Ruth Gilbert, 'My Big Fat Jewish TV Dinner: Reflections on British Jewishness in Friday Night Dinner and Grandma's House', *Jewish Film and Media*, 2:2 (2014), pp. 181–200 (p. 196).

117 Greengross, *Jewish and Homosexual*, p. 9.

118 Brown, 'Jewish and Gay', *Gay News*, 7 April 1977.

119 LMA/4653/PR/01/06/020, Rainbow Jews, leaflet from JGLG 40th Anniversary Party, 'Welcome from the President', 30 June 2012.

120 Interview with Russell Van Dyk, 19 March 2013.

121 Interview with Peggy Sherwood, 11 November 2013.

122 https://www.bky.org.uk (accessed 16 September 2024).

123 Weeks, *Sex, Politics and Society*, p. 261.

124 LSE Library, HCA/LGCM/7/30, JGG Newsletter, 9 December 1976.

125 LSE Library, HCA/LGCM/7/30, letter from Laurence Brown to Rev Richard Kirker, 26 September 1982.

126 LSE Library, HCA/LGCM/7/30, speech by Richard Kirker for the Silver Jubilee Weekend of Celebrations of the JGLG, 14–16 March 1997.

127 For Blue's engagement with Quaker services, see interview with Lionel Blue, 12 April 2013. For his establishment of an inclusive congregation on the Portobello Road in

London, see Blue, *Hitchhiking to Heaven*, p. 266. For the Sisters of Sion's support for BKY, see interview with Sheila Shulman, 23 October 2013.

128 Interview with Norman Goldner, 26 August 2014.

129 Interview with Lionel Blue, 12 April 2013.

130 Jacobs, 'Young, Gay and Jewish', *Jewish Chronicle*, 29 June 1979. For analysis of the idea that homosexuality was un-Jewish, see Schwartz, 'The Jewish View of Homosexuality', pp. 125–6.

131 Sweasey, *From Queer to Eternity*, p. 44.

132 Ibid., p. 48.

133 Naomi Alderman, *Disobedience* (London: Penguin, 2007), p. 250.

134 Sweasey, *From Queer to Eternity*, p. 48.

135 Blue, *Hitchhiking to Heaven*, pp. 309, 326.

6 The (un)forgivable sin

1 *Never Mind the Quality, Feel the Width* ran between 1967 and 1971 and was written by Vince Powell and Harry Driver. For analysis, see Gavin Schaffer, '"You Don't Cure a Problem by Sweeping it Under the Carpet": Jews, Sitcoms, and Race Relations in 1960s Britain', in Nathan Abrams (ed.), *Hidden in Plain Sight: Jews and Jewishness in British Film, Television, and Popular Culture* (Evanston, IL: Northwestern University Press, 2016), pp. 115–36.

2 'You Will Go the Ball, Manny Cohen' was broadcast on ITV on 26 January 1971. *Shiksa* is a pejorative Yiddish descriptor for a non-Jewish woman.

3 Bernice Rubens, *The Elected Member* (London: Sphere, 1980 [1969]), pp. 92, 141.

4 Maisie Mosco, *Between Two Worlds* (Sevenoaks: New English Library, 1983), p. 17.

5 Parental reactions to intermarriage were described in these terms in Beckman, *The Hackney Crucible*, p. 151.

6 Brook, *The Club*, p. 425.

7 Gerald Cromer, 'Intermarriage and Communal Survival in a London Suburb', *The Jewish Journal of Sociology*, 16:2 (1974), pp. 155–70.

8 Miriam Shaviv, 'Intermarriage is a Crisis which the US Ignores', *Jewish Chronicle*, 30 October 2020.

9 Jonathan Romain, *Till Faith Us Do Part: Couples who Fall in Love across the Religious Divide* (London: Fount, 1996), p. 51.

10 Ibid., p. 164. See also Marlena Schmool, 'British Jewry and its Attitude to Intermarriage', in Shulamit Reinharz and Sergio DellaPergola (eds), *Jewish Intermarriage Around the World* (Piscataway, NJ: Transaction Publishers, 2009), pp. 61–74.

11 Schmool, 'British Jewry and its Attitude to Intermarriage', p. 83.

12 Interview with Joyce Rothschild and Mark Pearson, 5 January 2023.

13 Maisie Mosco, *Almonds and Raisins* (London: Coronet Books, 1993 [1979]), p. 330.

14 Romain and Mitchell have noted the extent of concerns about interfaith marriage across religious communities in Jonathan Romain and David Mitchell, *Inclusive Judaism: The Changing Face of an Ancient Faith* (London: Jessica Kingsley, 2020), p. 143.

15 Romain, *Till Faith Us Do Part*, p. 9.

16 This was the view of a 20-year-old medical student from Hampstead, cited in Michael Wallach, 'Marrying Out', *Jewish Chronicle*, 23 May 1969, pp. 7–9.

17 Lionel Kochen, 'Anglo-Jewry Since World War II', *American Jewish Year Book*, 78 (1978), pp. 339–49 (p. 340). Rabbi Yitzchak Shochet cited in Martha Dixon, 'Intermarriage "threatens UK Jewry"', BBC News, 20 March 2005.

18 Jonathan Sacks, *Will We Have Jewish Grandchildren? Jewish Continuity and How to Achieve It* (London: Vallentine Mitchell, 1994), pp. 2, 14, 26.

19 This is the thinking of Mr Gabriel in Gerda Charles's *The Crossing Point* (London: Eyre and Spottiswoode, 1961), p. 172. In Maisie Mosco's *Almonds and Raisins*, Sarah describes intermarriage in these terms to her son (p. 214).

20 Immanuel Jakobovits, 'The Problem of Intermarriage', published transcript of speech, Jewish Marriage Education Council, 18 September 1967.

21 Statistics taken from Wallach, 'Marrying Out', *Jewish Chronicle*, 23 May 1969. Cromer argued that there was a perception of a marked increase ('Intermarriage and Communal Survival', p. 155).

22 S. J. Prais and Marlena Schmool, 'Statistics of Jewish Marriages in the United Kingdom: 1901–65', Report from the Statistical and Demographic Research Unit of the Board of Deputies, London Metropolitan Archives, Board of Deputies MSS, ACC3121/C18/1/3, 1965. Schmool's analysis of these statistics over a longer period can be found in Schmool, 'British Jewry and its Attitudes to Intermarriage'.

23 Kershen and Romain, *Tradition and Change*, p. 233. See also Romain, *Till Faith Us Do Part*, pp. 11–12.

24 For international comparative research in this period, see Moshe Davis, 'Mixed Marriages in Western Jewry: Historical Background to the Jewish Response', *Jewish Journal of Sociology*, 10:2 (1968), pp. 177–220.

25 Sacks, *Will We Have?*, p. 19.

26 Ruby Jo Reeves Kennedy, 'What has Social Science to Say about Intermarriage?', in Werner J. Cahnman (ed.), *Intermarriage and Jewish Life: A Symposium* (New York: Herzl Press and the Jewish Reconstructionist Press, 1963), pp. 36–7.

27 Endelman, *Radical Assimilation*, p. 181.

28 Cromer, 'Intermarriage and Communal Survival', p. 163.

29 Wallach, 'Marrying Out', *Jewish Chronicle*, 23 May 1969.

30 Ibid.

31 Research was published on Jewish student values in Vera West, 'The Influence of Parental Background on Jewish University Students', *Jewish Journal of Sociology*, 10:2 (1968), pp. 267–80.

32 Wallach, 'Marrying Out', *Jewish Chronicle*, 23 May 1969.

33 Interview with Jonathan Romain, 24 September 2020.

34 Jennifer Thompson, *Jewish on Their Own Terms: How Intermarried Couples are Changing American Judaism* (New Brunswick, NJ: Rutgers University Press, 2014), p. 15.

35 Karen Glaser, 'I Don't Need a Jewish Partner', *Jewish Chronicle*, 7 February 2020.

36 For the history of these laws in Judaism, see Mitchell and Romain, *Inclusive Judaism*, pp. 82–3.

37 Romain, *Till Faith Us Do Part*, p. 14.

38 Samira Mehta, *Beyond Chrismukkah: The Christian–Jewish Interfaith Family in the United States* (Chapel Hill, NC: University of North Carolina Press, 2018), p. 92.

39 Karen McGinity, *Marrying Out: Intermarriage and Fatherhood* (Bloomington, IN: Indiana University Press, 2014), p. 137.

40 Mehta, *Beyond Chrismukkah*, p. 88.

41 Tanya Wesker, 'Jewish or Not Jewish – Another Story', *Shifra*, 2 (May 1985).

42 See Elazar Barkan, *The Retreat of Scientific Racism: Changing Concepts of Race in Britain and the United States between the World Wars* (Cambridge: Cambridge University Press: 1992), and Schaffer, *Racial Science and British Society*.

43 Marshall Sklare, 'Intermarriage and Jewish Survival', *Commentary*, March 1970.

44 See Thompson, *Jewish on Their Own Terms*, p. 34.

45 Cromer, 'Intermarriage and Communal Survival', p. 166.

46 Recent research continues to assert that mixed marriages more frequently lead to divorce. See David Graham, 'Jews in Couples: Marriage, Intermarriage, Cohabitation and Divorce in Britain', Institute for Jewish Policy Research, July 2016, p. 31, https://www.jpr.org.uk/reports/jews-couples-marriage-intermarriage-cohabitation-and-divorce-britain (accessed 8 October 2024). This report argued that 'exogamous marriages are more than twice as likely to result in divorce as endogamous marriages'.

47 Wallach, 'Marrying Out', *Jewish Chronicle*, 23 May 1969.

48 Isaac Sutton, consultant psychiatrist, cited in Wallach, 'Marrying Out', *Jewish Chronicle*, 23 May 1969.

49 Dow Marmur, *Intermarriage* (RSGB pamphlet, 1978), p. 2.

50 Romain, *Till Faith Us Do Part*, pp. 74–5.

51 See McGinity, *Marrying Out*, p. 103.

52 Marmur, *Intermarriage*, p. 3. See also Romain, *Till Faith Us Do Part*, pp. 74–5.

53 McGinity, *Marrying Out*, p. 103.

54 Mosco, *Almonds and Raisins*, p. 44.

55 Brian Glanville, *The Bankrupts* (London: Secker and Warburg, 1958), pp. 159–60.

56 Ibid., p. 127.

57 Marmur, *Intermarriage*, p. 3.

58 Rubens, *The Elected Member*, p. 91.

59 Interview with Jo Schaffer, 17 August 2022.

60 Brook, *The Club*, p. 425.

61 Emma Klein, *Lost Jews: The Struggle for Identity Today* (Basingstoke: Macmillan, 1996), p. 127.

62 Thompson, *Jewish on Their Own Terms*, p. 171.

63 Marmur, *Intermarriage*, p. 2.

64 Ibid., p. 1, and Cromer, 'Intermarriage and Communal Survival', p. 161.

65 Wallach, 'Marrying Out', *Jewish Chronicle*, 23 May 1969.

66 Cromer, 'Intermarriage and Communal Survival', p. 158.

67 Endelman, *Radical Assimilation*, p. 203.

68 Interview with Joyce Rothschild and Mark Pearson, 5 January 2023.

69 Wallach, 'Marrying Out', *Jewish Chronicle*, 23 May 1969.

70 Marmur, *Intermarriage*, p. 2.

71 London Metropolitan Archives, Office of the Chief Rabbi MSS, ACC/2805/4/5/65, Cecil Roth to Hertz, 1 November 1944.

72 Endelman, *Radical Assimilation*, pp. 203–4.

73 Jakobovits, 'The Problem of Intermarriage', p. 21.

74 Office of the Chief Rabbi MSS, ACC/2805/6/1/5, Intermarriage, circular from the Court of the Chief Rabbi, 15 March 1945.

75 Jakobovits, 'The Problem of Intermarriage', p. 15.

76 Lee Levitt, 'Jet Launches "Safety Code"', *Jewish Chronicle*, 29 January 1988.

77 'An Urgent Call to World Jewry', *Jewish Chronicle*, 13 May 1988. Jet was operated by the Chofetz Chayim Torah Foundation, based in North London.

Notes

78 'Don't Make This Mistake', *Jewish Chronicle*, 8 July 1988.

79 'An Urgent Call to World Jewry', *Jewish Chronicle*, 13 May 1988.

80 Letters to the Editor, *Jewish Chronicle*, 3 June 1988 and 29 July 1988.

81 Letter to the Editor, 'Treated as a Gentile', *Jewish Chronicle*, 29 July 1988.

82 Letter to the Editor from the Voluntary Organising Secretary of the Chofetz Chayim Torah Foundation, *Jewish Chronicle*, 5 August 1988.

83 Letter to the Editor, 'No Racism in Campaign', *Jewish Chronicle*, 9 September 1988.

84 Letter to the Editor from the Voluntary Organising Secretary of the Chofetz Chayim Torah Foundation, *Jewish Chronicle*, 5 August 1988.

85 On 26 August 1988, Simon Palmer wrote to the *Jewish Chronicle* calling the Jet campaign 'strident and offensive'. Response to Palmer (7 October 1988) from Mervyn Kersh.

86 Office of the Chief Rabbi MSS, ACC/2805/7/8/12, Marriage and Conversion, leaflet of a sermon delivered at Marble Arch synagogue, 10 April 1969.

87 Cromer, 'Intermarriage and Communal Survival', p. 166.

88 Board of Deputies MSS, ACC3121/C18/1/8, Conference on Jewish Life in Modern Britain, 13 March 1977, paper given by S. J. Prais, 'Polarisation or Decline'.

89 Marmur, *Intermarriage*, p. 1.

90 Ibid., pp. 3–5.

91 Norma Spence, 'Facing Love's Dilemma', *Jewish Chronicle*, 9 December 1988.

92 Office of the Chief Rabbi MSS, ACC/2805/7/8/12, Marriage and Conversion, meeting on 2 September 1975.

93 Ibid.

94 Marmur, *Intermarriage*, p. 5

95 Interview with David and Anna (names changed at the request of the interviewees), 20 December 2022.

96 Ibid.

97 Spence, 'Facing Love's Dilemma', *Jewish Chronicle*, 9 December 1988.

98 'Intermarriage Probe', *Jewish Chronicle*, 7 October 1988.

99 Jonathan Romain, 'Marrying Out: Myths and Reality', *Jewish Chronicle*, 19 January 1990.

100 Romain, *Till Faith Us Do Part*, p. 103. See Thompson, *Jewish on their Own Terms*.

101 Ibid., p. 174.

102 Interview with Jonathan Romain, 24 September 2020.

103 Ibid.

104 Romain, 'Marrying Out: Myths and Reality', *Jewish Chronicle*, 19 January 1990.

105 'Megan Rowley and Pamela Sills Describe their Experience in the Light of Last Year's Progressive Seminar for Inter-Faith Couples', *Jewish Chronicle*, 19 January 1990.

106 Ibid.

107 Interview with Jonathan Romain, 24 September 2020.

108 Romain argues that only 50% of seminar participants came from Reform and Liberal synagogues. Interview with Jonathan Romain, 24 September 2020.

109 Jefferey Blumenfeld, letter to the Editor, *Jewish Chronicle*, 6 January 1989.

110 Interview with Jonathan Romain, 24 September 2020.

111 Ian S. Goodhardt, letter to the Editor, *Jewish Chronicle*, 26 January 1990.

112 Klein, *Lost Jews*, pp. 101–5. *Beit Klal Yisrael* moved from Reform to Liberal affiliation, having been founded in 1990 by Rabbi Sheila Shulman.

113 Interview with David and Anna, 20 December 2022, and interview with Joyce Rothschild and Mark Pearson, 5 January 2023.

114 The Liberal Synagogue has accepted the Jewishness of children with a Jewish father since the 1950s. For details of Reform and Liberal policies, see Romain and Mitchell, *Inclusive Judaism*, pp. 87–96.

115 Dixon, 'Intermarriage "threatens UK Jewry"', BBC News, 20 March 2005.

116 Gerald Cromer, 'Intermarriage Handbooks', *The Jewish Journal of Sociology*, 47:1–2 (2005), p. 48.

117 Marmur, *Intermarriage*, p. 11.

118 Interview with Jonathan Romain, 24 September 2020.

119 Glaser, 'I Don't Need a Jewish Partner', *Jewish Chronicle*, 7 February 2020.

120 Graham, 'Jews in Couples', p. 15. Graham argued that 78% of married Jews were married to Jews, while 68% of cohabiting Jews lived with non-Jews (pp. 2–3).

121 Interview with David and Anna, 20 December 2022.

122 Darieck Scott, 'Jungle Fever? Black Gay Identity Politics, White Dick, and the Utopian Bedroom', *GLQ: A Journal of Lesbian and Gay Studies*, 1 (1994), pp. 299–321 (p. 317).

123 Meredith McGuire, *Lived Religion: Faith and Practice in Everyday Life* (Oxford: Oxford University Press, 2008), p. 12. See also Lynn Davidman, 'The New Voluntarism and the Case of Unsynagogued Jews', in Nancy Ammerman (ed.), *Everyday Religion: Observing Modern Religious Lives* (Oxford: Oxford University Press, 2007), pp. 52–64.

124 Mehta, *Beyond Chrismukkah*, p. 205.

125 Thompson, *Jewish on their Own Terms*, p. 166.

126 McGinity, *Marrying Out*, p. 137.

127 Marmur, *Intermarriage*, p. 2.

128 Louis Golding, *Magnolia Street* (St Albans: Gainsborough Press, 1932), p. 473.

7 The nice Jewish boy (who believes in Jesus)

1 'Jesus? He's Gone South', *Jewish Chronicle*, 26 July 2019, p. 10.

2 David Aaronovitch, 'Jews for Jesus Leaflets Always Put Me in an Extremely Bad Mood', *Jewish Chronicle*, 3 June 2022.

3 David A. Rausch, *Messianic Judaism: Its History, Theology, and Polity* (New York: Edwin Mellen, 1982), pp. 21–4; Richard Harvey, *Mapping Messianic Jewish Theology: A Constructive Approach* (Milton Keynes: Paternoster, 2009), p. 3; and Kelvin Crombie, *Restoring Israel: 200 Years of the CMJ Story* (Jerusalem: Nicolayson's, 2008), p. 17.

4 See Michael Darby, *The Emergence of the Hebrew Christian Movement in Nineteenth-Century England* (Leiden: Brill, 2010), pp. 53–7.

5 Walter Barker, *A Fountain Opened: A Short History of the Church's Ministry among the Jews, 1809–1982* (London: Olive Press, 1983), pp. 16–17.

6 Anne Summers, 'False Start or Brave Beginning? The Society of Jews and Christians, 1924–1944', *Journal of Ecclesiastical History*, 65:4 (2014), pp. 827–51 (p. 828). See also Marcus Braybrooke, *Children of One God: A History of the Council of Christians and Jews* (London: Vallentine Mitchell, 1991), p. 1.

7 Shirley Jackson Case, 'Review of CG Montefiore's Commentary on the Synoptic Gospels', *American Journal of Theology*, 15:1 (1911), pp. 116–17.

8 Claude Montefiore, *The Synoptic Gospels: Vol. 1* (London: Macmillan, 1927), p. xxi, and Claude Montefiore, *Judaism and St Paul: Two Essays* (London: Max Goschen, 1914), p. 142. For analysis of Montefiore's thinking, see Daniel Langton, 'Claude Montefiore in the Context of Jewish Approaches to Jesus and the Apostle Paul', *Hebrew Union College Annual*, 70 (1999), pp. 405–28.

9   Braybrooke, *Children of One God*, pp. 1–3.

10 Summers, 'False Start', p. 834.

11 Ibid., pp. 838–9.

12 James Parkes, *The Jew and his Neighbour: A Study of the Causes of Anti-Semitism* (London: SCM Press, 1930). For analysis of Parkes's career, see Colin Richmond, *Campaigner against Antisemitism: The Reverend James Parkes 1896–1981* (London: Vallentine Mitchell, 2005), and Haim Chertock, *He also Spoke as a Jew: The Life of James Parkes* (London: Vallentine Mitchell, 2006).

13 William Simpson, *Youth and Anti-Semitism* (London: Epworth Press, 1938).

14 For analysis of the beginnings of CCJ, see Braybrooke, *Children of One God*, pp. 10–17.

15 Tony Kushner, 'The Beginnings of the Council of Christians and Jews', *Common Ground: The Journal of the Council of Christians and Jews*, 3–4 (1992), pp. 6–10 (p. 6).

16 Braybrooke, *Children of One God*, p. 5.

17 Temple to Parkes, cited in Kushner, 'The Beginnings of the Council', p. 7.

18 Council of Christians and Jews MSS (Manchester), Manchester Central Library, MS666/2000/82, Patrick Rodger's memories of working with CCJ sent in response to request by Canon Radcliffe, 19 July 1996.

19 Council of Christians and Jews MSS, Manchester Central Library, MS666/2000/82, Rt Rev David Sheppard to Liverpool Diocesan Synod, 11 March 1989.

20 Barker, *A Fountain Opened*, p. 45.

21 Council of Christians and Jews MSS, Manchester Central Library, MS666/2000/82, Rodger to Radcliffe, 19 July 1989.

22 Council of Christians and Jews MSS, Manchester Central Library, MS666/2000/82, Council of Christians and Jews (Manchester), Minutes, 17 February 1982.

23 London Metropolitan Archives, Chief Rabbi MSS, ACC/2805/16/41, draft included in correspondence between Marcus Braybrooke and Chief Rabbi Jakobovits, 12 January 1986.

24 Chief Rabbi MSS, ACC/2805/7/16/5, Peter Jennings to Moshe Davis, 13 July 1977.

25 'Carey is Praised for Cutting Link with Missionaries', *Jewish Chronicle*, 13 March 1992.

26 Interview with CMJ activist, 20 June 2019.

27 Chief Rabbi MSS, ACC/2805/7/16/30, Executive Director's Report to the CCJ Executive, 2 February 1989.

28 Chief Rabbi MSS, ACC/2805/16/41, notes on CCJ Seminar on Missionary Activity, November 1985.

29 Ruth A. Tucker, *Not Ashamed: The Story of Jews for Jesus* (Sisters, OR: Multnomah, 1999), pp. 78–86.

30 Ibid., pp. 84–5.

31 Richard Harvey, *But I'm Jewish! A Jew for Jesus tells his Story* (London: Jews for Jesus, 1996), p. 27.

32 Interview with Richard Harvey, 21 June 2019.

33 Ibid.

34 Harvey, *But I'm Jewish!*, pp. 31–40.

35 This advertisement appeared on page 4 of *The Times*, 17 December 1991.

36 Chief Rabbi's comments in Ruth Gledhill, 'Jewish Leaders Attack Advert', *The Times*, 17 December 1991. Bernard Levin attacked Jews for Jesus in his article, 'Clodhoppers on Crusade: The Vulgarity and Religious Ambiguity of Jews for Jesus are a Liability to Two Faiths', *The Times*, 27 January 1992.

Notes

37 This episode was entitled 'King of the Jews' and was broadcast on BBC 1 on 31 March 1991.

38 Interview with Richard Harvey, 21 June 2019.

39 See Rausch, *Messianic Judaism*, p. 241; Yaakov Ariel, 'A Different Kind of Dialogue? Messianic Judaism and Jewish-Christian Relations', *Crosscurrents*, September 2012, pp. 318–27; and Francine K. Samuelson, 'Messianic Judaism: Church, Denomination, Sect, or Cult?', *Journal of Ecumenical Studies*, 37:2 (2000), pp. 161–86.

40 Arkush made these comments in 'King of the Jews', *Heart of the Matter*, BBC 1, 31 March 1991.

41 Interview with CMJ activist, 20 June 2019.

42 Interview with a Messianic Jew, 31 May 2019.

43 Interview with Richard Harvey, 20 June 2019.

44 Chief Rabbi MSS, ACC/2805/16/41, M. Brian Ettlinger's response to Richard Harvey's paper on 'The Validity of Maintaining a Hebrew Christian Identity', presented at CCJ's Advisory Group on Missionary Activity, 19 October 1987.

45 Rabbi Sylvia Rothschild described Messianic Jewish theology in this way in 'King of the Jews', *Heart of the Matter*, BBC 1, 31 March 1991.

46 Harvey recalls this meeting with Julia Neuberger and John Rayner in *But I'm Jewish!*, p. 27.

47 Harvey, *But I'm Jewish!*, p. 30.

48 Dan Cohn-Sherbok, *Messianic Judaism* (London: Cassell, 2000), p. 79.

49 Rausch, *Messianic Judaism*, p. 248.

50 Interview with Richard Harvey, 20 June 2019, and interview with Shmuel Arkush, 18 July 2019.

51 'N16 Double Agents', *Jewish Chronicle*, 11 July 1986. Richard Harvey's recollection of this meeting is very different. He recalls that Messianic Jews attended the meeting but kept silent, so that 'no controversy ensued'. Notes from Richard Harvey, 15 April 2024.

52 Chief Rabbi MSS, ACC/2805/16/41, Weissman to Sacks, 11 January 1992.

53 Dan Cohn-Sherbok, 'If Jews Can Accept Radicals, Why Can't we Accept Messianic Jews?', *Church of England Newsletter*, 20 April 2000.

54 Arye Forta, 'Dishonest Conversion of Jews', *The Times*, 16 January 1989.

55 Arkush on 'King of the Jews', *Heart of the Matter*, BBC 1, 31 March 1991.

56 Letter by Barry Karsberg in *The Times*, 11 January 1989.

57 Lee Levitt, 'Decade of Danger', *Jewish Chronicle*, 5 January 1990.

58 Interview with Shmuel Arkush, 18 July 2019.

59 'King of the Jews', *Heart of the Matter*, BBC 1, 31 March 1991.

60 Samuelson, 'Messianic Judaism', p. 162.

61 Ibid., p. 184.

62 Arye Forta, 'Misguided Missions', *Jewish Chronicle*, 9 June 1989.

63 Ibid. Richard Harvey notes that these claims were investigated and although 'no evidence' was found, he wrote a 'Code of Practice' for CMJ in response. Notes from Richard Harvey, 15 April 2024.

64 'Warning to Elderly', *Jewish Chronicle*, 17 February 1989.

65 Chief Rabbi MSS, ACC/2805/16/41, Operation Judaism Pamphlet, 'Danger: Missionaries at Work', 1990.

66 Interview with Shmuel Arkush, 18 July 2019.

67 Clifford Longley, 'Jews Deplore Conversion Drive by "Outside" Protestants', *The Times*, 8 November 1985.

Notes

68 David Goodkin, 'Fight Against Missionaries', *Jewish Chronicle*, 26 October 1984.

69 Interview with Richard Harvey, 20 June 2019.

70 'Parents Accuse', *Jewish Chronicle*, 18 January 1980.

71 'TV Points at Threat of Missionaries', *Jewish Chronicle*, 7 March 1980. The story was covered in an episode of London Weekend Television's religious affairs programme, *Credo*.

72 Interview with Shmuel Arkush, 18 July 2019.

73 Ibid. Arkush recalled being told by tutors that he would be stopped from progressing unless he agreed to shave off his beard and remove his skull cap.

74 David Goodkin, 'How Students Fight the Campus War', *Jewish Chronicle*, 17 December 1982.

75 'Student Plea', *Jewish Chronicle*, 4 April 1980.

76 Keren David, 'How Vulnerable are our Students?', *Jewish Chronicle*, 30 August 1985.

77 Interview with Shmuel Arkush, 18 July 2019.

78 Cohn-Sherbok, *Messianic Judaism*, p. 188.

79 Interview with Shmuel Arkush, 18 July 2019.

80 'Missionary Fight is On', *Jewish Chronicle*, 23 May 1986.

81 Interview with Shmuel Arkush, 18 July 2019.

82 Chief Rabbi MSS, ACC/2805/16/40, notes from Shimon Cohen on Operation Judaism, 3 November 1988.

83 Chief Rabbi MSS, ACC/2805/16/40, Operation Judaism, Report to Management Committee, Undated (c. 1988).

84 Ibid., p. 46.

85 Andrew White, *The Vicar of Baghdad: My Journey So Far* (Oxford: Lion, 2015), p. 201. In the aftermath of Mission Week, White established the Cambridge University Jews and Christians group (CUJAC) to improve relations (p. 203).

86 Chief Rabbi MSS, ACC/2805/16/40, Paul Ellerman and Jeremy Callman, 'The Cambridge Mission Week, 12–19 February 1989, Assessment and Report', April 1989.

87 Ibid.

88 Chief Rabbi MSS, ACC/2805/16/40. For the article, see Paul Ellerman, 'Jesus Made Me Kosher', *The Forum: Weekly Newsletter of the Cambridge Jewish Society*, Lent Term, 4, Week Ending 17 February 1989. The letter is attached to the report as Appendix 2.

89 Chief Rabbi MSS, ACC/2805/16/40, Paul Ellerman and Jeremy Callman, 'The Cambridge Mission Week, 12–19 February 1989, Assessment and Report', April 1989.

90 'N16 Double Agents', *Jewish Chronicle*, 23 May 1986.

91 Interview with Shmuel Arkush, 18 July 2019.

92 Chief Rabbi MSS/ACC/2805/16/41, Cohen to Arkush, 20 January 1987.

93 'Anti-Messianic Action Starts in Redbridge', *Jewish Chronicle*, 21 July 1989.

94 Letter to *Jewish Chronicle*, 23 June 1989. See also Helen Shapiro, *Walking Back to Happiness* (London: Harper Collins, 1993), pp. 189–92.

95 Rausch, *Messianic Judaism*, p. 22.

96 Interview with a Messianic Jew, 31 May 2019.

97 Interview with a Messianic Jewish activist, 20 June 2019.

98 Barker, *A Fountain Opened*, p. 3, and Michael Lawson, 'Christians, Reach Out to Jews with Love', *The Times*, 6 July 1992.

99 Interview with a Messianic Jewish activist, 20 June 2019.

100 Cohn-Sherbok, 'If Jews can Accept Radicals', *Church of England Newsletter*, 20 April 2000.

Notes

101 Sylvia Barack Fishman, *Double or Nothing? Jewish Families and Mixed Marriage* (Waltham, MA: Brandeis University Press, 2004), p. 97.

102 Howard Jacobson, *Roots Schmoots: Journeys among Jews* (London: Viking, 1993), p. 233.

103 Harvey, *But I'm Jewish!*, pp. 20–1.

104 Interview with Richard Harvey, 21 June 2019.

105 Interview with a Messianic Jew, 31 May 2019.

106 Barry Toberman, 'Disc Jockey Convert', *Jewish Chronicle*, 15 February 1980.

107 Ariel highlights a 1980s opinion poll in Israel which showed a Jewish inclination to accept Messianic Jews ('A Different Kind of Dialogue?', p. 323).

108 Interview with a CMJ activist, 20 June 2019.

109 Interview with a Messianic Jew, 31 May 2019.

110 Interview with Richard Harvey, 21 June 2019.

111 Gerald Jacobs, 'Turning the Other Cheek', *Jewish Chronicle*, 5 April 1991. See also Chaim Bermant, 'Idle Talk between Parkway and Ponevez', *Jewish Chronicle*, 13 March 1992. Here, Bermant dismissed Jews for Jesus as a 'handful of individuals' and questioned whether the Lubavitch movement itself didn't pose a threat to the community.

112 Ariel, 'A Different Kind of Dialogue?', p. 326.

113 Faith and Order Commission of the Church of England, *God's Unfailing Word: Theological and Practical Perspectives on Jewish–Christian Relations* (2019), p. 58. Harvey recalls that this was his contribution. Notes from Richard Harvey, 15 April 2024. See also Harvey, *Mapping Messianic Jewish Theology*.

114 Interview with a Messianic Jew, 31 May 2019.

115 Interview with a CMJ activist, 20 June 2019.

116 Ibid.

117 Interview with a Messianic Jew, 31 May 2019.

118 Richard Harvey speaking on 'King of the Jews', *Heart of the Matter*, BBC 1, 31 March 1991.

119 See Lipson, *Jews for Jesus*, p. 10.

120 Interview with a CMJ activist, 20 June 2019.

121 Cohn-Sherbok explained that 'the history of Christian anti-Semitism' had 'profoundly affected Jewish consciousness' ('If Jews can Accept Radicals', *Church of England Newsletter*, 20 April 2000).

122 Interview with Shmuel Arkush, 18 July 2019.

123 'King of the Jews', *Heart of the Matter*, BBC 1, 31 March 1991.

124 Interview with Shmuel Arkush, 18 July 2019.

125 Forta, 'Misguided Missions', *Jewish Chronicle*, 9 June 1989.

126 Chief Rabbi MSS, ACC/2805/16/40, Paul Ellerman and Jeremy Callman, 'The Cambridge Mission Week, 12–19 February 1989, Assessment and Report', April 1989.

127 'Mock Missionaries Unmasked', *Jewish Chronicle*, 3 November 1989.

128 Chief Rabbi MSS/ACC/2805/16/41. The attendance was reported in Arkush's report to the Management Committee of Operation Judaism, 1 May 1989.

129 Interview with a CMJ activist, 20 June 2019.

130 See Steven Jaffe, 'Cross Purposes', *Jewish Chronicle*, 1 January 2021. Jaffe argued that most of the Jews who have taken on Christian faith 'have had tenuous connections with Judaism'.

131 Nathan Jeffay, 'Calls to Ban "Offensive" Ad', *Jewish Chronicle*, 1 August 2003.

132 Interview with Richard Harvey, 21 June 2019.

133 David, 'How Vulnerable are our Students', *Jewish Chronicle*, 30 August 1985.

134 *God's Unfailing Word*, pp. 103–4.
135 Interview with Richard Harvey, 21 June 2019.

8 The last outpost of the British Empire

1   Ephraim Myer Raines, *Identity Card* (unpublished personal memoir), c. 2012, pp. 3–5.
2   Ibid., p. 10.
3   Interview with Myer Raines, 21 March 2017.
4   It was, ex-activist Antony Lerman argues, 'created from above by thoughtful and sensitive Anglo-Jews in a manner that closely resembled the origins of the Scout movement'. See Antony Lerman, *History of Habonim* (unpublished MS, provided by author), p. 34.
5   Ibid.
6   Raines, *Identity Card*, p. 17.
7   Interview with Myer Raines.
8   Raines, *Identity Card*, pp. 87–8.
9   Central Zionist Archive, Jerusalem, F13/637, Treasurer of Kfar Hanassi to Mr Litav, 12 September 1966. Adding the fifteen parents of members who also lived at Kfar Hanassi, this took the number of Anglophone (nearly all British) members to 185. Kibbutz statistics from ten years later number the community of adult members at 219, with an additional 25 parents. See Kfar Hanassi Archive, 'Village Voice', 8 October 1976.
10 Baruch Kimmerling, 'History Caught in the Cross-Fire: The Case of Israeli-Jewish Historiography', *History and Memory*, 7:1 (1995), pp. 41–65 (p. 49).
11 On the periodisation of Zionist *aliyah*, see Hizky Shoham, 'From "Great History" to "Small History": The Genesis of the Zionist Periodization', *Israel Studies*, 18:1 (2013), pp. 31–55; Yoav Gelber, *Nation and History: Israeli Historiography between Zionism and Post-Zionism* (London: Vallentine Mitchell, 2011), pp. 107–11; and S. Ilan Troen, *Imagining Zion: Dreams, Designs and Realities in a Century of Jewish Settlement* (New Haven, CT: Yale University Press, 2003), pp. 5–10.
12 For an early description of the differences between *aliyah* and other migration, see Aryeh Tartakower, 'The Sociological Implications of the Present-Day Aliyah', *Jewish Social Studies*, 13:4 (1951), pp. 291–310.
13 Elazar Leshem and Judith T. Shuval, *Immigration to Israel: Sociological Perspectives* (New Brunswick, NJ: Transaction Publishers, 1998), pp. 10–13.
14 Kimmerling, 'History Caught in the Cross-Fire', p. 49.
15 Shoham, 'From "Great History" to "Small History"', p. 33.
16 Kimmerling, 'History Caught in the Cross-Fire', p. 49.
17 Gur Alroey, 'Two Historiographies: Israeli Historiography and the Mass Jewish Migration to the United States, 1881–1914', *Jewish Quarterly Review*, 105:1 (2015), pp. 99–129 (p. 110).
18 Chaim Waxman, '"In the End is it Ideology?" Religio-Cultural and Structural Factors in American Aliya', *Contemporary Jewry*, 16 (1995), pp. 50–67 (pp. 63–4).
19 Bermant, *Troubled Eden*, p. 113.
20 Wendehorst notes that Zionism did not become 'a mass phenomenon' among British Jewry until the late 1930s (*British Jewry*, p. 266).
21 Levenberg, *The Board and Zion*, pp. 60–1.
22 Ibid., pp. 151–2.

Notes

23 For example, the Glasgow Jewish community established a committee 'composed of young people who have in mind to emigrate to Israel' in 1953. Scottish Jewish Archives Centre, Garnett Hill Synagogue, Glasgow, Glasgow Zionist Organization Annual Report, 1953–4, Chairman's Report by Sidney Haase.

24 The Board of Deputies formally 'pledged the full support of the Board' to the World Zionist Organisation's 'aliyah department' in London during an Aliyah Seminar in 1978. London Metropolitan Archives, Board of Deputies MSS, ACC3121 E4 402, Summary of Aliyah Seminar for Deputies, 18 February 1979.

25 Omer-Jackaman, *The Impact of Zionism*, p. 139.

26 Wendehorst, *British Jewry*, p. 263.

27 Barry Kosmin and Caren Levy, *Jewish Identity in an Anglo-Jewish Community: The Findings of the 1978 Redbridge Survey* (London: Research Unit of the Board of Deputies of British Jews, 1983), pp. 27–8, https://archive.jpr.org.uk/download?id=2509 (accessed 8 October 2024).

28 Wendehorst, *British Jewry*, p. 263. Wendehorst notes that ten members of the British Zionist movement were killed in this war.

29 For accounts of activities of the Machal (Mitnadvei Chutz L'Aretz – Volunteers from Abroad), see Jason Fenton, *Strength and Courage: The Untold Story of the Machal Volunteers who Helped Win Israel's War of Independence* (Irvine, CA: ProtoMet Media, 2009). For the perspective of a non-Jewish British volunteer, see Gordon Levett, *Flying Under Two Flags: An Ex-RAF Pilot in Israel's War of Independence* (London: Frank Cass, 1994).

30 L. D. Staetsky, Marina Sheps and Jonathan Boyd, 'Immigration from the United Kingdom to Israel', Institute for Jewish Policy Research, October 2013, p. 5, https://www.jpr.org.uk/reports/immigration-united-kingdom-israel (accessed 8 October 2024).

31 Bermant, *Troubled Eden*, p. 113.

32 Staetsky, Sheps and Boyd, 'Immigration from the United Kingdom to Israel', p. 18.

33 Ibid., p. 21.

34 Veidat Habonim, 20th Anniversary, 1949, in Melvin Cohen (ed.), *Habonim in Britain 1929–55* (Yad Tabenkin: Habonim, 1999), p. 307.

35 Lerman, *The Making and Unmaking of a Zionist*, p. 193.

36 Bermant, *Coming Home*, p. 98.

37 Interview with British migrant to Amiad (AB), June 2017.

38 Interview with British migrant to Kfar Hanassi (DC), June 2017.

39 Interview with British migrant to Lavi (HR), June 2017.

40 Interview with British migrant to Amiad (JB), June 2017.

41 Interview with British migrant to Kfar Hanassi (AC), June 2017.

42 Interview with JB.

43 One Habonim report asserted that fewer than 5% of senior members migrated to Israel. See Avraham Tachav, 'The Movement: A Scientific Approach', *Habonim Newsletter*, 27 November 1959.

44 See Omer-Jackaman, *The Impact of Zionism*, p. 131.

45 Interview with British migrant to Amiad (EC), June 2017.

46 Lariks, 'The One Reality', *Habonim Newsletter*, 29 January 1960.

47 Vic, 'Why I Joined Garin Vav', *Habonim Newsletter*, 29 January 1960.

48 Interview with DC.

49 'Garin Supplement No 1: What is Garin Vav', *Habonim Newsletter*, 15 January 1960. *Chevra* describes a semi-formalised friendship group.

Notes

50 Interview with British migrant, now living in Rehovot (MS), June 2017.

51 Interview with EC.

52 Lerman, *The Making and Unmaking of a Zionist*, p. 31. In Britain, the prominent David Eder Farm was established by the Zionist Federation in 1935 in Harrietsham in Kent. See Cohen (ed.), *Habonim in Britain*, p. 22. Cohen notes that Zionist youth had been posted to *hachsharah* training on other farms from 1933.

53 Cohen (ed.), *Habonim in Britain*, p. 158.

54 Kibbutz Lavi Archive, File 1/9, Souvenir Brochure: Consecration of the Herbert Laster Memorial Hostel, 8 September 1957.

55 Cohen (ed.), *Habonim in Britain*, p. 301.

56 'Editorial: Towards the Second Million', *Chayenu: The Organ of Jewish Religious Labour*, 13:11–12 (November–December 1949).

57 Max Mordechai-Kopfstein, for example, arrived in Britain as part of the Kindertransport, spent the war in *Bachad hachsharah* centres, and worked as a *hachsharah* leader in Thaxted before making *aliyah* himself in 1955. Obituary, *Jewish Chronicle*, 24 September 2021.

58 Kibbutz Lavi MSS, Box 2/8, Bachad Fellowship: Tenth Anniversary Celebration, Kibbutz Lavi. Aryeh Handler, 'From Bachad to Lavi'.

59 Cohen (ed.), *Habonim in Britain*, pp. 155–8, 196–205.

60 Board of Deputies MSS, ACC3121/d2/07, Belfast, note from A. G. Brotman, 13 January 1941.

61 Bermant, *Coming Home*, p. 118.

62 Raines, *Identity Card*, p. 19.

63 Kibbutz Lavi Archive, Joseph Muller Hartmann, 'Report on Hachshara Work of Hechalutz B'Anglia'.

64 Bermant, *Coming Home*, p. 114.

65 L. F. Easterbrook, 'The Strangest Farm in the Country', *News Chronicle*, 11 July 1946.

66 Schaffer, 'Unmasking the "Muscle Jew"', pp. 375–96.

67 Shalom Namali, 'The House on the Hill', *Jewish Chronicle Supplement*, 30 May 1958.

68 Merron, *Collectively Yours*, p. 16. *Goyim* is a pejorative term for non-Jewish people. More broadly, Goldberg notes, Jews in Israel frequently took on habits typical of non-Jews in their previous homes. See Harvey E. Goldberg, 'Historical and Cultural Dimensions of Ethnic Phenomena in Israel', in Alex Weingrod (ed.), *Studies in Israeli Ethnicity: After the Ingathering* (New York: Gordon and Breach, 1985), pp. 179–200 (p. 188).

69 Interview with British migrant to Lavi (HR), June 2017. See also Ephraim Gatwirth, 'A Walk Down Allenby Street', *Chayenu*, 13:11–12 (November–December 1949).

70 Namali, 'House on the Hill', *Jewish Chronicle Supplement*, 30 May 1958.

71 Interview with British migrant to Kfar Hanassi (AW), March 2017.

72 Interview with EC.

73 Letter in response to Avraham Tachav, *Habonim Newsletter*, 4 December 1959.

74 Interview with AW, March 2017.

75 *Habonim Newsletter*, 26 May 1967.

76 Merron, *Collectively Yours*, p. 227.

77 Bermant, *Coming Home*, p. 124.

78 Kibbutz Lavi Archive, Box 1/9, Report by Yaacov Lomas on Northern Bachad Farm, Ollerton, August 1953.

79 Interview with DC.

80 Interview with JB.

Notes

81 Interview with EC.

82 Interview with JB.

83 See Omer-Jackaman, *The Impact of Zionism*, p. 132.

84 Interview with EC.

85 *Habonim Newsletter*, 23 December 1959.

86 Ibid.

87 Goldberg, 'Historical and Cultural Dimensions', p. 186.

88 Interview with MS.

89 *Jewish Chronicle* supplement, 'Aliyah', interview with Norman and Evelyn Cohen, 3 November 1978.

90 Interview with British migrant to Kfar Hanassi (PB), March 2017.

91 On fundraising for the Churchill forest, see *Glasgow Evening Citizen*, 27 May 1966. The Queen Elizabeth Coronation Forest was planted in 1955 near Nazareth. Board of Deputies minutes show that Harold Wilson had agreed to a forest being planted in his name. See Board of Deputies MSS, ACC 3121/E4/135, letter from Harold Miller (Zionist Federation), 10 December 1976.

92 Omer-Jackaman, *The Impact of Zionism*, p. 139.

93 Central Zionist Archive, F13/637, letter from Eric Lucas (Zionist Federation of Great Britain and Ireland) to Edward Sieff, 10 November 1966.

94 Kfar Hanassi Archive, 'Village Voice', 12 September 1975.

95 Interview with AC.

96 Interview with AC.

97 'Kfar Hanassi', in Cohen (ed.), *Habonim in Britain*, pp. 260–1.

98 Interview with AC.

99 Norman Appelton, 'The Rise and Fall of the Zig', in Cohen (ed.), *Habonim in Britain*, pp. 236–7.

100 Interview with AC.

101 Interview with AW.

102 Kfar Hanassi archive, 'Village Voice', 28 January 1977. 11,179 English books were borrowed against 4,010 in Hebrew.

103 Kfar Hanassi archive, 'Village Voice', 12 October 1975.

104 *Jewish Chronicle* supplement, 'Aliyah', interview with Susan Hazan, 3 November 1978.

105 Kfar Hanassi archive, 'Village Voice', 'A Trip with a Difference', 16 May 1975.

106 Interview with PB.

107 Interview with British migrant to Kfar Hanassi (CP), June 2017.

108 'Kfar Hanassi', in Cohen (ed.), *Habonim in Britain*, pp. 260–1.

109 Ibid.

110 Interview with PB.

111 Gilbert, *Writing Jewish*, p. 86.

112 Bermant, *Coming Home*, p. 108.

113 *Chayenu*, 13:1–2 (January–February 1949), 'Torah V'Avodah Organisation: Twenty-First Conference and Winter School'.

114 Yad Tabenkin, Ramat Efal, Habonim Archive, Box 11/1, 72308, *Habonim Newsletter*, 'A New Year', 14 September 1956.

115 Of course, Zionism writ large has often been constructed in this way as a settler-colonial project. See, for discussion, R. Busbridge, 'Israel-Palestine and the Settler Colonial "Turn": From Interpretation to Decolonization', *Theory, Culture & Society*, 35:1 (2018), pp. 91–115.

116 Interview with British migrant to Lavi (SC), March 2017.

117 Interview with PB.

118 Interview with AW.

119 Interview with British migrant to Lavi (MH), June 2017.

120 *Jewish Chronicle*, 'Aliyah 80s', a supplement published for the Aliyah department, WZO (Britain), and the National Aliyah and Volunteers Council, 1 February 1980. Interview with Susan Wolff.

121 Interview with JB.

122 Interview with SC.

123 Interview with Myer Raines.

124 Interview with AB.

125 For analysis, see Wendehorst, *British Jewry*, pp. 128–9.

126 Central Zionist Archive, F13/175, essay on 'The Work of the Zionist Society' by Harry Levine (1943).

127 Interview with AW.

128 Interview with CP.

129 Comments of Captain David Rebak in Fenton, *Strength and Courage*.

130 Interview with British migrant to kibbutz Hazorea (ML), March 2017.

131 Bermant, *Coming Home*, p. 210.

132 Interview with JB.

133 Baum, *Feeling Jewish*, p. 55.

134 Gabriel Sheffer, *Diaspora Politics: At Home Abroad* (Cambridge: Cambridge University Press, 2003), p. 15, and M. Kearney, 'The Local and the Global: The Anthropology of Globalization and Transnationalism', *Annual Review of Anthropology*, 24 (1995), pp. 547–65.

135 Tamar Horowitz, 'Value-Orientated Parameters in Migration Policies in the 1990s: The Israeli Experience', *International Migration*, 34:4 (1996), pp. 513–37 (p. 517).

136 Raines, *Identity Card*, p. 79.

137 Interview with Myer Raines.

138 Interview with AC.

Conclusion

1 Howard Jacobson, *The Mighty Walzer* (London: Vintage, 1999), p. 374. *Tsemisht* translates as confused or mixed up; *meshuggener* as crazy.

2 Golding, *Magnolia Street*, p. 225.

3 Louis Golding, *Forward from Babylon* (London: Cristofers, 1920), p. 159.

4 Cited in Blue, *Hitchhiking to Heaven*, p. 124.

5 Grant, *Remind Me Who I Am, Again*, p. 162.

6 Linda Grant, *When I Lived in Modern Times* (London: Granta, 2000), p. 68.

7 Elisa Bray, 'The March Reminded People what our Community is About', *Jewish Chronicle*, 1 December 2023. The march took place on 26 November 2023.

8 Karen Glaser and Gaby Wine, 'Thousands of Non-Jews Marched Alongside Us', *Jewish Chronicle*, 1 December 2023.

9 Louis Golding, 'The Israeli State', *The Literary Guide and Rationalist Review*, 64:11 (1949), pp. 205–6 (p. 206).

Select bibliography

Abrams, Nathan (ed.), *Hidden in Plain Sight: Jews and Jewishness in British Film, Television, and Popular Culture* (Evanston, IL: Northwestern University Press, 2016)

Alderman, Geoffrey, 'British Jewry: The Disintegration of a Community', in Sol Encel and Leslie Stein (eds), *Continuity, Commitment, and Survival: Jewish Communities in the Diaspora* (Westport, CT: Praeger, 2003), pp. 49–65

Alderman, Geoffrey, *Controversy and Crisis: Studies in the History of the Jews in Modern Britain* (Boston: Academic Studies Press, 2008)

Alderman, Geoffrey, *The Federation of Synagogues: A New History* (London: Federation of Synagogues, 2018)

Alderman, Geoffrey, *Modern British Jewry* (Oxford: Clarendon, 1988)

Alderman, Geoffrey (ed.), *New Directions in Anglo-Jewish History* (Boston: Academic Studies Press, 2010)

Alderman, Naomi, *Disobedience* (London: Penguin, 2007)

Améry, Jean, 'On the Necessity and Impossibility of Being a Jew', trans. Sidney and Stella Rosenfeld, *New German Critique*, 20:2 (1980), pp. 15–29

Ammerman, Nancy (ed.), *Everyday Religion: Observing Modern Religious Lives* (Oxford: Oxford University Press, 2007)

Andrusier, Adam, *Two Hitlers and a Marilyn* (London: Headline, 2021)

Aurell, Jaume, 'Making History by Contextualizing Oneself: Autobiography as Historiographical Intervention', *History and Theory*, 54:2 (2015), pp. 244–68

Aviv, Caryn, and Shneer, David, *New Jews: The End of the Jewish Diaspora* (New York: New York University Press, 2005)

Baker, Cynthia, *Jew* (New Brunswick, NJ: Rutgers University Press, 2017)

Barker, Walter, *A Fountain Opened: A Short History of the Church's Ministry among the Jews, 1809–1982* (London: Olive Press, 1983)

Baron, Alexander, *The Lowlife* (London: Black Spring, 2021 [1963])

Batnitzky, Liora, *How Judaism Became a Religion* (Princeton, NJ: Princeton University Press, 2011)

Baum, Devorah, *Feeling Jewish (A Book for Just about Anyone)* (New Haven, CT: Yale University Press, 2017)

Bayfield, Tony, *Being Jewish Today: Confronting the Real Issues* (London: Bloomsbury, 2019)

Beckman, Morris, *The Hackney Crucible* (London: Vallentine Mitchell, 1996)

Benski, Tova, 'Identification, Group Survival and Inter-Group Relations: The Case of a Middle-Class Jewish Community in Scotland', *Ethnic and Racial Studies*, 4:3 (1981), pp. 307–20

Select bibliography

Ben-Ur, Aviva, 'Identity Imperative: Ottoman Jews in Wartime and Interwar Britain', *Immigrants and Minorities*, 33:2 (2015), pp. 165–95

Bermant, Chaim, *Coming Home* (London: George Allen and Unwin, 1976)

Bermant, Chaim, *Troubled Eden: An Anatomy of British Jewry* (London: Vallentine Mitchell, 1969)

Blue, Lionel, 'European Jewry after the War', in Dow Marmur (ed.), *Reform Judaism: Essays on Reform Judaism in Britain* (Oxford: Reform Synagogues of Great Britain, 1973), pp. 215–27

Blue, Lionel, *Hitchhiking to Heaven: An Autobiography* (London: Hodder and Stoughton, 2004)

Blue, Lionel, *To Heaven, with Scribes and Pharisees: The Lord of Hosts in Suburbia, the Jewish Path to God* (London: Darton, Longman and Todd, 1975)

Boyarin, Daniel, *A Traveling Homeland: The Babylonian Talmud as Diaspora* (Philadelphia, PA: University of Pennsylvania Press, 2015)

Boyarin, Daniel, and Boyarin, Jonathan, 'Diaspora: Generation and the Ground of Jewish Identity', *Critical Inquiry*, 19:4 (1993), pp. 693–725

Braybrooke, Marcus, *Children of One God: A History of the Council of Christians and Jews* (London: Vallentine Mitchell, 1991)

Brod, Harry (ed.), *A Mensch Among Men: Explorations in Jewish Masculinity* (Freedom, CA: The Crossing Press, 1988)

Brook, Stephen, *The Club: The Jews of Modern Britain* (London: Constable, 1989)

Brown, Callum, *The Death of Christian Britain: Understanding Secularisation 1800–2000* (London: Routledge, 2001)

Brown, Callum, *Religion and Society in Twentieth-Century Britain* (Harlow: Pearson Longman, 2006)

Carrington, David (ed.), *Light on Soviet Jewry* (London: Ranelagh Press, 1969)

Cesarani, David, 'A Funny Thing Happened on the Way to the Suburbs: Social Change in Anglo-Jewry between the Wars, 1914–45', *Jewish Culture and History*, 1:1 (1998), pp. 5–26

Cesarani, David, 'One Hundred Years of Zionism in England', *European Judaism*, 25:1 (1992), pp. 40–7

Charles, Gerda, *The Crossing Point* (London: Eyre and Spottiswoode, 1961)

Cohen, Melvin (ed.), *Habonim in Britain 1929–55* (Ramat Efal: Yad Tabenkin, 1999)

Cohen, Stuart, *English Zionists and British Jews: The Communal Politics of Anglo-Jewry, 1895–1920* (Princeton, NJ: Princeton University Press, 1982)

Cohn-Sherbok, Dan, *Messianic Judaism* (London: Cassell, 2000)

Cole, Tim, *Images of the Holocaust: The Myth of 'Shoah Business'* (London: Duckworth, 1999)

Cooper, John, *The British Campaign for Soviet Jewry 1966–1991: Human Rights and Exit Permits* (Manchester: i2i, 2023)

Cooperman, Alan, and Alper, Becka, 'Introduction to the Special Issue', *Contemporary Jewry*, 43 (2023), pp. 193–200.

Coyle, Adrian, and Rafalin, Deborah, 'Jewish Gay Men's Accounts of Negotiating Cultural, Religious, and Sexual Identity: A Qualitative Study', *Journal of Psychology & Human Sexuality*, 12:4 (2000), pp. 21–47

Cromer, Gerald, 'Intermarriage and Communal Survival in a London Suburb', *The Jewish Journal of Sociology*, 16:2 (1974), pp. 155–70

Dansky, Miriam, *Gateshead: Its Community, Its Personalities, Its Institutions* (Southfield, MI: Targum, 1992)

Select bibliography

Diemling, Maria, and Ray, Larry (eds), *Boundaries, Identity and Belonging in Modern Judaism* (Abingdon: Routledge, 2015)

Elton, Benjamin, 'British Orthodox Jewry 1945–90: Swing to the Right or Shift to the Centre?', *Journal of Modern Jewish Studies*, 13:2 (2014), pp. 264–83

Endelman, Todd, 'Anglo-Jewish Historiography and the Jewish Historical Mainstream', in Tony Kushner and Hannah Ewence (eds), *Whatever Happened to British Jewish Studies?* (London: Vallentine Mitchell, 2012), pp. 31–42

Endelman, Todd, *Broadening Jewish History: Towards a Social History of Ordinary Jews* (Oxford: The Littman Library of Jewish Civilisation, 2011)

Endelman, Todd, *The Jews of Britain, 1656 to 2000* (Berkeley, CA: University of California Press, 2002)

Endelman, Todd, *Radical Assimilation in English Jewish History, 1645–1945* (Bloomington, IN: Indiana University Press, 1990)

Fackenheim, Emil, 'The 614th Commandment', *Judaism*, 16:3 (1967), pp. 269–73

Fein, Leonard, *Where Are We? The Inner Life of American Jews* (New York: Harper and Row, 1998)

Feldman, David, 'Conceiving Difference: Religion, Race and the Jews in Britain, c. 1750–1900', *History Workshop Journal*, 76 (2013), pp. 160–86

Feldman, David, *Englishmen and Jews: Social Relations and Political Culture 1840–1914* (New Haven, CT: Yale University Press, 1994)

Fenton, Jason, *Strength and Courage: The Untold Story of the Machal Volunteers who Helped Win Israel's War of Independence* (Irvine, CA: ProtoMet Media, 2009)

Feuchtwang, Stephan, 'Mythical Moments in National and Other Family Histories', *History Workshop Journal*, 59 (2005), pp. 179–93

Flint Ashery, Shlomit, *Spatial Behavior in Haredi Communities in Great Britain* (Cham: Springer, 2020)

Frank, Michael, *The Mighty Franks: A Memoir* (London: 4th Estate, 2017)

Freedman, Maurice (ed.), *A Minority in Britain: Social Studies of the Anglo-Jewish Community* (London: Vallentine Mitchell, 1955)

Freud-Kandel, Miri, *Orthodox Judaism in Britain since 1913: An Ideology Forsaken* (London: Vallentine Mitchell, 2006)

Gartner, Lloyd, *The Jewish Immigrant in England: 1870–1914* (London: Vallentine Mitchell, 2001 [1960]).

Gelber, Yoav, *Nation and History: Israeli Historiography between Zionism and Post-Zionism* (London: Vallentine Mitchell, 2011)

Gerlis, Daphne, *Those Wonderful Women in Black: Story of the Women's Campaign for Soviet Jewry* (London: Minerva Press, 1996)

Gilbert, Ruth, *Writing Jewish: Contemporary British-Jewish Literature* (Basingstoke: Palgrave 2013)

Goldberg, David, *This is Not the Way: Jews, Judaism and the State of Israel* (London: Faber and Faber, 2012)

Golding, Louis, *Forward from Babylon* (London: Cristofers, 1920)

Golding, Louis, *Magnolia Street* (St Albans: Gainsborough Press, 1932)

Goodman, Martin, *A History of Judaism* (London: Allen Lane, 2017)

Grant, Linda, *Remind Me Who I Am, Again* (London: Granta, 1998)

Grant, Linda, *The Story of the Forest* (London: Virago, 2023)

Grant, Linda, *When I Lived in Modern Times* (London: Granta, 2000)

Greenberg, Steven, *Wrestling with God and Men: Homosexuality in the Jewish Tradition* (Madison, WI: University of Wisconsin Press, 2004)

Select bibliography

Greengross, Wendy, *Jewish and Homosexual* (London: Reform Synagogues of Great Britain, 1980)

Gross, Rachel B., *Beyond the Synagogue: Jewish Nostalgia and Religious Practice* (New York: New York University Press, 2021)

Harris, Cyril, *For Heaven's Sake* (London: Vallentine Mitchell, 2000)

Harvey, Richard, *But I'm Jewish! A Jew for Jesus Tells his Story* (London: Jews for Jesus, 1996)

Harvey, Richard, *Mapping Messianic Jewish Theology: A Constructive Approach* (Milton Keynes: Paternoster, 2009)

Harway, Danielle, Schwartz, Ros, and Johnson, Val (eds), *A Word in Edgeways* (London: JF Publications, 1988)

Heilman, Samuel, *Defenders of the Faith: Inside Ultra-Orthodox Jewry* (New York: Schocken, 1992)

Henriques, Ursula, *The Jews of South Wales* (Cardiff: University of Wales Press, 2013)

Hill, Harvey, 'The Science of Reform: Abraham Geiger and the Wissenschaft des Judentum', *Modern Judaism*, 27:3 (2007), pp. 329–49

Hirschhorn, Sara, *City on a Hilltop: American Jews and the Israeli Settler Movement* (Cambridge, MA: Harvard University Press, 2017)

Homa, Bernard, *A Fortress in Anglo-Jewry: The Story of the Machzike Hadath* (London: Shapiro, Vallentine and Co., 1953)

Homa, Bernard, *Orthodoxy in Anglo-Jewry 1880–1940* (London: Jewish Historical Society of England, 1969)

Horn, Dara, *People Love Dead Jews: Reports from a Haunted Present* (New York: W.W. Norton, 2021)

Hughes, Aaron, *Rethinking Jewish Philosophy: Beyond Particularism and Universalism* (Oxford: Oxford University Press, 2014)

Huxley, Julian, and Haddon, Alfred, *We Europeans: A Survey of Racial Problems* (London: Jonathan Cape, 1935)

Jacobovits, Immanuel, *'If Only My People': Zionism in my Life* (London: Weidenfeld and Nicolson, 1984)

Jacobovits, Immanuel, *Journal of a Rabbi* (London: W.H. Allen, 1967)

Jacobs, Joseph, *Jewish Contributions to Civilization* (Philadelphia, PA: The Jewish Publication Society of America, 1919)

Jacobs, Louis, *Beyond Reasonable Doubt* (London: The Littman Library of Jewish Civilisation, 1999)

Jacobs, Louis, *Helping with Inquiries: An Autobiography* (London: Vallentine Mitchell, 1989)

Jacobs, Louis, *We Have Reason to Believe: Some Aspects of Jewish Theology Examined in the Light of Modern Thought*, 4th edn (London: Vallentine Mitchell, 1995)

Jacobson, Howard, *The Finkler Question* (London: Bloomsbury, 2010)

Jacobson, Howard, *Kalooki Nights* (London: Vintage, 2006)

Jacobson, Howard, *The Mighty Walzer* (London: Vintage, 1999)

Jacobson, Howard, *Roots Schmoots: Journeys among Jews* (London: Viking 1993)

Kadish, Sharman, *The Synagogues of Britain and Ireland: An Architectural and Social History* (New Haven, CT: Yale University Press, 2011)

Kahn-Harris, Keith, and Gidley, Ben, *Turbulent Times: The British Jewish Community Today* (London: Continuum, 2010)

Karpf, Anne, Klug, Brian, Rose, Jacqueline, and Rosenbaum, Barbara (eds), *A Time to Speak Out: Independent Jewish Voices on Israel, Zionism and Jewish Identity* (London: Verso, 2008)

Select bibliography

Kershen, Anne, *Strangers, Aliens and Asians: Huguenots, Jews and Bangladeshis in Spitalfields, 1660–2000* (Abingdon: Routledge, 2005)

Kershen, Anne, and Romain, Jonathan, *Tradition and Change: A History of Reform Judaism in Britain, 1840–1995* (London: Vallentine Mitchell, 1995)

Kessler, Edward, *A Reader of Early Liberal Judaism: The Writings of Israel Abrahams, Claude Montefiore, Lily Montagu and Israel Mattuck* (London: Vallentine Mitchell, 2004)

Kimmerling, Baruch, 'History Caught in the Cross-Fire: The Case of Israeli-Jewish Historiography', *History and Memory*, 7:1 (1995), pp. 41–65

Kirshenblatt-Gimblett, Barbara (ed.), *Writing a Modern Jewish History: Essays in Honor of Salo Baron* (New York: Jewish Museum, 2006)

Klein, Emma, *Lost Jews: The Struggle for Identity Today* (Basingstoke: Macmillan, 1996)

Kosmin, Barry, and Levy, Caren, *Jewish Identity in an Anglo-Jewish Community: The Findings of the 1978 Redbridge Survey* (London: Research Unit of the Board of Deputies of British Jews, 1983), https://archive.jpr.org.uk/download?id=2509 (accessed 8 October 2024)

Krausz, Ernest, 'The Economic and Social Structure of Anglo Jewry', in Julius Gould and Shaul Esh (eds), *Jewish Life in Modern Britain* (London: Routledge, 1964), pp. 27–40

Krausz, Ernest, 'The Edgware Survey: Factors in Jewish Identification', *Jewish Journal of Sociology*, 11:2 (1969), pp. 151–64

Kureishi, Hanif, *My Ear at His Heart: Reading My Father* (London: Faber and Faber, 2004)

Kushner, Tony, *Anglo-Jewry since 1066: Place, Locality and Memory* (Manchester: Manchester University Press, 2009)

Kushner, Tony, *The Battle of Britishness: Migrant Journeys: 1685 to the Present* (Manchester: Manchester University Press, 2012)

Kushner, Tony, 'Jewish Local Studies and Memory Work: A Case Study of Cornwall', *Journal of Jewish Studies*, 55:1 (2004), pp. 157–62

Kushner, Tony (ed.), *The Jewish Heritage in British History: Englishness and Jewishness* (London: Frank Cass, 1992)

Landy, David, *Jewish Identity and Palestinian Rights: Diaspora Jewish Opposition to Israel* (London: Zed Books, 2011)

Lerman, Antony, *The Making and Unmaking of a Zionist: A Personal and Political Journey* (London: Pluto, 2012)

Lerman, Antony, *Whatever Happened to Antisemitism? Definition and the Myth of the 'Collective Jew'* (London: Pluto, 2022)

Leshem, Elazar, and Shuval, Judith, *Immigration to Israel: Sociological Perspectives* (New Brunswick, NJ: Transaction Publishers, 1998)

Levenberg, Schneier, *The Board and Zion: An Historical Survey* (Hull: Rare Times, 1985)

Light, Alison, *Common People: The History of an English Family* (London: Penguin, 2015)

Lipman, Vivian, *A History of the Jews in Britain since 1858* (Leicester: Leicester University Press, 1990)

Longworth, Philip (ed.), *Confrontations with Judaism* (London: Anthony Blond, 1967)

Marber, Patrick, *Howard Katz* (London: Faber and Faber, 2001)

Marmur, Dow, *Intermarriage* (London: RSGB Pamphlet, 1978)

Marqusee, Mark, *If I Am Not for Myself: Journey of an Anti-Zionist Jew* (London: Verso, 2008)

Mattuck, Israel, *Jewish Ethics* (London: Hutchinson, 1953)

Maybaum, Ignaz, *The Jewish Mission* (London: James Clarke, 1951)

Maybaum, Ignaz, 'Jewish Understanding of the Christian, Christian Understanding of the Jew', in Dow Marmur (ed.), *A Genuine Search: God – Torah – Israel: A Reform Perspective* (London: Reform Synagogues of Great Britain, 1979), pp. 221–5.

Select bibliography

McGinity, Karen, *Marrying Out: Intermarriage and Fatherhood* (Bloomington, IN: Indiana University Press, 2014)

McGuire, Meredith, *Lived Religion: Faith and Practice in Everyday Life* (Oxford: Oxford University Press, 2008)

Mehta, Samira, *Beyond Chrismukkah: The Christian–Jewish Interfaith Family in the United States* (Chapel Hill, NC: University of North Carolina Press, 2018)

Merron, David, *Collectively Yours: Tales from the Borderline* (Bakewell: Country Books, 1999)

Meyer, Michael, *Response to Modernity: A History of the Reform Movement in Judaism* (Oxford: Oxford University Press, 1988)

Miller, Rory, *Divided Against Zion: Anti-Zionist Opposition in Britain to a Jewish State in Palestine, 1945–8* (London: Frank Cass, 2000)

Mitchell, Bruce, 'London's Haredi Publications in Yiddish: Language, Literature and Ultra-Orthodox Ideology', *European Judaism*, 32:2 (1999), pp. 51–66

Mosco, Maisie, *Almonds and Raisins* (London: Coronet Books, 1993 [1979])

Mosco, Maisie, *Between Two Worlds* (Sevenoaks: New English Library, 1983)

Mosco, Maisie, *The Waiting Game* (Sevenoaks: New English Library, 1987)

Myerhoff, Barbara, *Number Our Days: A Triumph of Continuity and Culture Among Jewish Old People in an Urban Ghetto* (New York: Simon and Schuster, 1978)

Nash, Catherine, *Of Irish Descent: Origin Stories, Genealogy, and the Politics of Belonging* (Syracuse, NY: Syracuse University Press, 2008)

Newman, Aubrey, *The United Synagogue 1870–1970* (London: Routledge and Kegan Paul, 1976)

Novick, Peter, *The Holocaust in American Life* (Boston: Houghton Mifflin, 1999)

Omer-Jackaman, Jack, *The Impact of Zionism and Israel on Anglo-Jewry's Identity, 1948–82: Caught Somewhere between Zion and Galut* (London: Vallentine Mitchell, 2019)

Parkes, James, *The Jew and his Neighbour: A Study of the Causes of Anti-Semitism* (London: SCM Press, 1930).

Pearce, Andy, *Holocaust Consciousness in Contemporary Britain* (Abingdon: Routledge, 2014)

Persoff, Meir, *Faith Against Reason: Religious Reform and the British Chief Rabbinate 1840–1990* (London: Vallentine Mitchell, 2008)

Pinkus, Benjamin, *The Jews of the Soviet Union: The History of a National Minority* (Cambridge: Cambridge University Press, 1988)

Rabinowicz, Harry, *A World Apart: The Story of the Chasidism in Britain* (London: Vallentine Mitchell, 1997)

Rabinowitz, Richard, *Objects of Love and Regret: A Brooklyn Story* (Cambridge, MA: Belknap Press of Harvard University Press, 2022)

Rabkin, Yakov, *A Threat from Within: A Century of Jewish Opposition to Zionism*, trans. Fred A. Reed (London: Zed Books, 2006)

Rapoport, Chaim, *Judaism and Homosexuality: An Authentic Orthodox View* (London: Vallentine Mitchell, 2004)

Rausch, David, *Messianic Judaism: Its History, Theology, and Polity* (New York: Edwin Mellen Press, 1982)

Rawidowicz, Simon, *Israel: The Ever-Dying People and Other Essays*, ed. Benjamin Ravid (Cranbury, NJ: Associated University Presses, 1986)

Rich, Dave, 'The Activist Challenge: Women, Students, and the Board of Deputies of British Jews in the British Campaign for Soviet Jewry', *Jewish History*, 29 (2015), pp. 163–85

Select bibliography

Richmond, Colin, *Campaigner against Antisemitism: The Reverend James Parkes 1896–1981* (London: Vallentine Mitchell, 2005)

Regal, Lawrence, and Rosenberg, Rosita, *Liberal Judaism: The First Hundred Years* (London: Liberal Judaism, 2004)

Roi, Yaacov, *The Struggle for Soviet-Jewish Emigration, 1948–67* (Cambridge: Cambridge University Press, 1991)

Romain, Gemma, *Connecting Histories: A Comparative Exploration of African-Caribbean and Jewish History and Memory in Modern Britain* (London: Kegan Paul, 2006)

Romain, Jonathan, *Till Faith Us Do Part: Couples who Fall in Love across the Religious Divide* (London: Fount, 1996)

Romain, Jonathan (ed.), *Renewing the Vision: Rabbis Speak Out on Modern Jewish Issues* (London: SCM Press, 1996)

Romain, Jonathan, and Mitchell, David, *Inclusive Judaism: The Changing Face of an Ancient Faith* (London: Jessica Kingsley, 2020)

Roth, Cecil, 'The Jewish Community in the Context of World Jewry', in Julius Gould and Shaul Esh (eds), *Jewish Life in Modern Britain* (London: Routledge and Kegan Paul, 1964), pp. 93–110

Roth, Cecil, *The Jewish Contribution to Civilization* (London: Macmillan, 1938)

Rubens, Bernice, *The Elected Member* (London: Sphere, 1980 [1969])

Rubens, Bernice, *I Dreyfus* (London: Little Brown, 1999)

Rubinstein, William, *A History of the Jews in the English-Speaking World: Great Britain* (Basingstoke: Macmillan, 1996)

Sacks, Jonathan, *Future Tense* (London: Hodder and Stoughton, 2009)

Sacks, Jonathan, *One People? Tradition, Modernity, and Jewish Unity* (London: The Littman Library of Jewish Civilisation, 1993)

Sacks, Jonathan, *Will We Have Jewish Grandchildren? Jewish Continuity and How to Achieve It* (London: Vallentine Mitchell, 1994)

Samuelson, Francine, 'Messianic Judaism: Church, Denomination, Sect, or Cult?', *Journal of Ecumenical Studies*, 37:2 (2000), pp. 161–86

Sartre, Jean-Paul, *Anti-Semite and Jew: An Explanation of the Etiology of Hate*, trans. George. J Becker (New York: Schocken, 1948)

Saunders, Diane, and Lester, Philippa, *From the Leylands to Leeds 17: Jewish Leeds in Words and Images* (Leeds: Leyland Books, 2014)

Schaffer, Gavin, 'Unmasking the "Muscle Jew": The Jewish Soldier in British War Service, 1899–1945', *Patterns of Prejudice*, 46:3–4 (2012), pp. 375–96

Segev, Tom, *The Seventh Million: The Israelis and the Holocaust*, trans Haim Watzman (New York: Hill and Wang, 1993)

Shapiro, Helen, *Walking Back to Happiness* (London: Harper Collins, 1993)

Sharot, Stephen, 'Reform and Liberal Judaism in London 1840–1940', *Jewish Social Studies*, 41:3/4 (1979), pp. 211–28

Sheffer, Gabriel, *Diaspora Politics: At Home Abroad* (Cambridge: Cambridge University Press, 2003)

Sheridan, Sybil (ed.), *Hear Our Voice: Women Rabbis Tell Their Stories* (London: SCM Press, 1994)

Shneer, David, and Aviv, Caryn (eds), *Queer Jews* (London: Routledge, 2002)

Shoham, Hizky, 'From "Great History" to "Small History": The Genesis of the Zionist Periodization', *Israel Studies*, 18:1 (2013), pp. 31–55

Simpson, William, *Youth and Anti-Semitism* (London: Epworth, 1938)

Select bibliography

Slezkine, Yuri, *The Jewish Century* (Princeton, NJ: Princeton University Press, 2006)

Staetsky, L. D., Sheps, Marina, and Boyd, Jonathan, 'Immigration from the United Kingdom to Israel', Institute for Jewish Policy Research, October 2013, https://www.jpr.org.uk/reports/immigration-united-kingdom-israel (accessed 8 October 2024)

Steedman, Carolyn, *Landscape for a Good Woman* (London: Virago, 1986)

Steyn, Juliet, *The Jew: Assumptions of Identity* (London: Cassell, 1999)

Summers, Anne, 'False Start or Brave Beginning? The Society of Jews and Christians, 1924–1944', *Journal of Ecclesiastical History*, 65:4 (2014), pp. 827–51

Sweasey, Peter, *From Queer to Eternity: Spirituality in the Lives of Lesbian, Gay and Bisexual People* (London: Cassell, 1997)

Thomlinson, Natalie, *Race, Ethnicity and the Women's Movement in England, 1968–93* (Basingstoke: Palgrave, 2016)

Thompson, Jennifer, *Jewish on Their Own Terms: How Intermarried Couples are Changing American Judaism* (New Brunswick, NJ: Rutgers University Press, 2014)

Troen, S. Ilan, *Imagining Zion: Dreams, Designs and Realities in a Century of Jewish Settlement* (New Haven, CT: Yale University Press, 2003)

Tucker, Ruth, *Not Ashamed: The Story of Jews for Jesus* (Sisters, OR: Multnomah, 1999)

Vital, David, *The Future of the Jews* (Cambridge, MA: Harvard University Press, 1990)

Wasserstein, Bernard, *Vanishing Diaspora: The Jews in Europe since 1945* (London: Penguin, 1997)

Wendehorst, Stephan, *British Jewry, Zionism, and the Jewish State, 1936–1956* (Oxford: Oxford University Press, 2012)

Wiesel, Elie, *The Jews of Silence: A Personal Report on Soviet Jewry* (Philadelphia, PA: The Jewish Publication Society of America, 1967)

Wistrich, Robert (ed.), *Anti-Zionism and Antisemitism in the Contemporary World* (Basingstoke: Macmillan, 1990)

Yerushalmi, Yosef Hayim, *Zakhor: Jewish History and Memory* (New York: Schocken, 1989)

Young, James, *The Texture of Memory: Holocaust Memorials and Meaning* (New Haven, CT: Yale University Press, 1993)

Zerubavel, Eviatar, *Ancestors and Relatives: Genealogy, Identity, and Community* (Oxford: Oxford University Press, 2012)

Index

35s, the 78–80, 82, 83, 86, 87–8, 88–9, 89

Aaronovitch, David 150
Abrahams, Israel 52
Abse, Leo 82, 112
Aziza, Nudrat, *Kehillah* 20–1, 194, fig. 1
Agudath Israel 45
AIDS crisis 118, 128
Albany Trust 114, 118
Alderman, Geoffrey 25, 30–1, 42, 91–2, 98
Alderman, Naomi 129
Alexander, David Lindo 95
aliyah 174, 176–80, 188–92
Allen, Jim, *Perdition* 105–6
Aman, Shloimy 21
Amias, Saul 77–8, 114
Amnesty International 86
Andrusier, Adam 12
Anglo-Jewish Association (AJA) 96–7
anti-missionary campaign 160–5, 170–1
antisemitism 2–3, 4–5, 7, 33, 58, 71, 71–2,
    90–2, 91, 94, 107, 136, 152, 158, 161,
    169, 170, 189–90, 191, 193, 196
anti-Zionism 90, 93, 97–8, 103–7, 161
Appelton, Norman 186–7
Ariel, Yaakov 168
Arkush, Shmuel 156, 157–8, 158–9, 160–5,
    168, 169, 170, 172
Aron, Wellesley 175
Ashkenazi Judaism 45, 51
Associated British Synagogues 53, 55
Associated Synagogues of Great Britain
    (ASGB) 53, 59–60
Aviv, Caryn 125

Balfour Declaration 71, 95, 177
Bard, Julia 92, 99
Barker, Walter 154, 166
Baron, Alexander 12
Baron, Salo 6
Bauer, Yehuda 94–5
Baum, Devorah 2, 8, 190
Bayfield, Tony 124, 142
Beckman, Morris 27
Beit Klal Yisrael 113, 123, 127, 128
Benski, Tova 84
Benson, Simon 116
Bermant, Chaim 23, 41, 61, 82, 84, 87,
    116, 178, 179, 181, 184, 188, 190,
    239n111
Bernstein, Fanny 14, 15
Bernstein, Marks 14–15, 17–18
Bernstein, Sophie 14–15
Birmingham, Singers Hill cathedral
    synagogue 1, 33
Black, George 23–4
Bloomfield, Irene 121
Blue, Lionel 18–19, 56, 58, 65, 69, 113,
    114, 121, 124, 128, 129
Bnei Akiva 179–80, 183, 188
Board of Deputies 22, 26, 31, 53, 62, 63,
    71–2, 76, 79, 91, 141, 171, 178
    Demographic and Statistical Research
    Unit 8, 133
Bradford 20–1, 35, 51
Braine, Naomi 125
British Jewish experience 1–3
British Jewish studies 10
Britishness 71, 78, 96–8, 185–8

Index

Brodie, Israel 60, 65–6, 70
Brook, Stephen 22, 130–1, 138
Brown, Callum 4
Brown, Laurence 117
Brown, Michael 118
Bruegel, Irene 100
Brunner, Lazar Dovid 63

Cable Street mural 34
caesurae 12
Cambridge University 163, 170
Campaign Against Antisemitism 195
Cardiff 59
Carey, George, Archbishop of Canterbury
    154–5
cemeteries and graves, preservation
    31–5
Cesarani, David 91, 92
Charles, Gerda, *The Crossing Point* 3
Chasidim 45, 47–8
Chester, Gail 106
Chevra Machzike Hadath 45
Cheyette, Bryan 91
Church's Ministry among Jewish People
    (CMJ) 150–1, 151, 153–5
Clause 43 crisis 67–8
Cohen, Brunel 96
Cohen, Jeffrey 40
Cohen, Norman 9–10
Cohen, Ruth 70
Cohen, Shimon 164
Cohn-Sherbok, Dan 158, 166
Cole, Tim 82
communal anxiety 22
communal life 5
community history 11–13
community safety 1
Conjoint Foreign Committee 95
Consultative Committee on Jewish–
    Christian Relations 61
conversion to Judaism 56–7
Cooper, John 82, 86
Corre, John 109
Council of Christians and Jews (CCJ)
    152–3, 153–4, 155, 157
Coyle, Adrian 122
Cromer, Gerald 131, 133, 136, 138, 141,
    146–7

Davis, Bernard 115
de Lange, Nicholas 31–2, 94
demographic decline 24–5
discord thesis, the 136
divorce 233n46
Dryan, Dovid 45
dual loyalty charges 71–2
Dunitz, Alfred 31–2

Edelman, Maurice 72
education 48–9
Edwards, Jackie 24–5, 37
EMETH (Emunah Mitzvah Torah) 60–1,
    62
Endelman, Todd 42, 201n11
Enlightenment, the 50–1, 93
Epstein, Brian 126
Eshkol, Levi 62
ethnic identity 30–1
European immigration 42–3, 43–8
evangelism, challenge of 153–5
ever-dying people narratives 6

Fackenheim, Emil 13
Falmouth 34–5, 35
Federation of Synagogues 45
Fein, Leonard 5–6
feminist movement 104–5, 106
Feuchtwang, Stephan 12
Fidler, Michael 62, 63
Finestein, Israel 7
First Zionist Congress 94
Fishman, Sylvia 166
Forta, Arye 159, 170
Foundation for Jewish Heritage 23
Fox, Pam 11
Frankel, William 67, 115–16
Freedland, Michael 39
Freedman, Maurice 8
Freeman, Alan 76–7
Freud-Kandel, Miri 48
Frey, Joseph 151
future, the 36–7

Gainsford, Doreen 78–9
Gartner, Lloyd 26
Gay Liberation Front (GLF) 113, 114
Gay News 114–15, 117, 127

Index

Gay Times 112
genealogy 26–31, 34, 35
Gerlis, Daphne 78, 85
German Jews 42–3
Gidley, Ben 11–12, 25–6
Gilbert, Clive 100
Gilbert, Martin 88–9
Gilbert, Ruth 126
Glancy, Josh 22
Glanville, Brian 137
Glaser, Karen 134, 147
Glasgow 36–7, 52, 59, 81, 84, 87–8, 179
Gluzman, Semyon 83
God's Unfailing Word 172
Goldberg, David J. 42, 99, 185
Goldberg, Selwyn 56–7
Golding, Louis 149, 193–4, 196, 202n22
Golditch, Dayan 44, 46, 47, 48, 48–9
Goldner, Norman 128
Golds, Peter 115
Grant, Linda 5, 26, 89, 194
Greenberg, Steven 121
Greengross, Wendy 121–2, 126
Grey, Antony 118
Gross, Rachel 28, 35
Gryn, Hugo 39–42, 53, 55, 58, 69, 70–1,
    210n17
Guardian 101

Habonim 87, 174–6, 179–80, 181, 184, 188,
    240n4
hachsharah 179–80, 181–4
Haddon, A. C. 95
Haley, Alex, *Roots* 28–9
Handler, Aryeh 181
Hanoar Hatzioni 126
Hardman, Leslie 114
Harris, Cyril 39–40
Harvey, Richard 150, 155–6, 157, 160, 163,
    166–7, 167–8, 172
Heart of the Matter (TV documentary
    series) 156, 158, 159, 168
Heilpern, Abraham 50
Heilpern, Chaim 43, 44, 46, 48, 49–50
Helsinki Accords 79–80, 86–7
Henriques, Basil 97
Henriques, Ursula 23
Heritage England 34, 35

Herman, Clem 124–5
Hertz, Joseph 139–40
Hillel Foundation 139
Hirsch, Samson Raphael 46–7
Historic England 1
history
    communal 11–13
    personal 12–18
History Workshop movement 30
HIV/AIDS 118
Holocaust (TV programme) 28
Holocaust, the 1, 4, 5, 12, 13, 27–8, 33, 41,
    69–70, 73, 82–3, 89, 96, 135, 153,
    170, 189, 191
Homa, Bernard 63, 64–5
homophobia 110, 113, 120
homosexuality 56, 109–29
    coming out 126
    Greengross study 121–2, 126
    Jewish gay life 112–17
    and Jewish law 116, 117
    and Jewish life 125–8
    and Jewishness 120, 126
    opposition to 109–11
    Orthodox position on 111, 116–17,
        117–19
    Progressive position on 116, 119–25,
        125–6
    Rapoport's analysis 119–21
Horn, Dara 35
Horowitz, Tamar 191
Hull 59
Huxley, Julian 95

Independent Jewish Voices (IJV) 92, 101,
    102, 103, 107, 224n70
Institute for Jewish Policy Research (JPR) 7
interfaith marriage 24, 25, 56–8, 130–49,
    195
    Jewish worries 132–9
    Orthodox position on 139–41, 142–3,
        145–6
    Progressive position on 142–6, 147
    Sternberg seminars 144–6
    stigma of 130–2
    threat of 132
interfaith work 58
Invisible Church, the 160–1, 167

Ireland, Jewish Museum 33
Irn-Ju 36–7
Israel, State of 5, 61, 99
   British Jewish support for 71, 72
   as central to Jewish life 107–8
   foundation 12, 96, 178
   Jewish migration to 174–6, 176–80,
      184–8, 188–92
Israel criticism 90–108
   roots 93–100
   twenty-first century 100–2
   and the Zionist majority 102–7
Israeli Liaison Bureau 78

Jacobs, David 30, 49
Jacobs, Gerald 168
Jacobs, Louis 44, 65–8, 69
Jacobs Affair 60, 65–8, 69, 118
Jacobson, Howard 12, 103, 166, 193
Jacobson, Israel 50
Jaffe, Richard 31
Jakobovits, Immanuel 7, 9, 40, 41, 42,
      60–2, 63–7, 67–8, 71, 88, 117–18,
      124, 132, 139–40, 141, 161–2
Janner, Barnett 71–2
Janner, Greville 76, 81
Jennings, Peter 154
Jesus 9, 150, 152, 156, 157, 162
Jet 140–1
Jewish activism
   cultures of 86–9
   Israel criticism 90–108
   and Jewish identification 83–6, 89
   Six-Day War 12, 71–3, 73, 78, 80–1, 82,
      84, 85–6, 87, 89
   Soviet Jewry campaign 61, 72, 73–80,
      80–1, 81, 81–3, 84, 86–7, 87–9,
      218n31
Jewish affiliation, decline in 24–5
Jewish Agency 80
Jewish AIDS Trust 118
Jewish Book Week 195
Jewish Chronicle 2, 22, 23, 28–9, 31, 32, 38,
      40, 41, 42, 61, 67, 82–3, 85–6, 91–2,
      100, 111, 114, 115, 115–16, 118–19,
      126, 128, 131, 132, 133, 134, 136, 140,
      147, 150, 164–5, 165, 167, 168, 185,
      187–8, 189, 195

Jewish community 4, 7, 8–10
Jewish decline 20–2, 22–6, 35–8, 71
Jewish Defense League 157
Jewish Echo 30, 82
Jewish Fellowship 96–7, 99, 101
Jewish Film Festival 195
Jewish Gay and Lesbian Group (JGLG)
   194
Jewish Gay Group (JGG) 115–16, 119, 122,
   128, fig. 5
Jewish Genealogical Society of Great
   Britain (JGSGB) 26–7, 31, 32, 195
Jewish Guardian 95–6
Jewish heritage
   interest in 26–31
   preservation 31–5, 35–8
Jewish history 1–5, 8
Jewish Homophile Liaison Group 114
Jewish immigrant experience 2, 13–18
Jewish law 50
Jewish Lesbian and Gay Helpline (JLGH)
   109–11, 113, 115, 126
Jewish Marriage Council 145
Jewish Museum, Ireland 33
Jewish nationalism 95–6
Jewish nationhood 95
Jewish Observer and Middle East Review 80
Jewish Outlook, The 96, 97, 104
Jewish population 22
Jewish Quarterly Review 52, 90–1
Jewish Question, the 8
Jewish Religious Union 52
Jewish Socialist 94, 100, 102, 106, 108
Jewish Socialists' Group (JSG) 90, 99, 100,
   107
Jewish Telegraph 117
Jewish Tribune 41, 47, 59, 60, 63, 68, 69, 85,
   104
Jewish–Christian relations 151, 151–5,
   168–73
Jewishness 1–2, 37–8, 81, 92–3, 107, 111,
   189
   of gay Jews 120, 126
   inclusive definition 10
   and political action 83–6
   preservation of 193–6
   public declarations of 2
   relevance 4–5

Index

Jews' College 49
Jews for Jesus 150–1, 155–60, 157–8, 170, 171, 239n111
Jews for Justice for Palestinians (JfJfP) 100, 101, 107
Joint Emergency Committee for the Religious Education of Refugee Children 53
Joint Palestine Appeal (JPA) 80–1
Joseph, Anthony 26–7, 27
Judaism, relevance 4, 93, 193–4
Julius, Myra 111, 126

Kadish, Sharman 33
Kahn-Harris, Keith 11–12, 25–6
Kaplan, Harvey 27, 30, 31, 36
Kershen, Anne 43
Kfar Hanassi kibbutz 175, 176, 182–3, 185–8, 192
kibbutzim and the kibbutz movement 87, 174–6
  aliyah 188–92
  Britishness 185–8
  kibbutz life 184–8
  motivation 180, 188–92
  preparations 181–4
  zigging 186–7
Kimmerling, Baruch 177
King-Hamilton, Alan 62
Klein, Emma 138
Klug, Brian 107
Kochen, Lionel 132
Kosmin, Barry 7, 178
Kramrisch, Faye 20
Krausz, Ernest 84
Kravitz, Bentzion 162
Kushner, Tony 2, 26, 30, 34–5, 35, 153

Landy, David 102, 107
last Jew trope 22, 23–5, 196
Lawrence, Dashiel 108
Leavor, Rudi 21, 35, fig. 1
Lebanon War, 1982 99–100
Lee, Michael 110
Leigh, Michael 50, 51, 53
Leo Baeck College 55, 55–6, 64, 70, 121–3
Lerman, Antony 73, 90, 240n4

Lesser, Benjamin, suicide of 160–1, 164, 165, 167, 171
Levenberg, Schneier 81
Levin, Bernard 4–5, 6, 71, 72, 78, 156
Levin, Salmond 68
Levine, Norman 32
Levy, Caren 178
Lewin, Harold 33
Liberal Judaism 9, 52, 56, 142, 143, 152
Lichtenstein, Rachel 21
Lipson, Daniel 101
Livshin, Ros 43
Lobenstein, Joe 63
London Society for the Promotion of Christianity among the Jews 151, 152
London Society for the Study of Religion 151–2
Lubavitch seminaries 49
Lubavitch/Chabad Orthodox sect 47

McGinity, Karen 136
McGuire, Meredith 148
Machzike Hadath 45
Maggid, Kamenitzer 98
majoritarian secularist trend 10
Manchester 23, 26, 29–30, 32, 44, 47, 51, 53, 56–7, 58, 88, 97, 193–4
  Machzikei Hadass 43, 45, 46, 49–50
Marber, Patrick 5
Marks, David Woolf 51
Marmur, Dow 56, 61–2, 116, 122, 136–7, 138, 139, 141–2, 146–7, 148
Marqusee, Mike 94
Marshall, Gordian 155
Masorti Judaism 41, 68
matrilineal descent 8–9
Mattuck, Israel 52
Maybaum, Ignaz 54, 70
Mendelssohn, Moses 93
Merron, David 184
Merthyr Tydfil 10, 14–15, 23, 23–5, 37, fig. 2, fig. 3
Messianic Judaism 9, 150–1, 155–6, 239n111
  Christian-Jewish identities 165–73
  coming out 165–8
  Jewish responses to 156–60, 160–5
  theology 157, 162–3, 171

Index

Meyer, Michael 50
Midlands Region Chaplaincy Board
161
Miller, David 44, 46
Mirvis, Ephraim 120, 172
Mizrahi Judaism 12, 44–5, 177
Moleman, Phil 184
Montagu, Lily 52
Montagu, Samuel 45
Montefiore, Claude 52, 65, 95, 152
Moonman, Eric 91
Mordechai-Kopfstein, Max 242n57
Morgenstern, Jack 43
Mosco, Maisie 84, 130, 131–2, 137
multiculturalism 3, 25, 37, 195
Museum of the Jewish East End 29, 30
Muslim community 35
Myerhoff, Barbara 71

Nash, Catherine 34
National Conference on Soviet Jewry
79
nationalism 174
Nazism 95–6, 153
refugees from 43, 181, 242n57
Neuberger, Julia 56
new historians 3
New Statesman 4
Newcastle upon Tyne 62
Newman, Jeffrey 58
Nodel, Isaac 116
non-affiliated Jews 10
Nurse, Nelson 160–1

Oberman, Barbara 82
Omer-Jackaman, Jack 72, 96, 178
Operation Judaism 156, 160–5, 168
Orthodox Judaism 39–41, 43, 43–50, 97–8,
209n9
definition of Jewish personhood 8–9
position on conversion 56–7
position on homosexuality 111, 116–17,
117–19
position on interfaith marriage 139–41,
142–3, 145–6, 147
relationship with Reform community
53, 59, 59–71
Outwrite 104–5

Padwa, Dayan Chanoch 210n17
Palatnik, Raiza 78
Palestine 4, 96–7, 99, 104–5, 175, 176, 177,
185
Paley, Grace 26
Parkes, James 66, 152, 153
Passover 124–5
patrilineal Jews 9, 135, 147, 194
personal history 12–18
Phillips, Melanie 92
Pink Paper 117
polarisation 43
post-war Britain 4–7
Prais, S. J. 141
Progressive Judaism 39–43, 97, 135, 194
Orthodox opposition to 59–62, 70–1
position on homosexuality 116, 119–25,
125–6
position on interfaith marriage 142–6
rise of 52, 55, 56, 58, 59, 64, 68

rabbinical training 55, 70
Rabinowicz, Richard 27, 47–8
Rabkin, Yakov 102
Rafalin, Deborah 122
Rager, Ijo 82
Raines, Myer 174–6, 178, 181, 189, 190,
191–2
Rapoport, Chaim 119–21
Rawidowicz, Simon 6
Rayner, John 62, 124
Reform Judaism 20–1, 39–40, 93–4
definition of Jewish personhood 9
origins 50
position on conversion 56–8
position on interfaith marriage 141–6,
147
relationship with Orthodox community
53, 59, 59–71
rise of 50–9
Reform Synagogues of Great Britain
(RSGB) 50, 54, 55, 56–7, 62, 63,
121–3, 146
refuseniks 5, 76, 81, 84, 88, 218n30
religion, relevance of 4
religiosity, decline in 4
Representative Council (Bournemouth) 69
Richardson, Jim 155

Index

Robinson, John 66
Rodger, Patrick 153, 154
Romain, Jonathan 43, 54–5, 56–7, 65, 131, 132, 134–5, 143–5, 146
Rosen, Moishe 155–6, 159
Rosenberg, David 94, 99, 106
Rosenstein, Pinchas 109–10
Roth, Cecil 2, 3, 10, 139
Rubens, Bernice 6, 31, 130

Sabel, Rose 33
Sabra refugee camp massacre 99–100
Sacks, Jonathan 6, 41, 59, 109–11, 119, 120, 132, 133, 158, 210n17
same-sex commitment ceremonies 55
same-sex marriage 116
Samuelson, Francine 159
Sarah, Rabbi Elizabeth Tikvah 55, 106–7, 122–3, 124
Schaffer, Gavin, family story 13–18
Schaffer, Sid 14–17
Schiller, Adrian 2
Schmool, Marlena 8, 131
Schochet, Jacob 159
Schonfeld, Avigdor (Victor) 45
Schonfeld, Solomon 46
Schwarcz, Tommy 164
Scotland, Tony 23–5, 37
Scottish Jewish Archives Project 29, 30
Second World War 15, 53, 96, 175, 181
Section 28 112
secularism 4–5, 30, 72, 84, 97, 125
Sephardi Judaism 51
Shapiro, Helen 165
Shatila refugee camp massacre 99–100
Shaviv, Miriam 131
Shaw, Henry 139
Shemot 31, 33
Sheppard, David, Bishop of Liverpool 153
Sherman, Alfred 67
Sherwood, Peggy 126, 127
Shifra: A Jewish Feminist Magazine 105, 135
Shindler, Colin 86
Shinwell, Emanuel 73
Shipman, Alfred 24
Shipman, Steve 24–5, 37, fig. 2
Shneer, David 125

Shulman, Sheila 54, 56, 106, 113, 122–3, 124, 129, 229n93
Simpson, William W. 152
Sinat Chinam 39
Singer, Charles 99
Six-Day War 12, 71–3, 73, 78, 80–1, 82, 84, 85–6, 87, 89, 183
Sklare, Marshall 135–6
Slepak, Leonid 81
Slowe, Malcolm 33
Society for the Advancement of the Science of Judaism 50–1
Society of Jews and Christians 152
Soetendorp, David 69, 85
Solomon, Mark 117, 118–19, 124
Soviet Jewry 61, 72, 73–80, 80–1, 81, 81–3, 84, 86–7, 87–9, 218n18, 218n30, 218n31
Soviet Jewry Actions Committee (SJAC) 76, 79, 80, 85
Spare Rib 104, 106
Stein, Leonard 96–7
Steinberg, Joseph 171
Suez Crisis 71–2
Sunday Telegraph 23
Sunderland 81
Sussman, Roberto 102, 105–6
synagogues 23, 44–5, 53

Tabick, Jackie 55–6
Tallen, Louise 47
Target Jews (video) 163–5, 171
Teff, Solomon 64, 83
Temple, William, Archbishop of Canterbury 152–3, 153, 154
Thompson, Jennifer 134
Times, The 76–7, 95, 96, 156, 158, 166
Torah, the 65–8, 70, 124

Union of Liberal and Progressive Synagogues (ULPS) 63
Union of Orthodox Hebrew Congregations (UOHC) 45–6, 48, 60–1, 63
United Nations 101
United States of America 9, 86, 113, 133, 134, 135–6, 146–7, 155–6, 159, 162, 177, 179, 209n112, 218n31

Index

United Synagogue 10, 41, 42, 45, 46,
    49–50, 93, 98, 107, 111
universal experience, Jews as brokers of 4
Universities' Committee for Soviet Jewry
    (UCSJ) 76
Unterman, Alan 114, 116–17, 117, 120
USSR 5, 74–5, 75–6, 85, 89, 218n18
    see also Soviet Jewry

Van Dyk, Russell 115, 127
Vital, David 10

Walkabout 1992 109–11, 126
Waxman, Chaim 177
Weissman, Robert 158
Wesker, Tanya 135
West London Synagogue of British Jews
    51, 53–4
White, Jerry 30
Wiesel, Elie 75, 83
Williams, Bill 3, 8, 26, 27, 30, 43
Wissenschaft des Judentums 51
Wittenberg, Jonathan 40
women rabbis 56, 123, 214n112

Women's Campaign for Soviet Jewry 82
The World at War (TV programme) 27–8
World Jewish Congress 84, 85
World Zionist Organisation 85
Writers for Israel 84
Written and Oral Law 68–9

Yiddish 47
Yitzchok, Ben 41
You Don't Have to Be Jewish (radio
    programme) 39–40
youth movements 179–80, 185, 191

Zelichenok, Alec and Galina 88
Zerubavel, Eviatar 34
Zionism 71, 86, 87, 89, 90–1, 92, 93, 95–6,
    97–8, 108, 174, 182, 188, 190, 191,
    193
    aliyah 176–80
    British Jewish support for 71
    ideology 184–5
    and Israel criticism 103–7
    turn to 84
Zionist Federation 80, 182